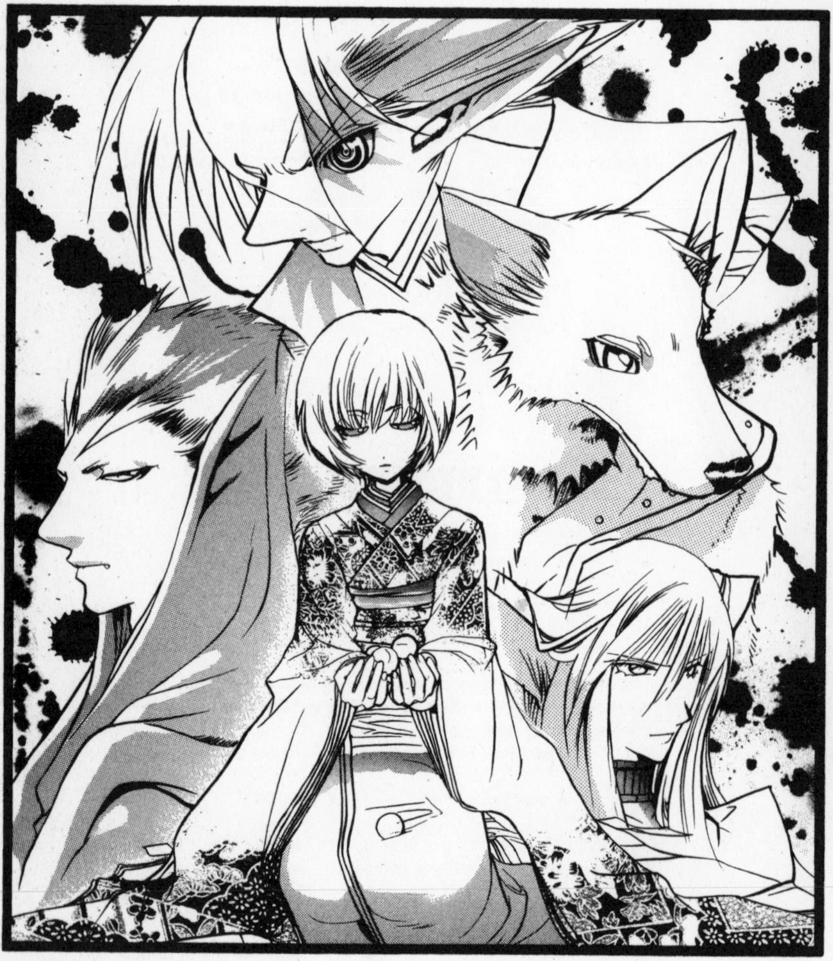

Translator - Nan Rymer
English Adaptation - Stuart Hazleton
Retouch and Lettering - Haruko Furukawa
Cover Layout - Patrick Hook
Graphic Designer - John Lo

Editor - Bryce P. Coleman
Digital Imaging Manager - Chris Buford
Pre-Press Manager - Antonio DePietro
Production Managers - Jennifer Miller, Mutsumi Miyazaki
Art Director - Matt Alford
Managing Editor - Jill Freshney
VP of Production - Ron Klamert
President & C.O.O. - John Parker
Publisher & C.E.O. - Stuart Levy

E-mail: info@TOKYOPOP.com
Come visit us online at www.TOKYOPOP.com

A 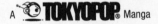 **TOKYOPOP**® Manga

TOKYOPOP Inc.
5900 Wilshire Blvd. Suite 2000
Los Angeles, CA 90036

Crescent Moon Vol. 2

Crescent Moon Volume 2 (originally published as Mikan no Tsuki) ©Haruko IIDA 2000 ©RED 2000.
First published in Japan 2000 by KADOKAWA SHOTEN PUBLISHING CO., LTD., Tokyo.
English translation rights arranged with KADOKAWA SHOTEN PUBLISHING CO., LTD., Tokyo
through TUTTLE-MORI AGENCY, INC., Tokyo.

English text copyright ©2004 TOKYOPOP Inc.

ISBN: 1-59182-793-0

First TOKYOPOP printing: July 2004

10 9 8 7 6 5 4 3 2 1

Printed in the USA

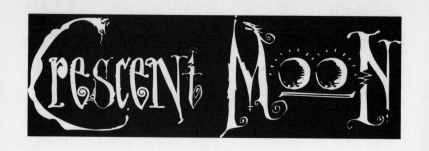

Haruko Iida
Original Works: Red Company/Takamura Matsuda
Volume 2

TOKYOPOP

Los Angeles • Tokyo • London • Hamburg

AFTER SHE LOST HER PARENTS IN A CAR ACCIDENT WHILE STILL JUST A KID, HIGH SCHOOL JUNIOR MAHIRU HAD AMAZING DREAMS AND VISIONS OF A DEMON YOUTH AND A PRINCESS ADORNED IN CEREMONIAL AND COURTLY GARB. ADDING TO MAHIRU'S QUESTIONS ABOUT HER RECURRING VISIONS WERE RUMORS STARTED BY THE SWIMMING CLUB SHE BELONGS TO. THEY BELIEVED THAT TOUCHING MAHIRU WOULD BRING GOOD LUCK.

AS MAHIRU STRUGGLED WITH HER IDENTITY, SHE WAS SUDDENLY APPROACHED BY FOUR MYSTERIOUS YOUTHS NAMED MITSURU, NOZOMU, AKIRA AND MISOKA. THEY CLAIMED HER TO BE THE "DESCENDENT OF THE PRINCESS," AND THEIR ONLY HOPE FOR RECLAIMING THE GEMS NAMED "THE TEARDROPS OF THE MOON" WHICH WERE STOLEN BY HUMANS OVER 1000 YEARS AGO.

THESE YOUTHS WERE NOT HUMANS BUT MEMBERS OF A "MONSTROUS" RACE NAMED THE PEOPLE OF THE MOON, WHO, WHILE IN TOKYO, HAD FORMED A BAND OF THIEVES KNOWN AS THE MOONLIGHT BANDITS. FROM THESE YOUTHS, MAHIRU LEARNED SHE IS THE DESCENDENT OF THE MINISTER OF THE LEFT'S PRINCESS, WHOSE ANCESTORS WERE RESPONSIBLE FOR STEALING THE TEARDROPS OF THE MOON SO MANY YEARS AGO. IT IS ALSO BECAUSE OF THIS HERITAGE THAT MAHIRU POSSESSES THE ABILITY TO DRAW OUT THE HIDDEN ABILITIES AND POWERS OF THE "LUNAR RACE."

ALTHOUGH AT FIRST, MAHIRU FEARED THE MOONLIGHT BANDITS AND WANTED NOTHING TO DO WITH THEM, SHE WAS TOUCHED BY NOZOMU AND HIS GANG'S KINDNESS. SINCE SHE ALSO WANTED TO LEARN MORE ABOUT HER ABILITIES AND DREAMS, MAHIRU DECIDED TO AID THE CREATURES IN THEIR ENDEAVORS.

AS SHE SLOWLY CAME TO UNDERSTAND THE BANDITS, ONLY MITSURU, BECAUSE OF HIS DEEP DISTRUST OF HUMANS, REFUSED TO ACCEPT MAHIRU AS A FRIEND RATHER THAN FOE. UNDAUNTED, MAHIRU WISHES TO SOMEHOW BEFRIEND MITSURU AND WORK WITH HIM BUT...

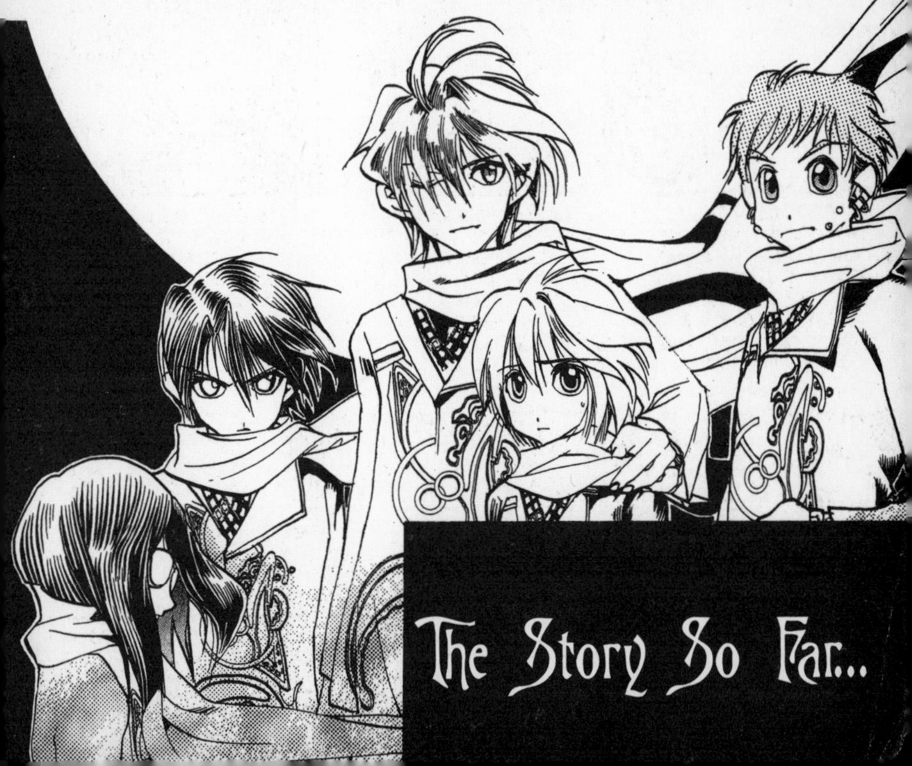

The Story So Far...

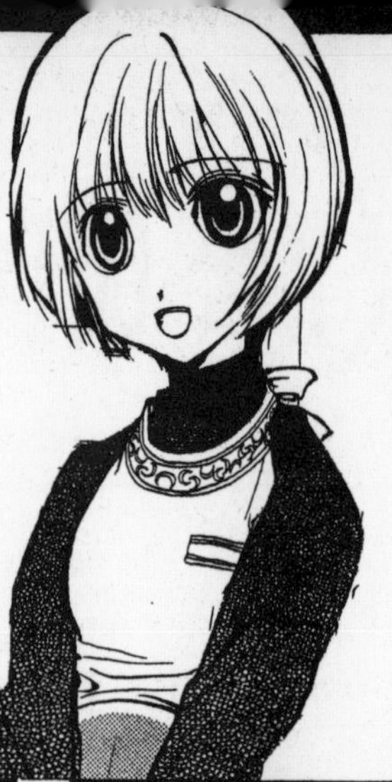

MAHIRU SHIRAISHI:

A JUNIOR IN HIGH SCHOOL. MAHIRU POSSESS THE ABILITY TO AWAKEN AND DRAW OUT THE HIDDEN POWERS OF THE "LUNAR RACE."

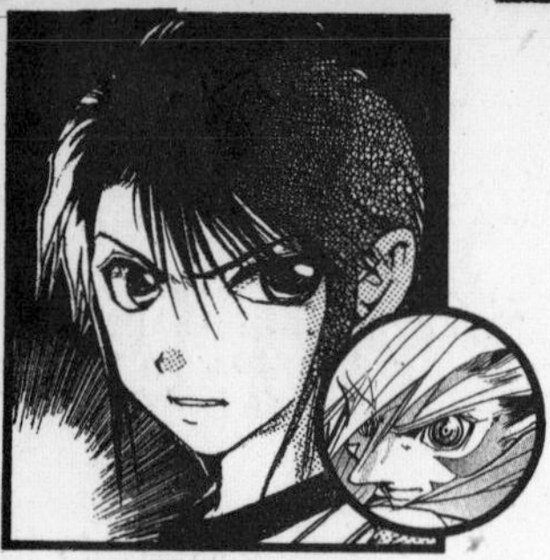

MITSURU SUOU:
A TENGU. DUE TO HIS COMPLICATED UPBRINGING, MITSURU NOT ONLY HATES AND BEGRUDGES THE HUMAN RACE, BUT DISTRUSTS THE LUNAR ONE AS WELL.

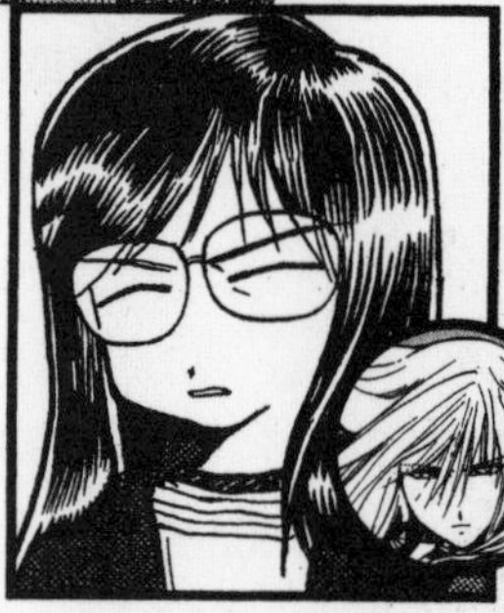

MISOKA ASAGI:
A FOX DEMON. COOL, CALM, COLLECTED AND TACIT, MISOKA ACTS INSTINCTIVELY AND IS RESPECTED AS THE UNSPOKEN LEADER.

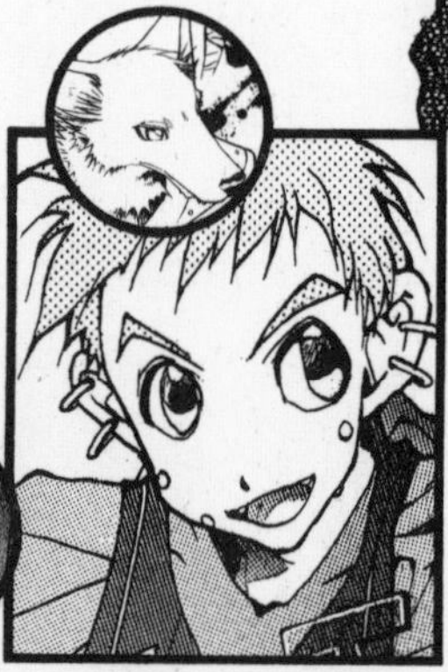

AKIRA YAMABUKI:
A WEREWOLF. A HAPPY-GO-LUCKY CHARACTER, AKIRA LOATHES DWELLING ON ANYTHING SERIOUS OR DEEP FOR TOO LONG. HE'S ALSO AN EXCELLENT CHEF.

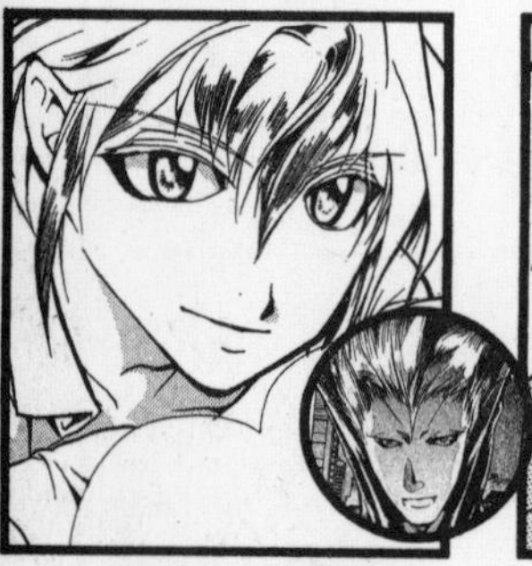

NOZOMU MOEGI:
A VAMPIRE. DESPITE HIS BLONDE HAIR AND BLUE EYES, HE SPEAKS WITH A KANSAI DIALECT. HE'S A SMOOTH TALKER AND LOVES THE LADIES.

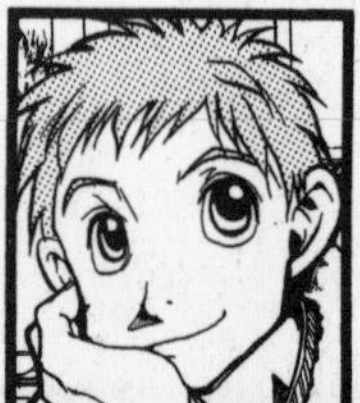

YOUHEI NISHINO:
DETECTIVE KUSAKABE'S SUBORDINATE. HE IS A POLICE SERGEANT.

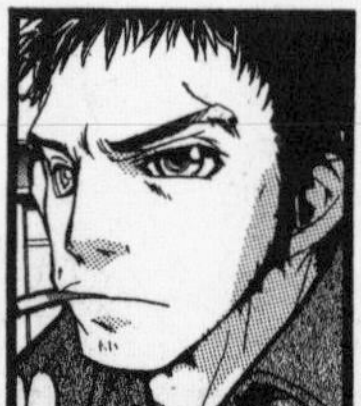

KIMITERU KUSAKABE:
A POLICE INSPECTOR INVESTIGATING THE "MOONLIGHT BANDITS."

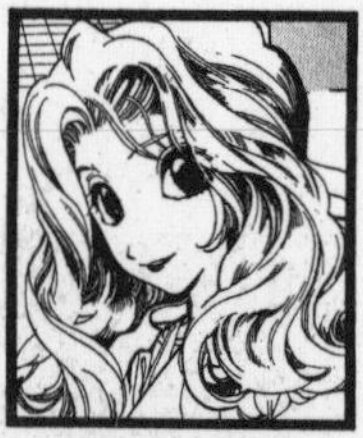

KATSURA SHION:
PIANIST FOR THE BAR, "MOONSHINE."

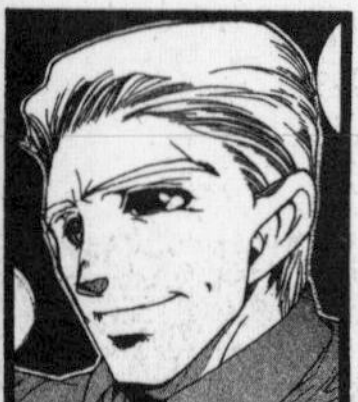

OBORO KUROSAKI:
OWNER OF THE BAR, "MOONSHINE."

Crescent Moon

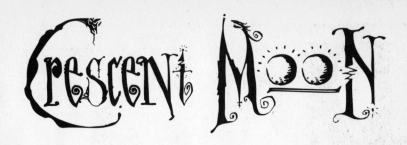

Contents

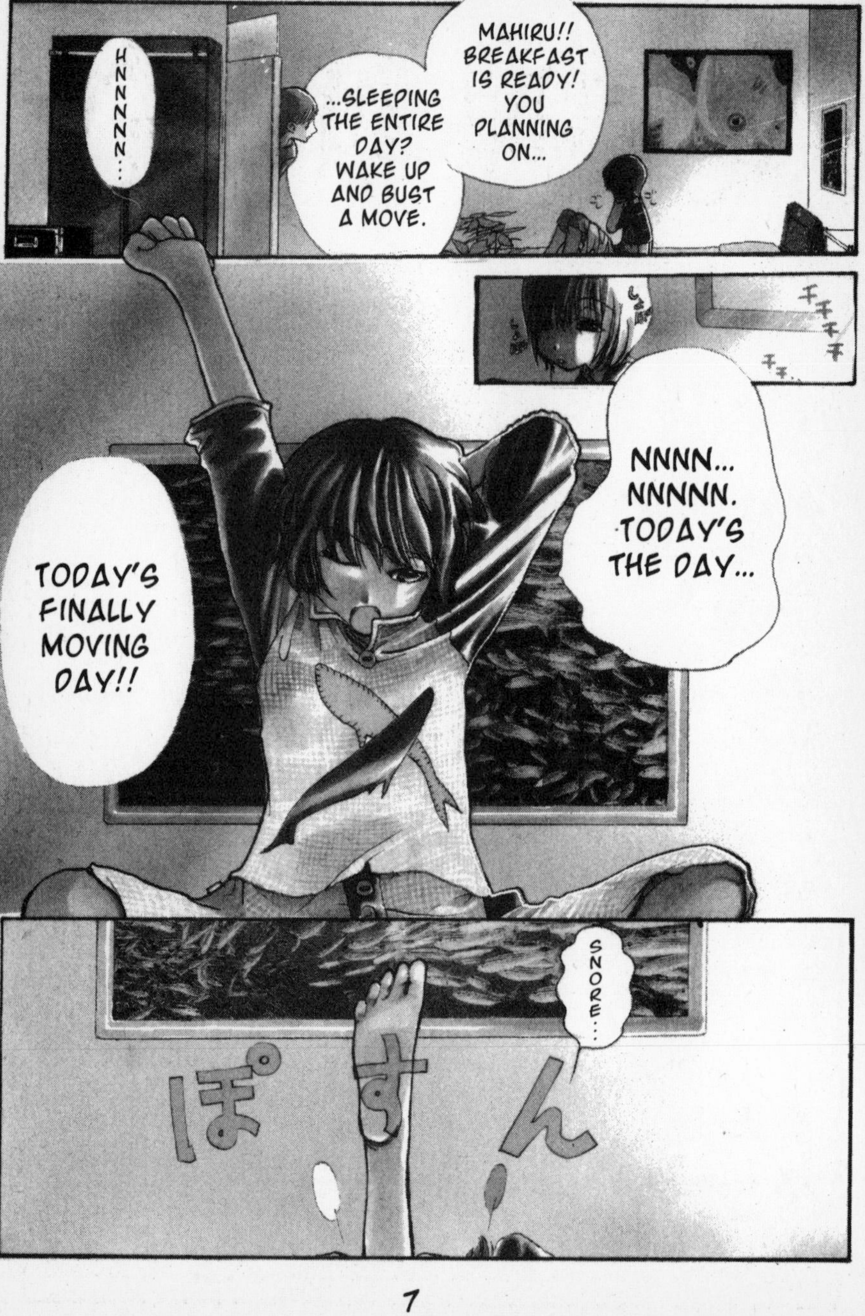
MAHIRU!! BREAKFAST IS READY! YOU PLANNING ON...
...SLEEPING THE ENTIRE DAY? WAKE UP AND BUST A MOVE.
HNNNNN...
NNNN... NNNNN. TODAY'S THE DAY...
TODAY'S FINALLY MOVING DAY!!
SNORE...
ぽすん

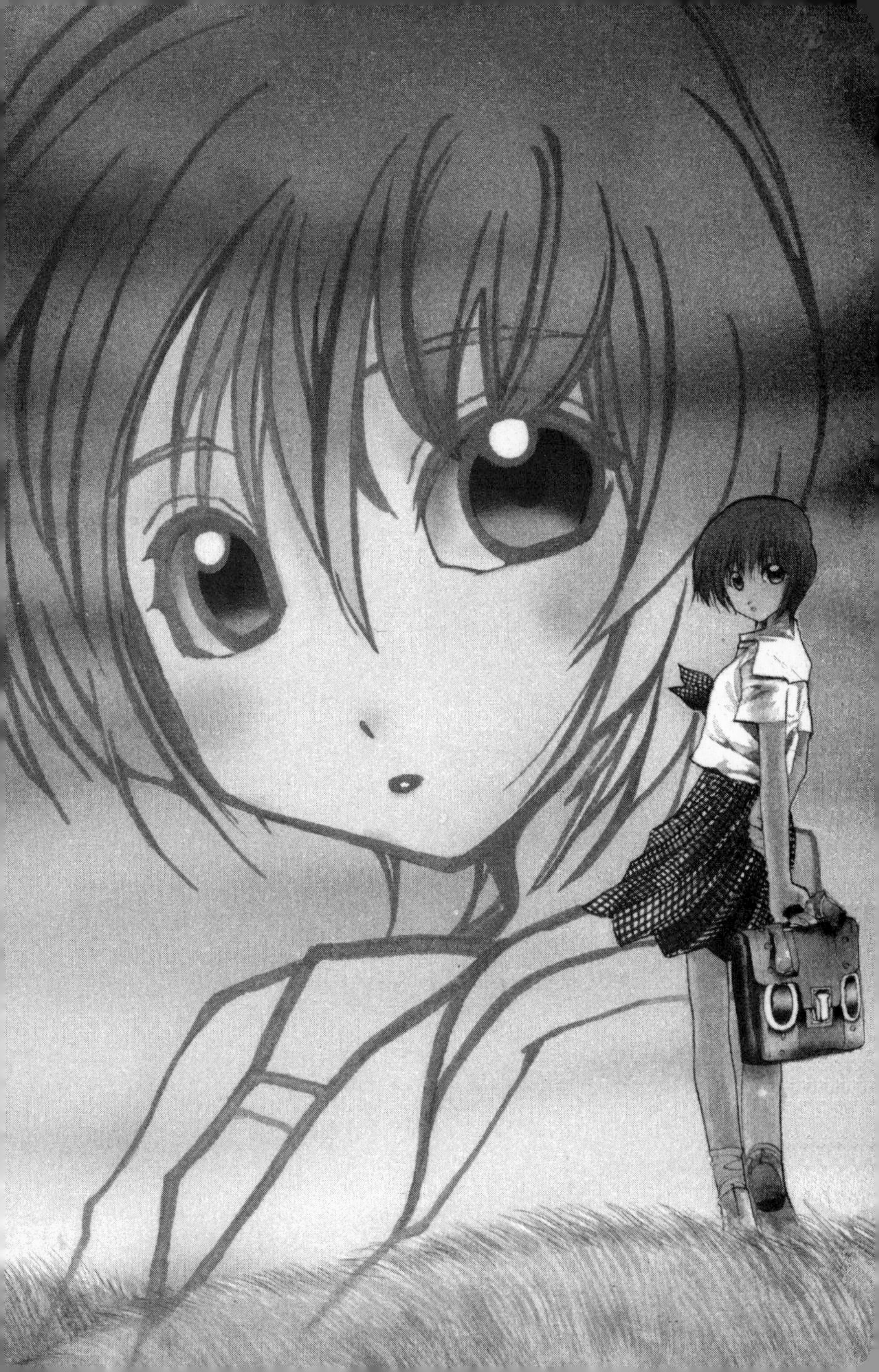

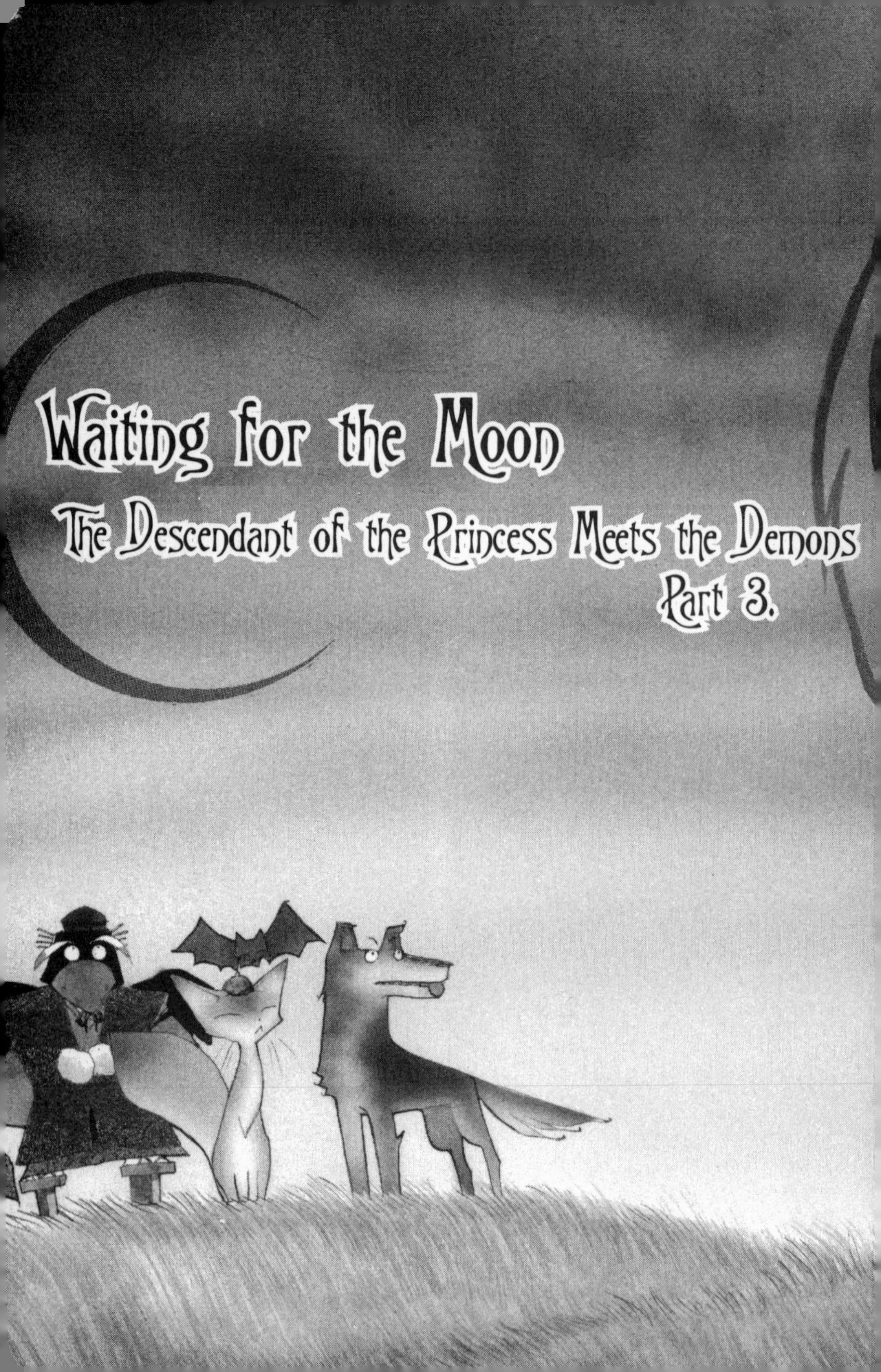
Waiting for the Moon
The Descendant of the Princess Meets the Demons
Part 3.

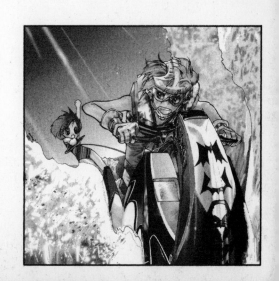

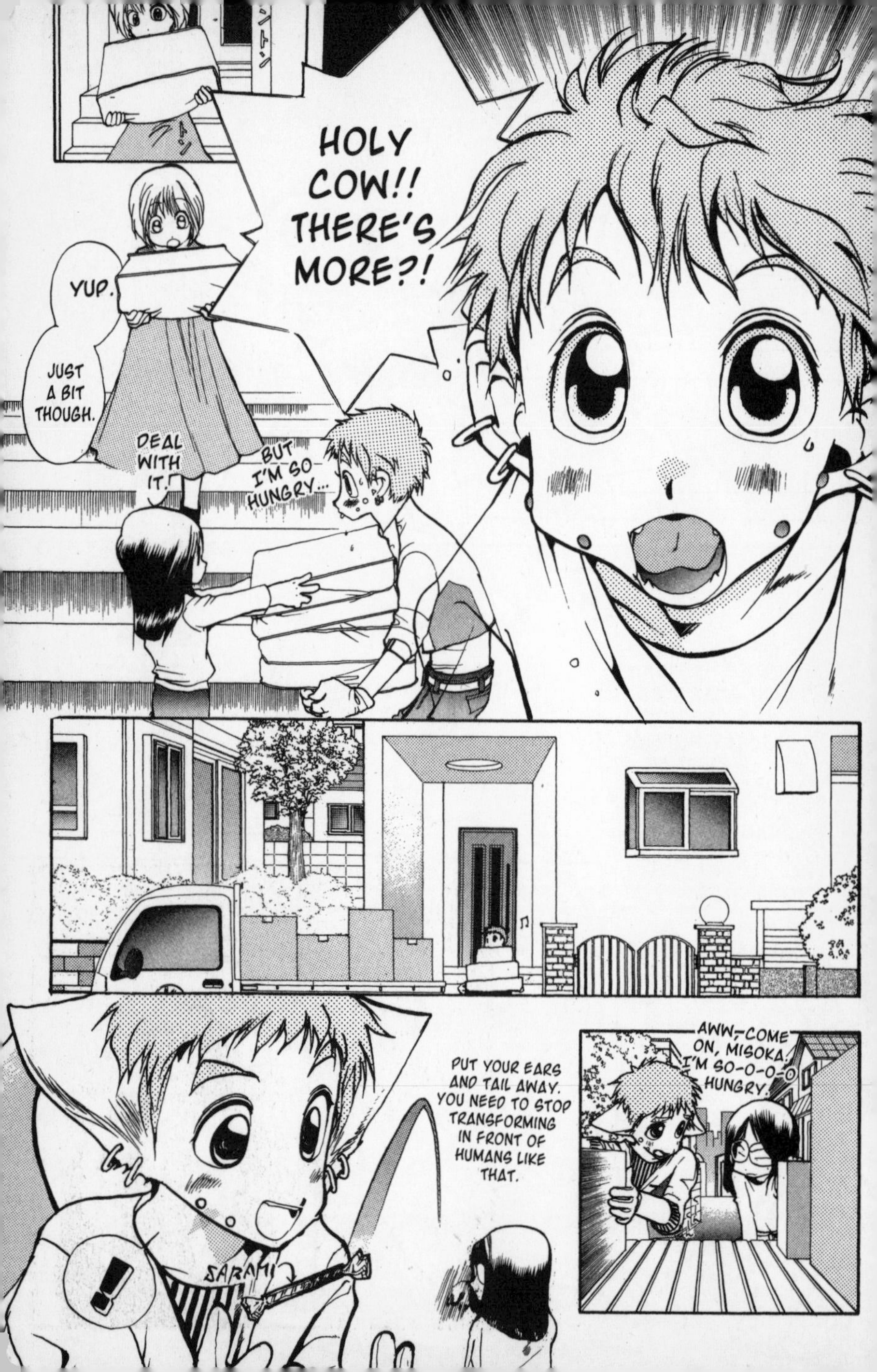
HOLY COW!! THERE'S MORE?!
YUP.
JUST A BIT THOUGH.
BUT I'M SO HUNGRY...
DEAL WITH IT.
AWW, COME ON, MISOKA. I'M SO-O-O-O HUNGRY.
PUT YOUR EARS AND TAIL AWAY. YOU NEED TO STOP TRANSFORMING IN FRONT OF HUMANS LIKE THAT.
SARAMI

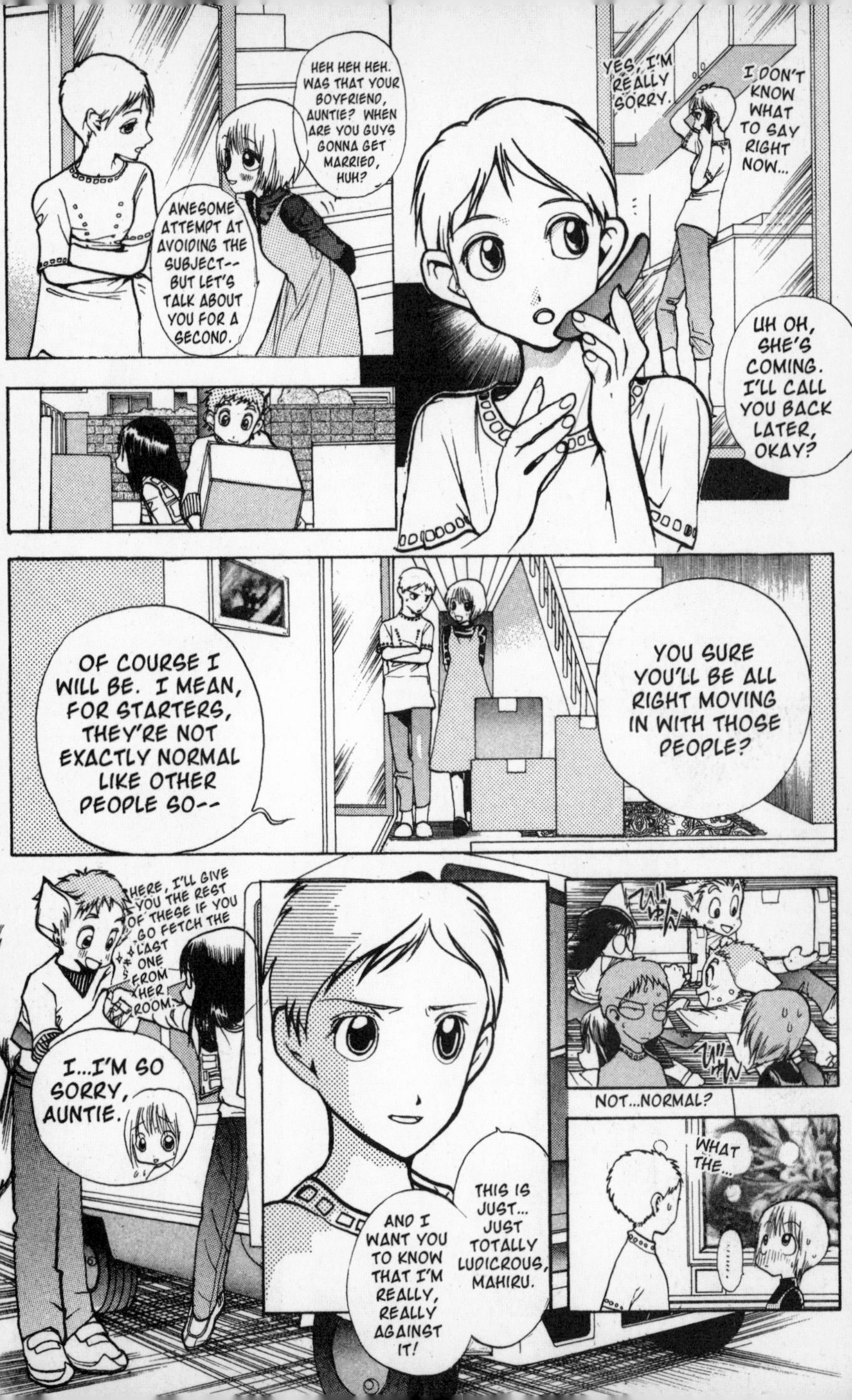
YES, I'M REALLY SORRY.
I DON'T KNOW WHAT TO SAY RIGHT NOW...
UH OH, SHE'S COMING. I'LL CALL YOU BACK LATER, OKAY?
HEH HEH HEH. WAS THAT YOUR BOYFRIEND, AUNTIE? WHEN ARE YOU GUYS GONNA GET MARRIED, HUH?
AWESOME ATTEMPT AT AVOIDING THE SUBJECT-- BUT LET'S TALK ABOUT YOU FOR A SECOND.
YOU SURE YOU'LL BE ALL RIGHT MOVING IN WITH THOSE PEOPLE?
OF COURSE I WILL BE. I MEAN, FOR STARTERS, THEY'RE NOT EXACTLY NORMAL LIKE OTHER PEOPLE SO--
NOT...NORMAL?
WHAT THE...
......
THIS IS JUST... JUST TOTALLY LUDICROUS, MAHIRU.
AND I WANT YOU TO KNOW THAT I'M REALLY, REALLY AGAINST IT!
HERE, I'LL GIVE YOU THE REST OF THESE IF YOU GO FETCH THE LAST ONE FROM HER ROOM.
I...I'M SO SORRY, AUNTIE.

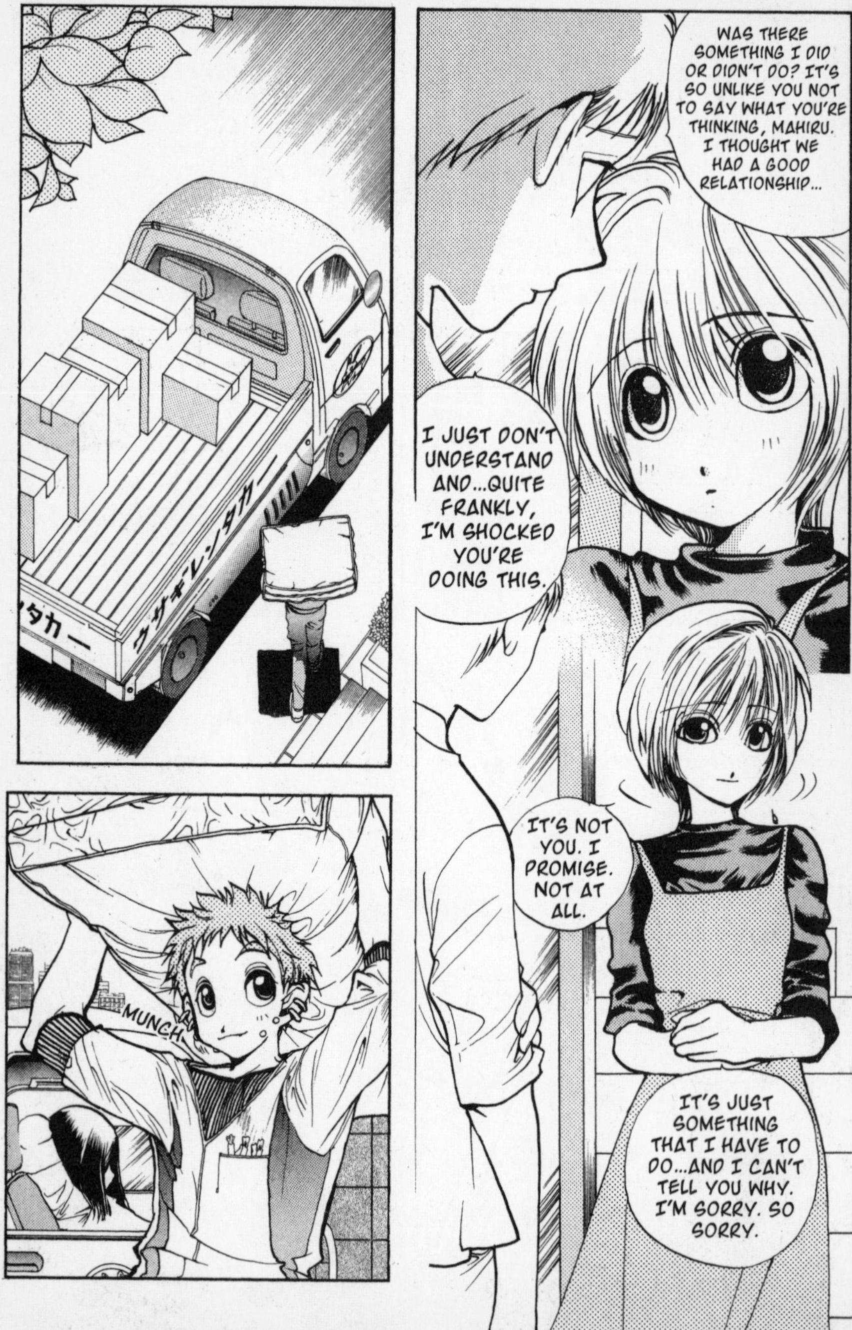
WAS THERE SOMETHING I DID OR DIDN'T DO? IT'S SO UNLIKE YOU NOT TO SAY WHAT YOU'RE THINKING, MAHIRU. I THOUGHT WE HAD A GOOD RELATIONSHIP...
I JUST DON'T UNDERSTAND AND...QUITE FRANKLY, I'M SHOCKED YOU'RE DOING THIS.
IT'S NOT YOU. I PROMISE. NOT AT ALL.
IT'S JUST SOMETHING THAT I HAVE TO DO...AND I CAN'T TELL YOU WHY. I'M SORRY. SO SORRY.
ウサギレンタカー
MUNCH

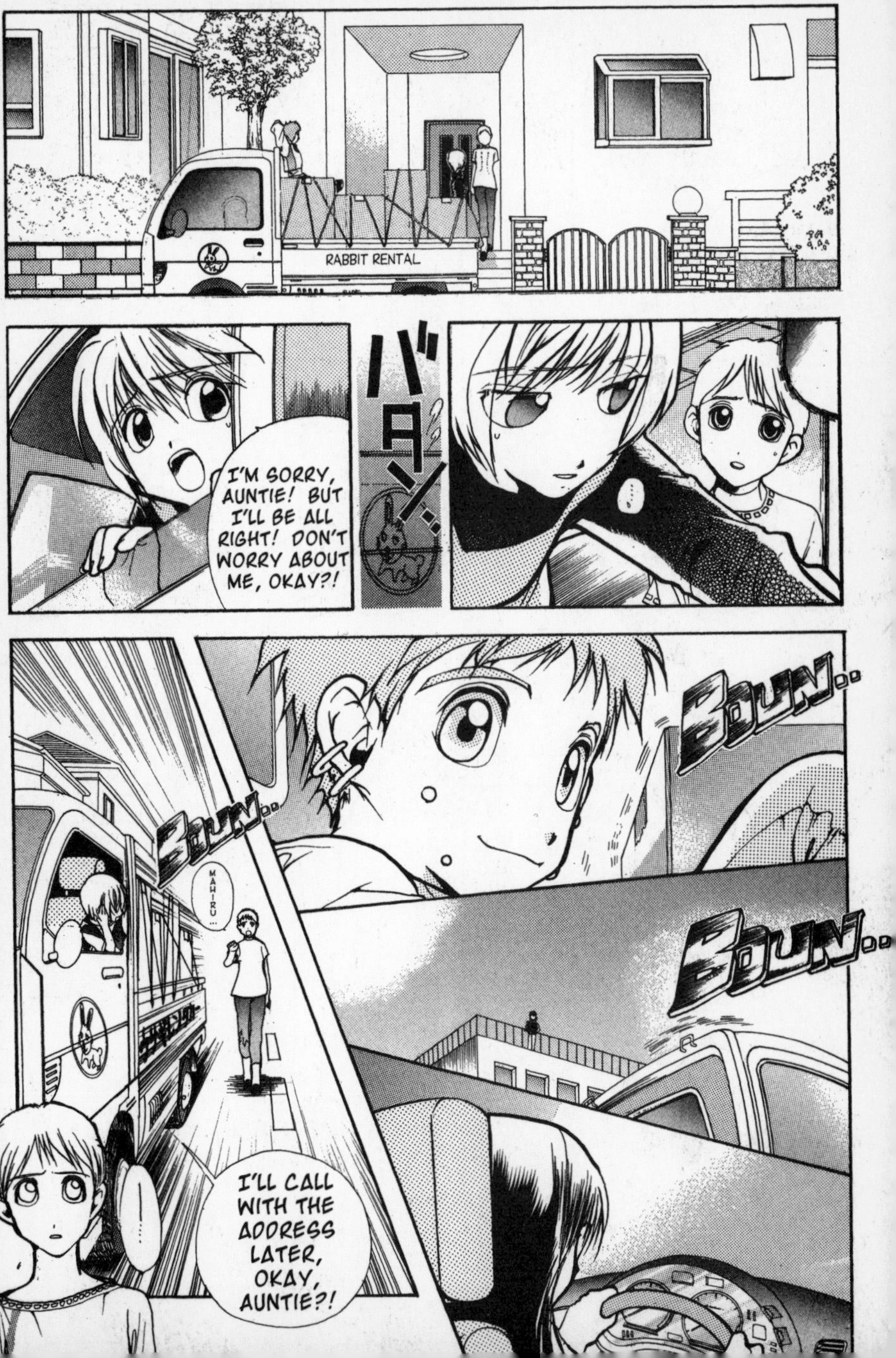
RABBIT RENTAL
...
バタン
I'M SORRY, AUNTIE! BUT I'LL BE ALL RIGHT! DON'T WORRY ABOUT ME, OKAY?!
BOUN..
BOUN..
BOUN..
MAHIRU...
I'LL CALL WITH THE ADDRESS LATER, OKAY, AUNTIE?!
...

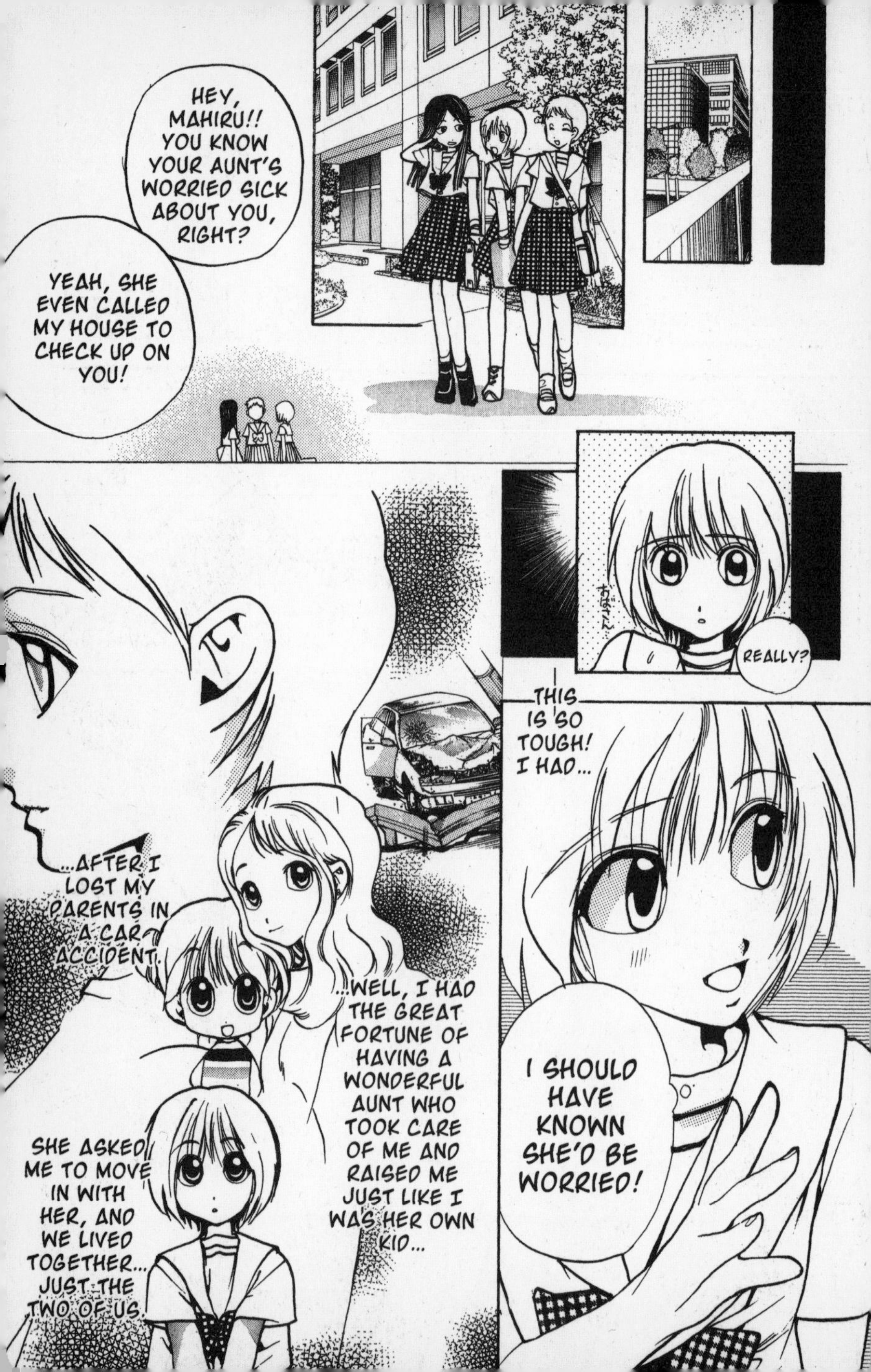
HEY, MAHIRU!! YOU KNOW YOUR AUNT'S WORRIED SICK ABOUT YOU, RIGHT?
YEAH, SHE EVEN CALLED MY HOUSE TO CHECK UP ON YOU!
REALLY?
THIS IS SO TOUGH! I HAD...
I SHOULD HAVE KNOWN SHE'D BE WORRIED!
...AFTER I LOST MY PARENTS IN A CAR ACCIDENT.
...WELL, I HAD THE GREAT FORTUNE OF HAVING A WONDERFUL AUNT WHO TOOK CARE OF ME AND RAISED ME JUST LIKE I WAS HER OWN KID...
SHE ASKED ME TO MOVE IN WITH HER, AND WE LIVED TOGETHER... JUST THE TWO OF US.

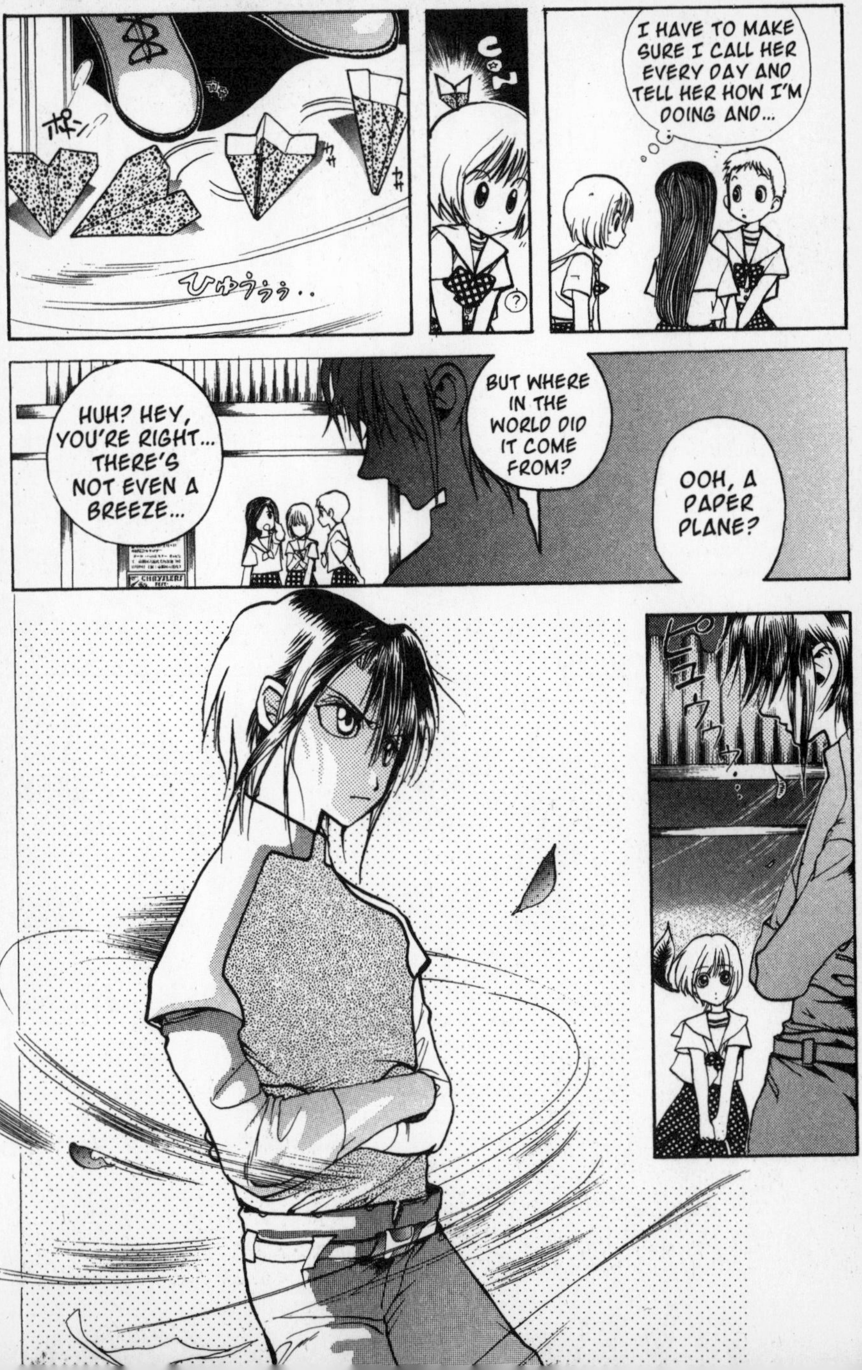
I HAVE TO MAKE SURE I CALL HER EVERY DAY AND TELL HER HOW I'M DOING AND...
?
OOH, A PAPER PLANE?
BUT WHERE IN THE WORLD DID IT COME FROM?
HUH? HEY, YOU'RE RIGHT... THERE'S NOT EVEN A BREEZE...

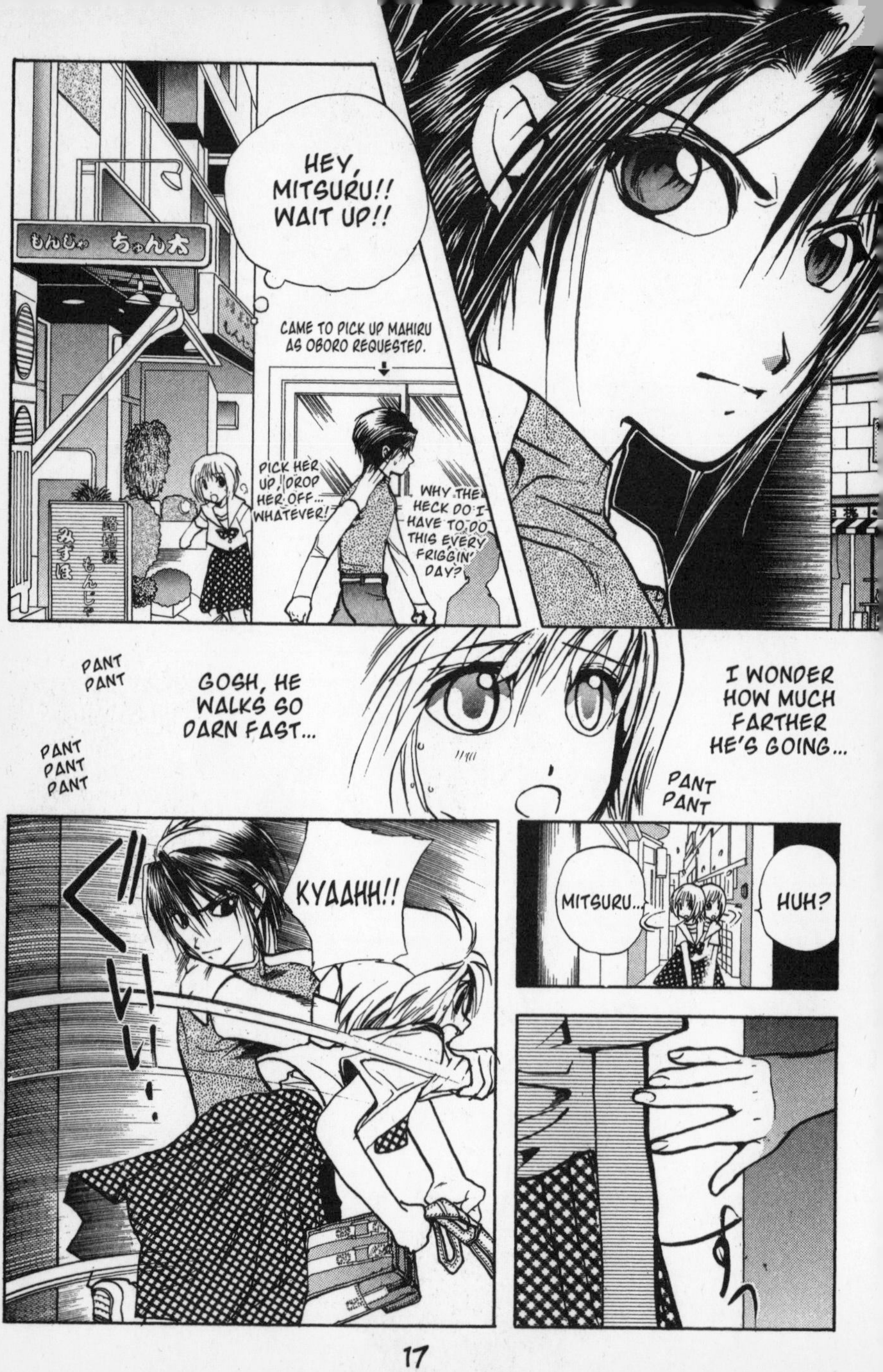
HEY, MITSURU!! WAIT UP!!
もんじゃ ちゃん太
CAME TO PICK UP MAHIRU AS OBORO REQUESTED.
WHY THE HECK DO I HAVE TO DO THIS EVERY FRIGGIN' DAY?
PICK HER UP, DROP HER OFF... WHATEVER!
I WONDER HOW MUCH FARTHER HE'S GOING...
PANT PANT
GOSH, HE WALKS SO DARN FAST...
PANT PANT
PANT PANT PANT
HUH?
MITSURU...
KYAAHH!!

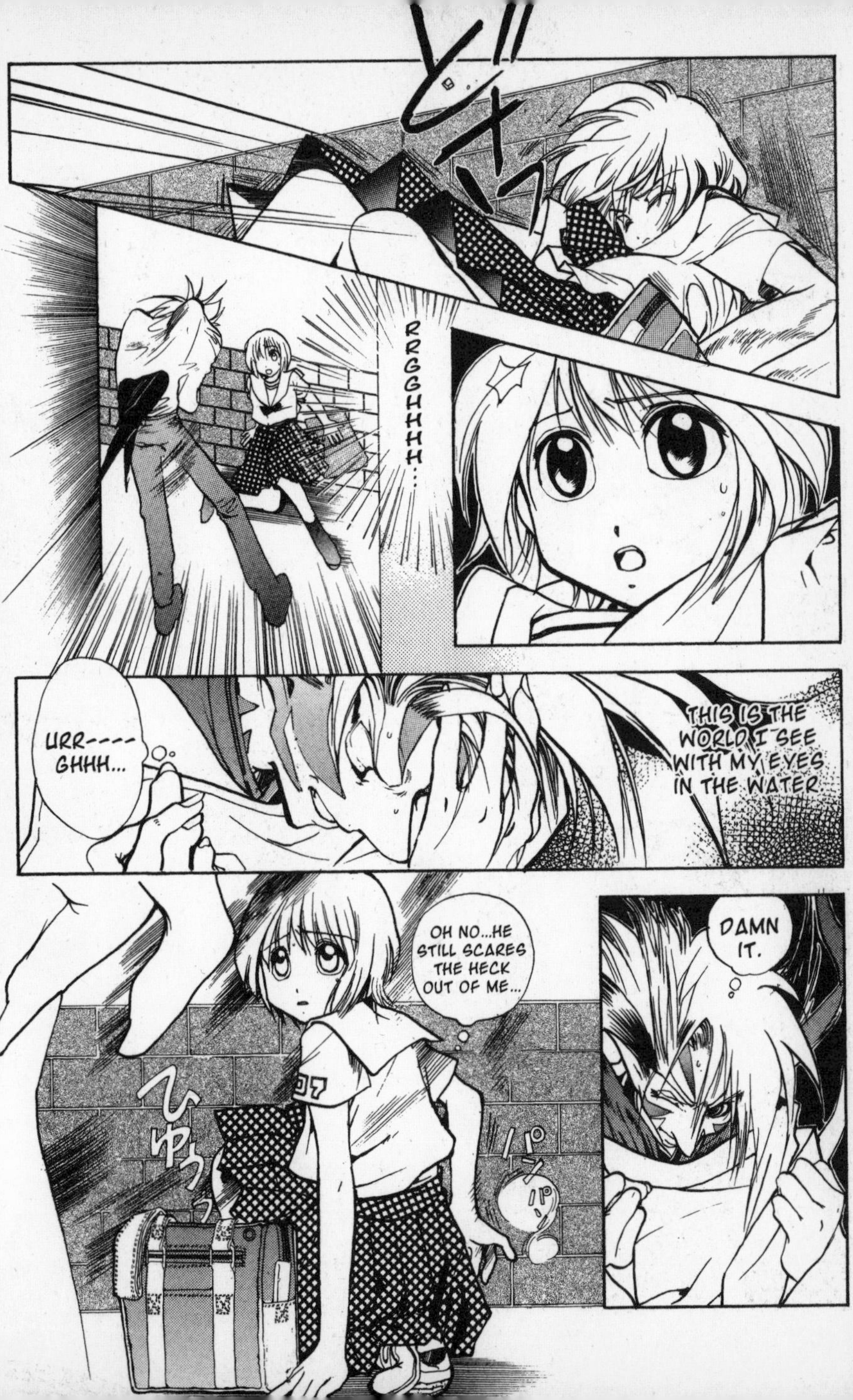
RRGGHHHH...
THIS IS THE WORLD I SEE WITH MY EYES IN THE WATER
URR----GHHH...
DAMN IT.
OH NO...HE STILL SCARES THE HECK OUT OF ME...

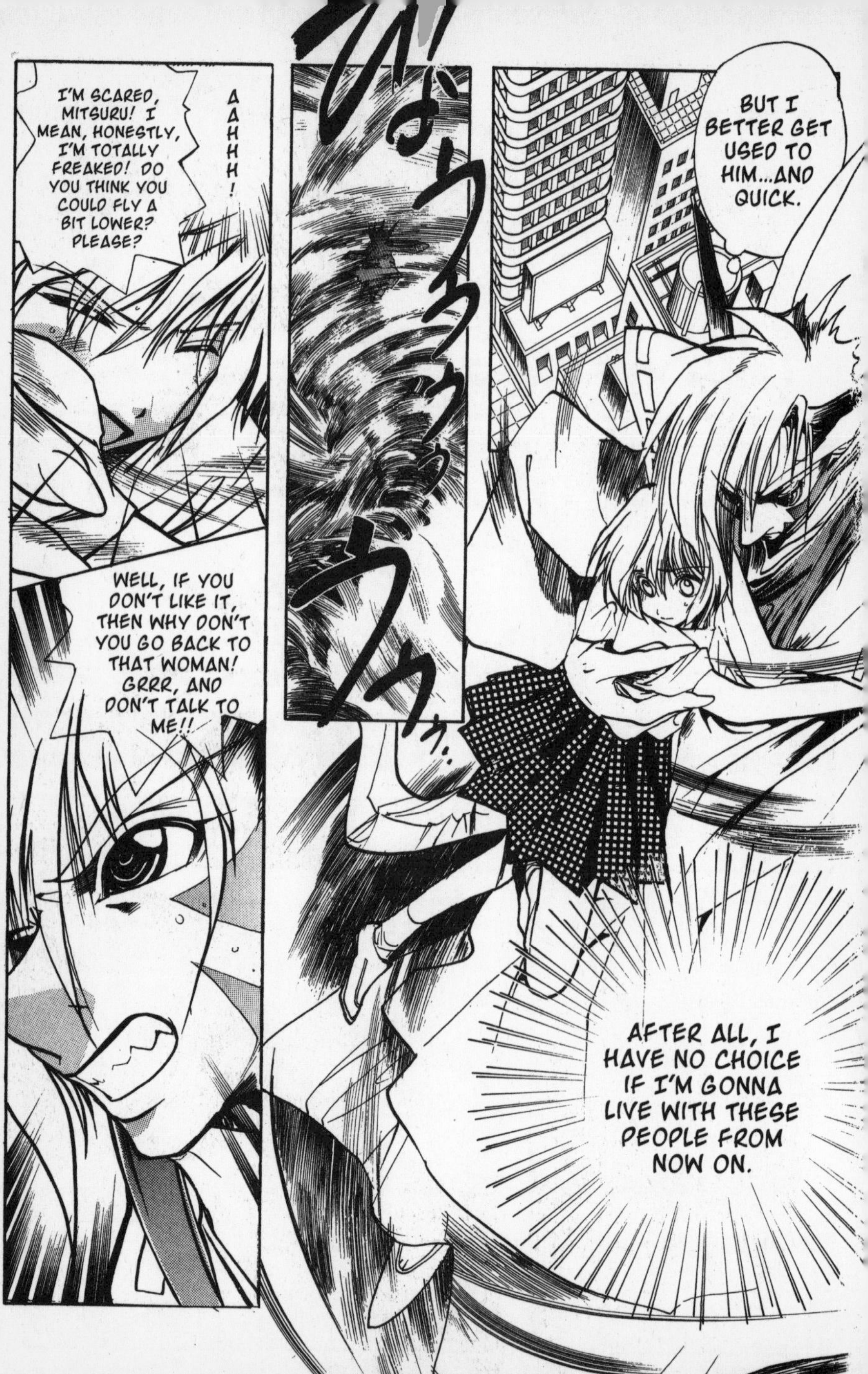
BUT I BETTER GET USED TO HIM...AND QUICK.
AFTER ALL, I HAVE NO CHOICE IF I'M GONNA LIVE WITH THESE PEOPLE FROM NOW ON.
AAHHHH!
I'M SCARED, MITSURU! I MEAN, HONESTLY, I'M TOTALLY FREAKED! DO YOU THINK YOU COULD FLY A BIT LOWER? PLEASE?
WELL, IF YOU DON'T LIKE IT, THEN WHY DON'T YOU GO BACK TO THAT WOMAN! GRRR, AND DON'T TALK TO ME!!

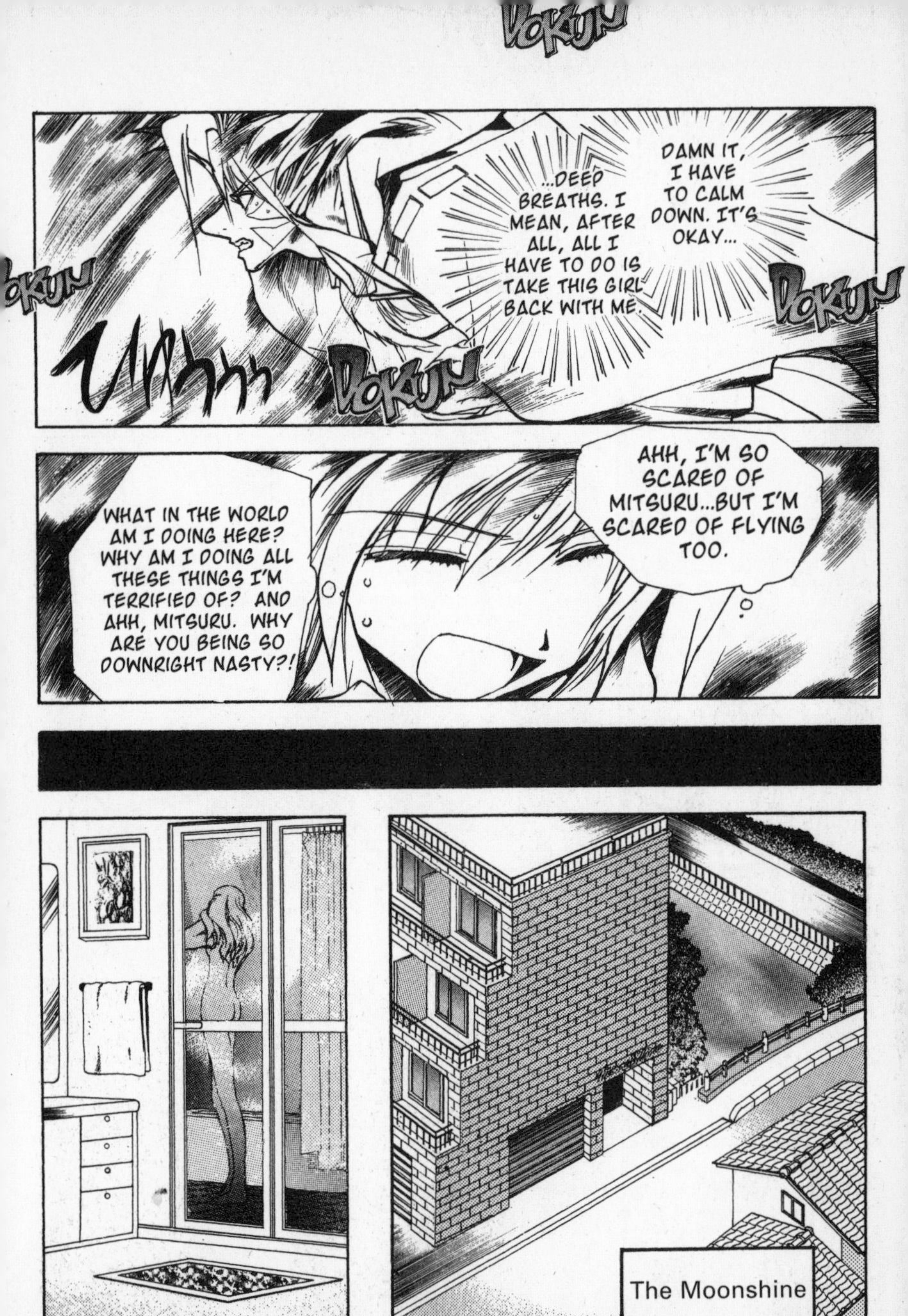
DOKUN
DAMN IT, I HAVE TO CALM DOWN. IT'S OKAY...
...DEEP BREATHS. I MEAN, AFTER ALL, ALL I HAVE TO DO IS TAKE THIS GIRL BACK WITH ME.
DOKUN
DOKUN
DOKUN
AHH, I'M SO SCARED OF MITSURU...BUT I'M SCARED OF FLYING TOO.
WHAT IN THE WORLD AM I DOING HERE? WHY AM I DOING ALL THESE THINGS I'M TERRIFIED OF? AND AHH, MITSURU. WHY ARE YOU BEING SO DOWNRIGHT NASTY?!
The Moonshine

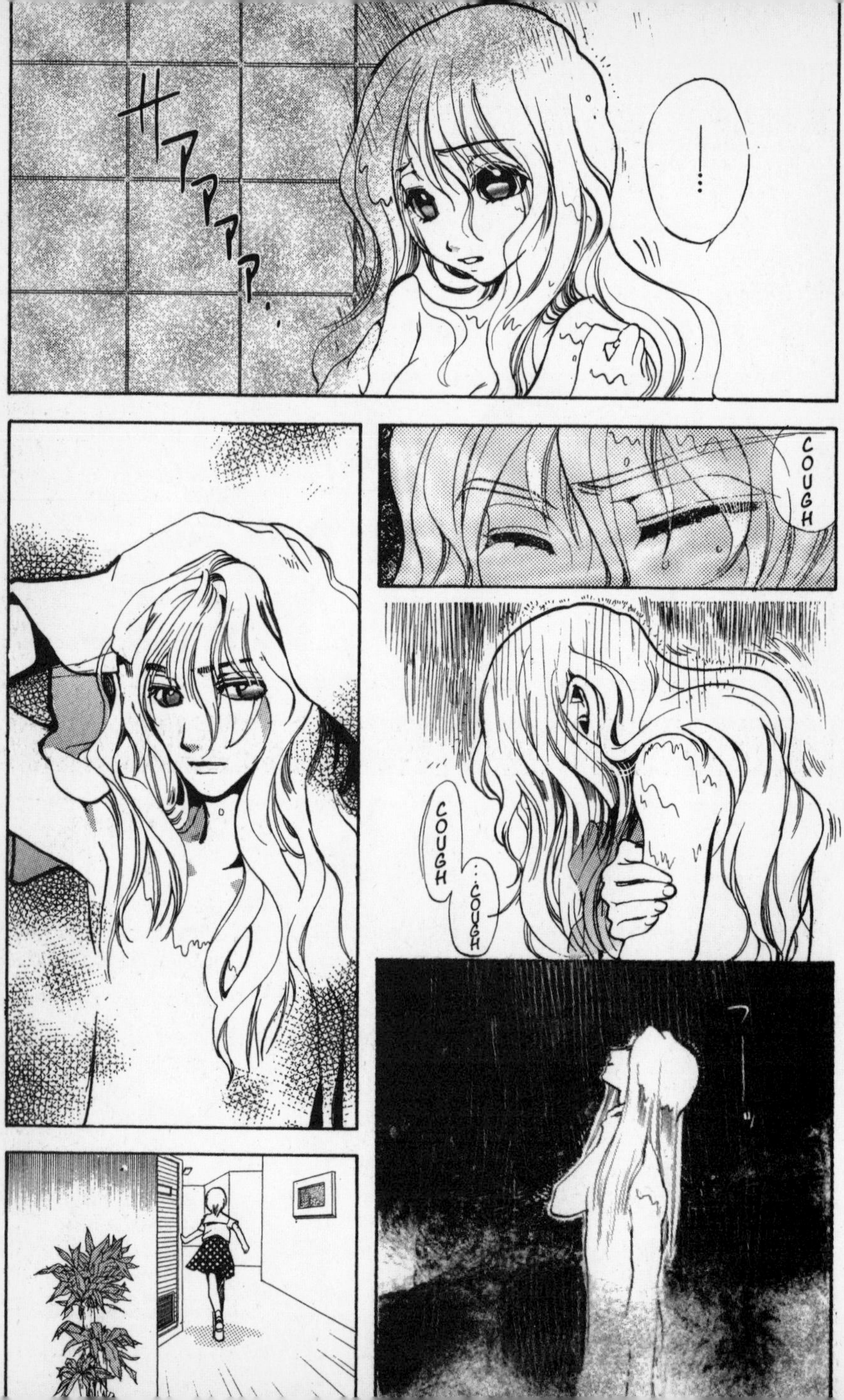
!...
COUGH
COUGH
...COUGH

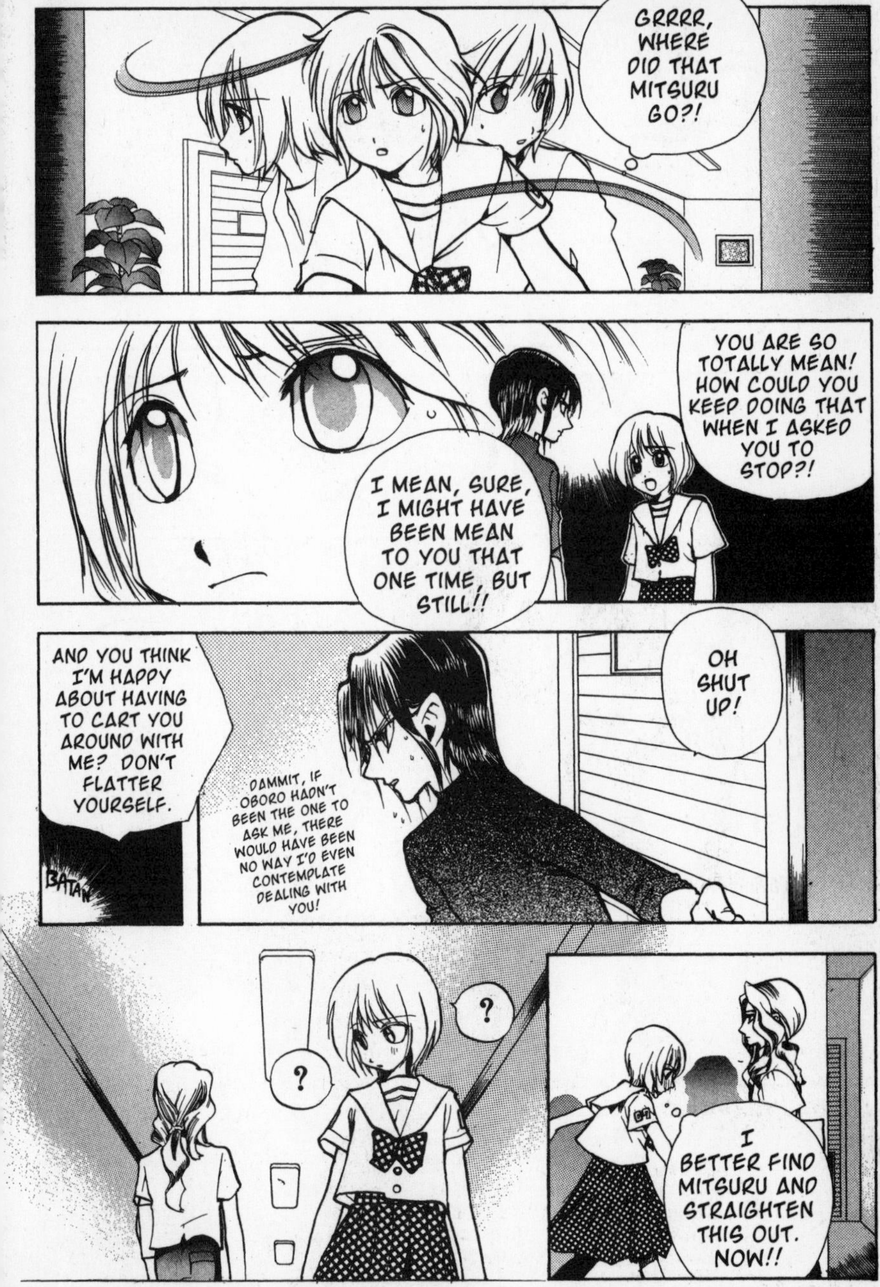
GRRRR, WHERE DID THAT MITSURU GO?!
YOU ARE SO TOTALLY MEAN! HOW COULD YOU KEEP DOING THAT WHEN I ASKED YOU TO STOP?!
I MEAN, SURE, I MIGHT HAVE BEEN MEAN TO YOU THAT ONE TIME, BUT STILL!!
OH SHUT UP!
DAMMIT, IF OBORO HADN'T BEEN THE ONE TO ASK ME, THERE WOULD HAVE BEEN NO WAY I'D EVEN CONTEMPLATE DEALING WITH YOU!
AND YOU THINK I'M HAPPY ABOUT HAVING TO CART YOU AROUND WITH ME? DON'T FLATTER YOURSELF.
BATAN
I BETTER FIND MITSURU AND STRAIGHTEN THIS OUT. NOW!!
?
?

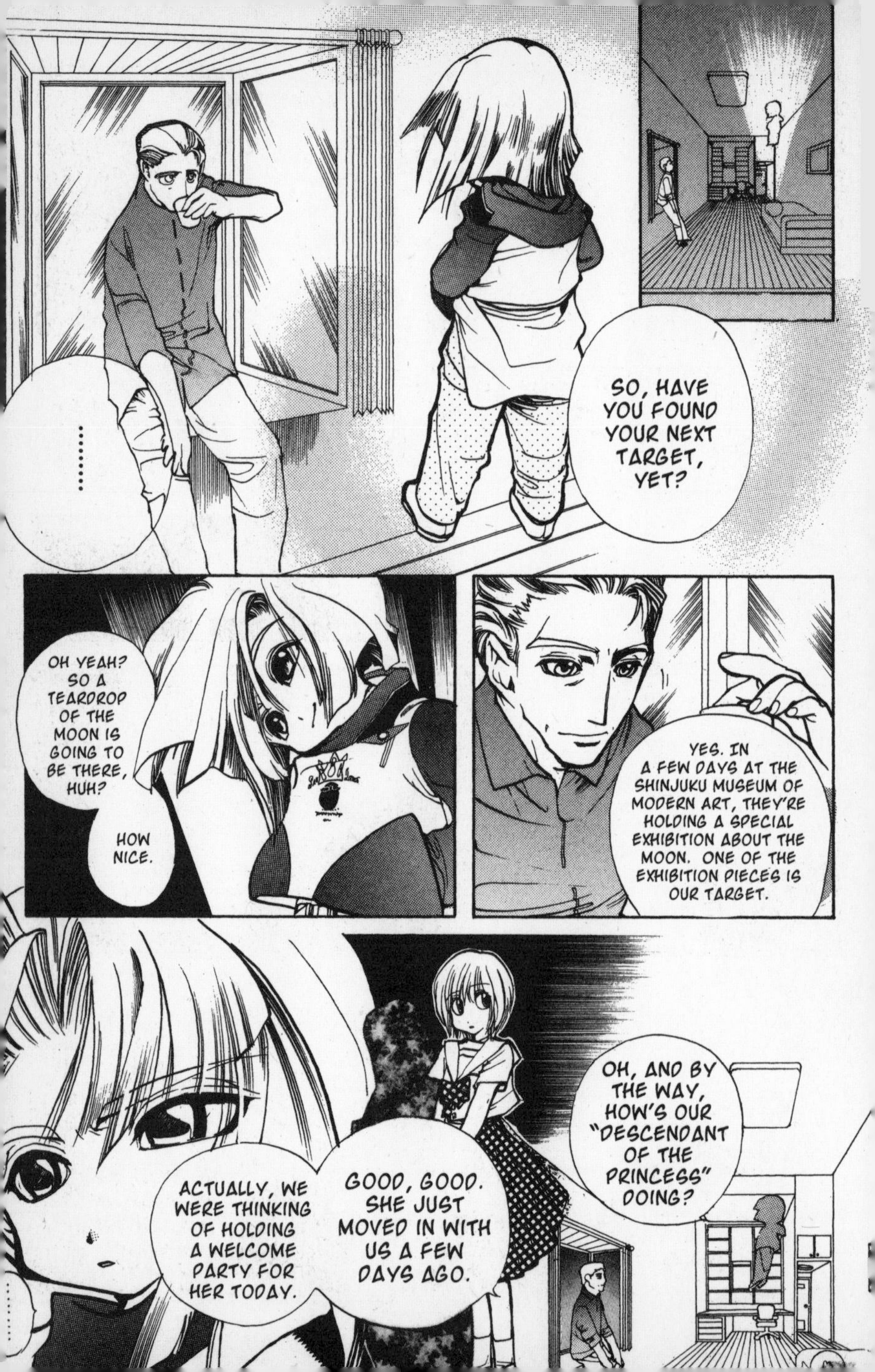
SO, HAVE YOU FOUND YOUR NEXT TARGET, YET?
......
YES. IN A FEW DAYS AT THE SHINJUKU MUSEUM OF MODERN ART, THEY'RE HOLDING A SPECIAL EXHIBITION ABOUT THE MOON. ONE OF THE EXHIBITION PIECES IS OUR TARGET.
OH YEAH? SO A TEARDROP OF THE MOON IS GOING TO BE THERE, HUH?
HOW NICE.
OH, AND BY THE WAY, HOW'S OUR "DESCENDANT OF THE PRINCESS" DOING?
GOOD, GOOD. SHE JUST MOVED IN WITH US A FEW DAYS AGO.
ACTUALLY, WE WERE THINKING OF HOLDING A WELCOME PARTY FOR HER TODAY.

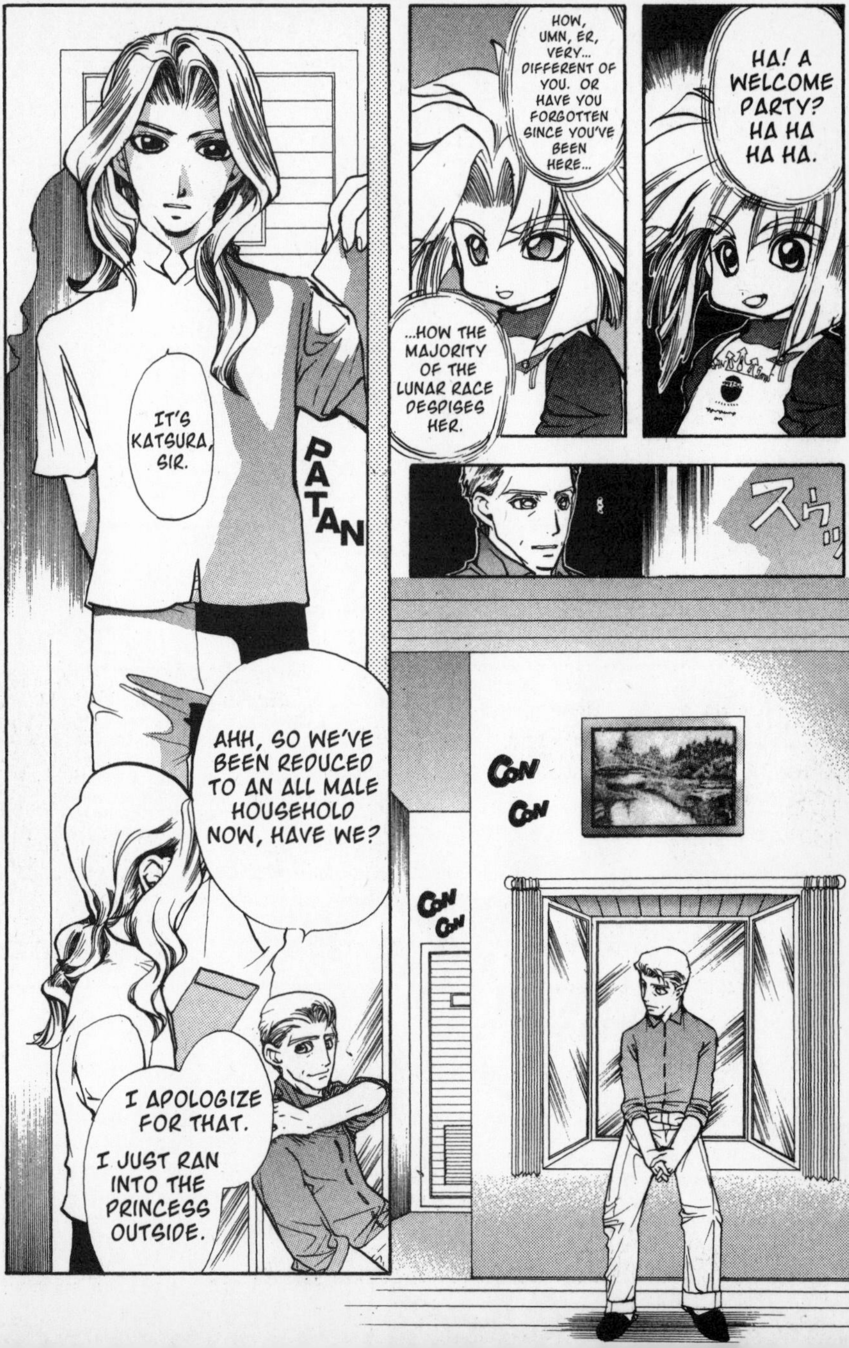
HA! A WELCOME PARTY? HA HA HA HA.
HOW, UMN, ER, VERY... DIFFERENT OF YOU. OR HAVE YOU FORGOTTEN SINCE YOU'VE BEEN HERE...
...HOW THE MAJORITY OF THE LUNAR RACE DESPISES HER.
スゥッ
CON CON
CON CON
PATAN
IT'S KATSURA, SIR.
AHH, SO WE'VE BEEN REDUCED TO AN ALL MALE HOUSEHOLD NOW, HAVE WE?
I APOLOGIZE FOR THAT.
I JUST RAN INTO THE PRINCESS OUTSIDE.

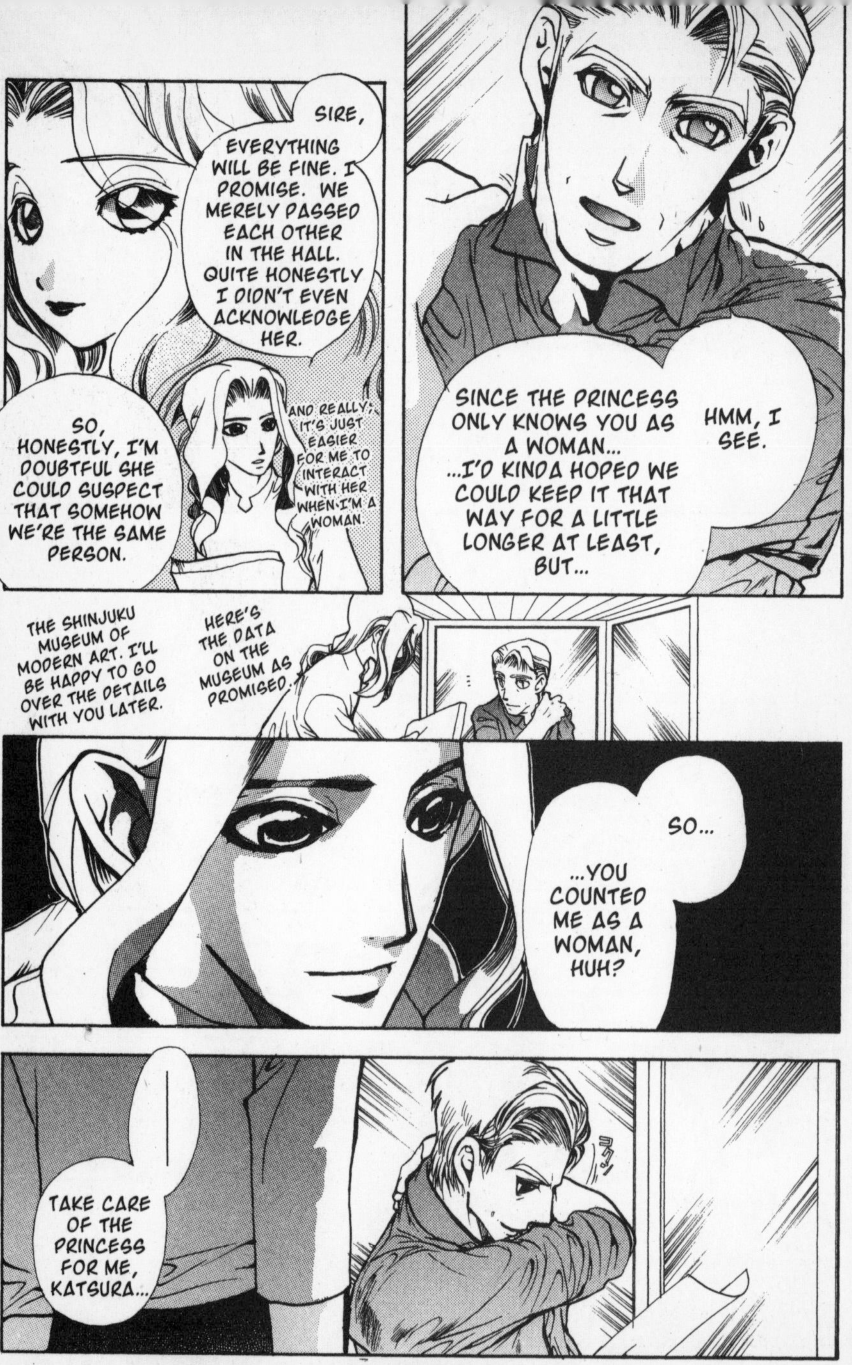
HMM, I SEE.
SINCE THE PRINCESS ONLY KNOWS YOU AS A WOMAN... ...I'D KINDA HOPED WE COULD KEEP IT THAT WAY FOR A LITTLE LONGER AT LEAST, BUT...
SIRE, EVERYTHING WILL BE FINE. I PROMISE. WE MERELY PASSED EACH OTHER IN THE HALL. QUITE HONESTLY I DIDN'T EVEN ACKNOWLEDGE HER.
AND REALLY, IT'S JUST EASIER FOR ME TO INTERACT WITH HER WHEN I'M A WOMAN.
SO, HONESTLY, I'M DOUBTFUL SHE COULD SUSPECT THAT SOMEHOW WE'RE THE SAME PERSON.
HERE'S THE DATA ON THE MUSEUM AS PROMISED.
THE SHINJUKU MUSEUM OF MODERN ART. I'LL BE HAPPY TO GO OVER THE DETAILS WITH YOU LATER.
SO...
...YOU COUNTED ME AS A WOMAN, HUH?
TAKE CARE OF THE PRINCESS FOR ME, KATSURA...

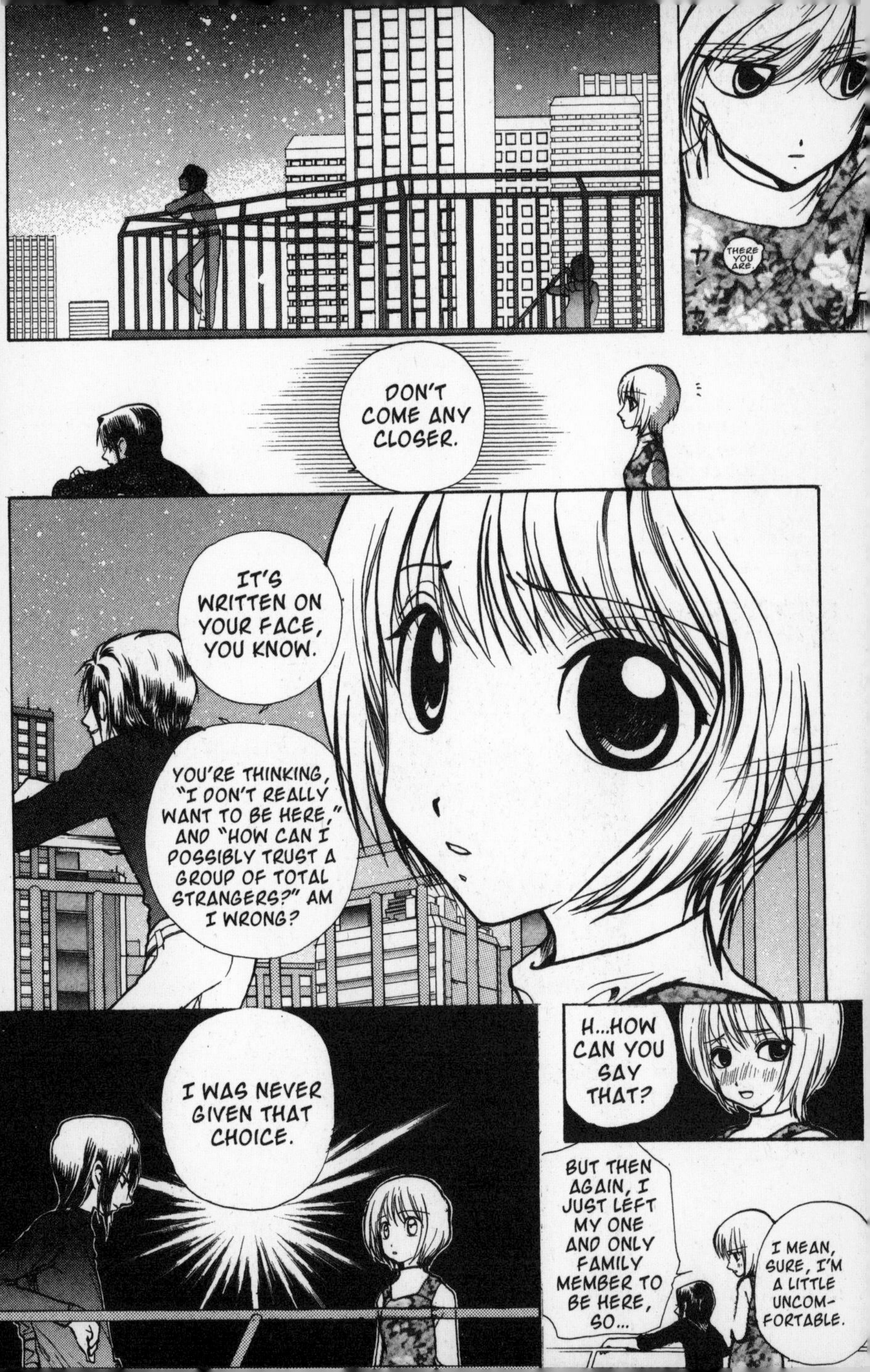
THERE YOU ARE.
DON'T COME ANY CLOSER.
IT'S WRITTEN ON YOUR FACE, YOU KNOW.
YOU'RE THINKING, "I DON'T REALLY WANT TO BE HERE," AND "HOW CAN I POSSIBLY TRUST A GROUP OF TOTAL STRANGERS?" AM I WRONG?
H...HOW CAN YOU SAY THAT?
I MEAN, SURE, I'M A LITTLE UNCOM-FORTABLE.
BUT THEN AGAIN, I JUST LEFT MY ONE AND ONLY FAMILY MEMBER TO BE HERE, SO...
I WAS NEVER GIVEN THAT CHOICE.

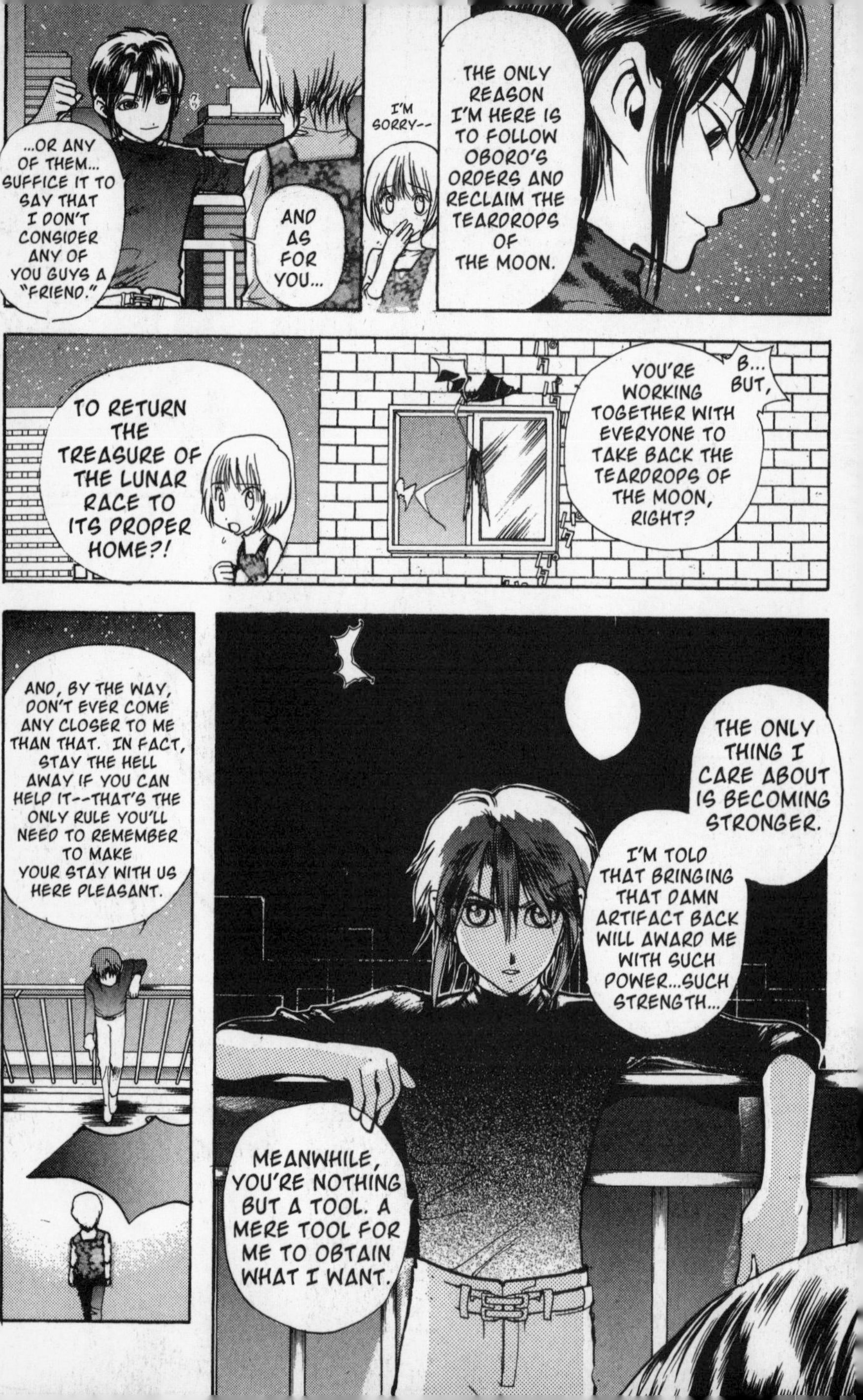

THE ONLY REASON I'M HERE IS TO FOLLOW OBORO'S ORDERS AND RECLAIM THE TEARDROPS OF THE MOON.
I'M SORRY--
AND AS FOR YOU...
...OR ANY OF THEM... SUFFICE IT TO SAY THAT I DON'T CONSIDER ANY OF YOU GUYS A "FRIEND."
B... BUT,
YOU'RE WORKING TOGETHER WITH EVERYONE TO TAKE BACK THE TEARDROPS OF THE MOON, RIGHT?
TO RETURN THE TREASURE OF THE LUNAR RACE TO ITS PROPER HOME?!
THE ONLY THING I CARE ABOUT IS BECOMING STRONGER.
I'M TOLD THAT BRINGING THAT DAMN ARTIFACT BACK WILL AWARD ME WITH SUCH POWER...SUCH STRENGTH...
MEANWHILE, YOU'RE NOTHING BUT A TOOL. A MERE TOOL FOR ME TO OBTAIN WHAT I WANT.
AND, BY THE WAY, DON'T EVER COME ANY CLOSER TO ME THAN THAT. IN FACT, STAY THE HELL AWAY IF YOU CAN HELP IT--THAT'S THE ONLY RULE YOU'LL NEED TO REMEMBER TO MAKE YOUR STAY WITH US HERE PLEASANT.

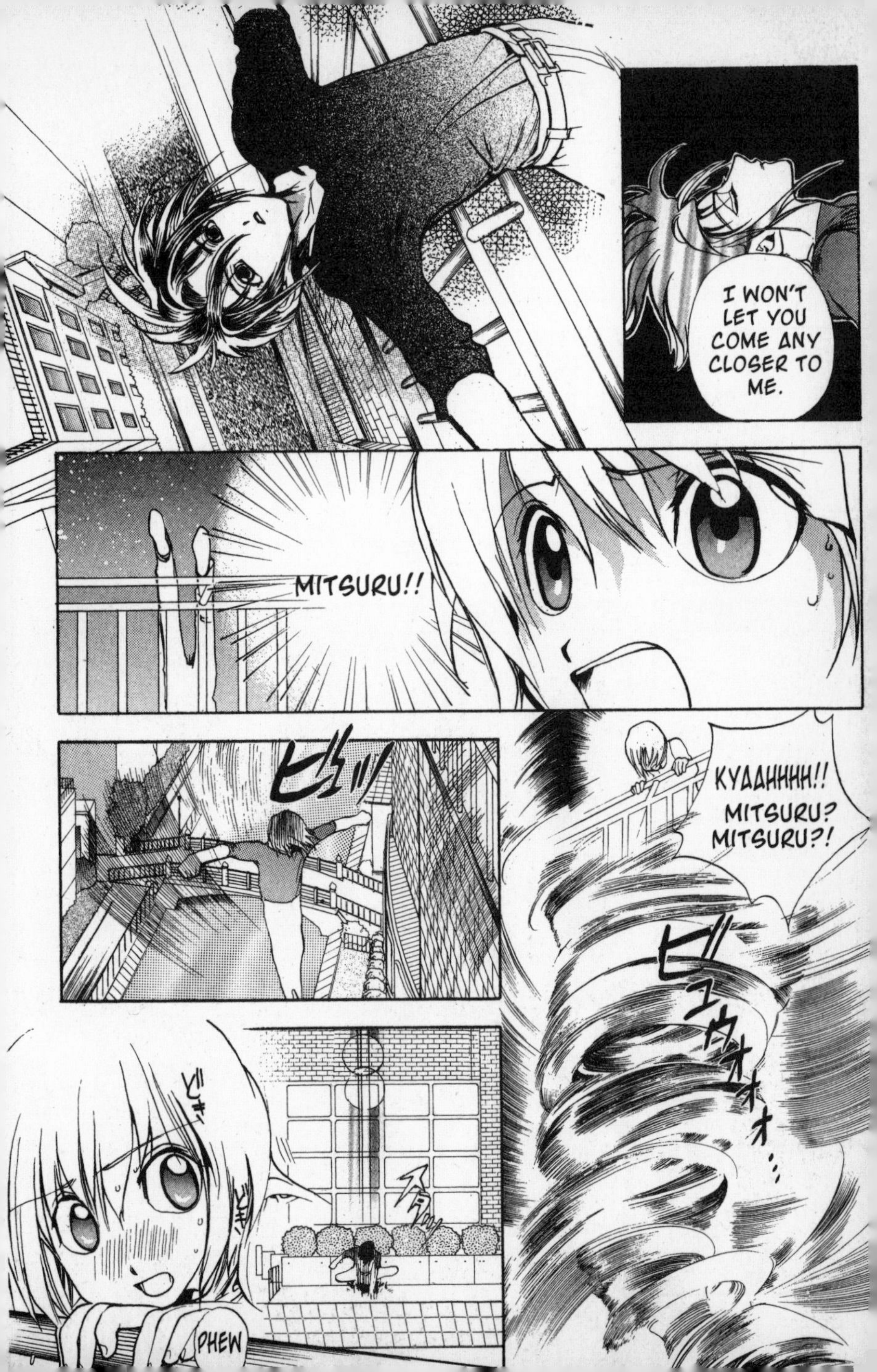
I WON'T LET YOU COME ANY CLOSER TO ME.
MITSURU!!
KYAAHHHH!!
MITSURU? MITSURU?!
PHEW

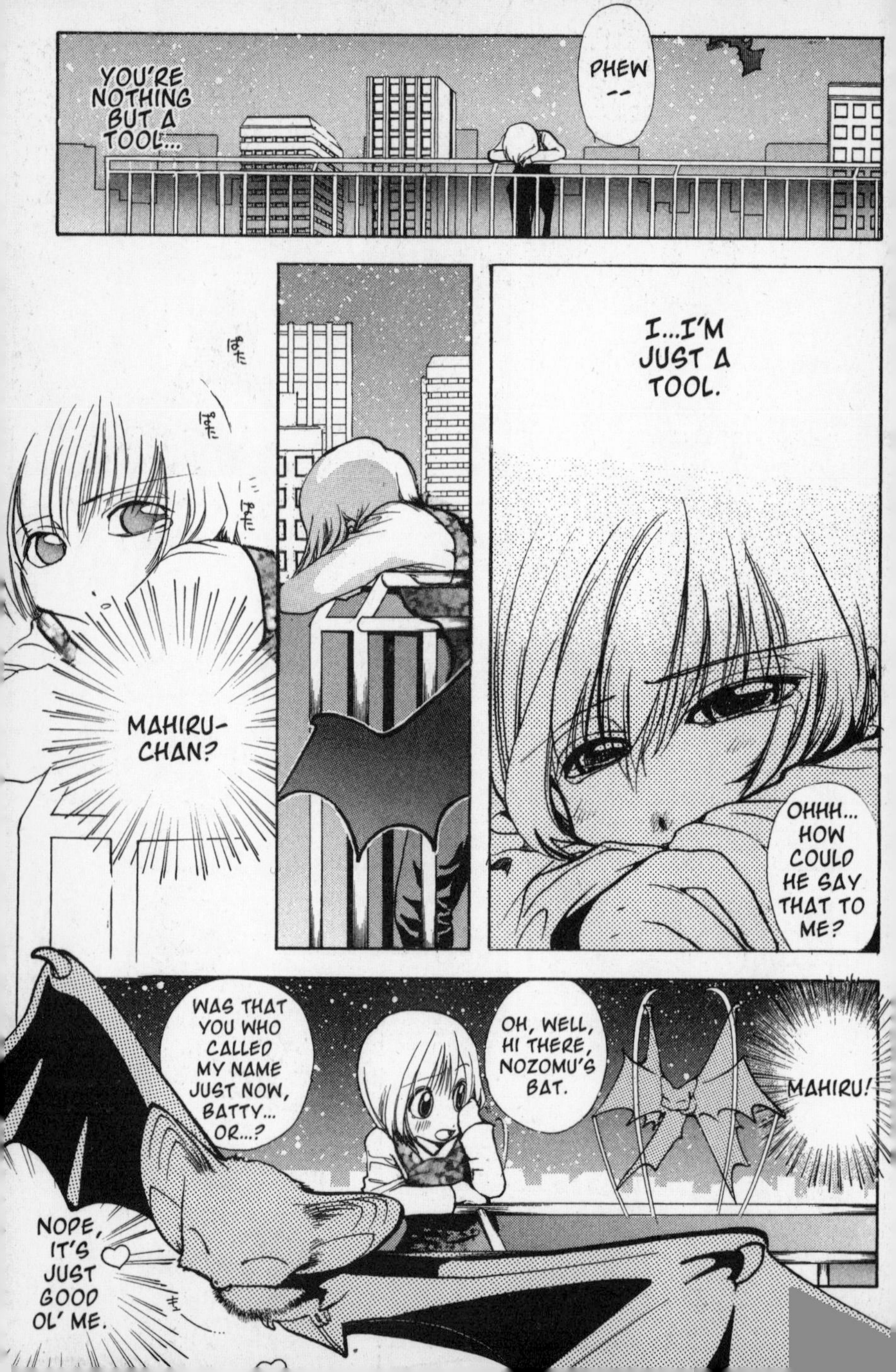
PHEW --
YOU'RE NOTHING BUT A TOOL...
I...I'M JUST A TOOL.
OHHH... HOW COULD HE SAY THAT TO ME?
MAHIRU-CHAN?
MAHIRU!
OH, WELL, HI THERE, NOZOMU'S BAT.
WAS THAT YOU WHO CALLED MY NAME JUST NOW, BATTY... OR...?
NOPE, IT'S JUST GOOD OL' ME.

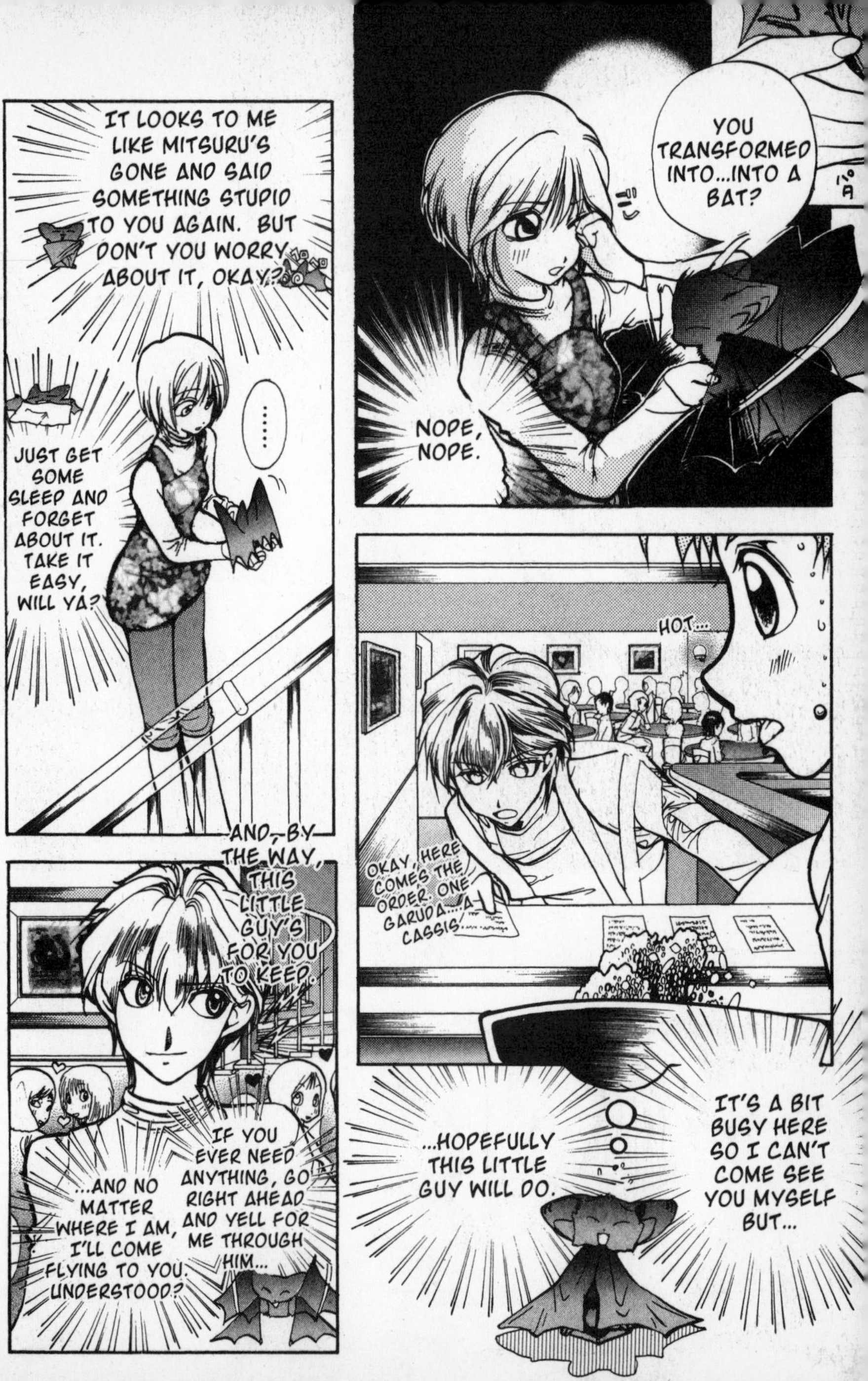

YOU TRANSFORMED INTO...INTO A BAT?
NOPE, NOPE.
HOT...
OKAY, HERE COMES THE ORDER. ONE GARUDA...A CASSIS!
IT'S A BIT BUSY HERE SO I CAN'T COME SEE YOU MYSELF BUT...
...HOPEFULLY THIS LITTLE GUY WILL DO.
IT LOOKS TO ME LIKE MITSURU'S GONE AND SAID SOMETHING STUPID TO YOU AGAIN. BUT DON'T YOU WORRY ABOUT IT, OKAY?
......
JUST GET SOME SLEEP AND FORGET ABOUT IT. TAKE IT EASY, WILL YA?
AND, BY THE WAY, THIS LITTLE GUY'S FOR YOU TO KEEP.
IF YOU EVER NEED ANYTHING, GO RIGHT AHEAD AND YELL FOR ME THROUGH HIM...
...AND NO MATTER WHERE I AM, I'LL COME FLYING TO YOU. UNDERSTOOD?

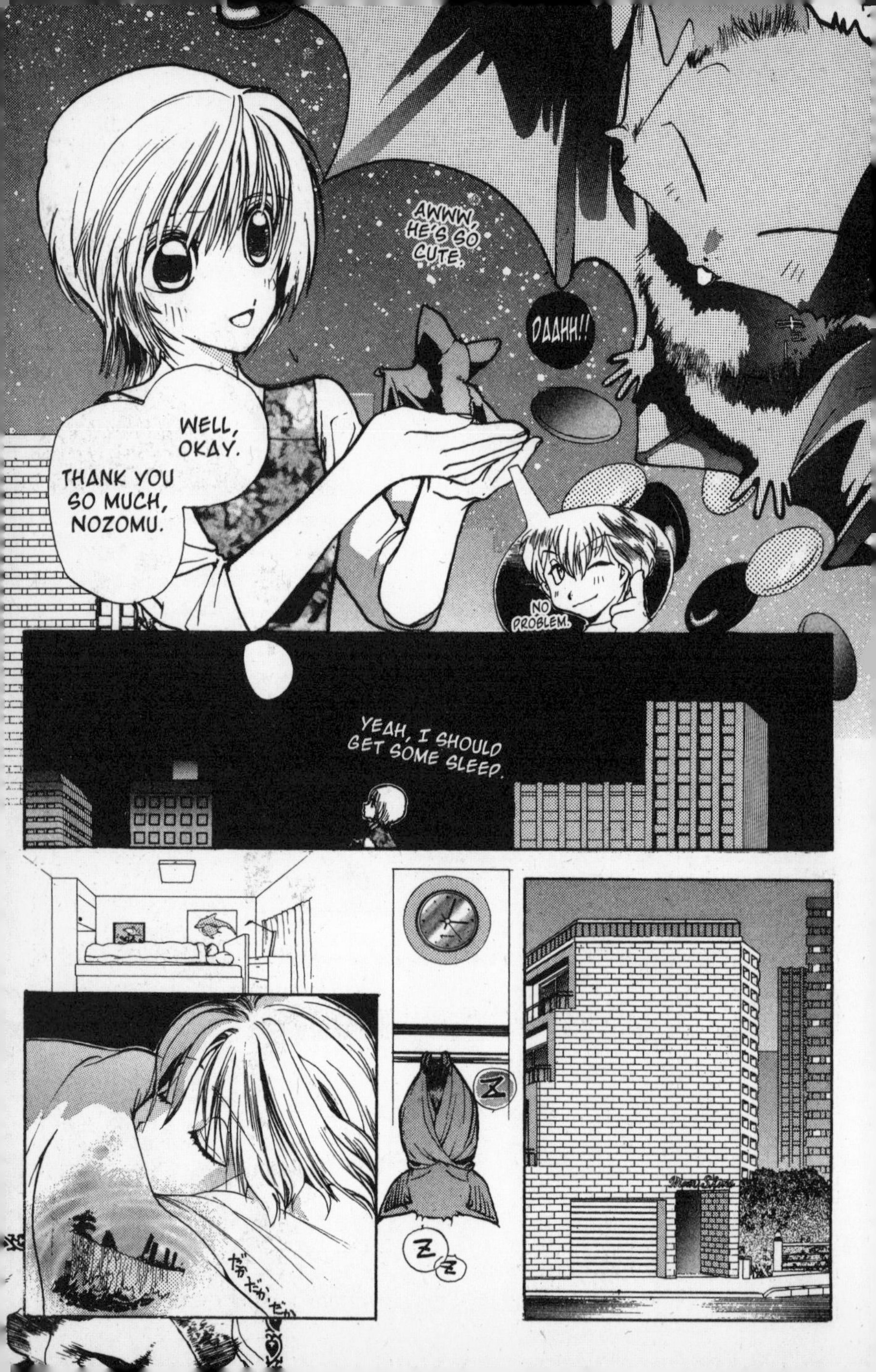
DAAHH!!
AWWW, HE'S SO CUTE.
WELL, OKAY. THANK YOU SO MUCH, NOZOMU.
NO PROBLEM.
YEAH, I SHOULD GET SOME SLEEP.
Z
Z Z

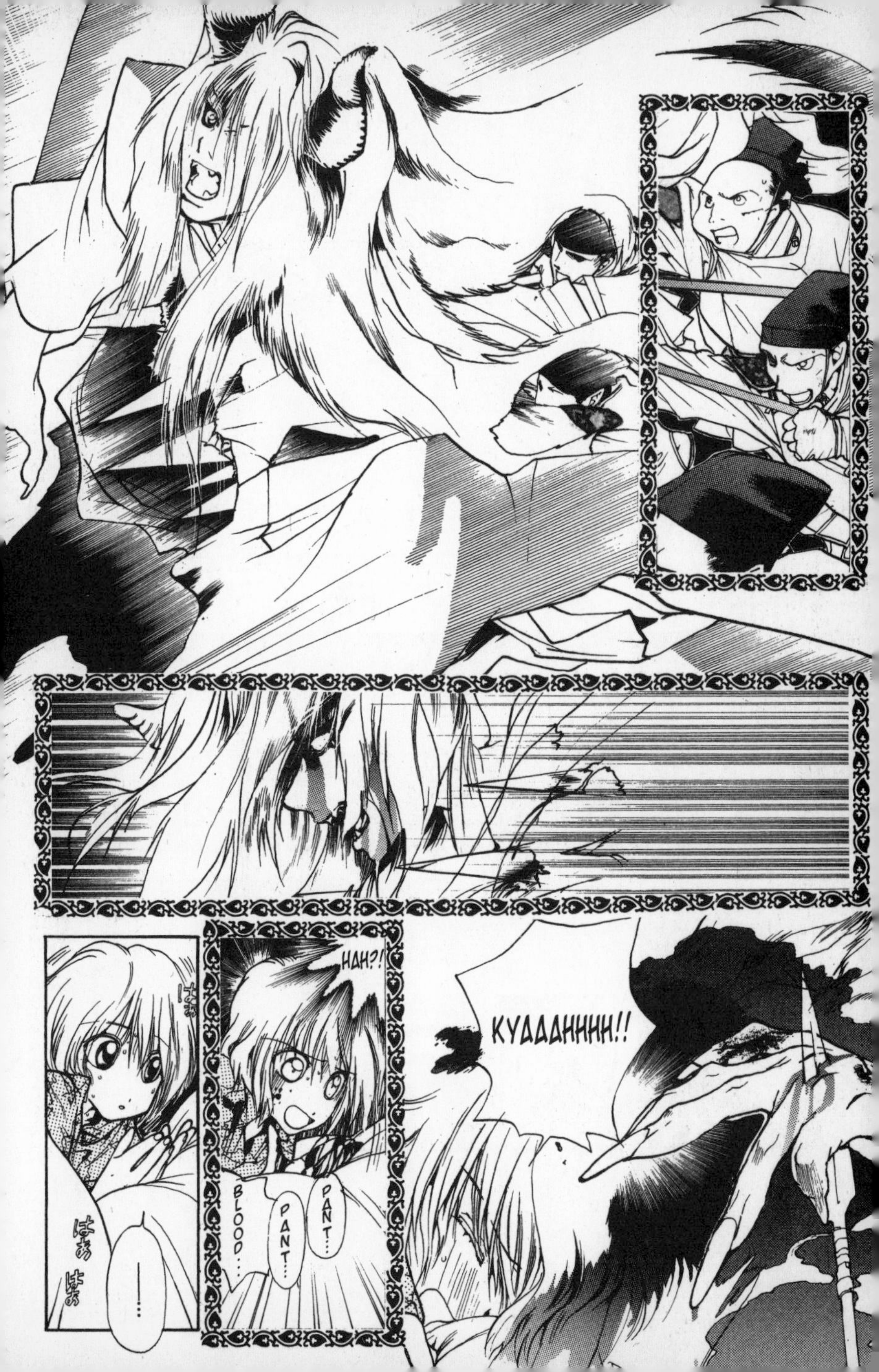
KYAAAHHHH!!
HAH?!
PANT PANT...
BLOOD...
......!
はあ はあ

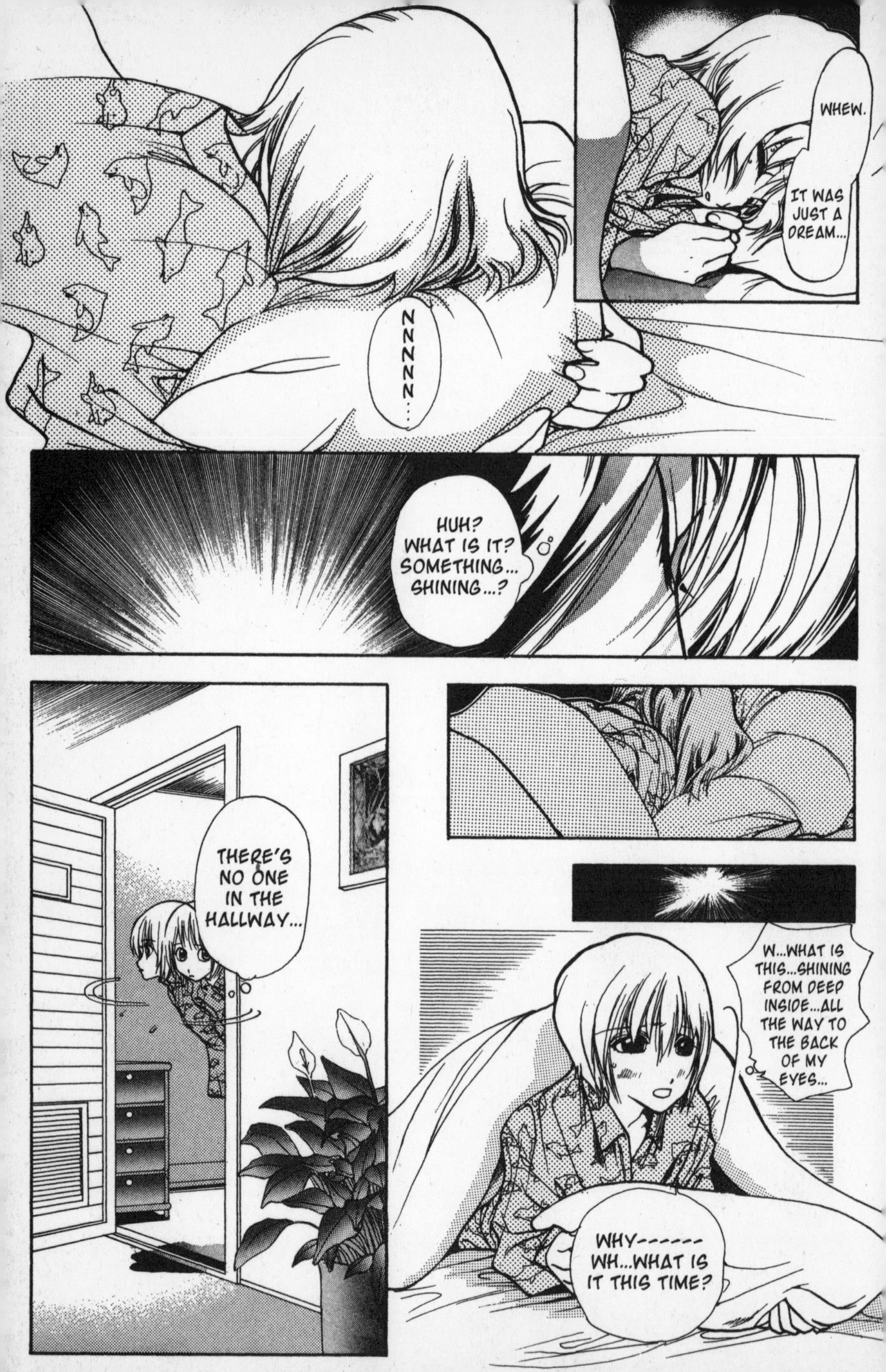
WHEW.
IT WAS JUST A DREAM...
NNNNN...
HUH? WHAT IS IT? SOMETHING... SHINING...?
W...WHAT IS THIS...SHINING FROM DEEP INSIDE...ALL THE WAY TO THE BACK OF MY EYES...
WHY------ WH...WHAT IS IT THIS TIME?
THERE'S NO ONE IN THE HALLWAY...

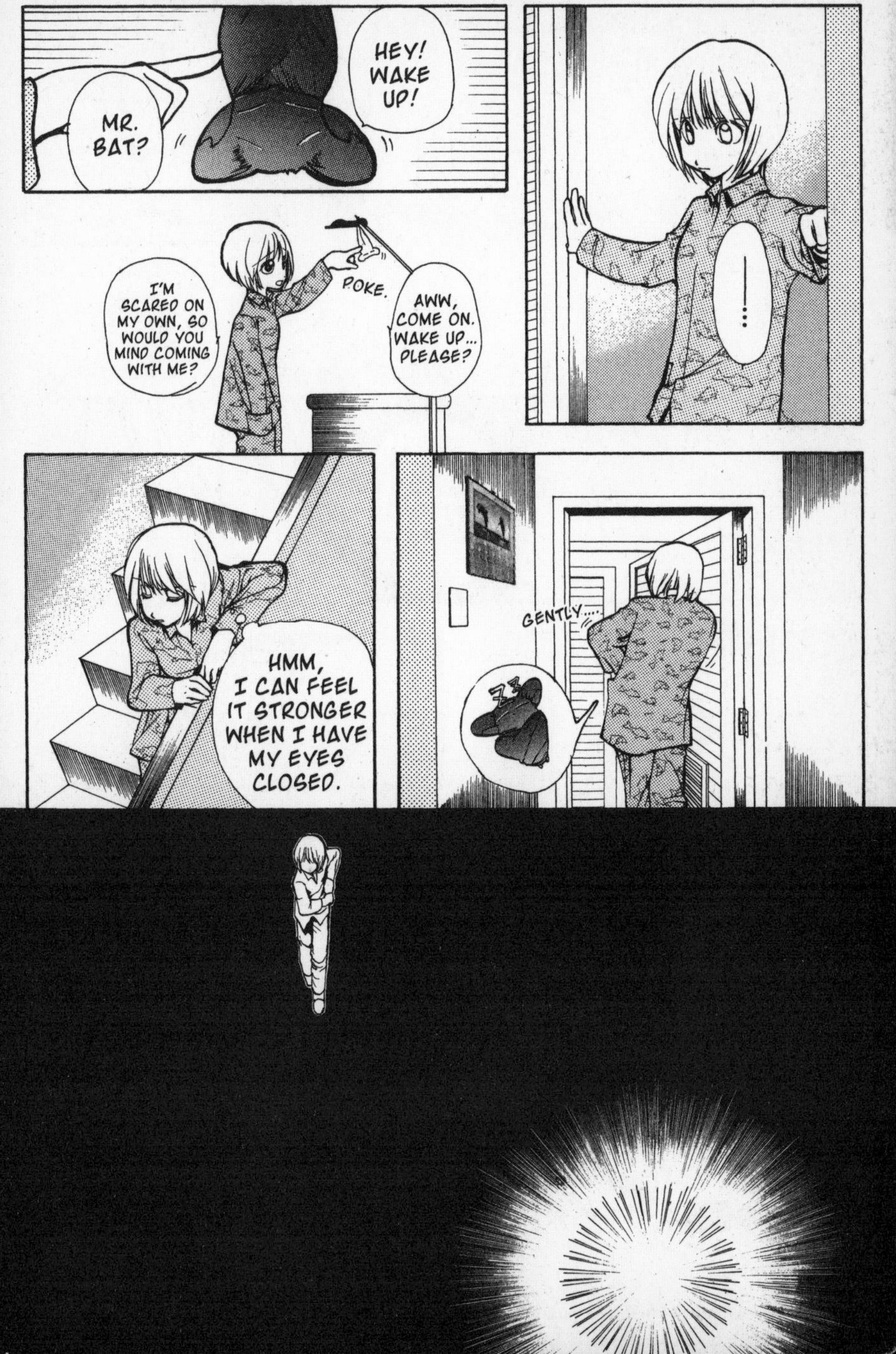
......
HEY! WAKE UP!
MR. BAT?
AWW, COME ON. WAKE UP... PLEASE?
POKE.
I'M SCARED ON MY OWN, SO WOULD YOU MIND COMING WITH ME?
GENTLY.....
HMM, I CAN FEEL IT STRONGER WHEN I HAVE MY EYES CLOSED.

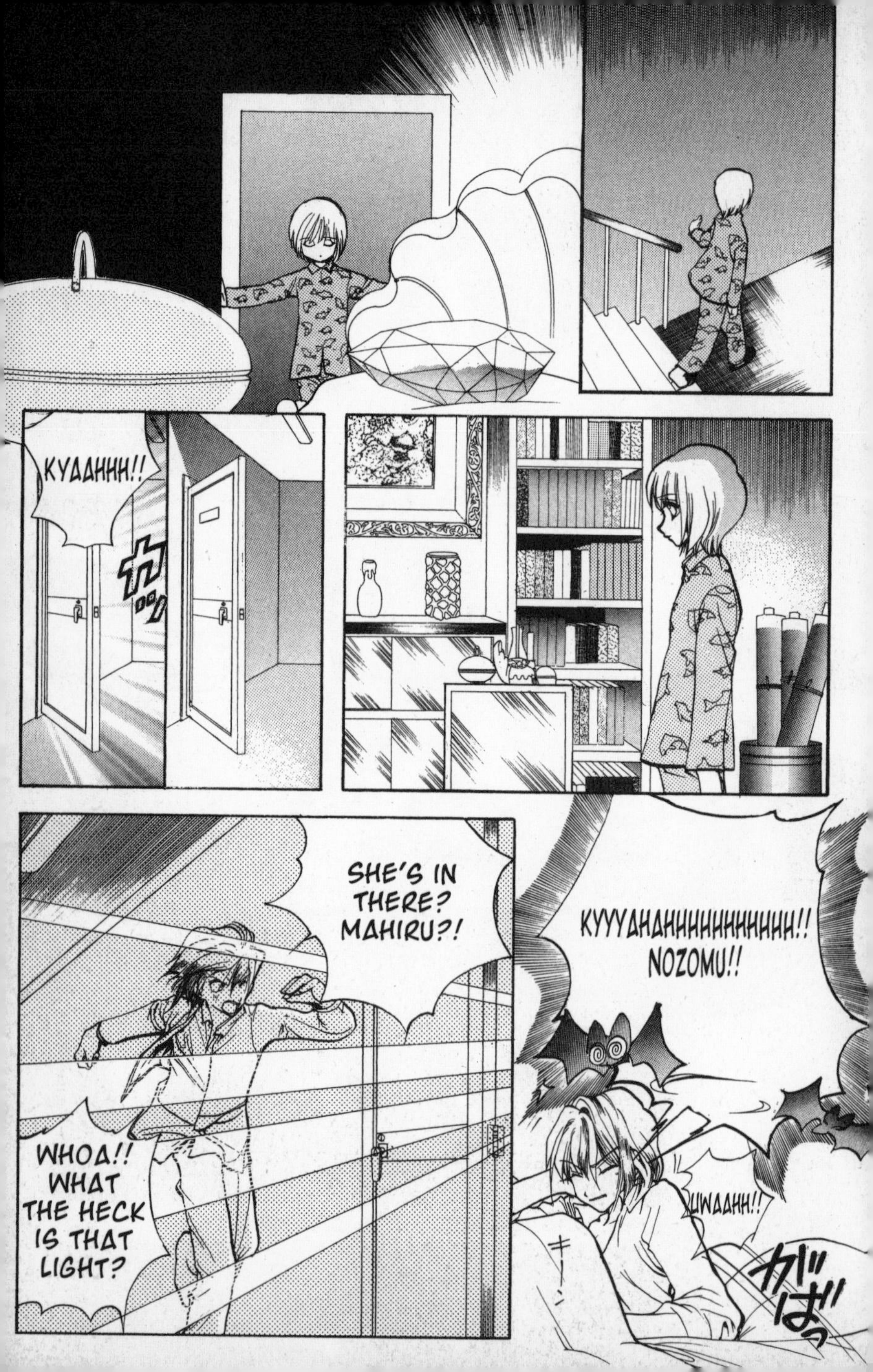
KYAAHHH!!
カッ
KYYYAHAHHHHHHHHHH!! NOZOMU!!
UWAAHH!!
ガバッ
SHE'S IN THERE? MAHIRU?!
WHOA!! WHAT THE HECK IS THAT LIGHT?

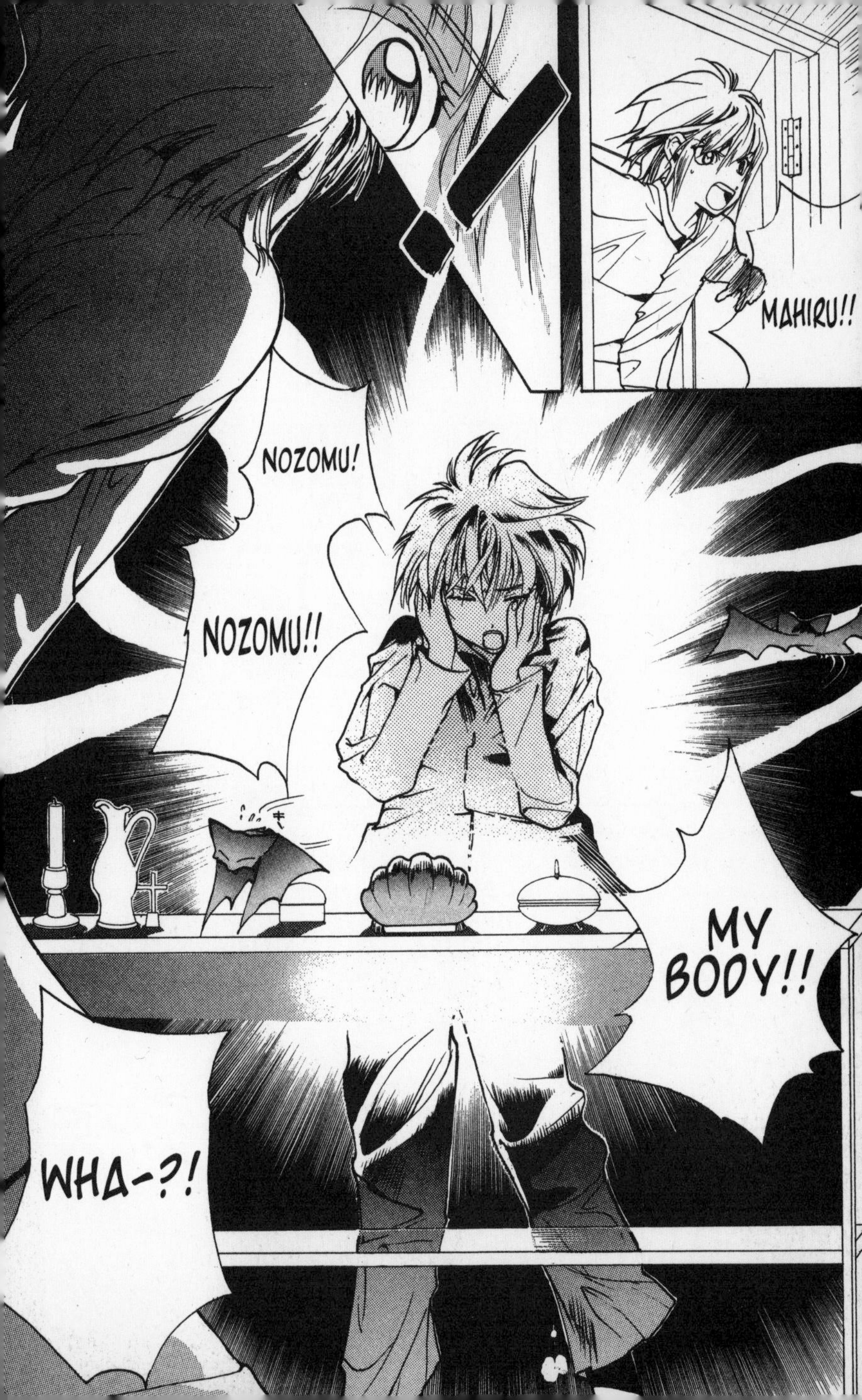
MAHIRU!!
NOZOMU!
NOZOMU!!
MY BODY!!
WHA-?!

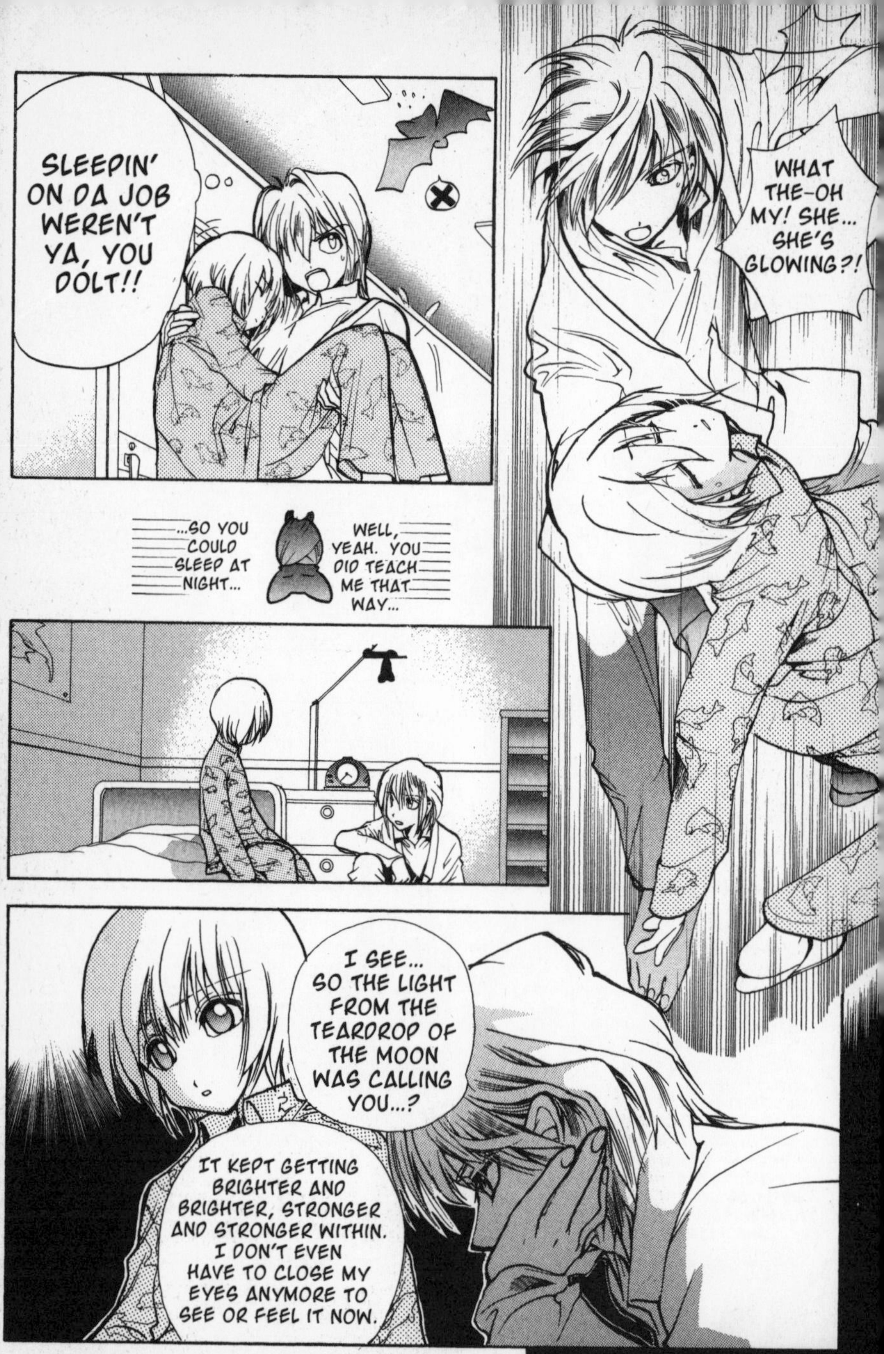
WHAT THE-OH MY! SHE... SHE'S GLOWING?!
SLEEPIN' ON DA JOB WEREN'T YA, YOU DOLT!!
WELL, YEAH. YOU DID TEACH ME THAT WAY...
...SO YOU COULD SLEEP AT NIGHT...
I SEE... SO THE LIGHT FROM THE TEARDROP OF THE MOON WAS CALLING YOU...?
IT KEPT GETTING BRIGHTER AND BRIGHTER, STRONGER AND STRONGER WITHIN. I DON'T EVEN HAVE TO CLOSE MY EYES ANYMORE TO SEE OR FEEL IT NOW.

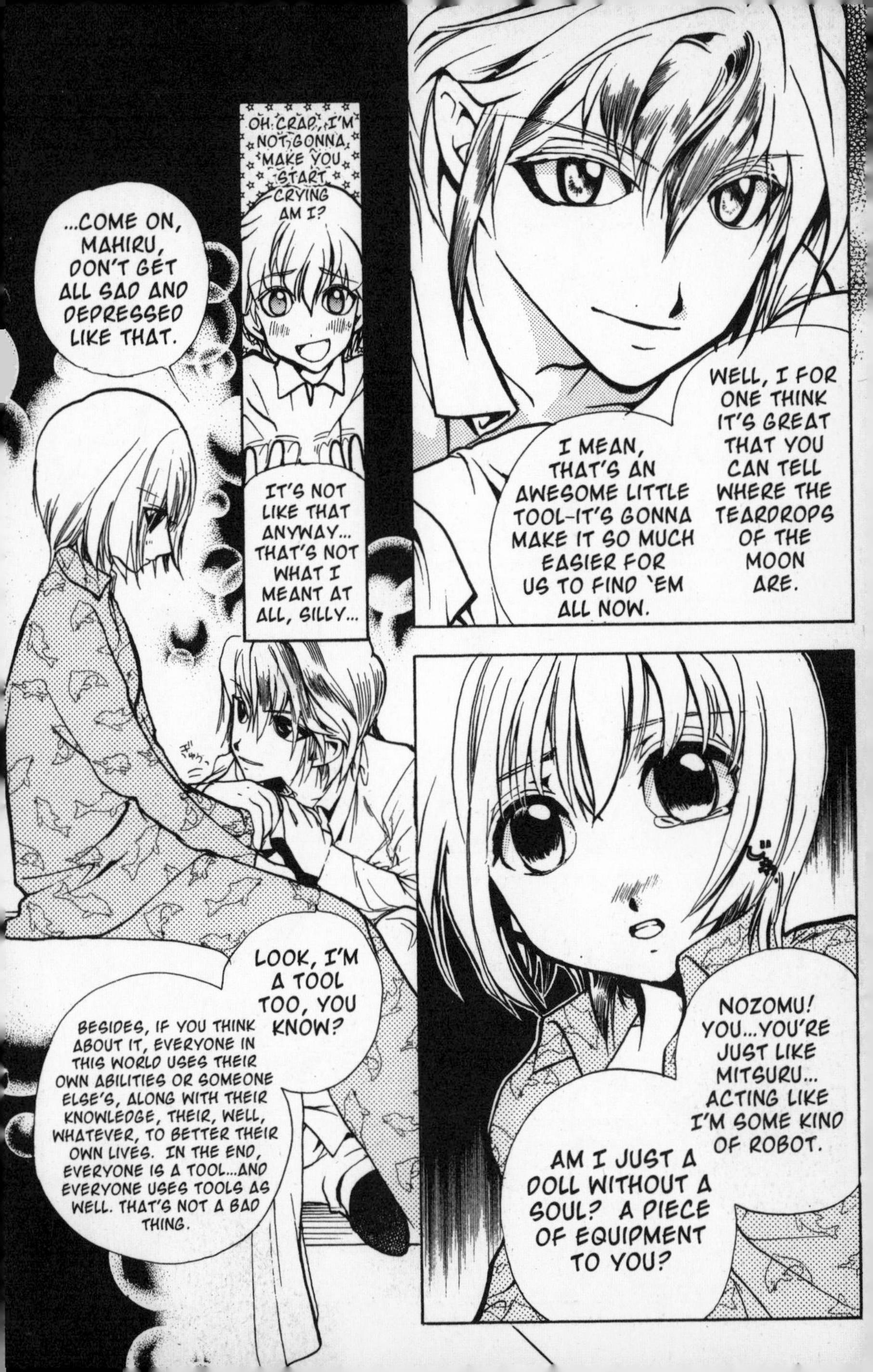
WELL, I FOR ONE THINK IT'S GREAT THAT YOU CAN TELL WHERE THE TEARDROPS OF THE MOON ARE.
I MEAN, THAT'S AN AWESOME LITTLE TOOL-IT'S GONNA MAKE IT SO MUCH EASIER FOR US TO FIND 'EM ALL NOW.
NOZOMU! YOU...YOU'RE JUST LIKE MITSURU... ACTING LIKE I'M SOME KIND OF ROBOT.
AM I JUST A DOLL WITHOUT A SOUL? A PIECE OF EQUIPMENT TO YOU?
...COME ON, MAHIRU, DON'T GET ALL SAD AND DEPRESSED LIKE THAT.
OH CRAP, I'M NOT GONNA MAKE YOU START CRYING AM I?
IT'S NOT LIKE THAT ANYWAY... THAT'S NOT WHAT I MEANT AT ALL, SILLY...
LOOK, I'M A TOOL TOO, YOU KNOW?
BESIDES, IF YOU THINK ABOUT IT, EVERYONE IN THIS WORLD USES THEIR OWN ABILITIES OR SOMEONE ELSE'S, ALONG WITH THEIR KNOWLEDGE, THEIR, WELL, WHATEVER, TO BETTER THEIR OWN LIVES. IN THE END, EVERYONE IS A TOOL...AND EVERYONE USES TOOLS AS WELL. THAT'S NOT A BAD THING.

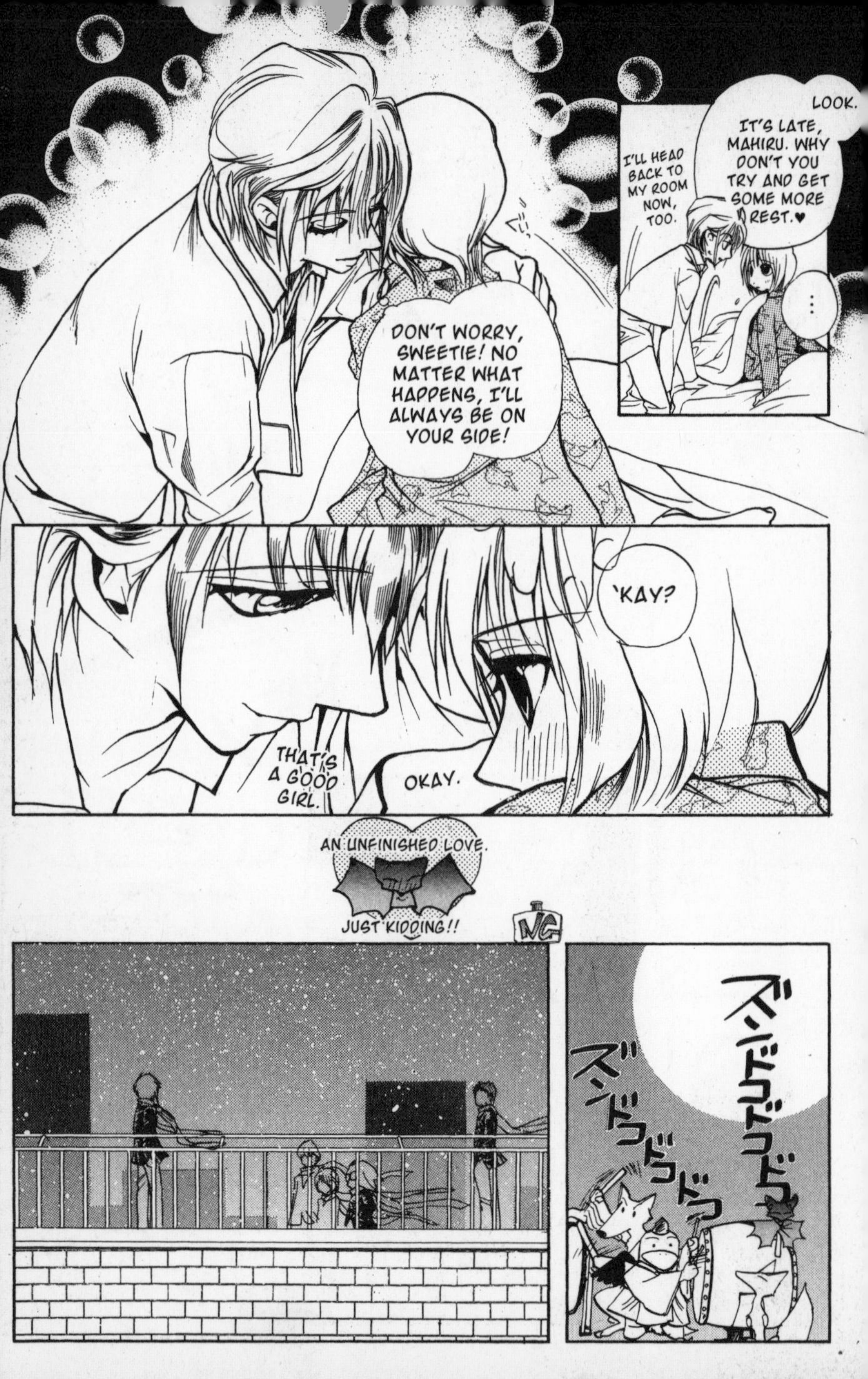
LOOK.
IT'S LATE, MAHIRU. WHY DON'T YOU TRY AND GET SOME MORE REST.♥
I'LL HEAD BACK TO MY ROOM NOW, TOO.
...
DON'T WORRY, SWEETIE! NO MATTER WHAT HAPPENS, I'LL ALWAYS BE ON YOUR SIDE!
'KAY?
OKAY.
THAT'S A GOOD GIRL.
AN UNFINISHED LOVE.
JUST KIDDING!!

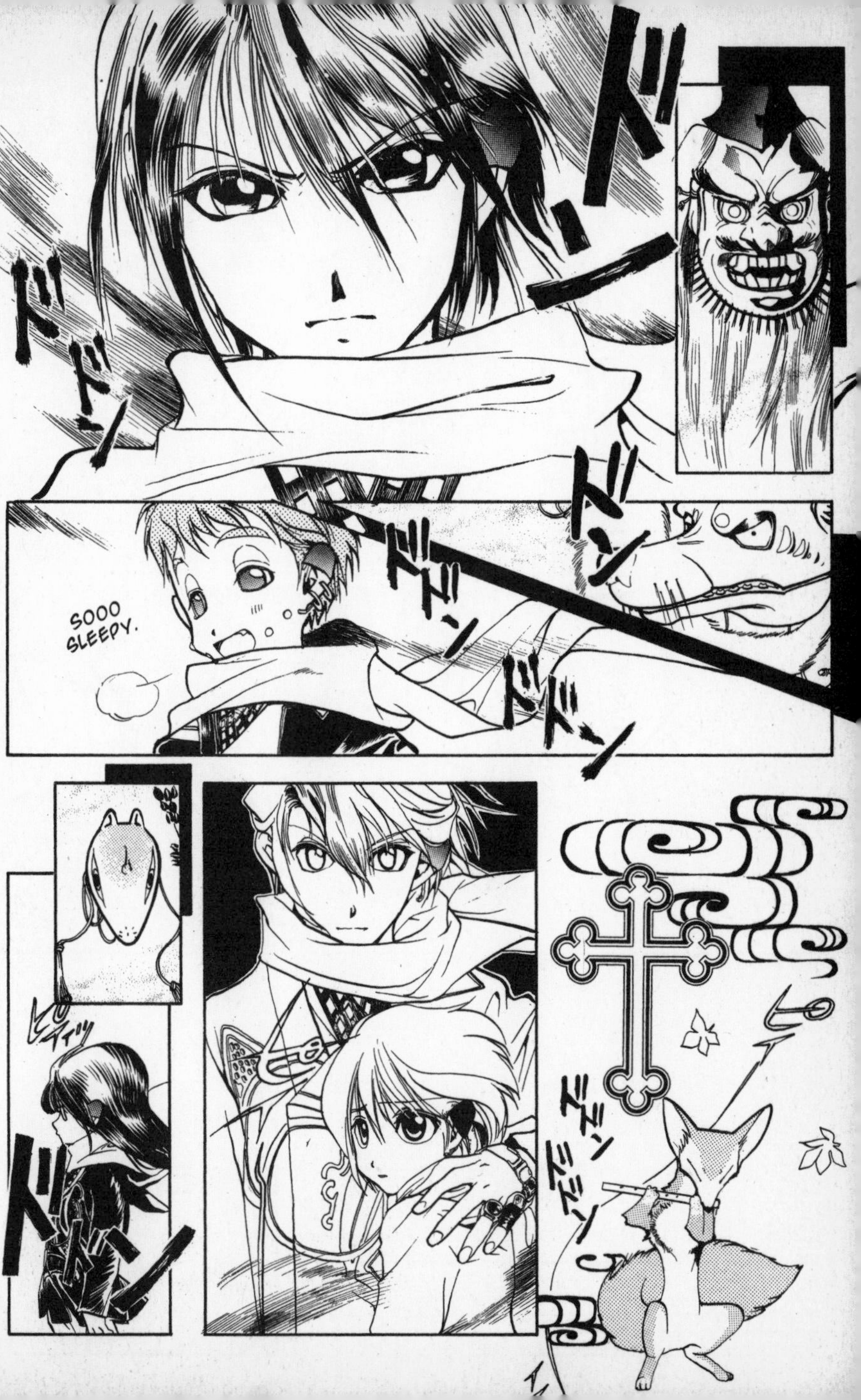
ドドン
ドドン
ドドン
ドドン
SOOO SLEEPY.
ドドン
ピィッ
ドドン
ドドン

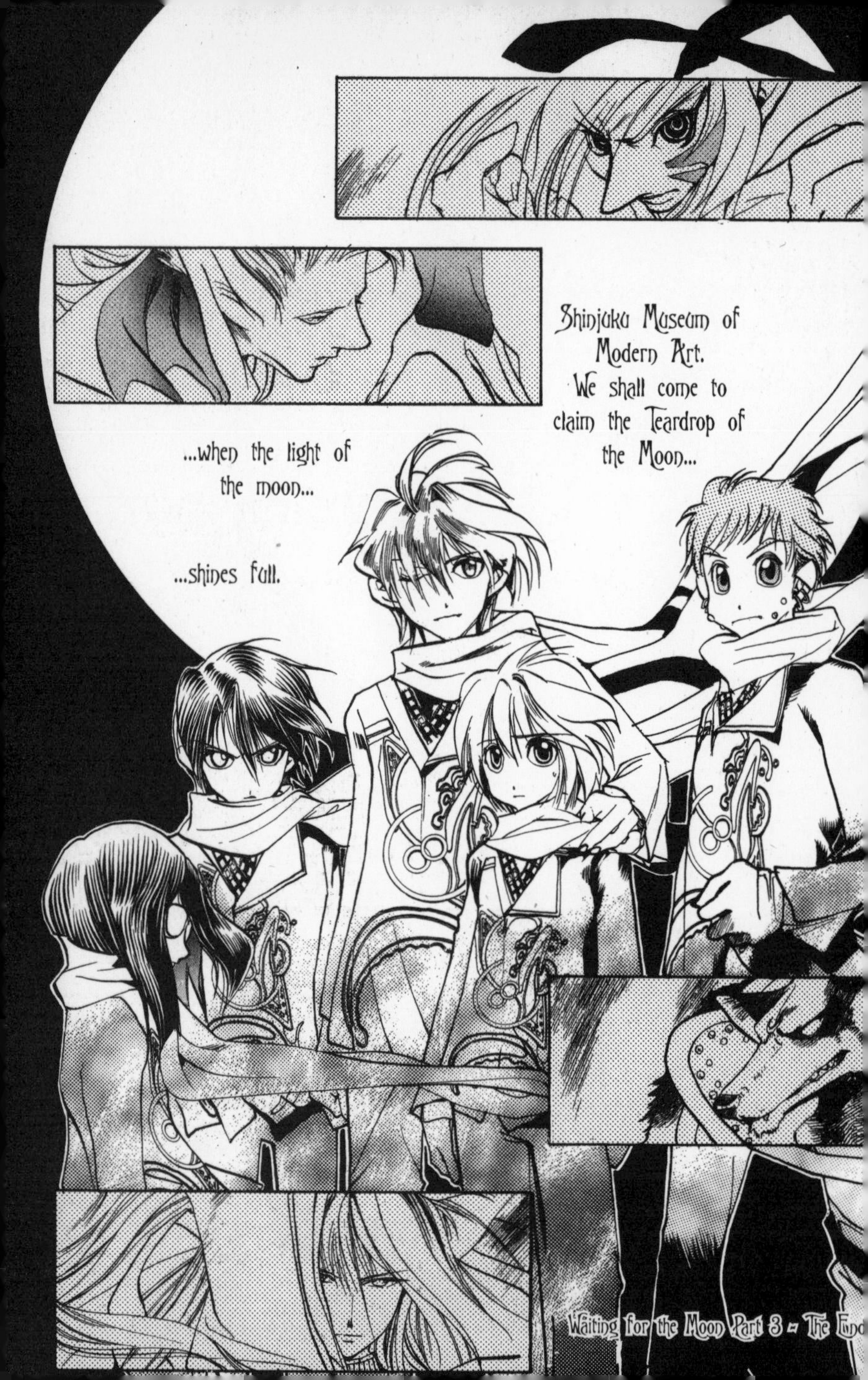
Shinjuku Museum of Modern Art. We shall come to claim the Teardrop of the Moon...
...when the light of the moon...
...shines full.
Waiting for the Moon Part 3 - The End

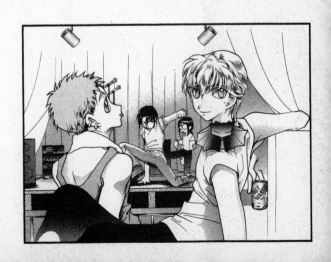

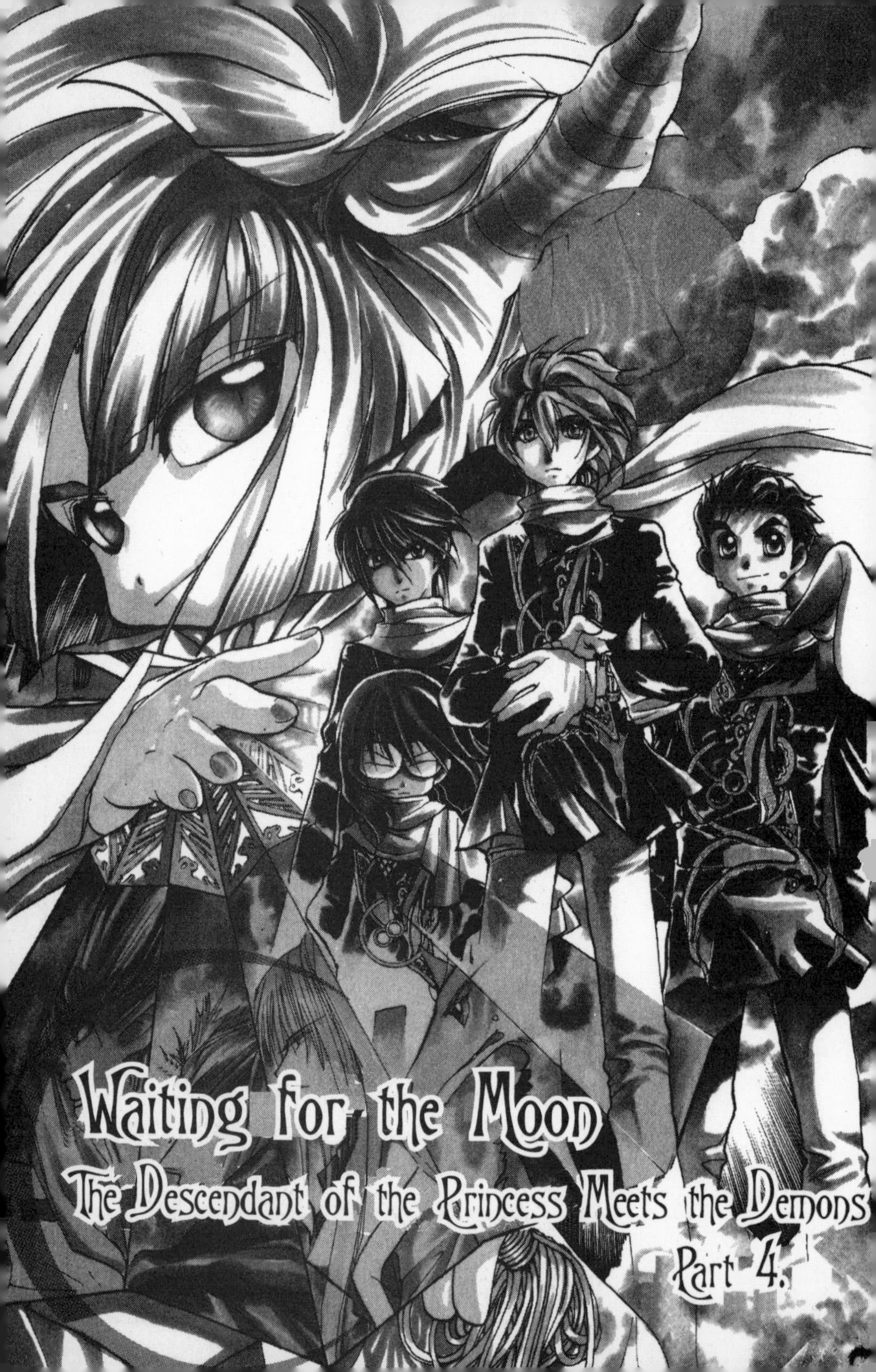
Waiting for the Moon
The Descendant of the Princess Meets the Demons
Part 4.

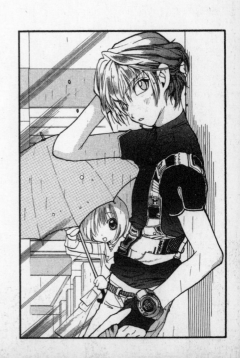

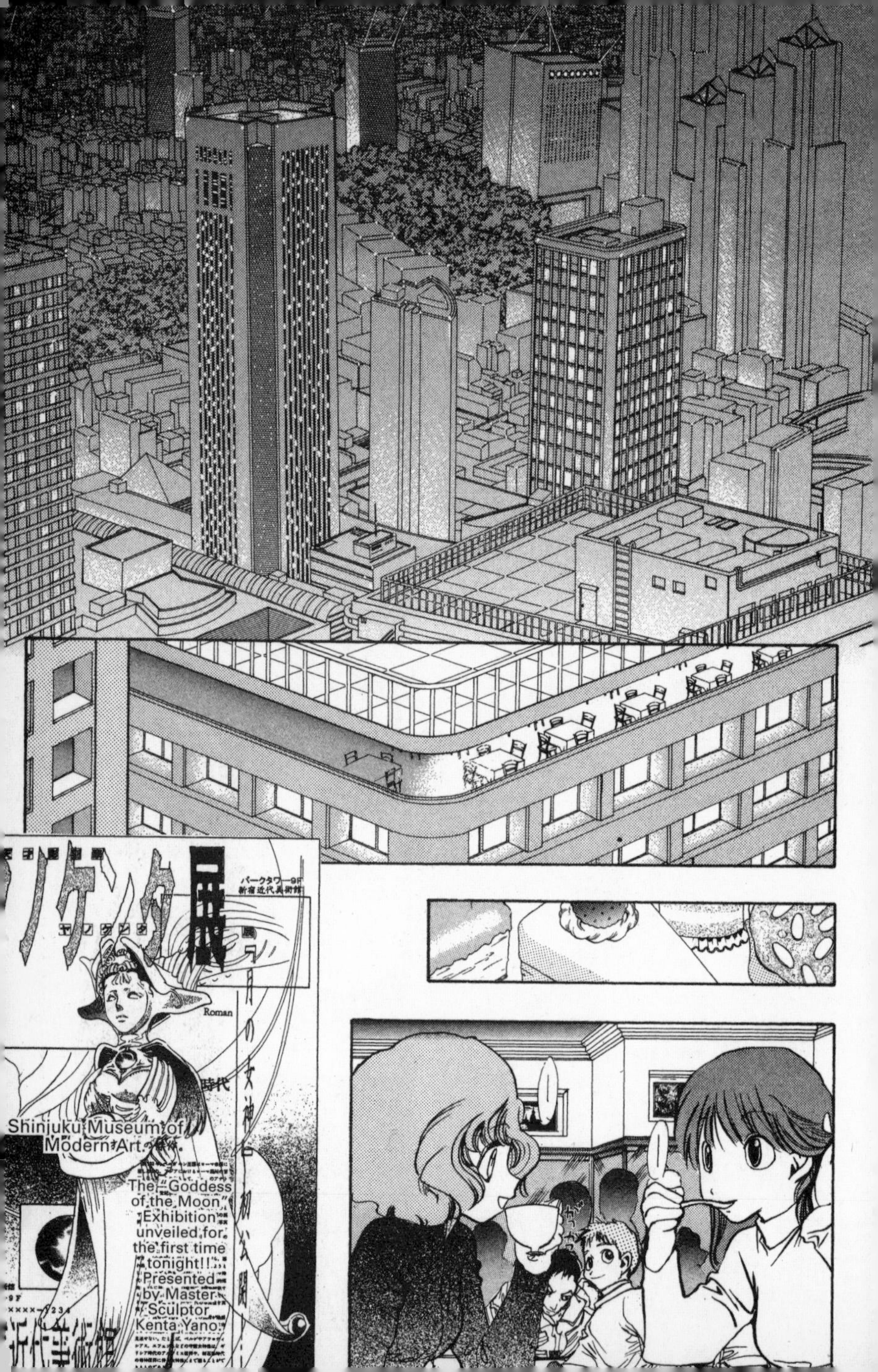
パークタワー9F
新宿近代美術館
ヤノケンタ
展
Roman
時代
月の女神
Shinjuku Museum of Modern Art.
The "Goddess of the Moon" Exhibition unveiled for the first time tonight!! Presented by Master Sculptor Kenta Yano.

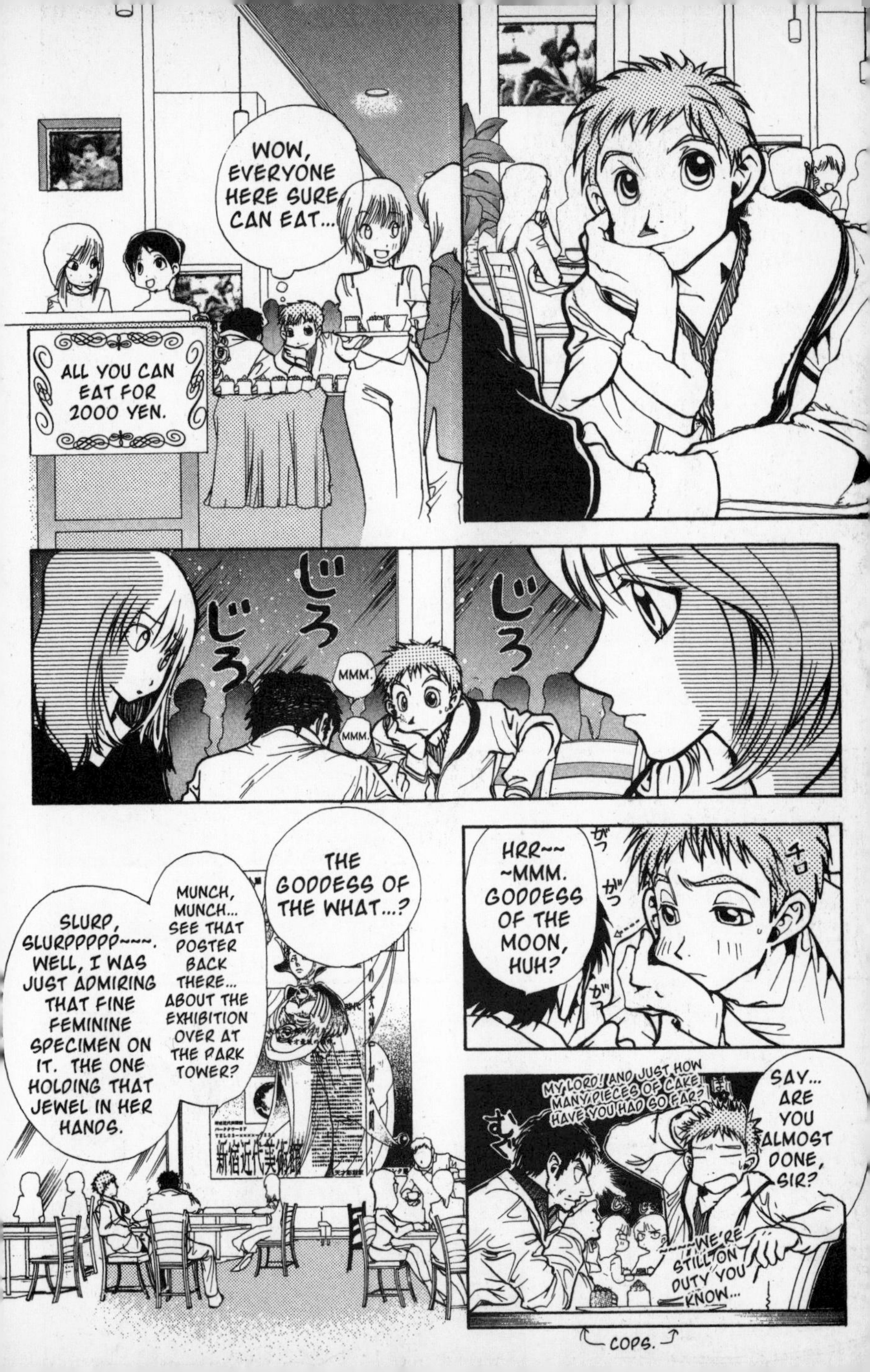
WOW, EVERYONE HERE SURE CAN EAT...
ALL YOU CAN EAT FOR 2000 YEN.
じろ
じろ
MMM.
MMM.
じろ
じろ
HRR~~ ~MMM. GODDESS OF THE MOON, HUH?
チロ
がつ
がつ
がつ
SAY... ARE YOU ALMOST DONE, SIR?
MY LORD! AND JUST HOW MANY PIECES OF CAKE HAVE YOU HAD SO FAR?
~~~WE'RE STILL ON DUTY YOU KNOW...
COPS.
THE GODDESS OF THE WHAT...?
MUNCH, MUNCH... SEE THAT POSTER BACK THERE... ABOUT THE EXHIBITION OVER AT THE PARK TOWER?
SLURP, SLURPPPPP~~~. WELL, I WAS JUST ADMIRING THAT FINE FEMININE SPECIMEN ON IT. THE ONE HOLDING THAT JEWEL IN HER HANDS.
新宿近代美術館
~~~

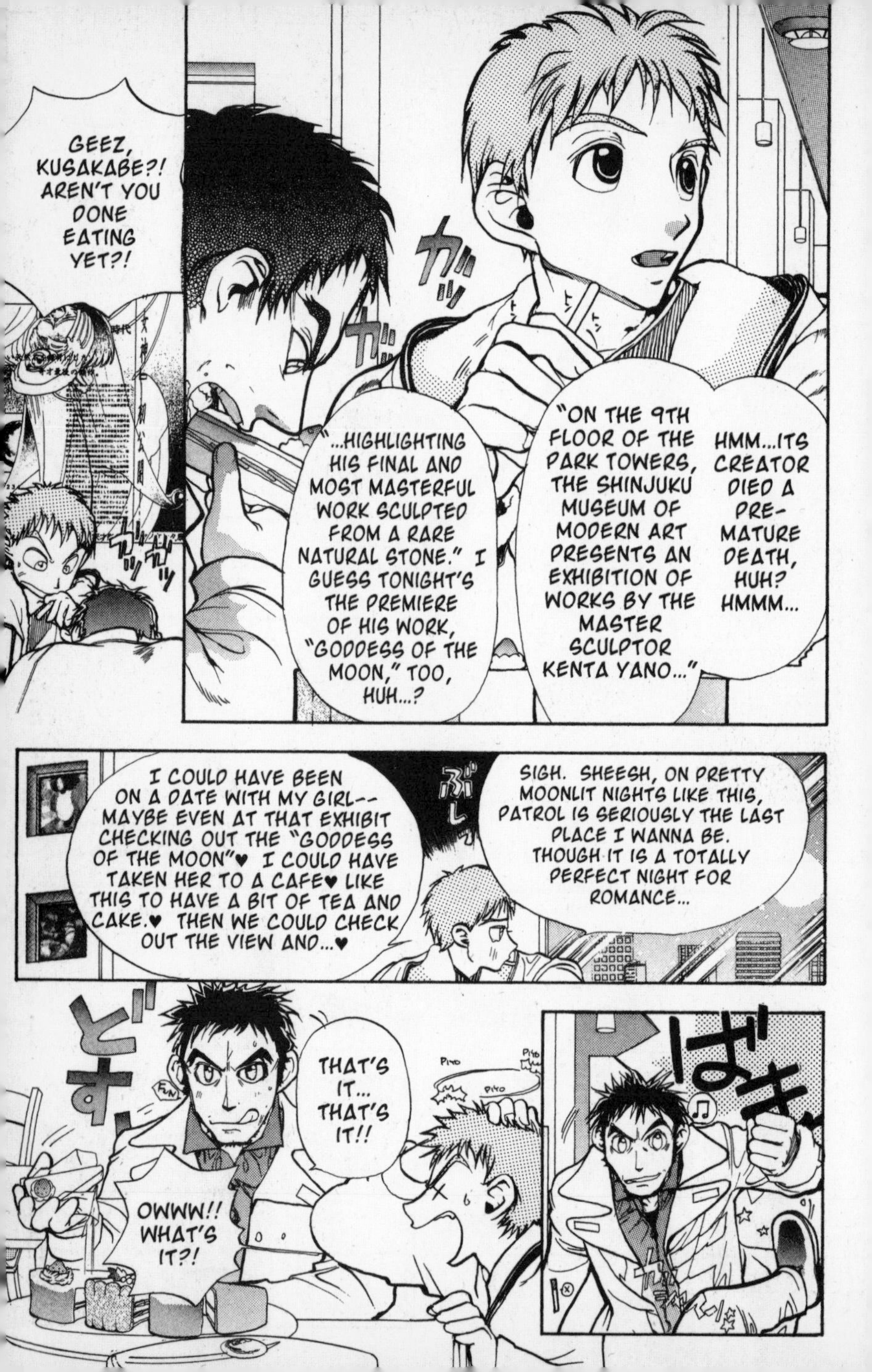
"ON THE 9TH FLOOR OF THE PARK TOWERS, THE SHINJUKU MUSEUM OF MODERN ART PRESENTS AN EXHIBITION OF WORKS BY THE MASTER SCULPTOR KENTA YANO..."
"...HIGHLIGHTING HIS FINAL AND MOST MASTERFUL WORK SCULPTED FROM A RARE NATURAL STONE." I GUESS TONIGHT'S THE PREMIERE OF HIS WORK, "GODDESS OF THE MOON," TOO, HUH...?
HMM...ITS CREATOR DIED A PRE-MATURE DEATH, HUH? HMMM...
GEEZ, KUSAKABE?! AREN'T YOU DONE EATING YET?!
SIGH. SHEESH, ON PRETTY MOONLIT NIGHTS LIKE THIS, PATROL IS SERIOUSLY THE LAST PLACE I WANNA BE. THOUGH IT IS A TOTALLY PERFECT NIGHT FOR ROMANCE...
I COULD HAVE BEEN ON A DATE WITH MY GIRL-- MAYBE EVEN AT THAT EXHIBIT CHECKING OUT THE "GODDESS OF THE MOON"♥ I COULD HAVE TAKEN HER TO A CAFE♥ LIKE THIS TO HAVE A BIT OF TEA AND CAKE.♥ THEN WE COULD CHECK OUT THE VIEW AND...♥
ばき
♪
THAT'S IT... THAT'S IT!!
PIYO
PIYO
PIYO
OWWW!! WHAT'S IT?!
FUN

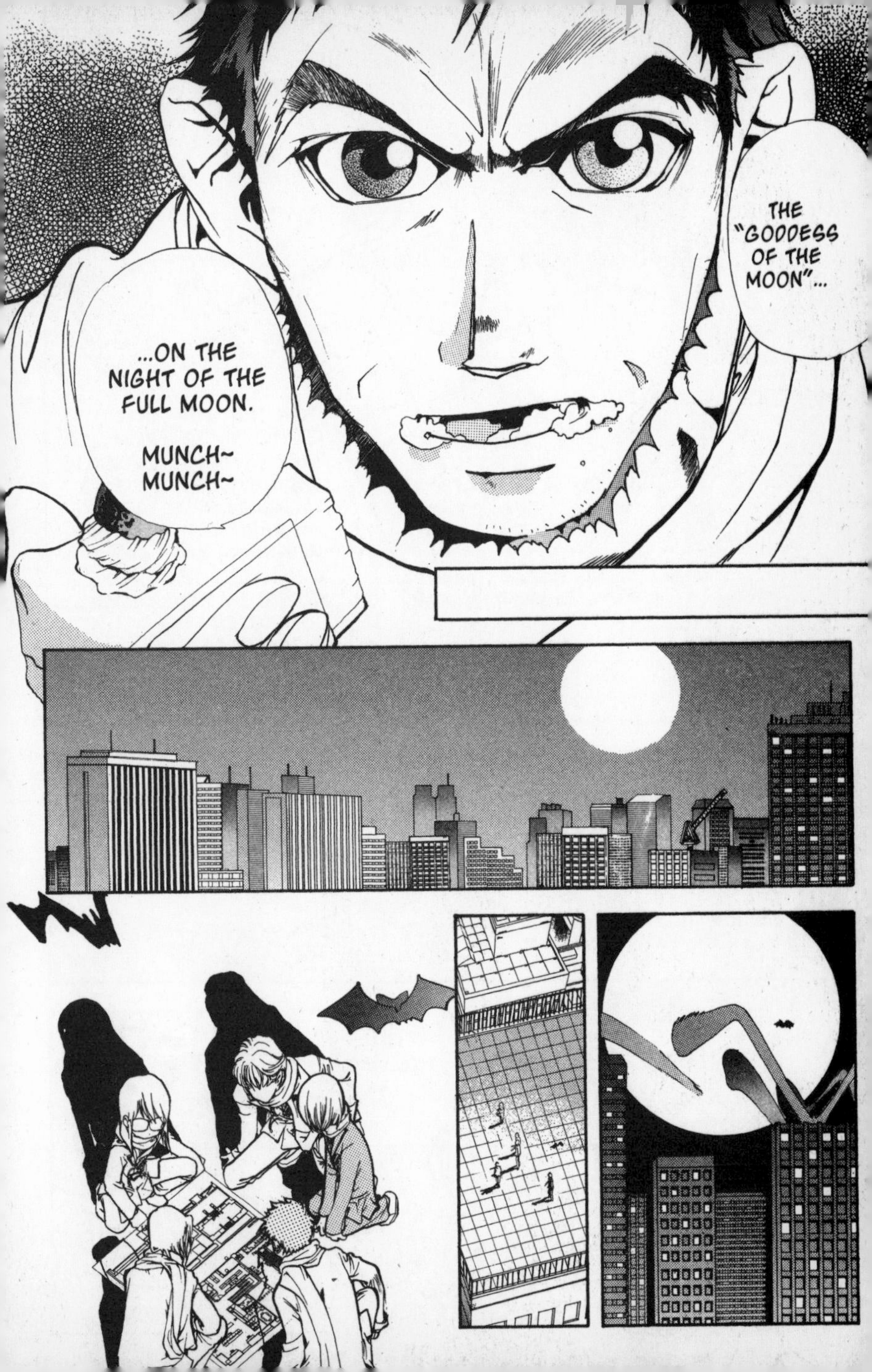
THE "GODDESS OF THE MOON"...
...ON THE NIGHT OF THE FULL MOON.
MUNCH~ MUNCH~

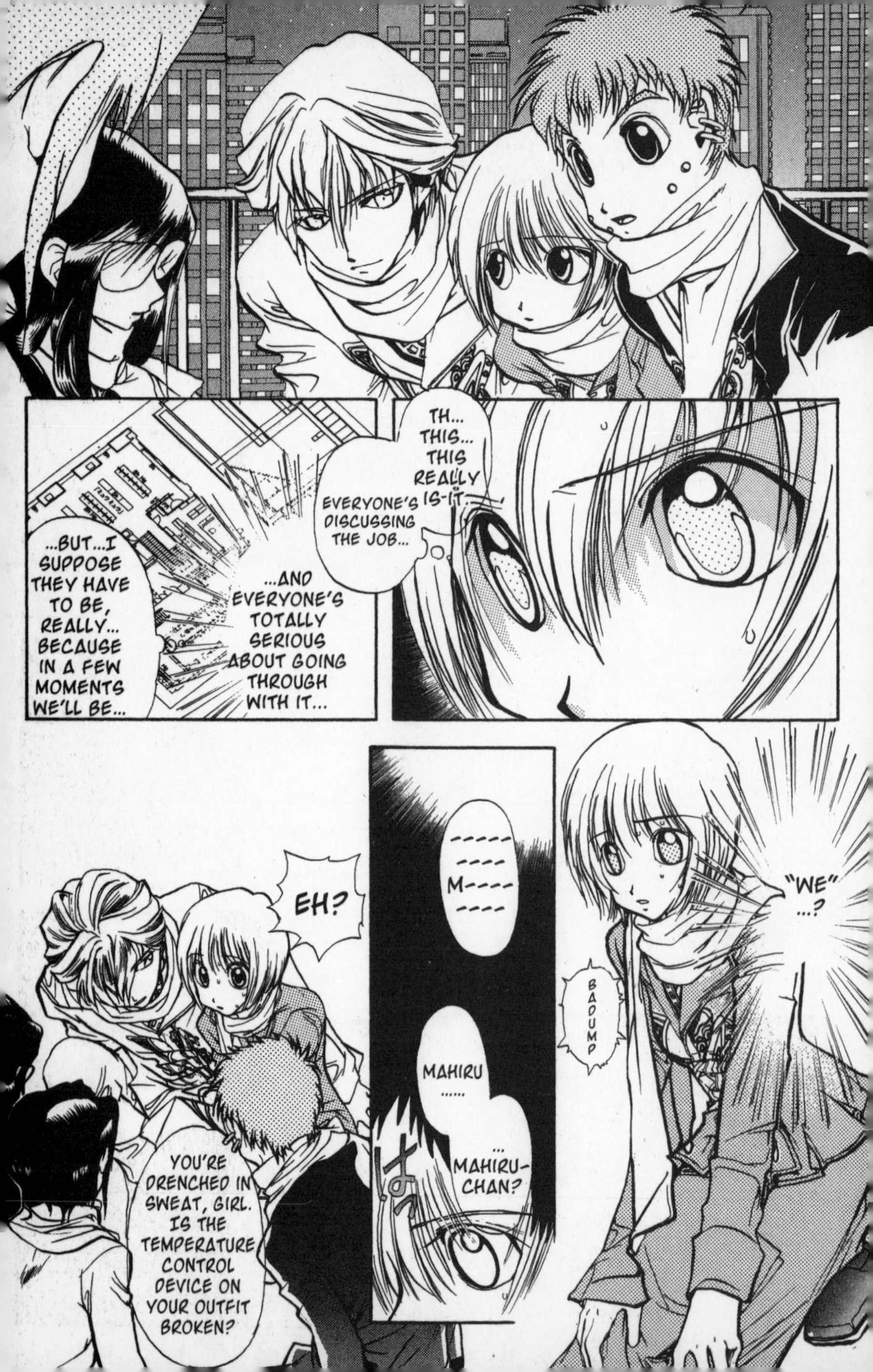
TH... THIS... THIS REALLY IS IT.
EVERYONE'S DISCUSSING THE JOB...
...AND EVERYONE'S TOTALLY SERIOUS ABOUT GOING THROUGH WITH IT...
...BUT...I SUPPOSE THEY HAVE TO BE, REALLY... BECAUSE IN A FEW MOMENTS WE'LL BE...
"WE" ...?
BADUMP
----- ---- M---- ----
MAHIRU ......
... MAHIRU-CHAN?
はっ
EH?
YOU'RE DRENCHED IN SWEAT, GIRL. IS THE TEMPERATURE CONTROL DEVICE ON YOUR OUTFIT BROKEN?

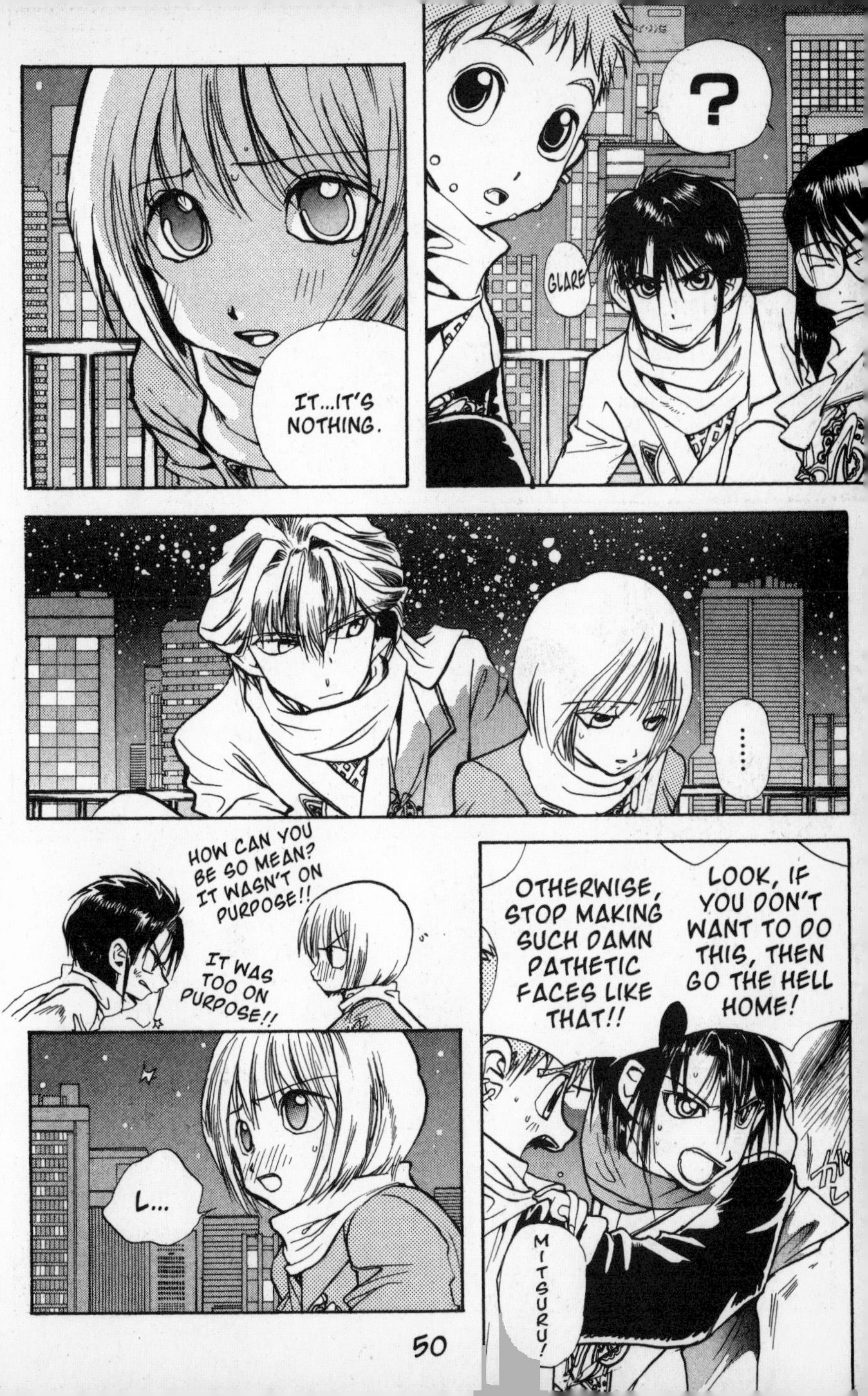
?
GLARE
IT...IT'S NOTHING.
......
LOOK, IF YOU DON'T WANT TO DO THIS, THEN GO THE HELL HOME!
OTHERWISE, STOP MAKING SUCH DAMN PATHETIC FACES LIKE THAT!!
MITSURU!
HOW CAN YOU BE SO MEAN? IT WASN'T ON PURPOSE!!
IT WAS TOO ON PURPOSE!!
I...

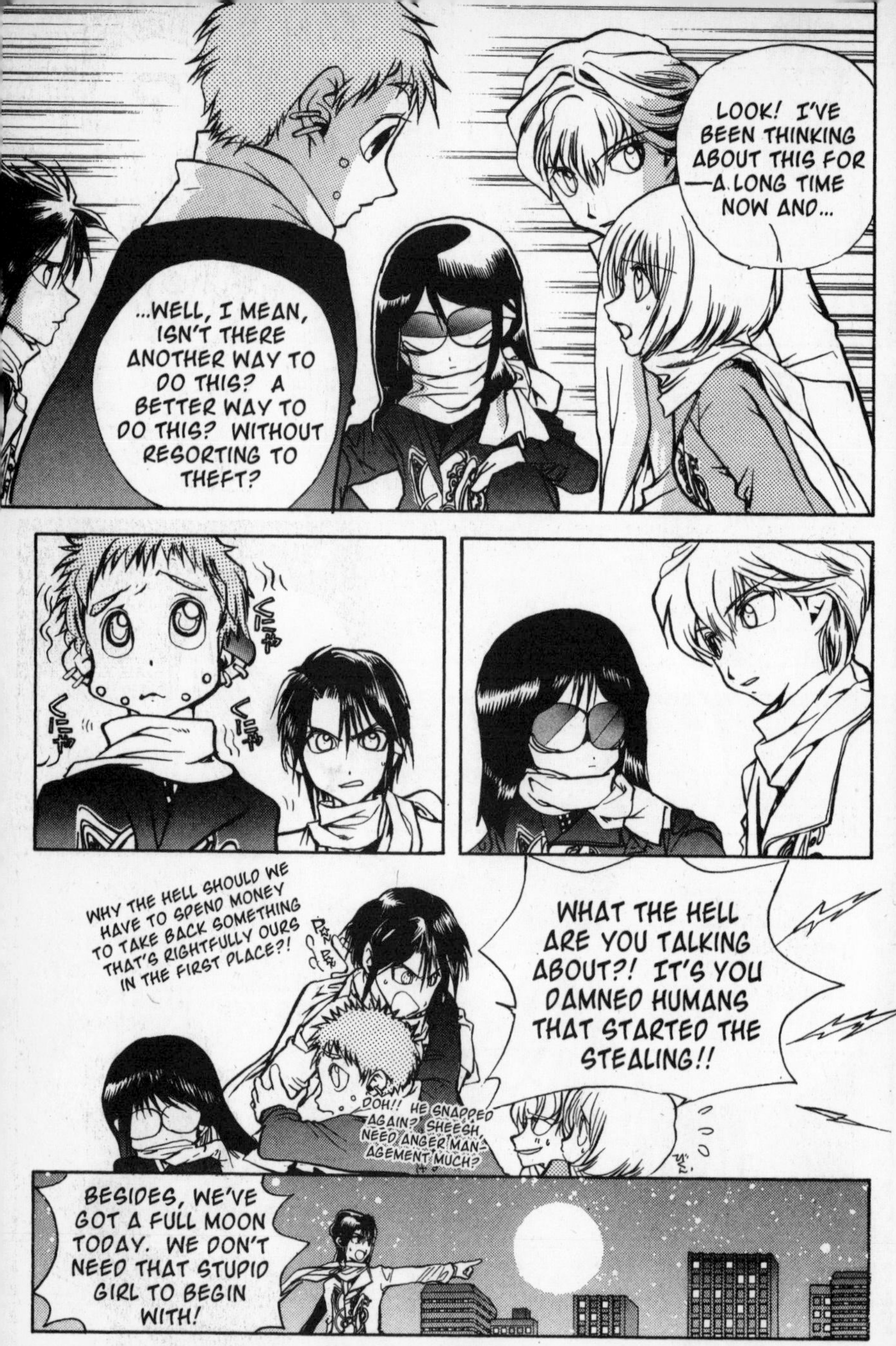
LOOK! I'VE BEEN THINKING ABOUT THIS FOR A LONG TIME NOW AND...
...WELL, I MEAN, ISN'T THERE ANOTHER WAY TO DO THIS? A BETTER WAY TO DO THIS? WITHOUT RESORTING TO THEFT?
WHAT THE HELL ARE YOU TALKING ABOUT?! IT'S YOU DAMNED HUMANS THAT STARTED THE STEALING!!
WHY THE HELL SHOULD WE HAVE TO SPEND MONEY TO TAKE BACK SOMETHING THAT'S RIGHTFULLY OURS IN THE FIRST PLACE?!
DOH!! HE SNAPPED AGAIN? SHEESH, NEED ANGER MAN-AGEMENT MUCH?
BESIDES, WE'VE GOT A FULL MOON TODAY. WE DON'T NEED THAT STUPID GIRL TO BEGIN WITH!

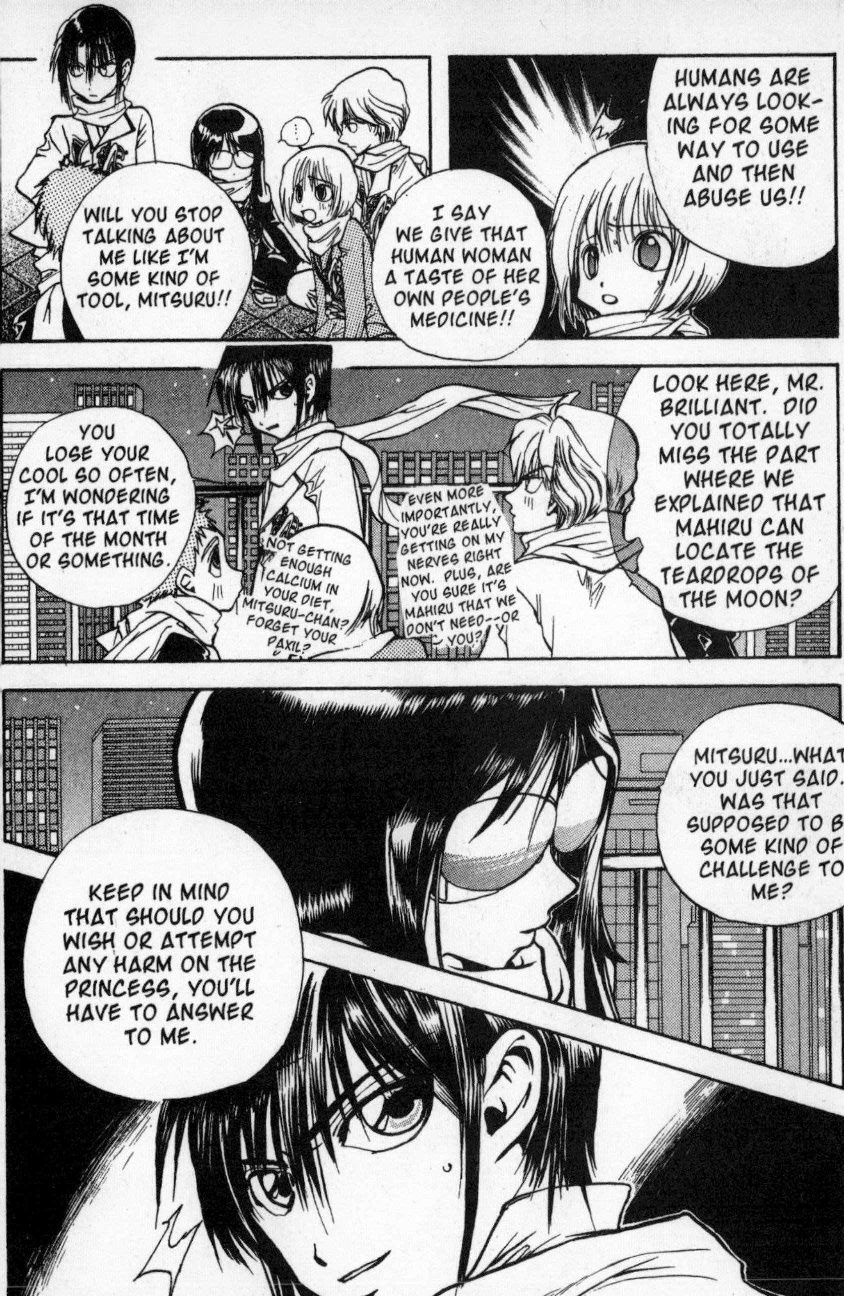
HUMANS ARE ALWAYS LOOKING FOR SOME WAY TO USE AND THEN ABUSE US!!
...
I SAY WE GIVE THAT HUMAN WOMAN A TASTE OF HER OWN PEOPLE'S MEDICINE!!
WILL YOU STOP TALKING ABOUT ME LIKE I'M SOME KIND OF TOOL, MITSURU!!
LOOK HERE, MR. BRILLIANT. DID YOU TOTALLY MISS THE PART WHERE WE EXPLAINED THAT MAHIRU CAN LOCATE THE TEARDROPS OF THE MOON?
EVEN MORE IMPORTANTLY, YOU'RE REALLY GETTING ON MY NERVES RIGHT NOW. PLUS, ARE YOU SURE IT'S MAHIRU THAT WE DON'T NEED--OR YOU?
NOT GETTING ENOUGH CALCIUM IN YOUR DIET, MITSURU-CHAN? FORGET YOUR PAXIL?
YOU LOSE YOUR COOL SO OFTEN, I'M WONDERING IF IT'S THAT TIME OF THE MONTH OR SOMETHING.
MITSURU...WHAT YOU JUST SAID... WAS THAT SUPPOSED TO BE SOME KIND OF CHALLENGE TO ME?
KEEP IN MIND THAT SHOULD YOU WISH OR ATTEMPT ANY HARM ON THE PRINCESS, YOU'LL HAVE TO ANSWER TO ME.

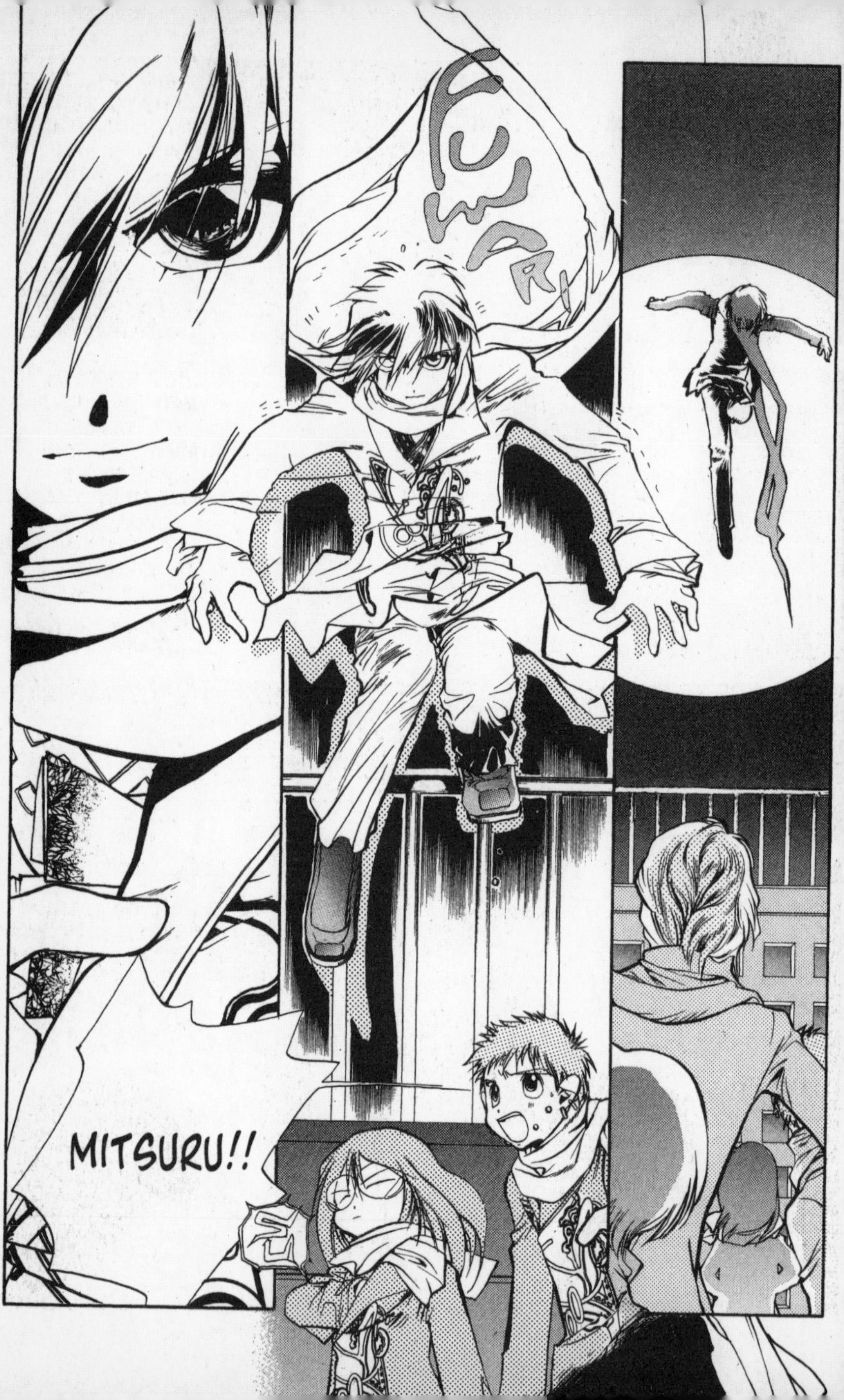
FUWARI
MITSURU!!

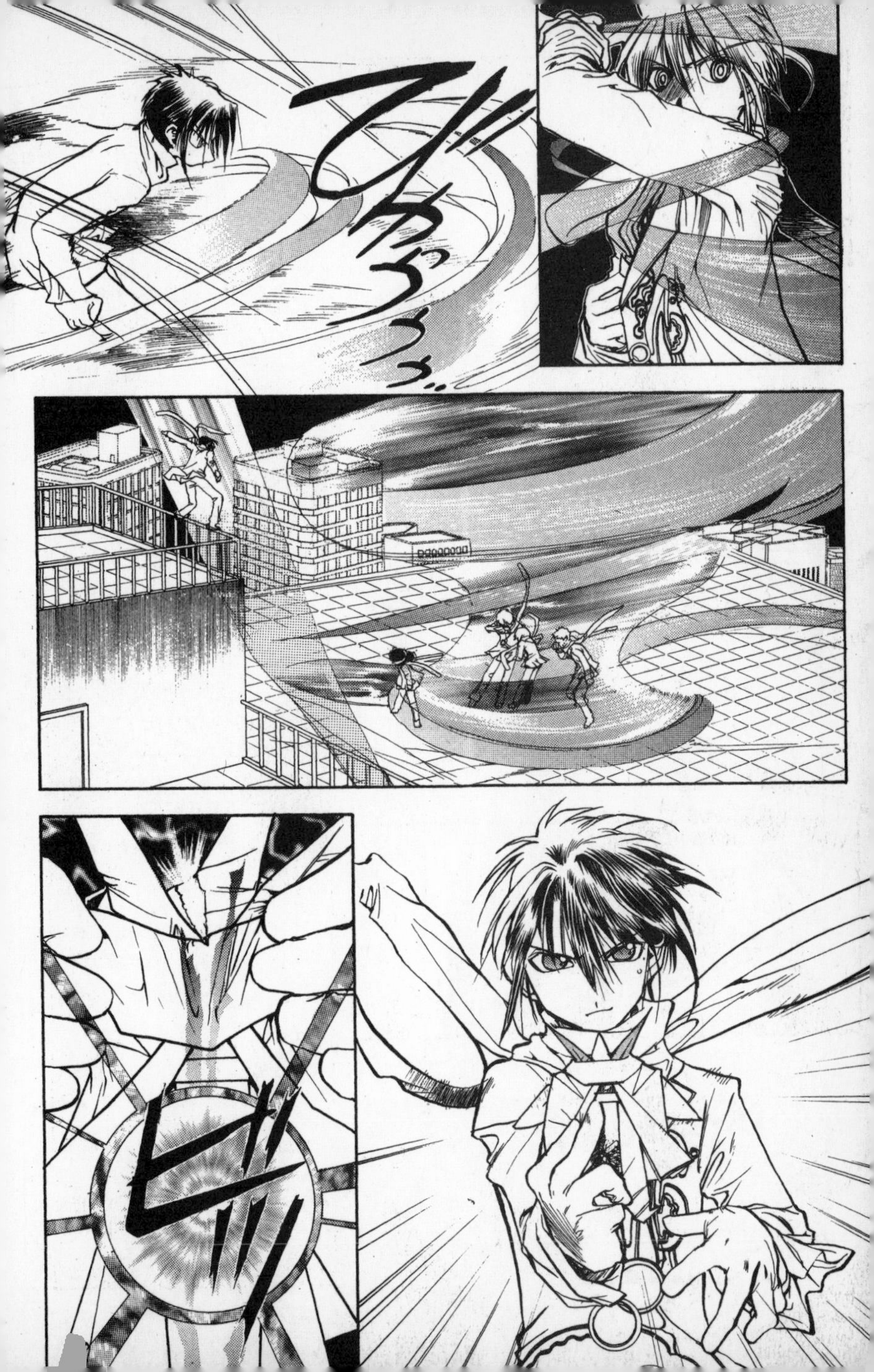

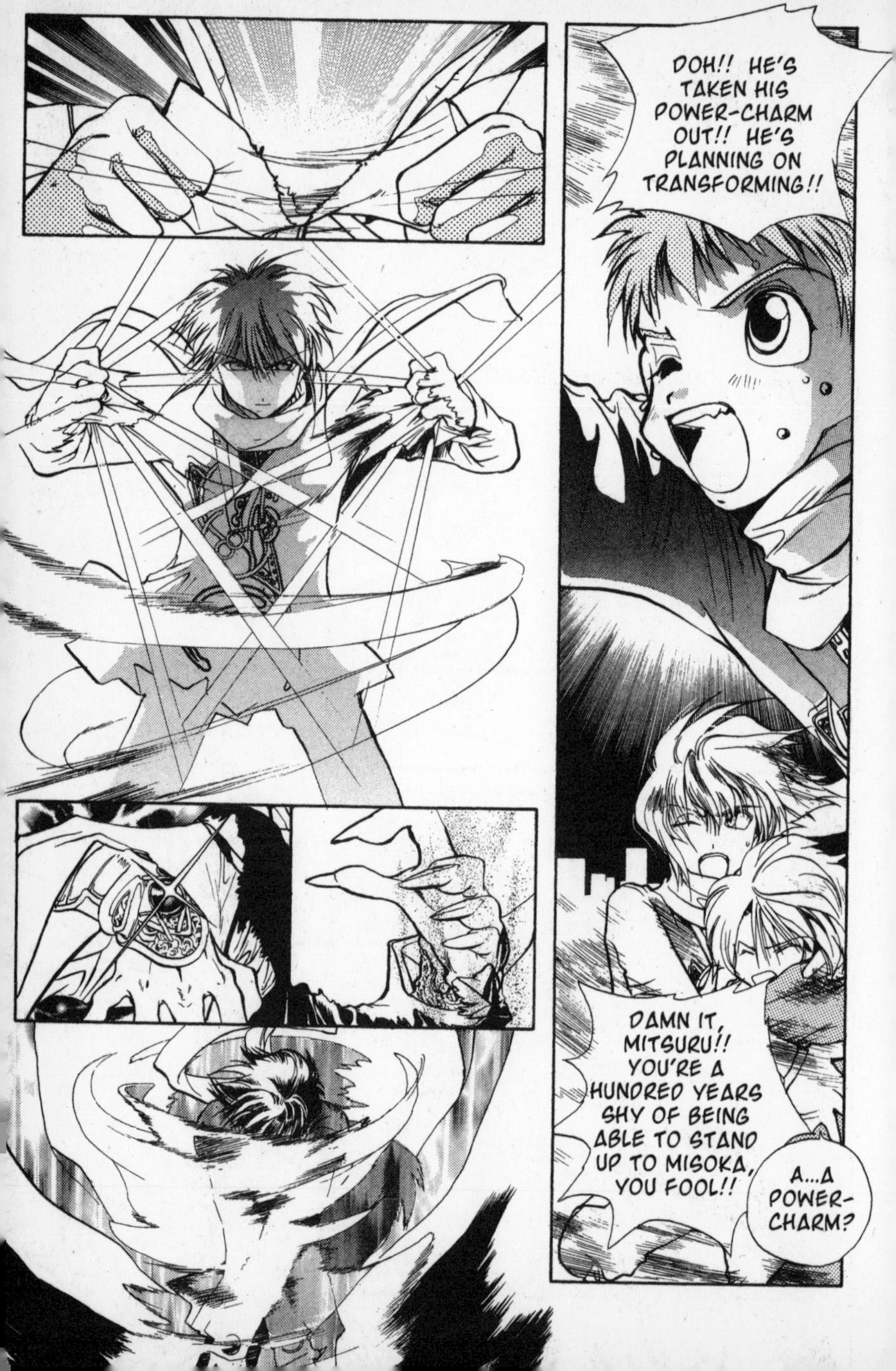
DOH!! HE'S TAKEN HIS POWER-CHARM OUT!! HE'S PLANNING ON TRANSFORMING!!
DAMN IT, MITSURU!! YOU'RE A HUNDRED YEARS SHY OF BEING ABLE TO STAND UP TO MISOKA, YOU FOOL!!
A...A POWER-CHARM?

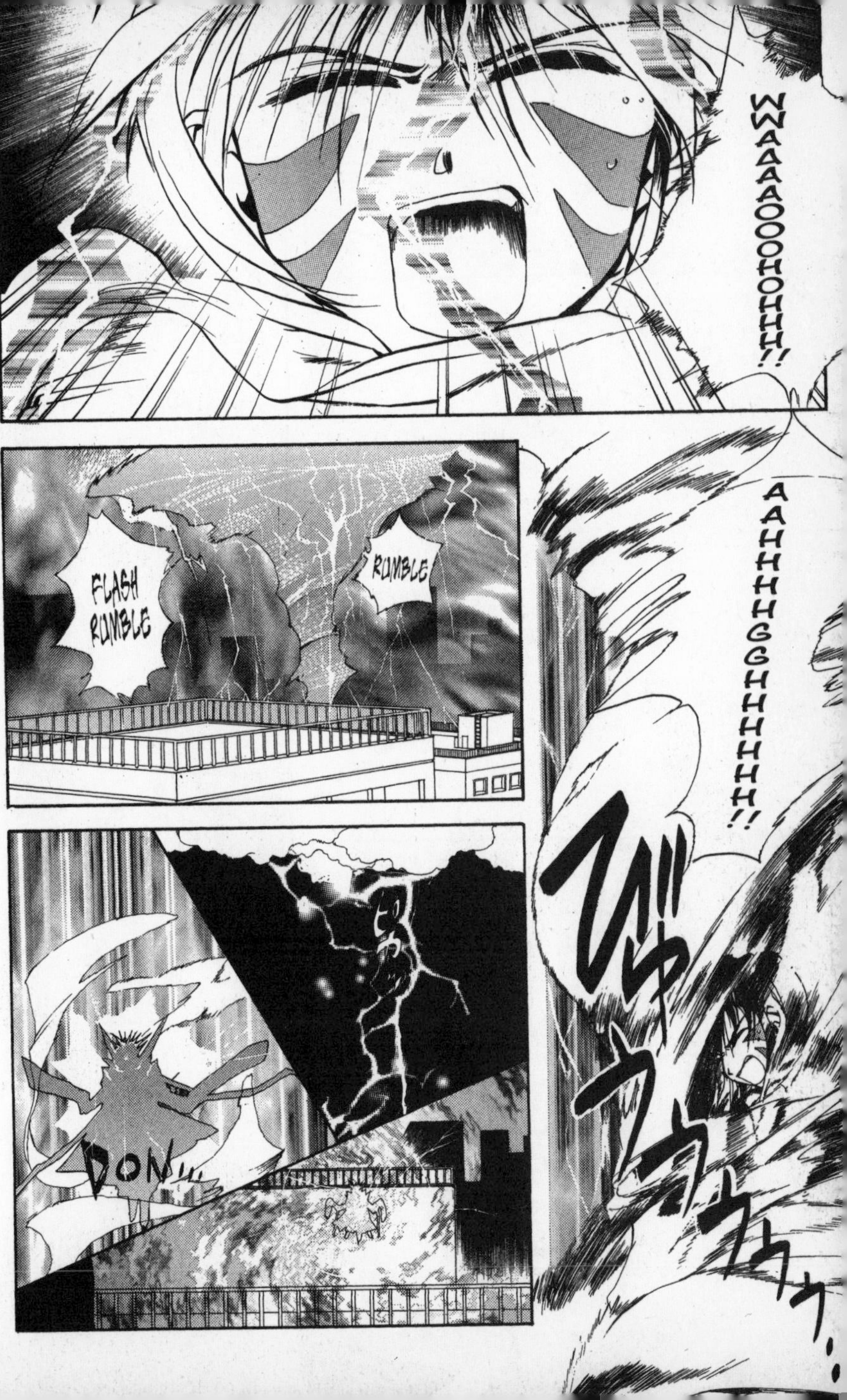
WWAAAAOOOHOHHH!!
AAHHHHGGHHHHHH!!
ひゅううう…
RUMBLE
FLASH RUMBLE
DON...

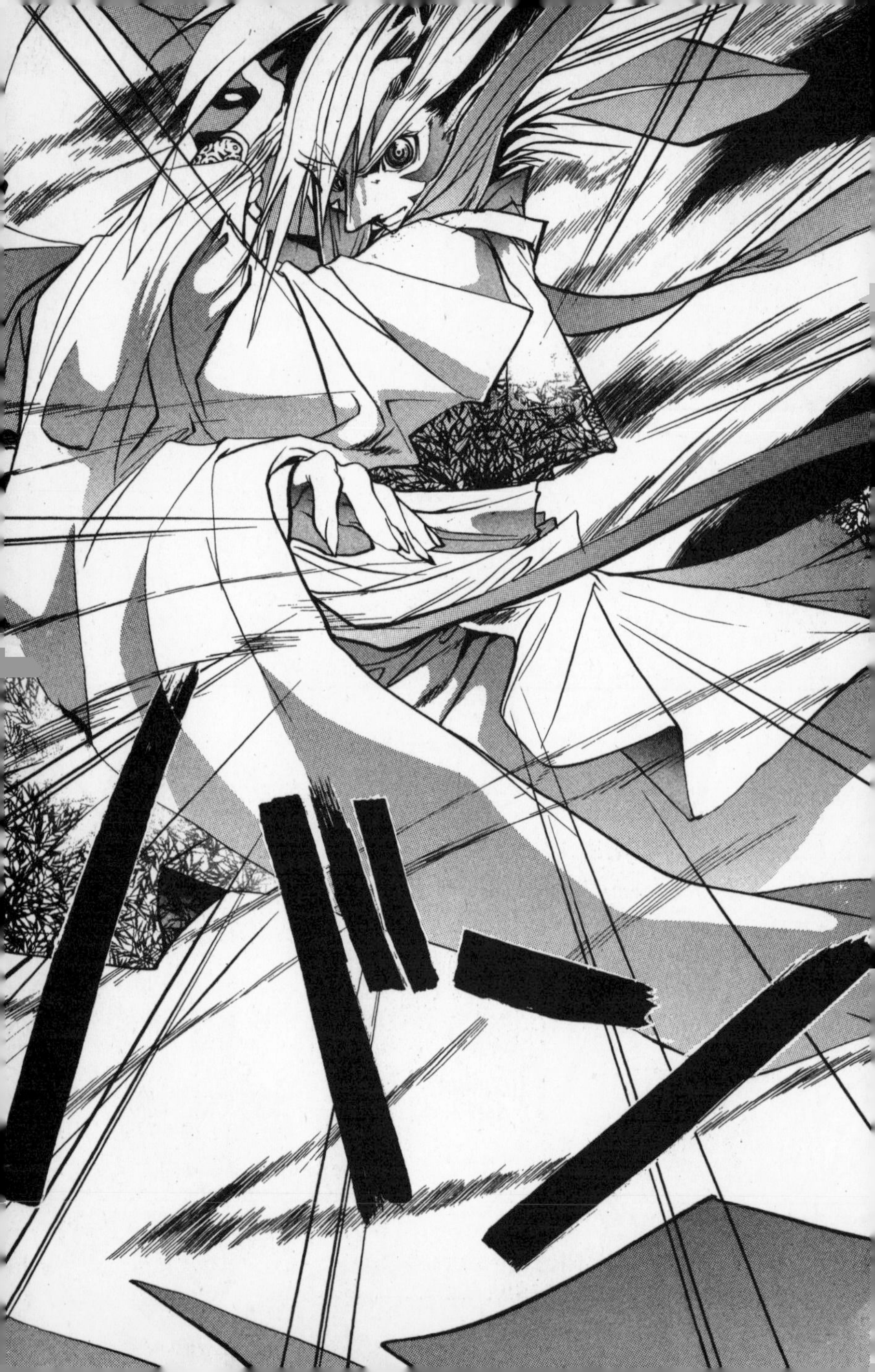

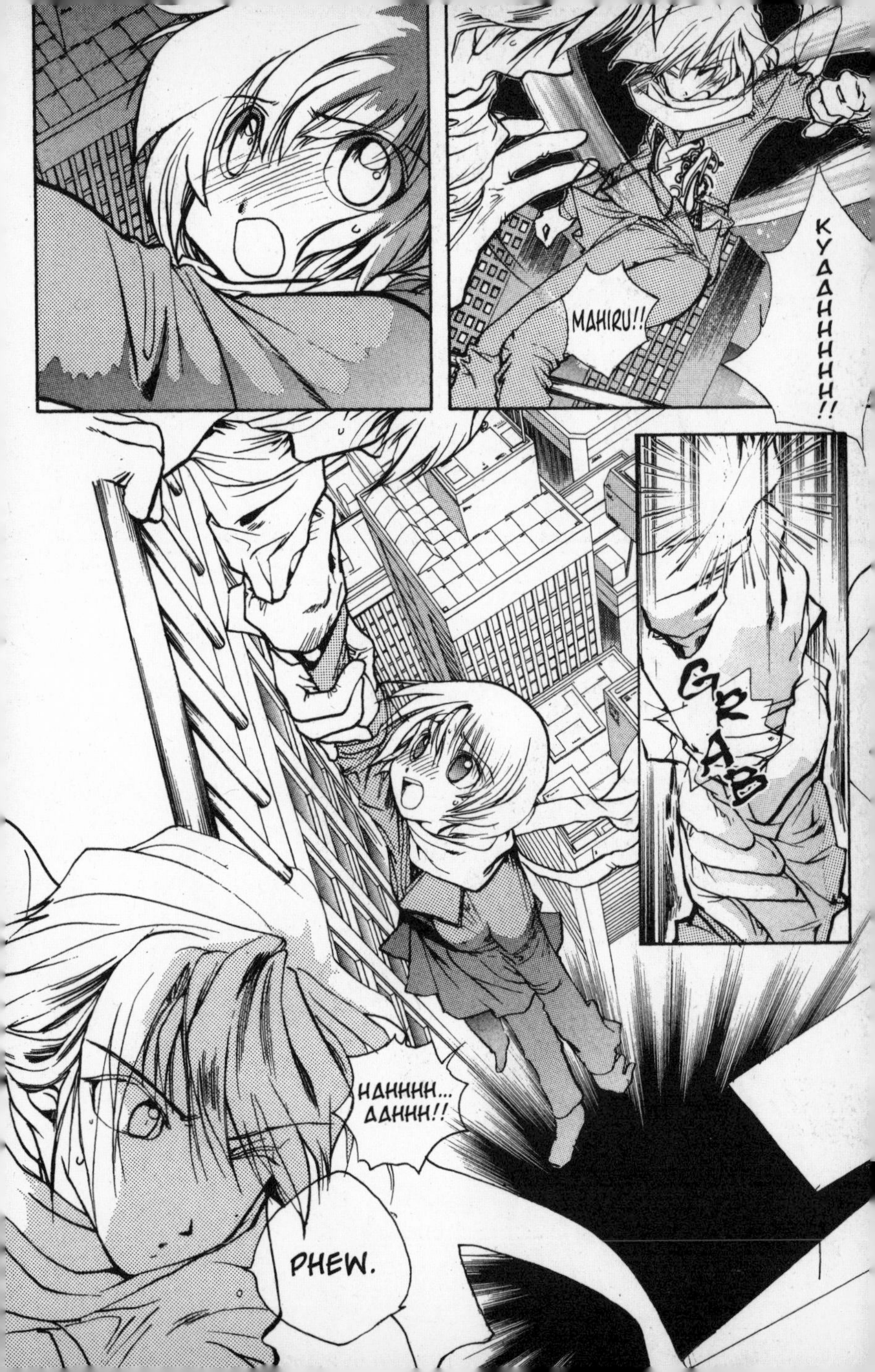
KYAAHHHHHH!!
MAHIRU!!
GRAB
HAHHHH... AAHHH!!
PHEW.

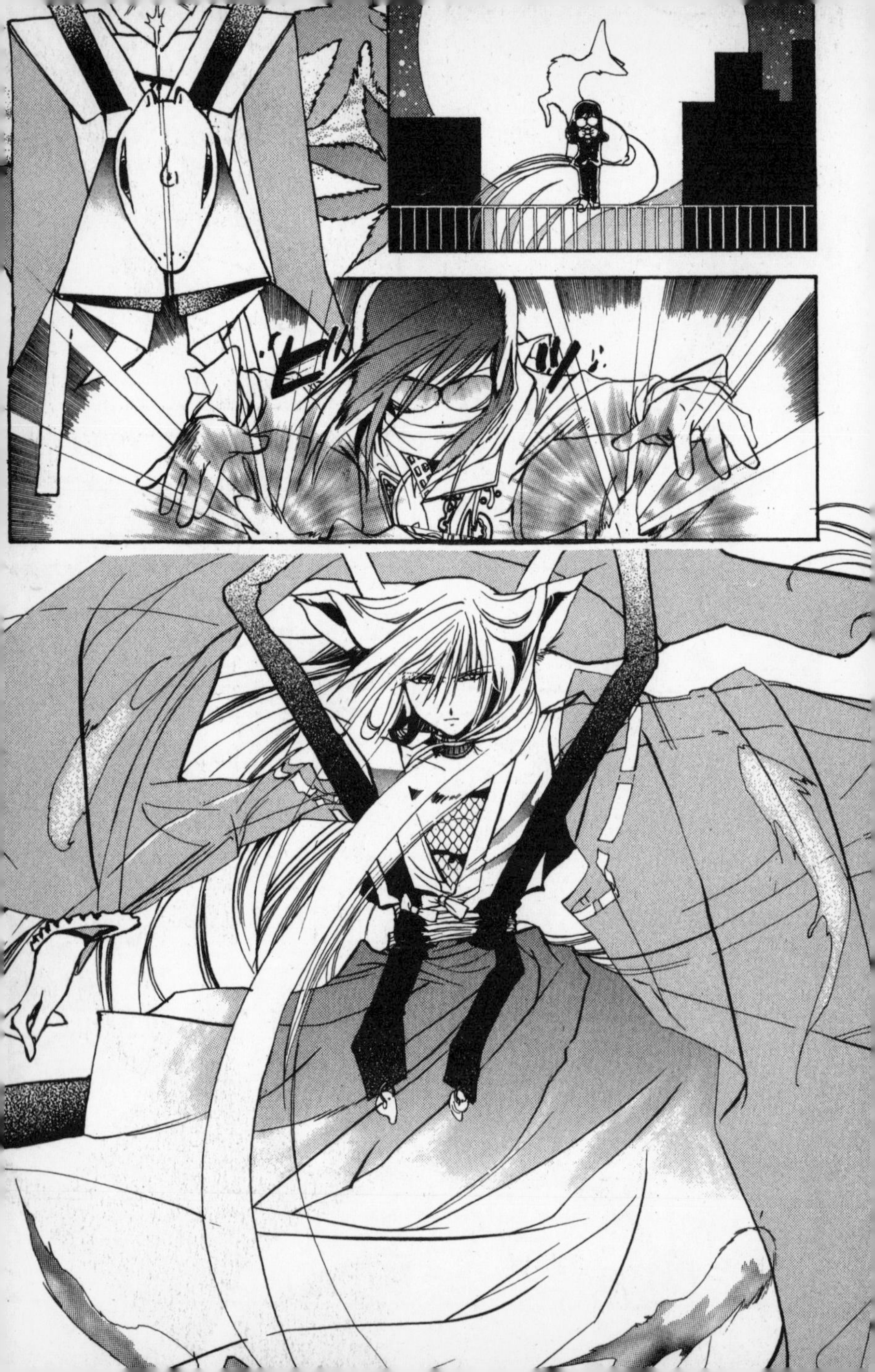
ビリッ

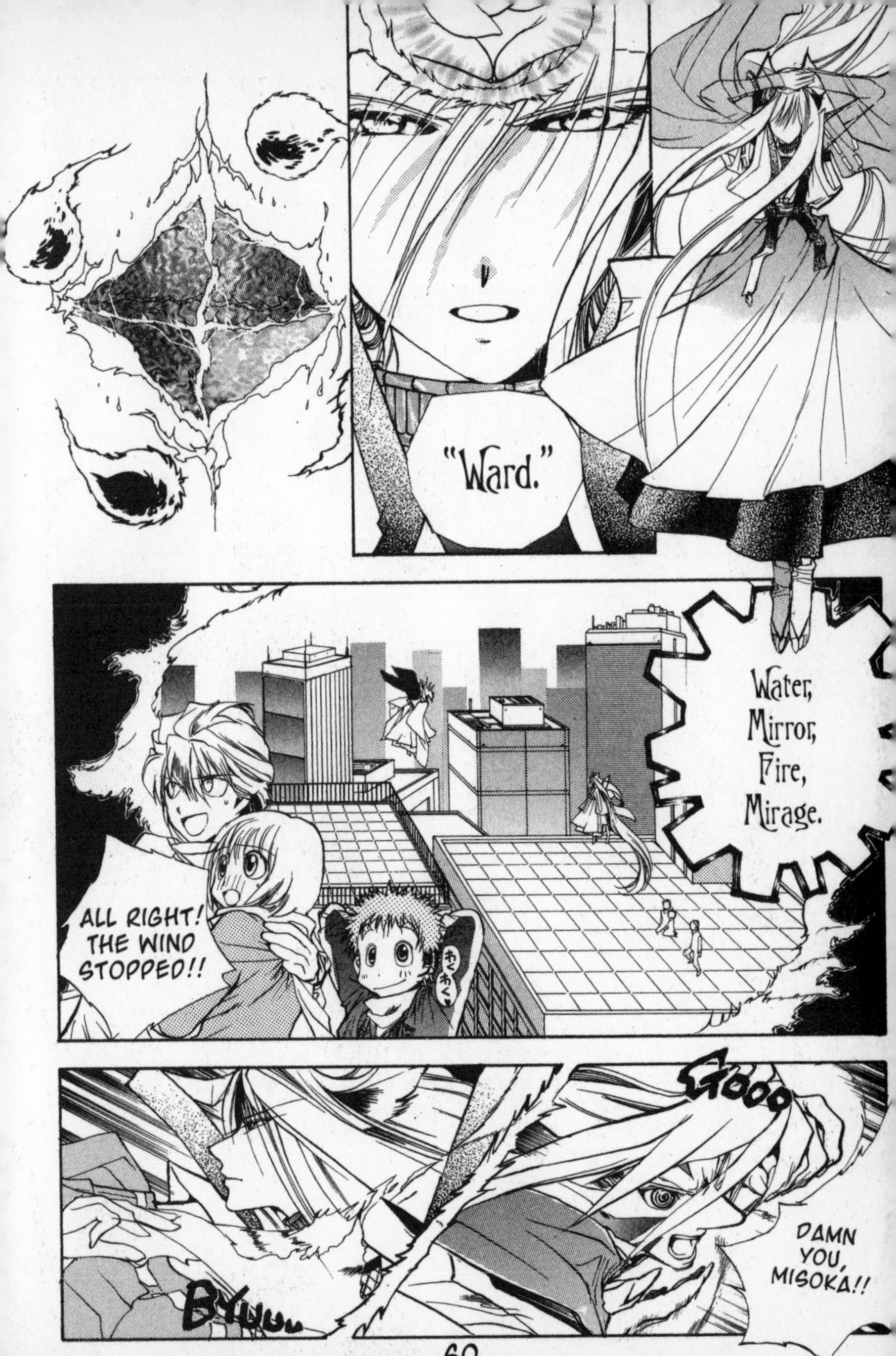
"Ward."
Water, Mirror, Fire, Mirage.
わくわく
ALL RIGHT! THE WIND STOPPED!!
GOOO
DAMN YOU, MISOKA!!
BYUUU

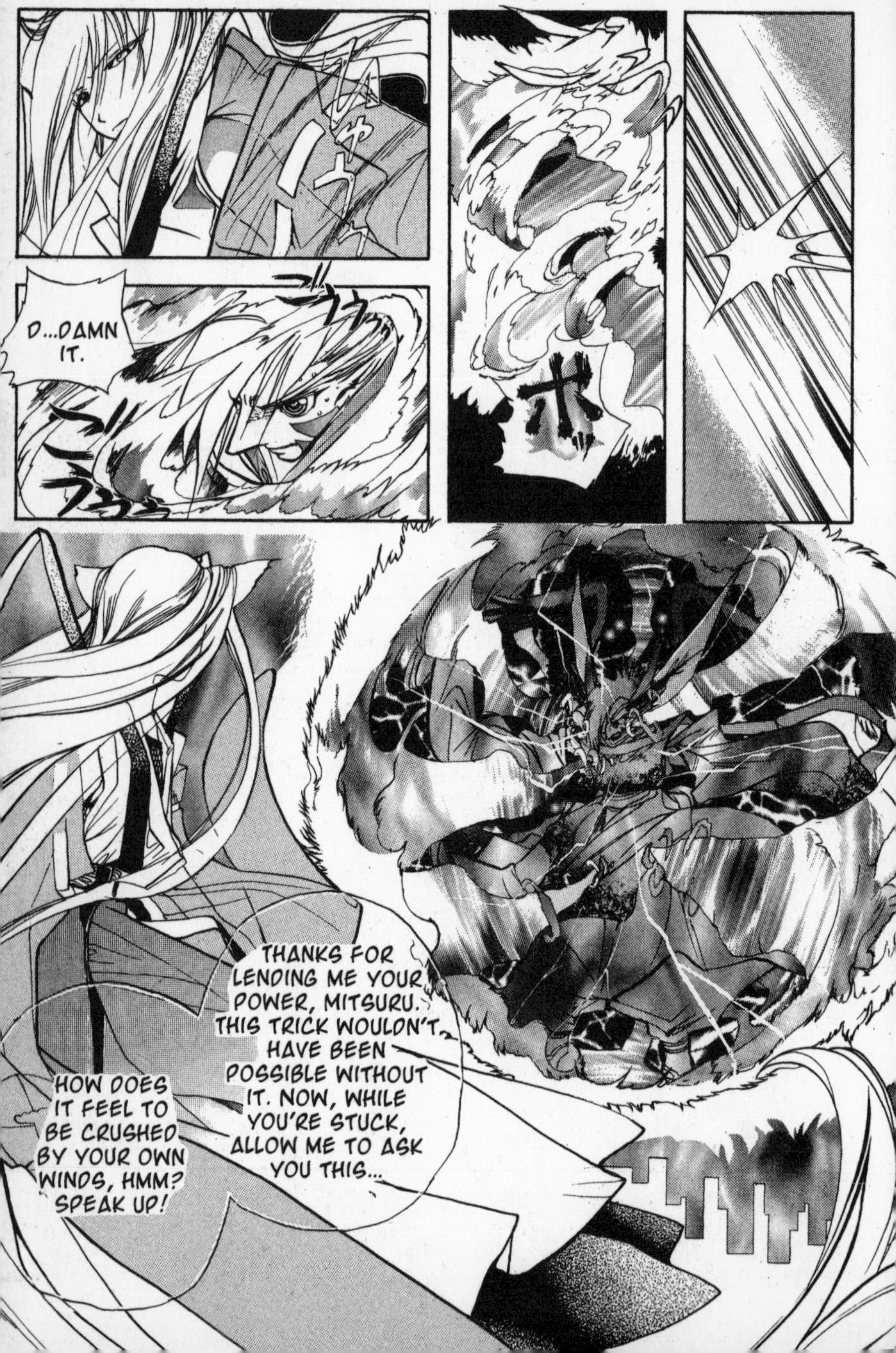
D...DAMN IT.
THANKS FOR LENDING ME YOUR POWER, MITSURU. THIS TRICK WOULDN'T HAVE BEEN POSSIBLE WITHOUT IT. NOW, WHILE YOU'RE STUCK, ALLOW ME TO ASK YOU THIS...
HOW DOES IT FEEL TO BE CRUSHED BY YOUR OWN WINDS, HMM? SPEAK UP!

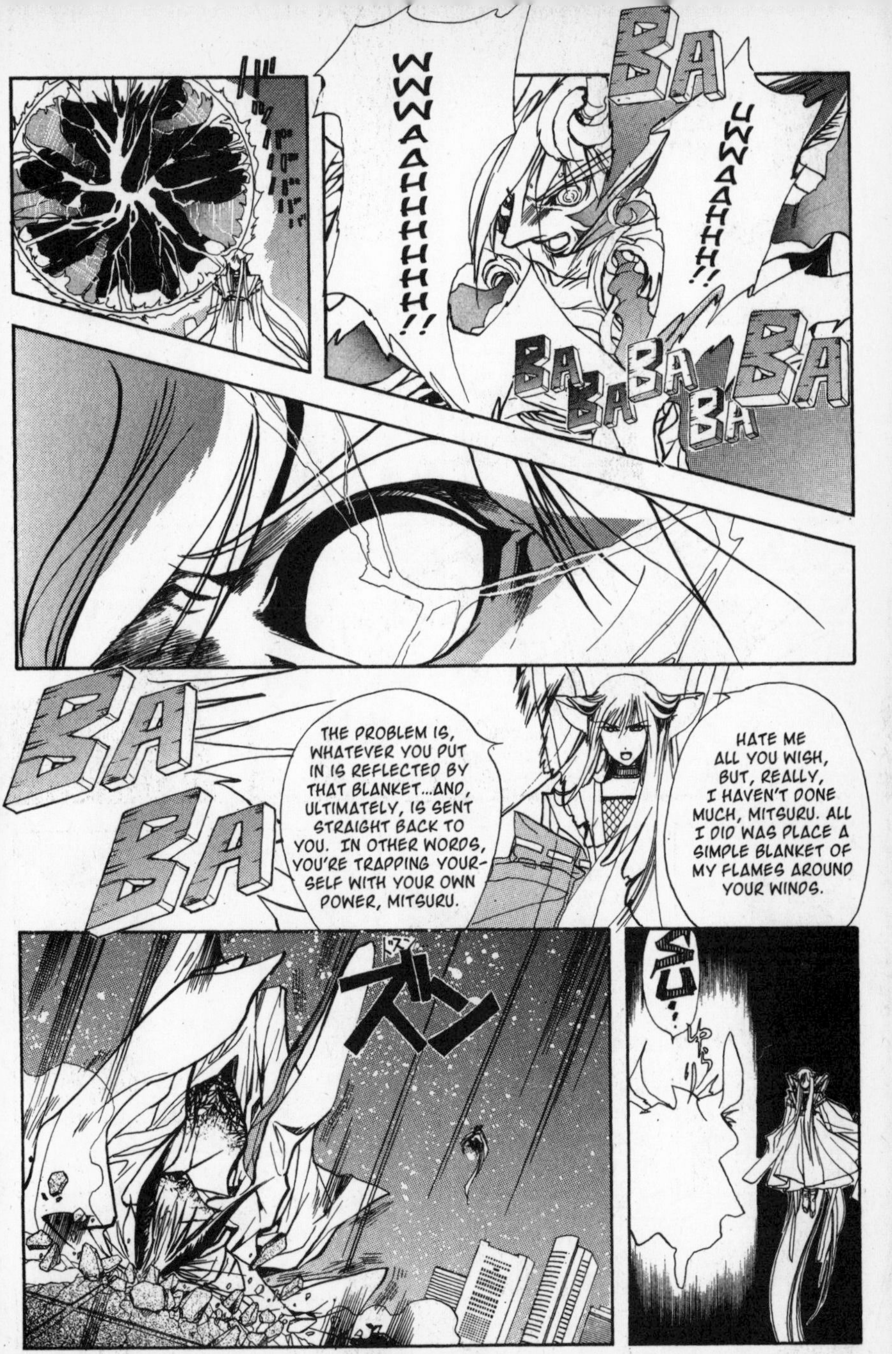
BA
UWWAAHHH!!
WWWAAHHHHHHHH!!
BABABABABA
HATE ME ALL YOU WISH, BUT, REALLY, I HAVEN'T DONE MUCH, MITSURU. ALL I DID WAS PLACE A SIMPLE BLANKET OF MY FLAMES AROUND YOUR WINDS.
THE PROBLEM IS, WHATEVER YOU PUT IN IS REFLECTED BY THAT BLANKET...AND, ULTIMATELY, IS SENT STRAIGHT BACK TO YOU. IN OTHER WORDS, YOU'RE TRAPPING YOURSELF WITH YOUR OWN POWER, MITSURU.
BA BA
SU
ズン

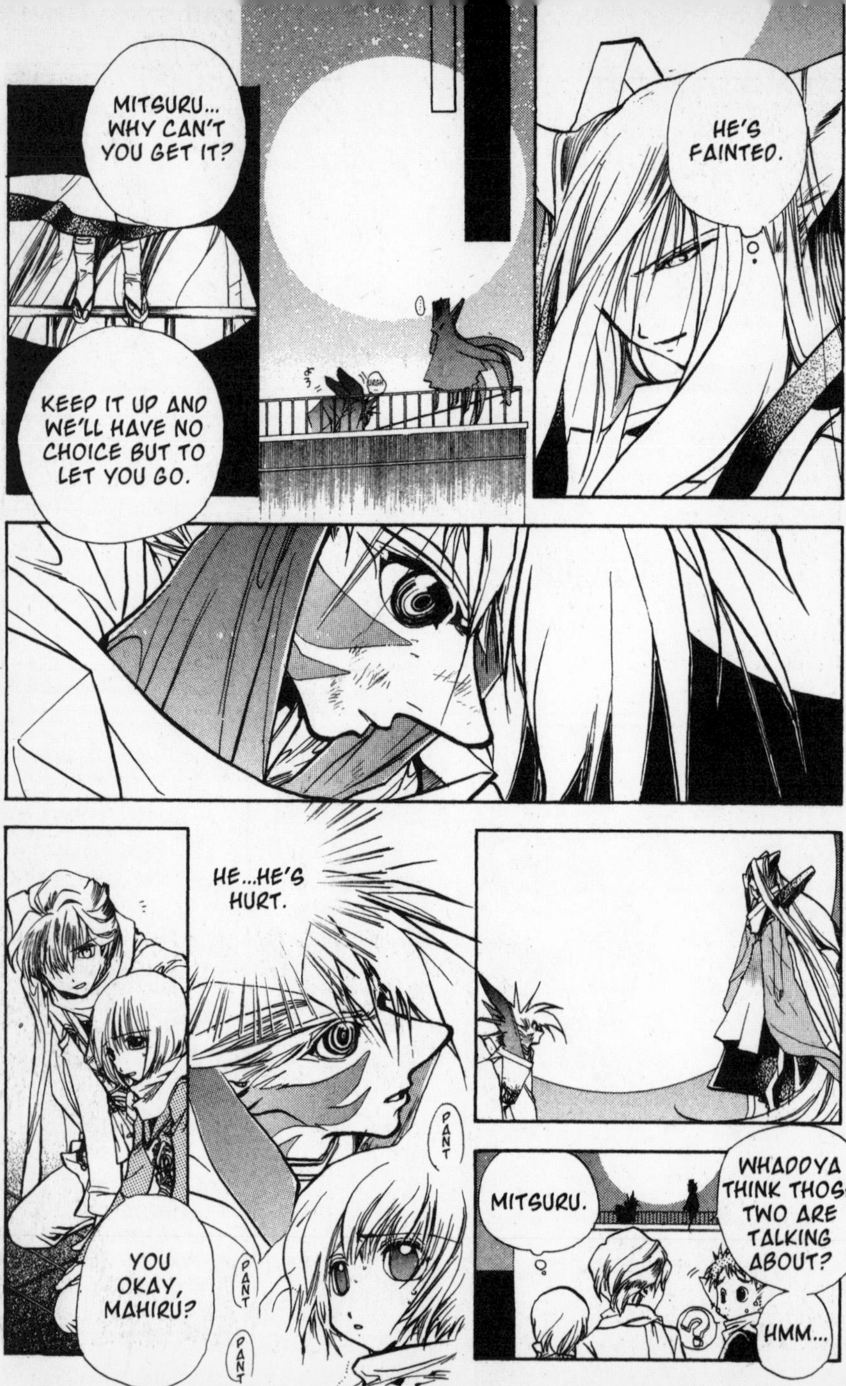
HE'S FAINTED.
URGH
MITSURU... WHY CAN'T YOU GET IT?
KEEP IT UP AND WE'LL HAVE NO CHOICE BUT TO LET YOU GO.
WHADDYA THINK THOSE TWO ARE TALKING ABOUT?
MITSURU.
HMM...
HE...HE'S HURT.
PANT
YOU OKAY, MAHIRU?
PANT
PANT

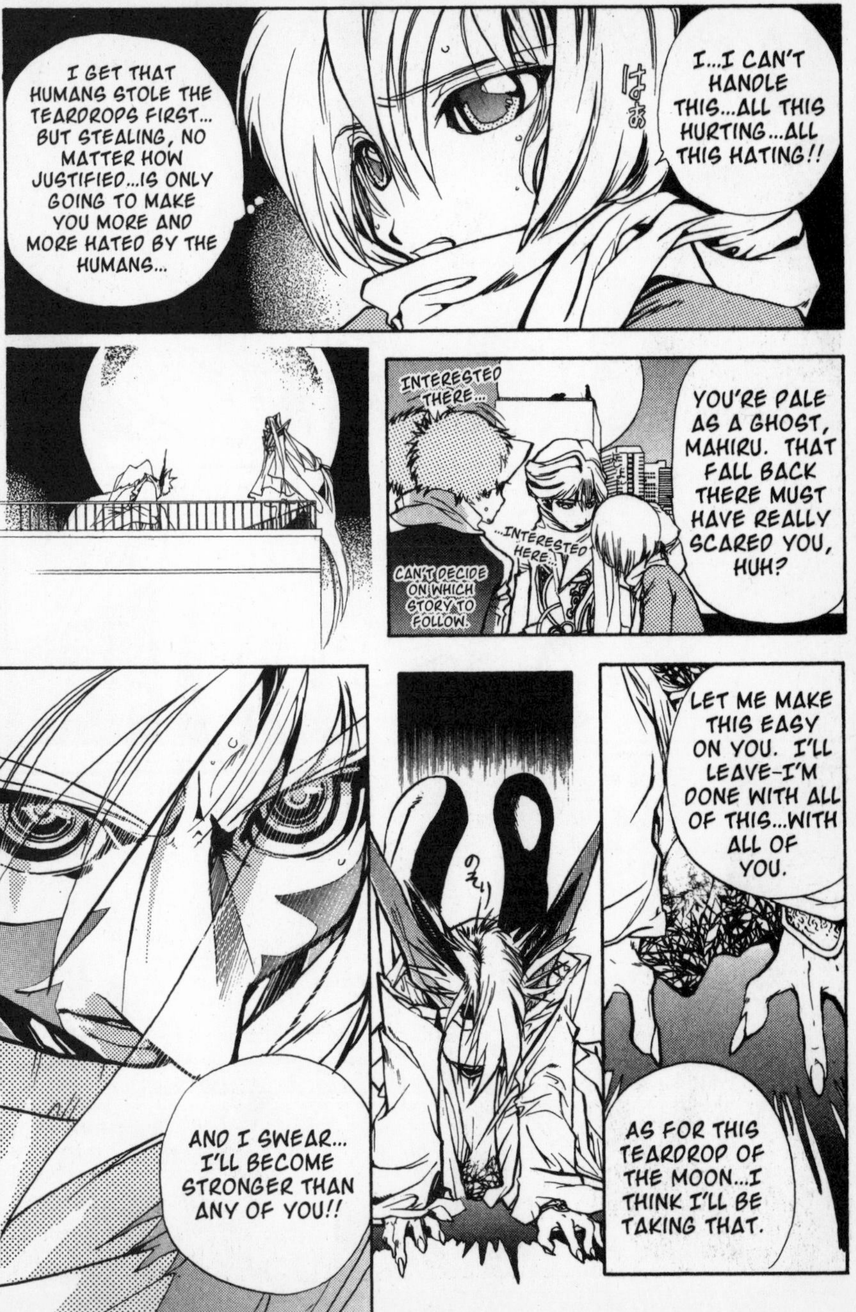
I...I CAN'T HANDLE THIS...ALL THIS HURTING...ALL THIS HATING!!
I GET THAT HUMANS STOLE THE TEARDROPS FIRST... BUT STEALING, NO MATTER HOW JUSTIFIED...IS ONLY GOING TO MAKE YOU MORE AND MORE HATED BY THE HUMANS...
YOU'RE PALE AS A GHOST, MAHIRU. THAT FALL BACK THERE MUST HAVE REALLY SCARED YOU, HUH?
INTERESTED THERE...
...INTERESTED HERE...
CAN'T DECIDE ON WHICH STORY TO FOLLOW.
LET ME MAKE THIS EASY ON YOU. I'LL LEAVE–I'M DONE WITH ALL OF THIS...WITH ALL OF YOU.
AS FOR THIS TEARDROP OF THE MOON...I THINK I'LL BE TAKING THAT.
AND I SWEAR... I'LL BECOME STRONGER THAN ANY OF YOU!!

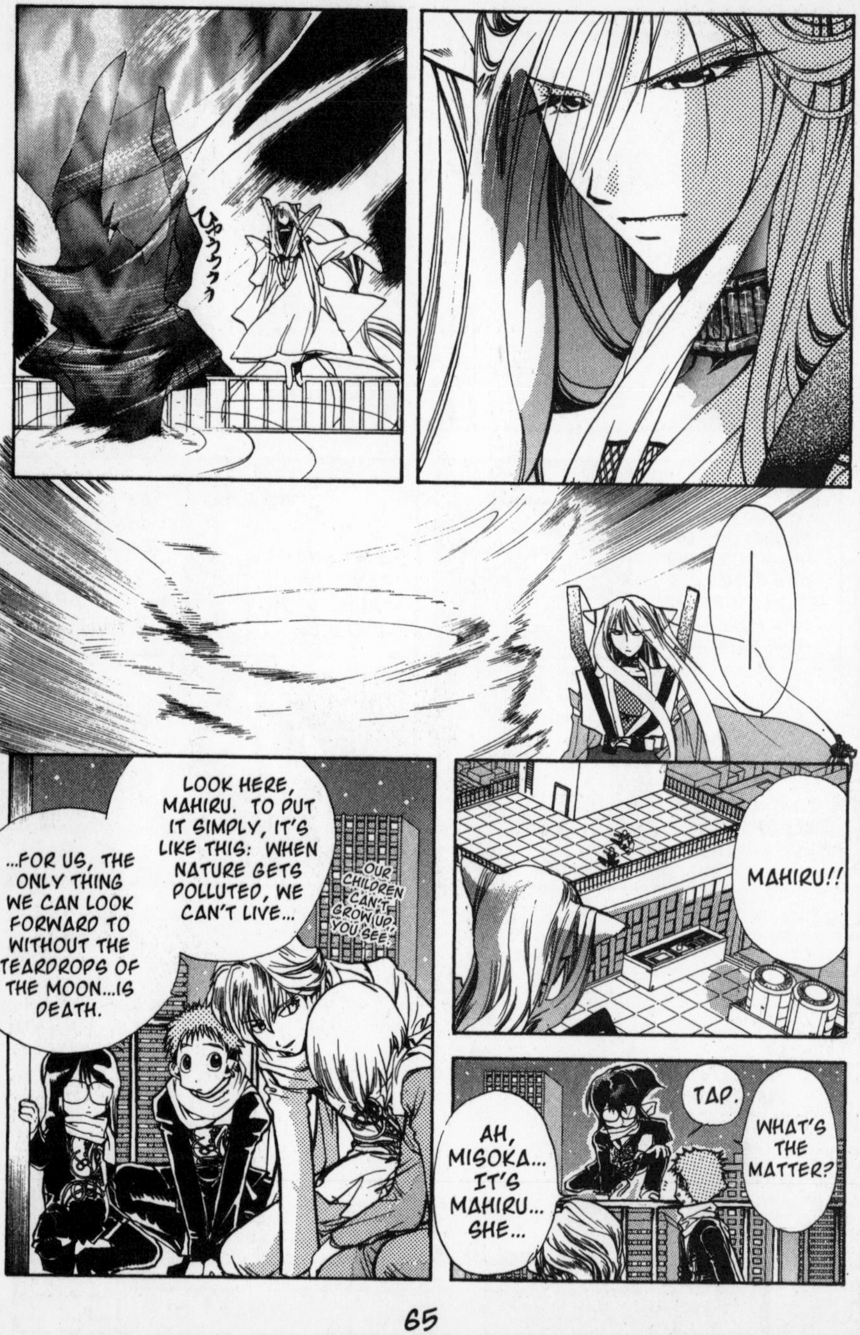
MAHIRU!!
TAP.
WHAT'S THE MATTER?
AH, MISOKA... IT'S MAHIRU... SHE...
LOOK HERE, MAHIRU. TO PUT IT SIMPLY, IT'S LIKE THIS: WHEN NATURE GETS POLLUTED, WE CAN'T LIVE...
OUR CHILDREN CAN'T GROW UP, YOU SEE.
...FOR US, THE ONLY THING WE CAN LOOK FORWARD TO WITHOUT THE TEARDROPS OF THE MOON...IS DEATH.

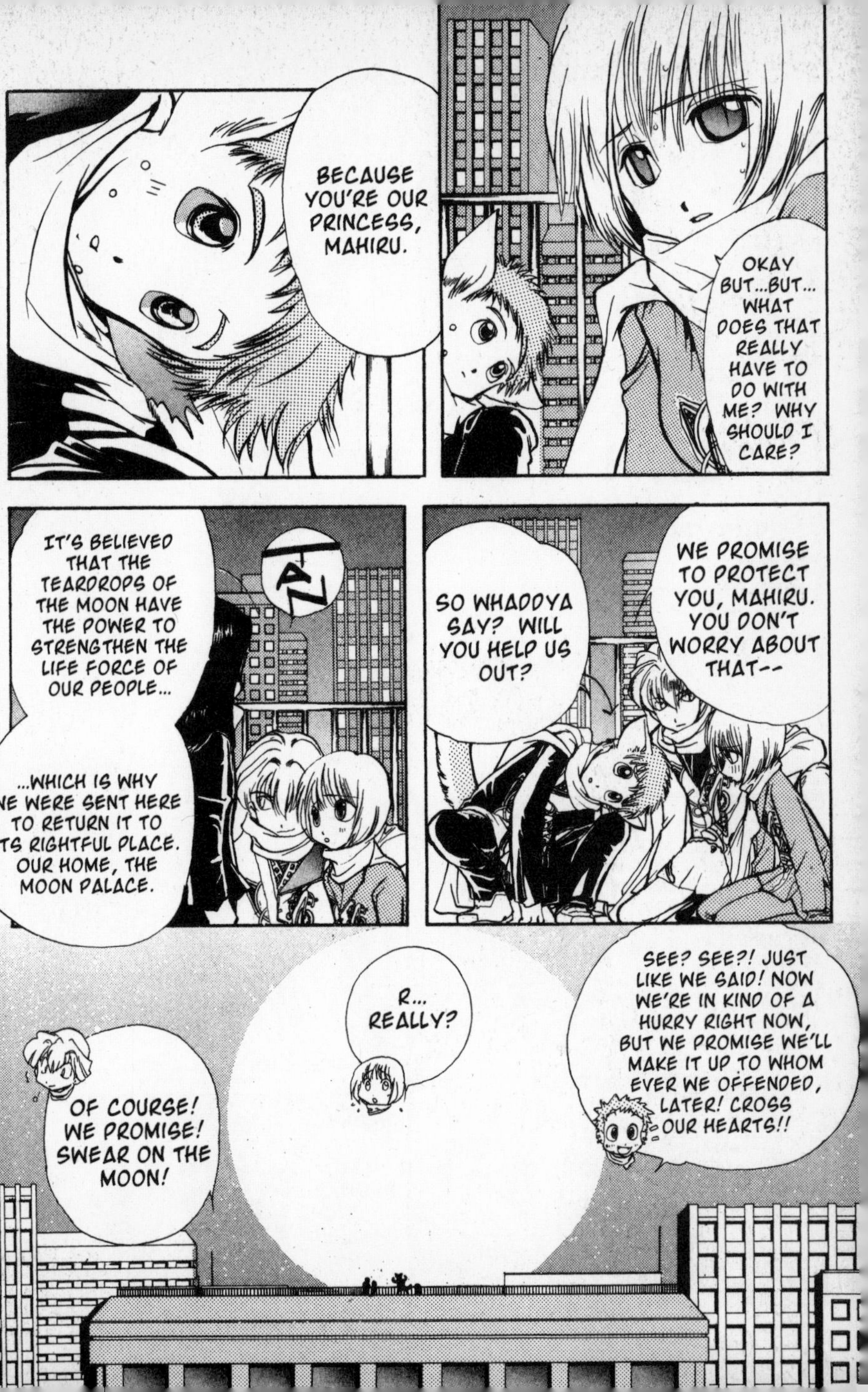
OKAY BUT...BUT... WHAT DOES THAT REALLY HAVE TO DO WITH ME? WHY SHOULD I CARE?
BECAUSE YOU'RE OUR PRINCESS, MAHIRU.
WE PROMISE TO PROTECT YOU, MAHIRU. YOU DON'T WORRY ABOUT THAT--
SO WHADDYA SAY? WILL YOU HELP US OUT?
IT'S BELIEVED THAT THE TEARDROPS OF THE MOON HAVE THE POWER TO STRENGTHEN THE LIFE FORCE OF OUR PEOPLE...
...WHICH IS WHY WE WERE SENT HERE TO RETURN IT TO ITS RIGHTFUL PLACE. OUR HOME, THE MOON PALACE.
SEE? SEE?! JUST LIKE WE SAID! NOW WE'RE IN KIND OF A HURRY RIGHT NOW, BUT WE PROMISE WE'LL MAKE IT UP TO WHOM EVER WE OFFENDED, LATER! CROSS OUR HEARTS!!
R... REALLY?
OF COURSE! WE PROMISE! SWEAR ON THE MOON!

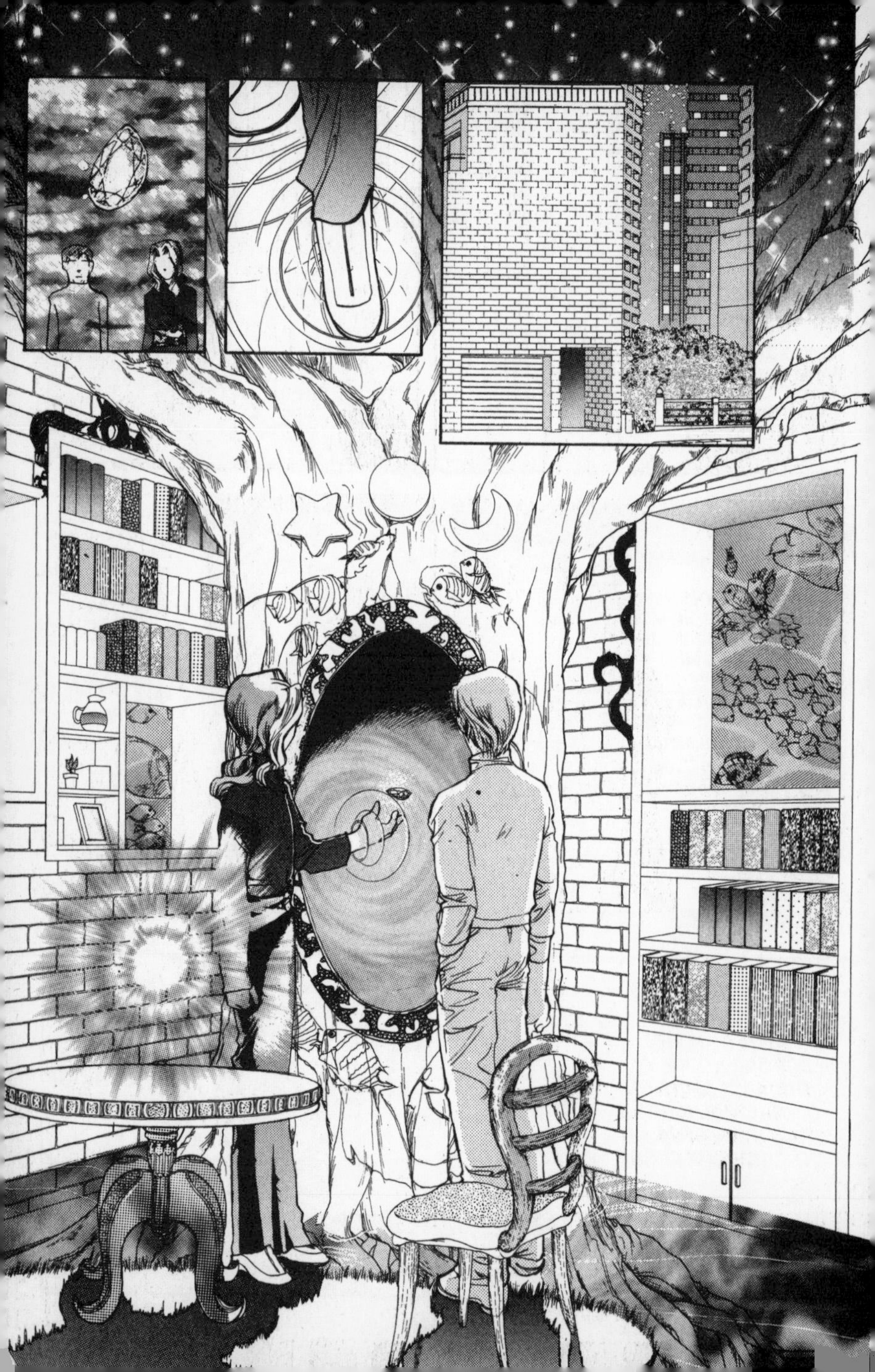

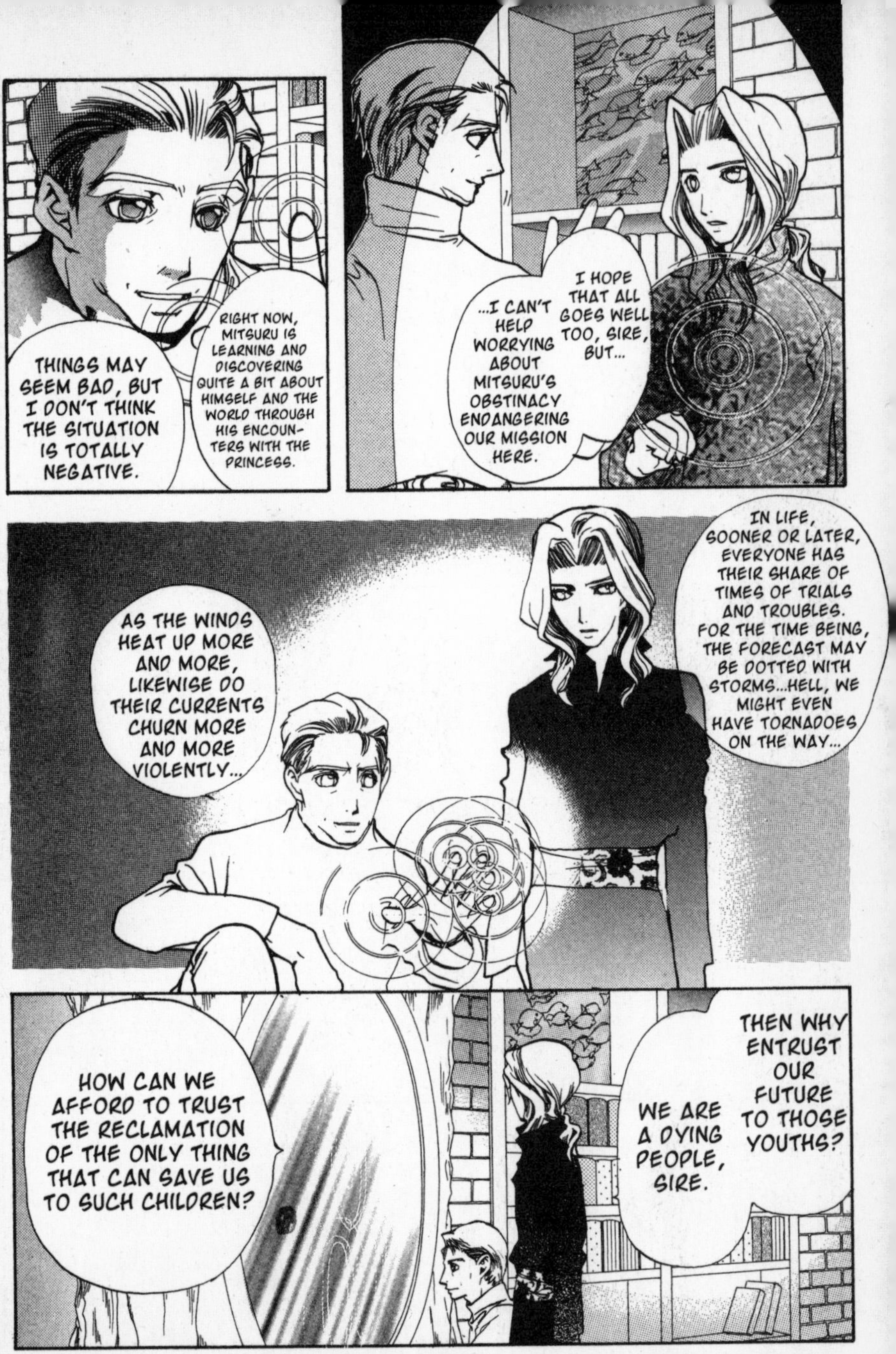
I HOPE THAT ALL GOES WELL TOO, SIRE, BUT...
...I CAN'T HELP WORRYING ABOUT MITSURU'S OBSTINACY ENDANGERING OUR MISSION HERE.
THINGS MAY SEEM BAD, BUT I DON'T THINK THE SITUATION IS TOTALLY NEGATIVE.
RIGHT NOW, MITSURU IS LEARNING AND DISCOVERING QUITE A BIT ABOUT HIMSELF AND THE WORLD THROUGH HIS ENCOUNTERS WITH THE PRINCESS.
IN LIFE, SOONER OR LATER, EVERYONE HAS THEIR SHARE OF TIMES OF TRIALS AND TROUBLES. FOR THE TIME BEING, THE FORECAST MAY BE DOTTED WITH STORMS...HELL, WE MIGHT EVEN HAVE TORNADOES ON THE WAY...
AS THE WINDS HEAT UP MORE AND MORE, LIKEWISE DO THEIR CURRENTS CHURN MORE AND MORE VIOLENTLY...
THEN WHY ENTRUST OUR FUTURE TO THOSE YOUTHS?
WE ARE A DYING PEOPLE, SIRE.
HOW CAN WE AFFORD TO TRUST THE RECLAMATION OF THE ONLY THING THAT CAN SAVE US TO SUCH CHILDREN?

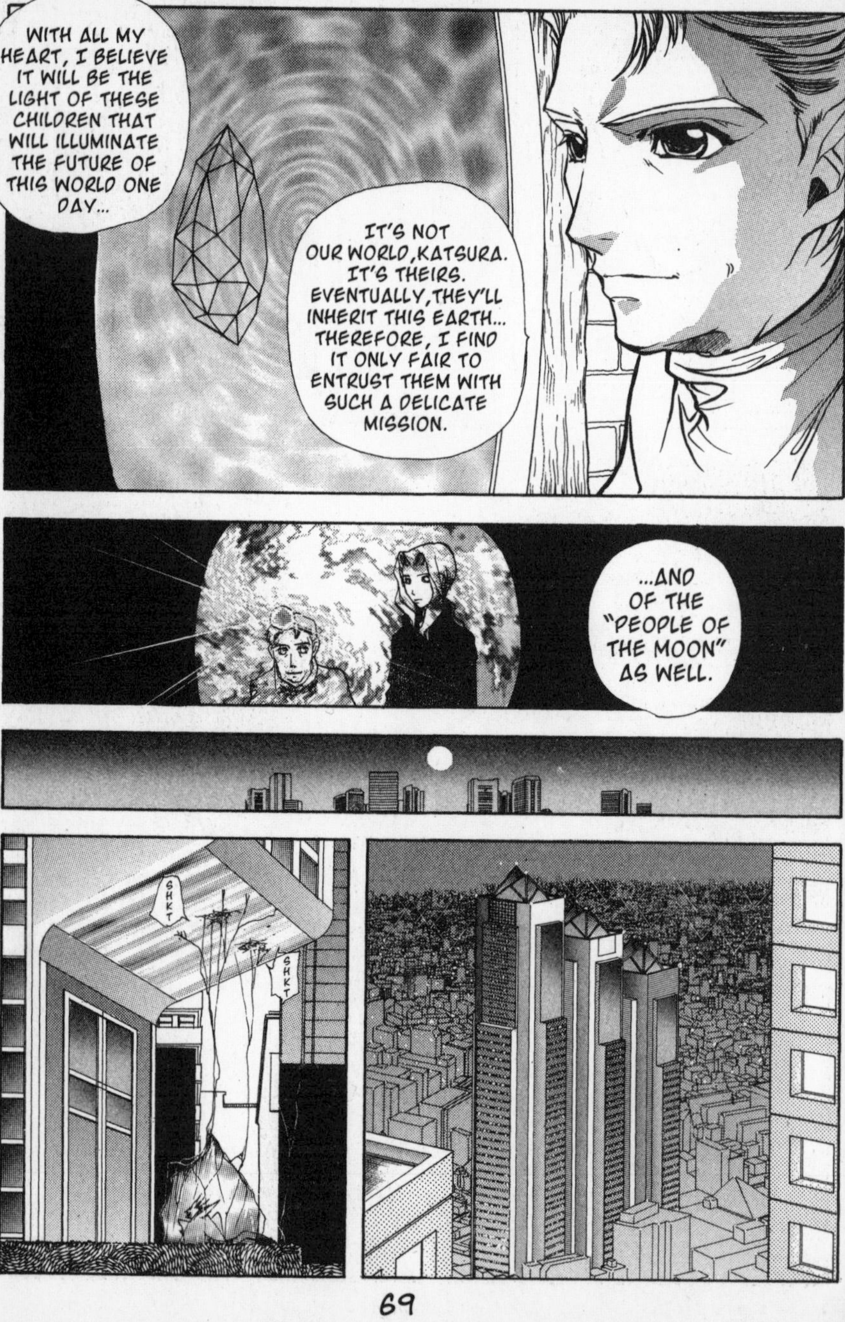
WITH ALL MY HEART, I BELIEVE IT WILL BE THE LIGHT OF THESE CHILDREN THAT WILL ILLUMINATE THE FUTURE OF THIS WORLD ONE DAY...
IT'S NOT OUR WORLD, KATSURA. IT'S THEIRS. EVENTUALLY, THEY'LL INHERIT THIS EARTH... THEREFORE, I FIND IT ONLY FAIR TO ENTRUST THEM WITH SUCH A DELICATE MISSION.
...AND OF THE "PEOPLE OF THE MOON" AS WELL.
SHKT
SHKT

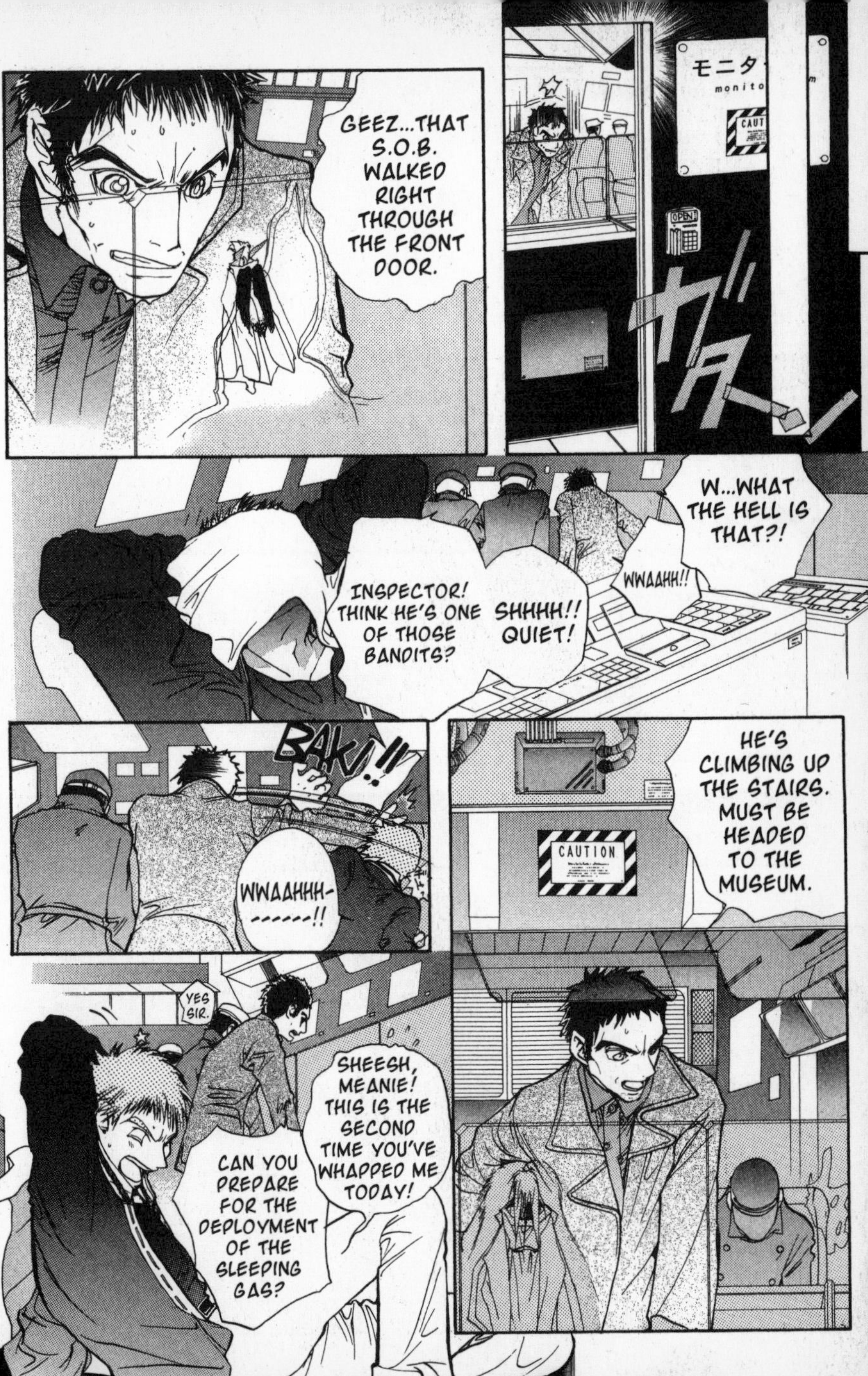
モニタ
monito
CAUT
OPEN
ガタ
GEEZ...THAT S.O.B. WALKED RIGHT THROUGH THE FRONT DOOR.
W...WHAT THE HELL IS THAT?!
WWAAHH!!
SHHHH!! QUIET!
INSPECTOR! THINK HE'S ONE OF THOSE BANDITS?
HE'S CLIMBING UP THE STAIRS. MUST BE HEADED TO THE MUSEUM.
CAUTION
BAKI!!
WWAAHHH-------!!
SHEESH, MEANIE! THIS IS THE SECOND TIME YOU'VE WHAPPED ME TODAY!
CAN YOU PREPARE FOR THE DEPLOYMENT OF THE SLEEPING GAS?
YES SIR.

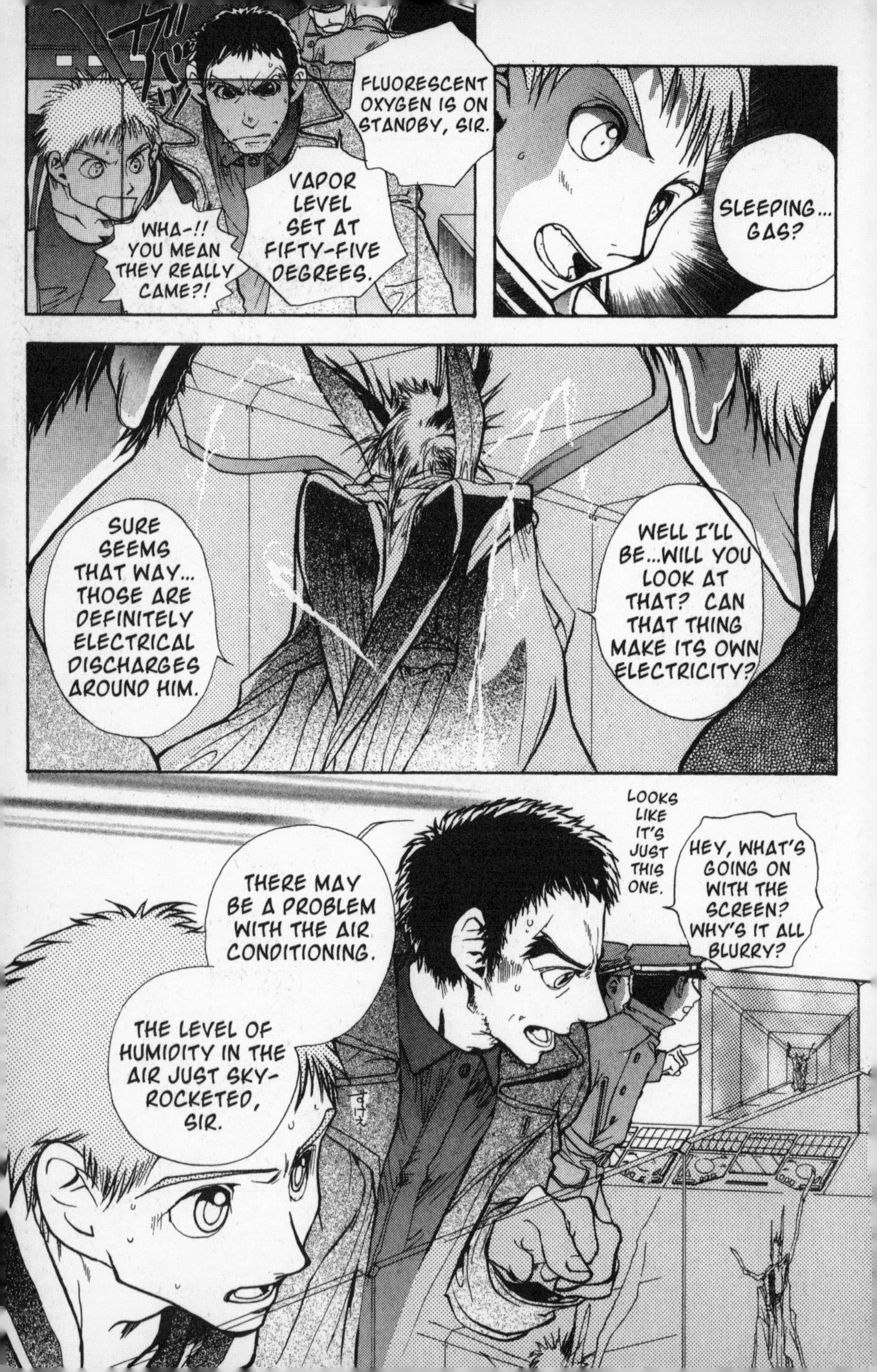
SLEEPING... GAS?
FLUORESCENT OXYGEN IS ON STANDBY, SIR.
VAPOR LEVEL SET AT FIFTY-FIVE DEGREES.
WHA-!! YOU MEAN THEY REALLY CAME?!
WELL I'LL BE...WILL YOU LOOK AT THAT? CAN THAT THING MAKE ITS OWN ELECTRICITY?
SURE SEEMS THAT WAY... THOSE ARE DEFINITELY ELECTRICAL DISCHARGES AROUND HIM.
HEY, WHAT'S GOING ON WITH THE SCREEN? WHY'S IT ALL BLURRY?
LOOKS LIKE IT'S JUST THIS ONE.
THERE MAY BE A PROBLEM WITH THE AIR CONDITIONING.
THE LEVEL OF HUMIDITY IN THE AIR JUST SKY-ROCKETED, SIR.

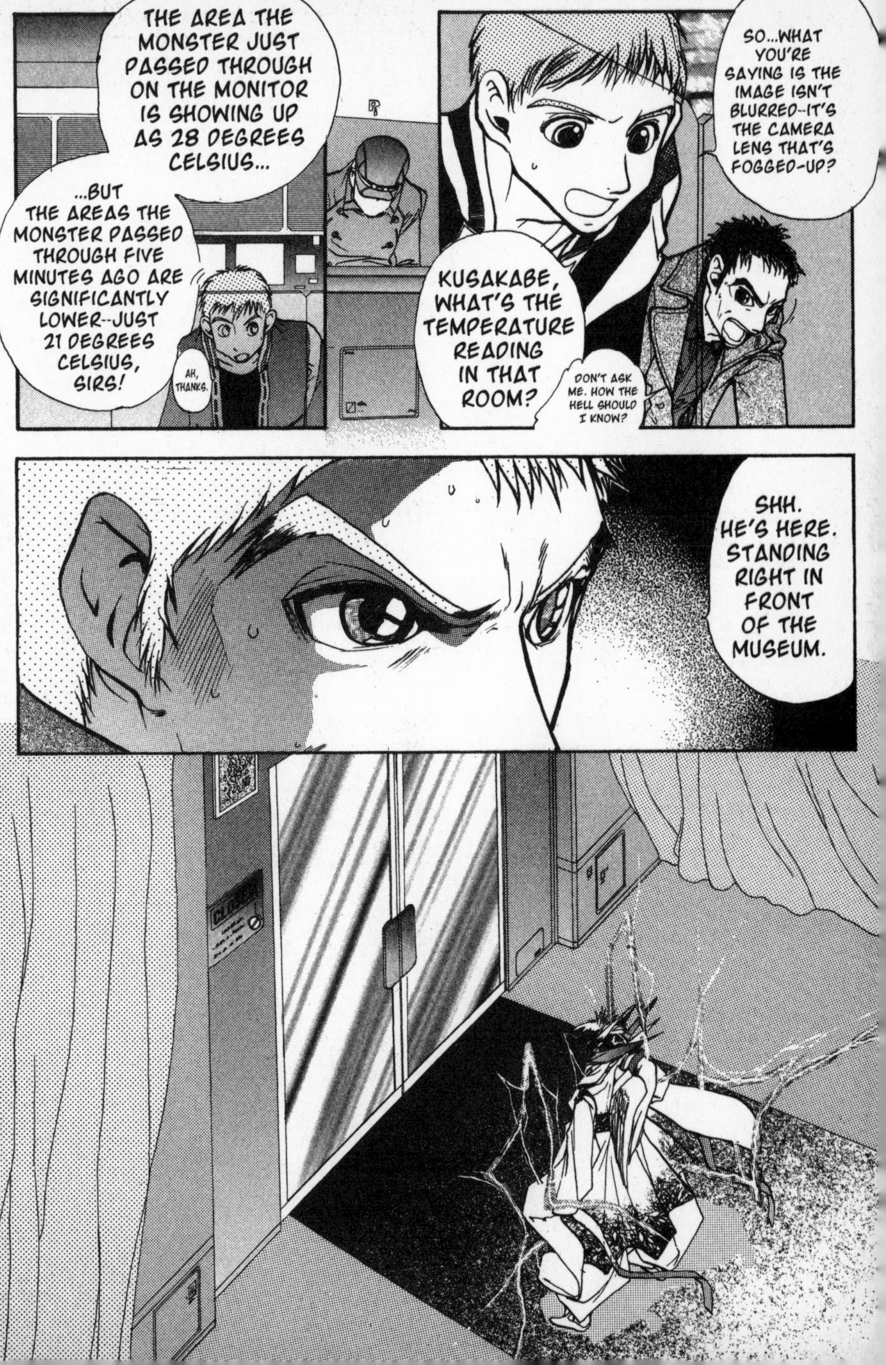
SO...WHAT YOU'RE SAYING IS THE IMAGE ISN'T BLURRED--IT'S THE CAMERA LENS THAT'S FOGGED-UP?
KUSAKABE, WHAT'S THE TEMPERATURE READING IN THAT ROOM?
DON'T ASK ME. HOW THE HELL SHOULD I KNOW?
THE AREA THE MONSTER JUST PASSED THROUGH ON THE MONITOR IS SHOWING UP AS 28 DEGREES CELSIUS...
...BUT THE AREAS THE MONSTER PASSED THROUGH FIVE MINUTES AGO ARE SIGNIFICANTLY LOWER--JUST 21 DEGREES CELSIUS, SIRS!
AH, THANKS.
SHH. HE'S HERE. STANDING RIGHT IN FRONT OF THE MUSEUM.

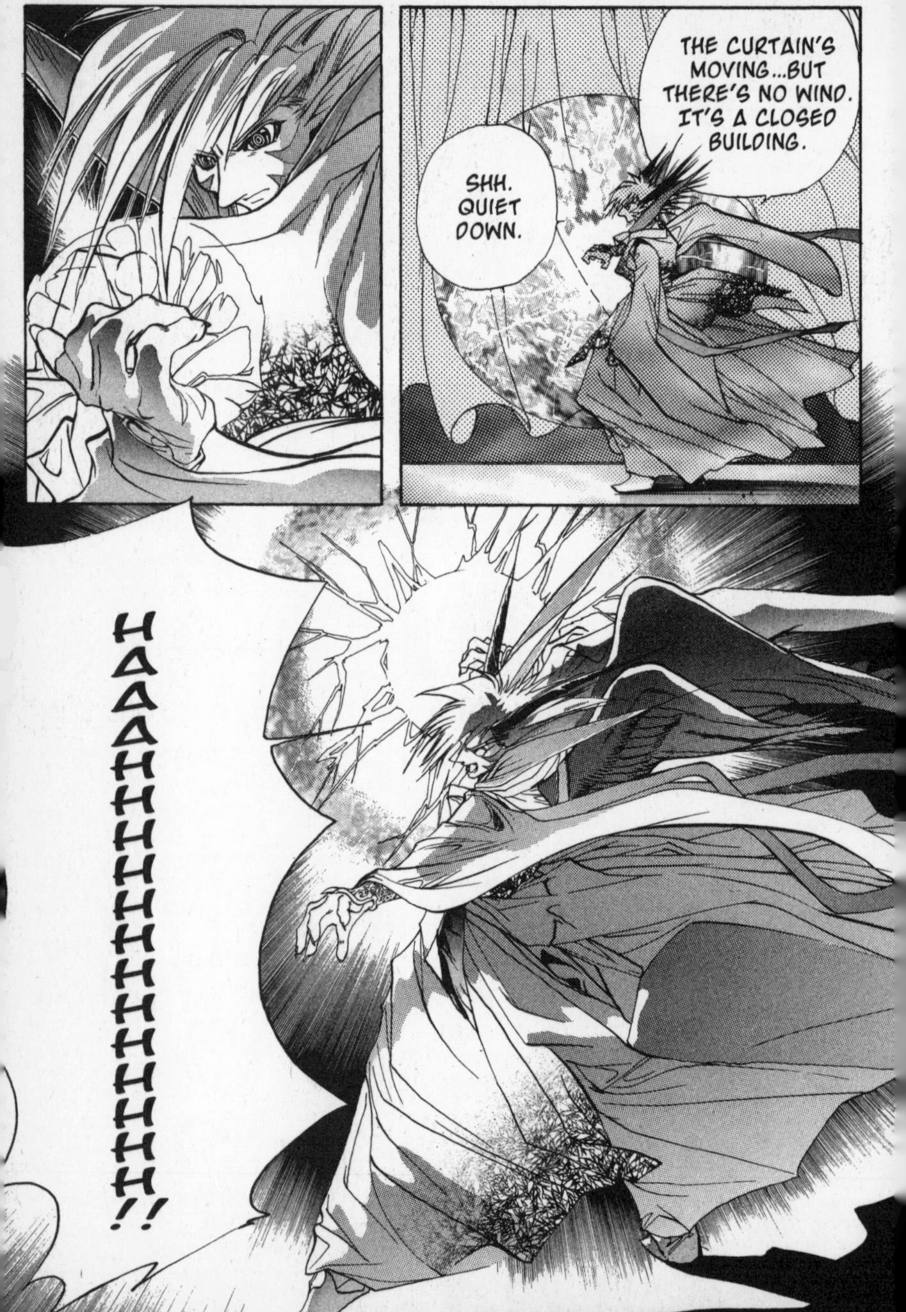
THE CURTAIN'S MOVING...BUT THERE'S NO WIND. IT'S A CLOSED BUILDING.
SHH. QUIET DOWN.
HAAAAHHHHHHHHHHHHHHHH!!

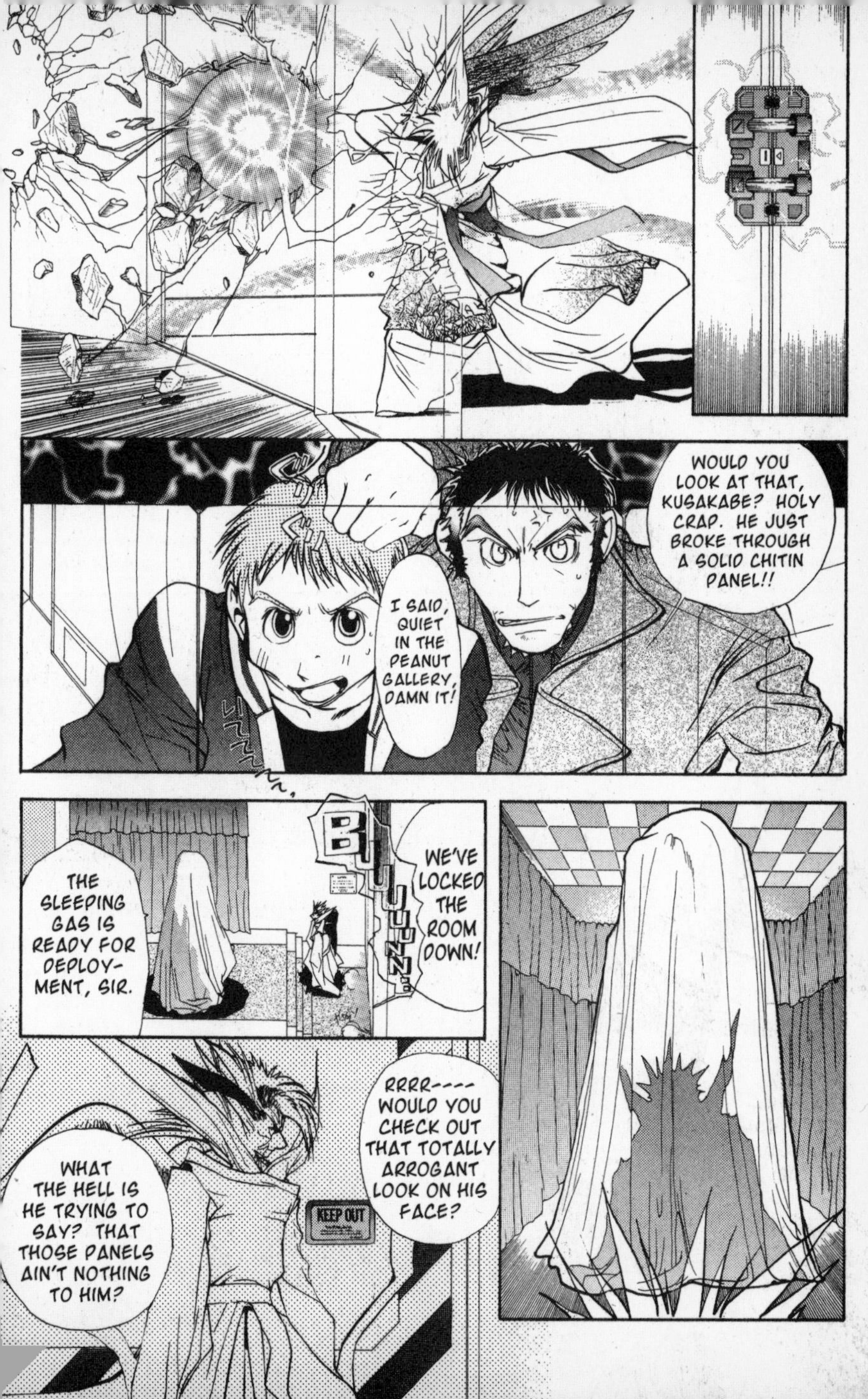
WOULD YOU LOOK AT THAT, KUSAKABE? HOLY CRAP. HE JUST BROKE THROUGH A SOLID CHITIN PANEL!!
I SAID, QUIET IN THE PEANUT GALLERY, DAMN IT!
WE'VE LOCKED THE ROOM DOWN!
THE SLEEPING GAS IS READY FOR DEPLOY-MENT, SIR.
RRRR---- WOULD YOU CHECK OUT THAT TOTALLY ARROGANT LOOK ON HIS FACE?
KEEP OUT
WHAT THE HELL IS HE TRYING TO SAY? THAT THOSE PANELS AIN'T NOTHING TO HIM?

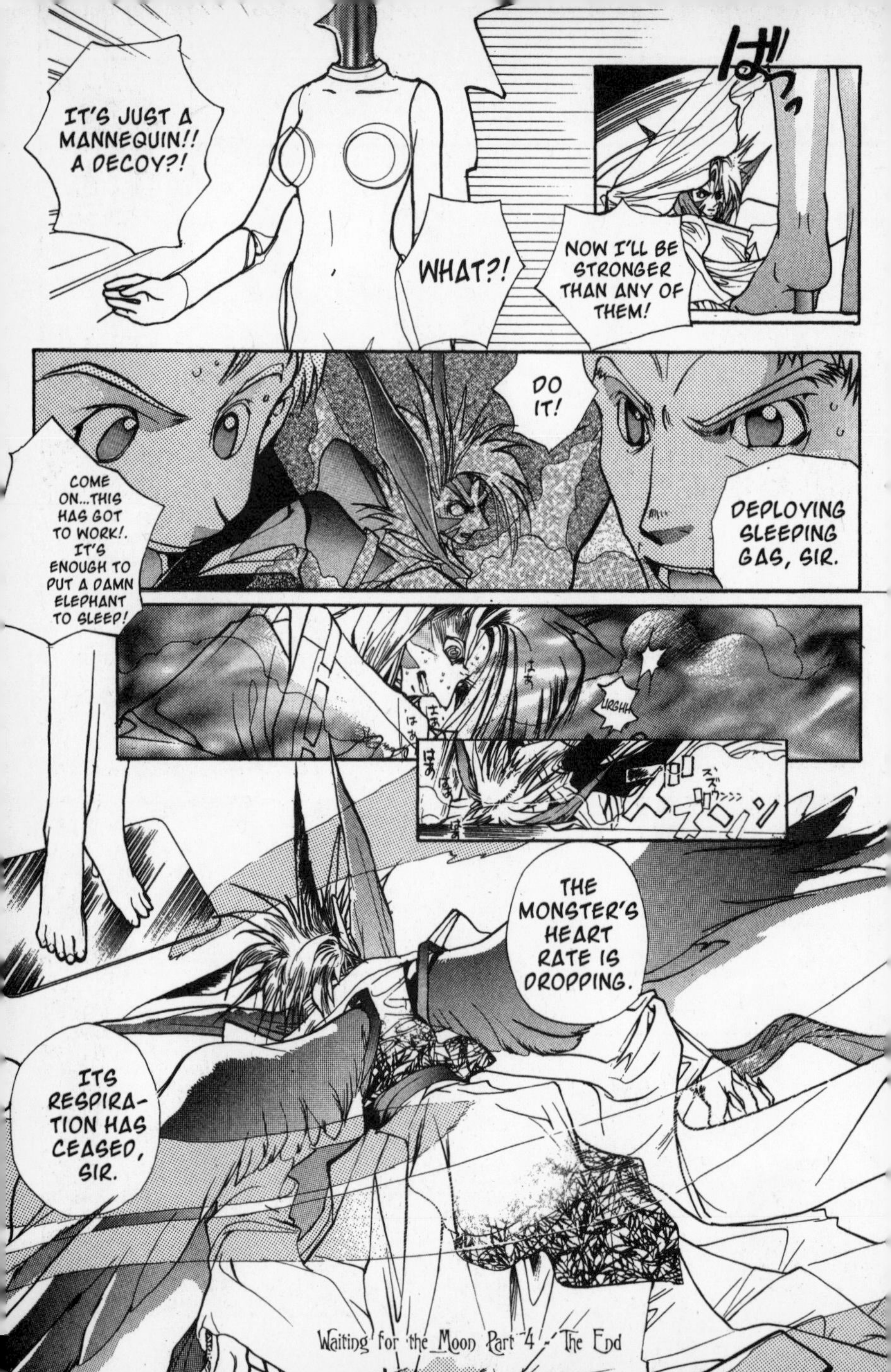
ばっ
NOW I'LL BE STRONGER THAN ANY OF THEM!
WHAT?!
IT'S JUST A MANNEQUIN!! A DECOY?!
DO IT!
DEPLOYING SLEEPING GAS, SIR.
COME ON...THIS HAS GOT TO WORK!. IT'S ENOUGH TO PUT A DAMN ELEPHANT TO SLEEP!
URGHH
THE MONSTER'S HEART RATE IS DROPPING.
ITS RESPIRATION HAS CEASED, SIR.

Waiting for the Moon Part 4 - The End

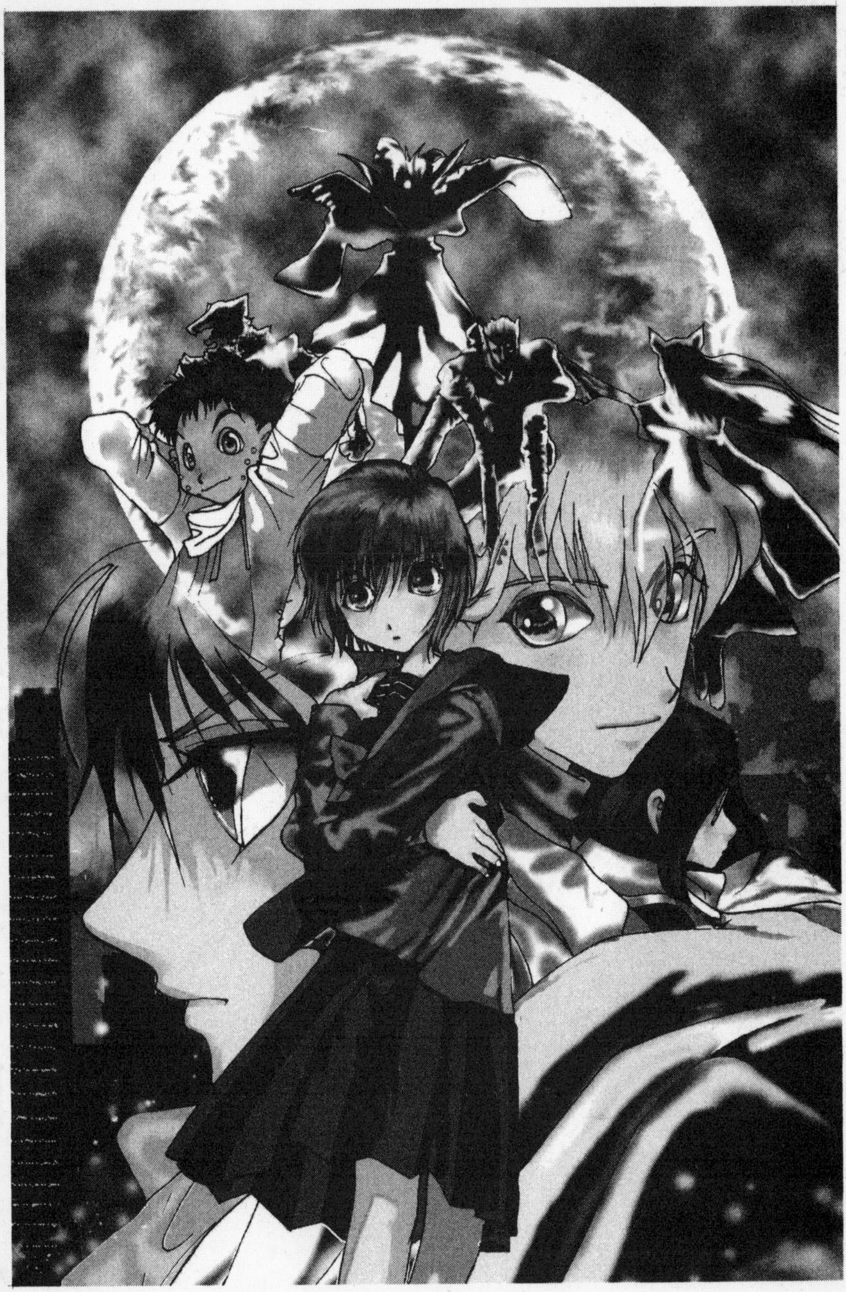

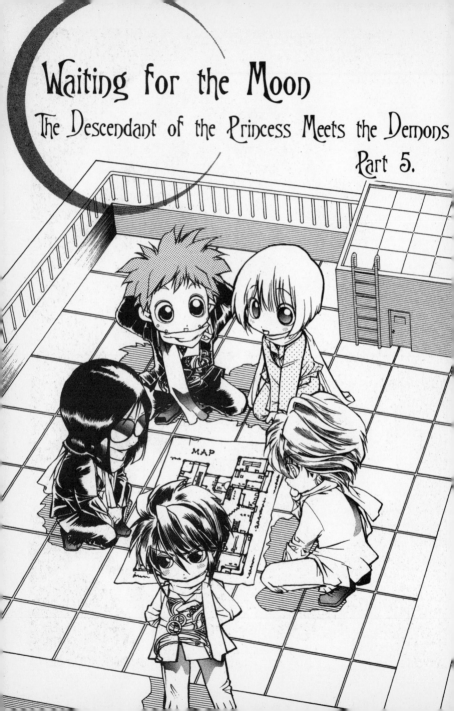

Waiting for the Moon

The Descendant of the Princess Meets the Demons Part 5.

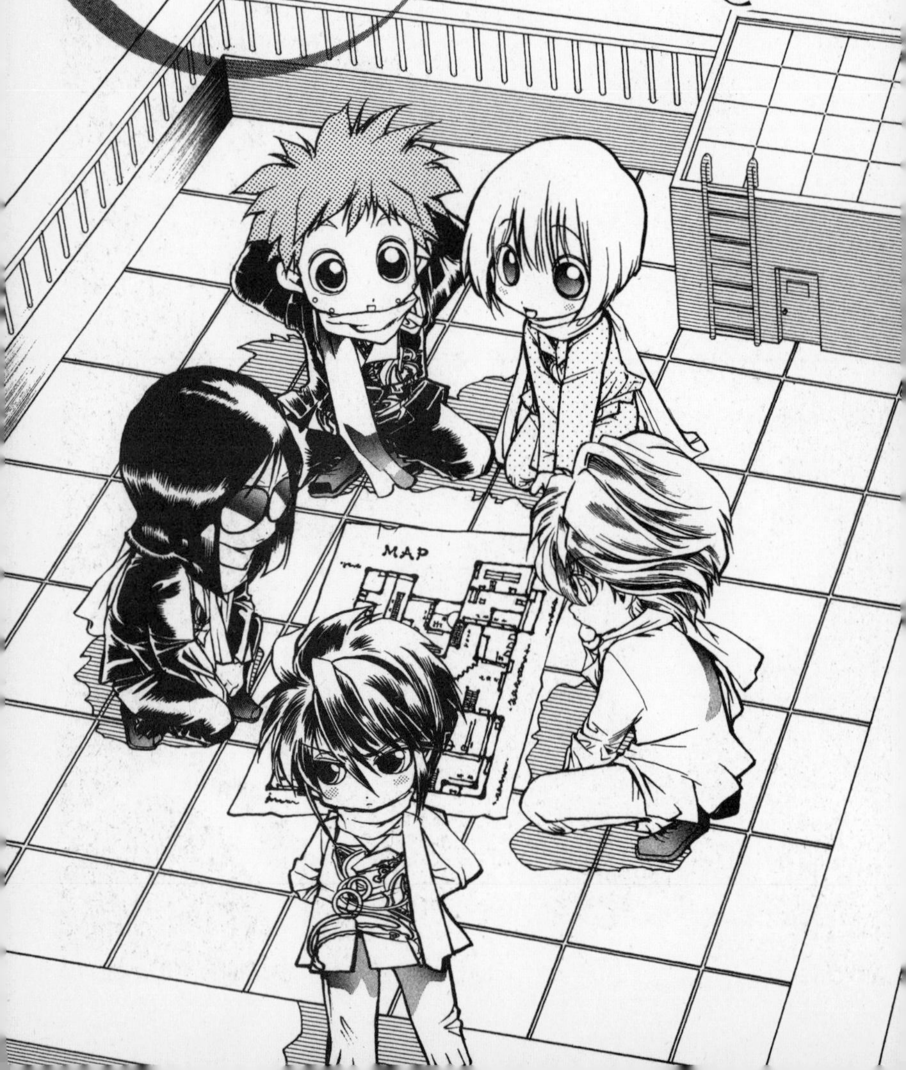
MAP

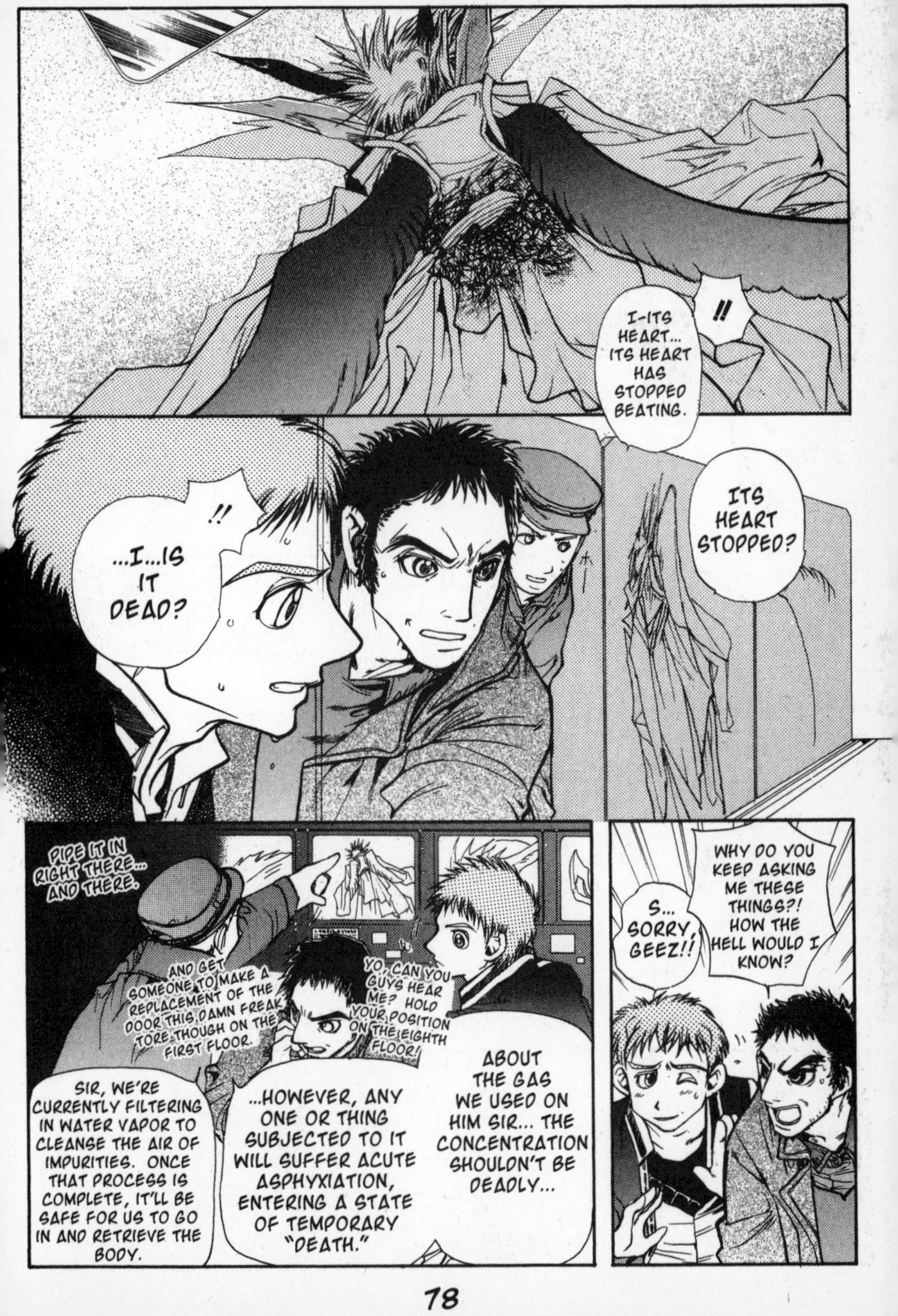
!!
I-ITS HEART... ITS HEART HAS STOPPED BEATING.
ITS HEART STOPPED?
!!
...I...IS IT DEAD?
WHY DO YOU KEEP ASKING ME THESE THINGS?! HOW THE HELL WOULD I KNOW?
S... SORRY, GEEZ!!
YO, CAN YOU GUYS HEAR ME? HOLD YOUR POSITION ON THE EIGHTH FLOOR!
PIPE IT IN RIGHT THERE... AND THERE.
AND GET SOMEONE TO MAKE A REPLACEMENT OF THE DOOR THIS DAMN FREAK TORE THOUGH ON THE FIRST FLOOR.
ABOUT THE GAS WE USED ON HIM SIR... THE CONCENTRATION SHOULDN'T BE DEADLY...
...HOWEVER, ANY ONE OR THING SUBJECTED TO IT WILL SUFFER ACUTE ASPHYXIATION, ENTERING A STATE OF TEMPORARY "DEATH."
SIR, WE'RE CURRENTLY FILTERING IN WATER VAPOR TO CLEANSE THE AIR OF IMPURITIES. ONCE THAT PROCESS IS COMPLETE, IT'LL BE SAFE FOR US TO GO IN AND RETRIEVE THE BODY.

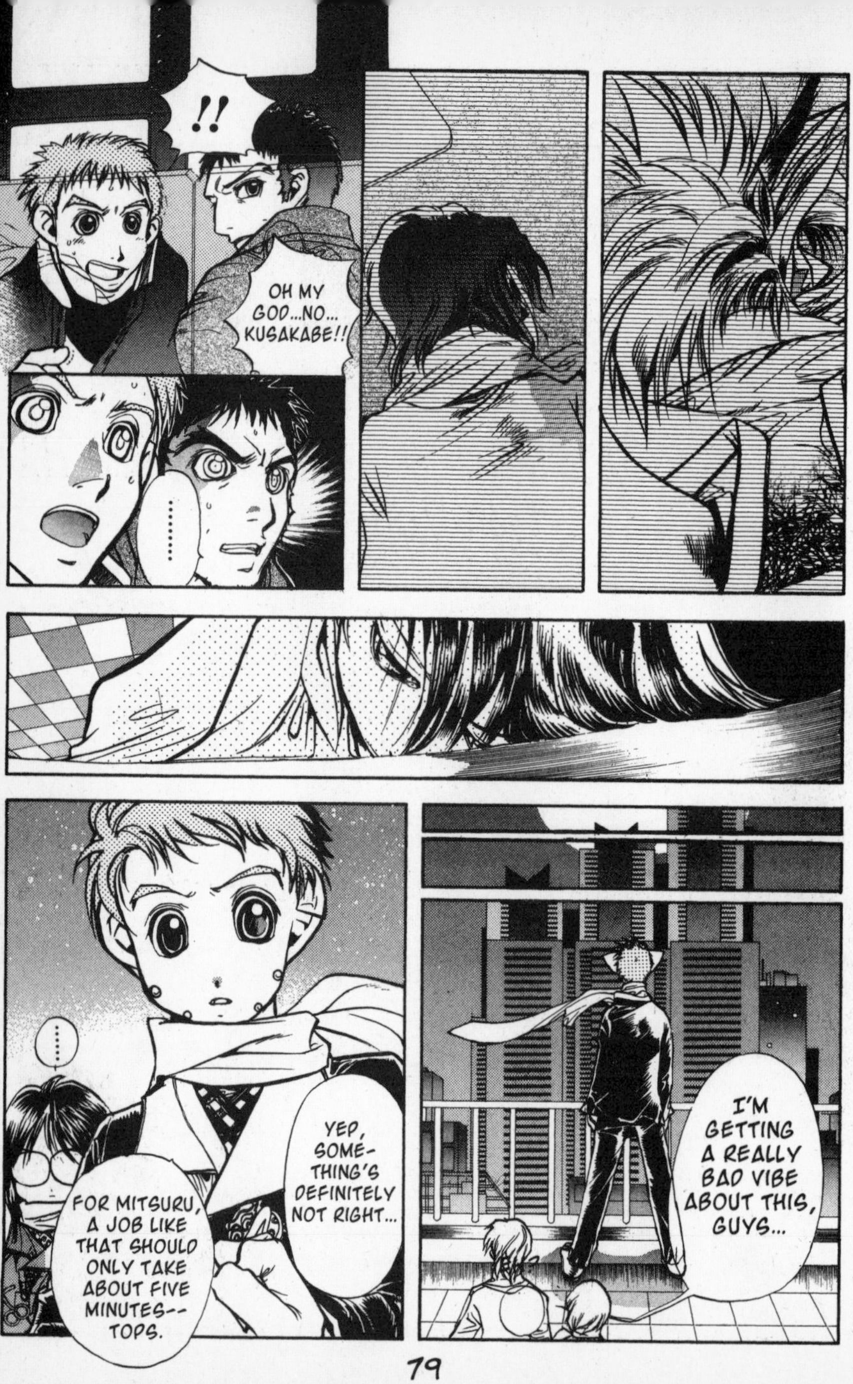
!!
OH MY GOD...NO... KUSAKABE!!
......
I'M GETTING A REALLY BAD VIBE ABOUT THIS, GUYS...
YEP, SOME-THING'S DEFINITELY NOT RIGHT...
FOR MITSURU, A JOB LIKE THAT SHOULD ONLY TAKE ABOUT FIVE MINUTES--TOPS.
......

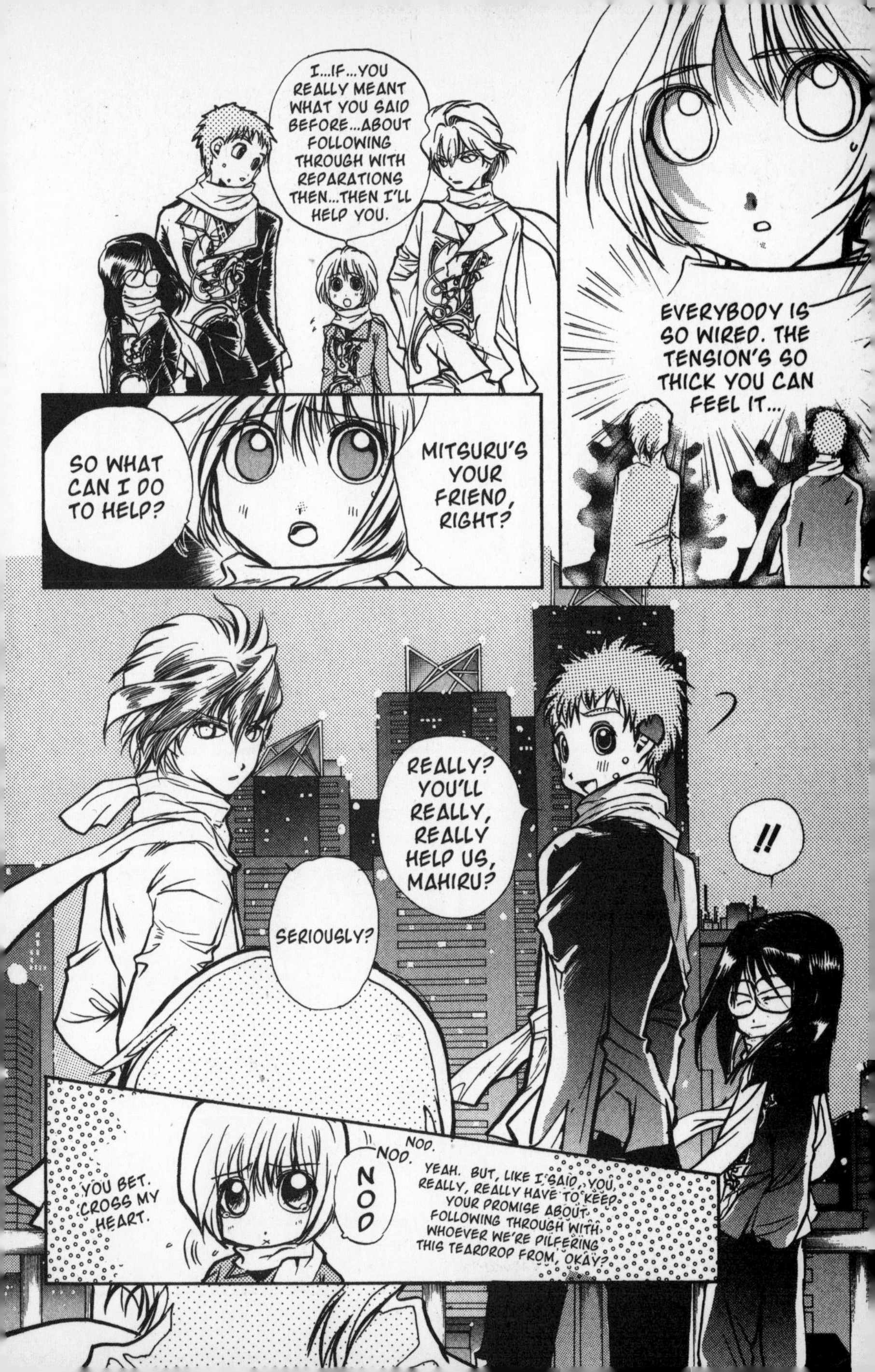
EVERYBODY IS SO WIRED. THE TENSION'S SO THICK YOU CAN FEEL IT...
I...IF...YOU REALLY MEANT WHAT YOU SAID BEFORE...ABOUT FOLLOWING THROUGH WITH REPARATIONS THEN...THEN I'LL HELP YOU.
MITSURU'S YOUR FRIEND, RIGHT?
SO WHAT CAN I DO TO HELP?
!!
REALLY? YOU'LL REALLY, REALLY HELP US, MAHIRU?
SERIOUSLY?
YEAH. BUT, LIKE I SAID, YOU REALLY, REALLY HAVE TO KEEP YOUR PROMISE ABOUT FOLLOWING THROUGH WITH WHOEVER WE'RE PILFERING THIS TEARDROP FROM, OKAY?
NOD. NOD.
NOD
YOU BET. CROSS MY HEART.

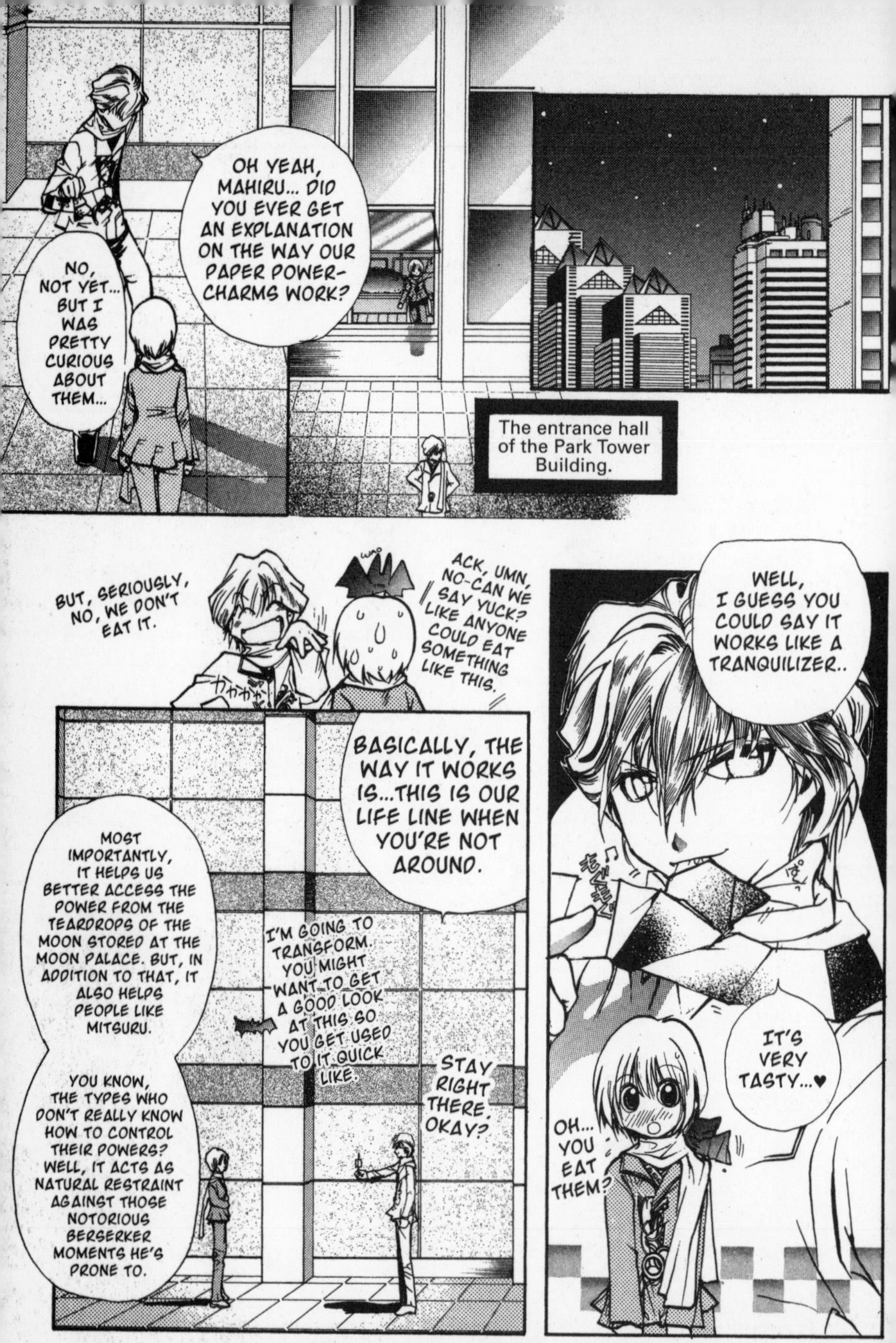
The entrance hall of the Park Tower Building.
OH YEAH, MAHIRU... DID YOU EVER GET AN EXPLANATION ON THE WAY OUR PAPER POWER-CHARMS WORK?
NO, NOT YET... BUT I WAS PRETTY CURIOUS ABOUT THEM...
WELL, I GUESS YOU COULD SAY IT WORKS LIKE A TRANQUILIZER..
IT'S VERY TASTY...♥
OH... YOU EAT THEM?
ACK, UMN, NO-CAN WE SAY YUCK? LIKE ANYONE COULD EAT SOMETHING LIKE THIS.
BUT, SERIOUSLY, NO, WE DON'T EAT IT.
BASICALLY, THE WAY IT WORKS IS...THIS IS OUR LIFE LINE WHEN YOU'RE NOT AROUND.
MOST IMPORTANTLY, IT HELPS US BETTER ACCESS THE POWER FROM THE TEARDROPS OF THE MOON STORED AT THE MOON PALACE. BUT, IN ADDITION TO THAT, IT ALSO HELPS PEOPLE LIKE MITSURU.
YOU KNOW, THE TYPES WHO DON'T REALLY KNOW HOW TO CONTROL THEIR POWERS? WELL, IT ACTS AS NATURAL RESTRAINT AGAINST THOSE NOTORIOUS BERSERKER MOMENTS HE'S PRONE TO.
I'M GOING TO TRANSFORM. YOU MIGHT WANT TO GET A GOOD LOOK AT THIS SO YOU GET USED TO IT QUICK LIKE.
STAY RIGHT THERE. OKAY?

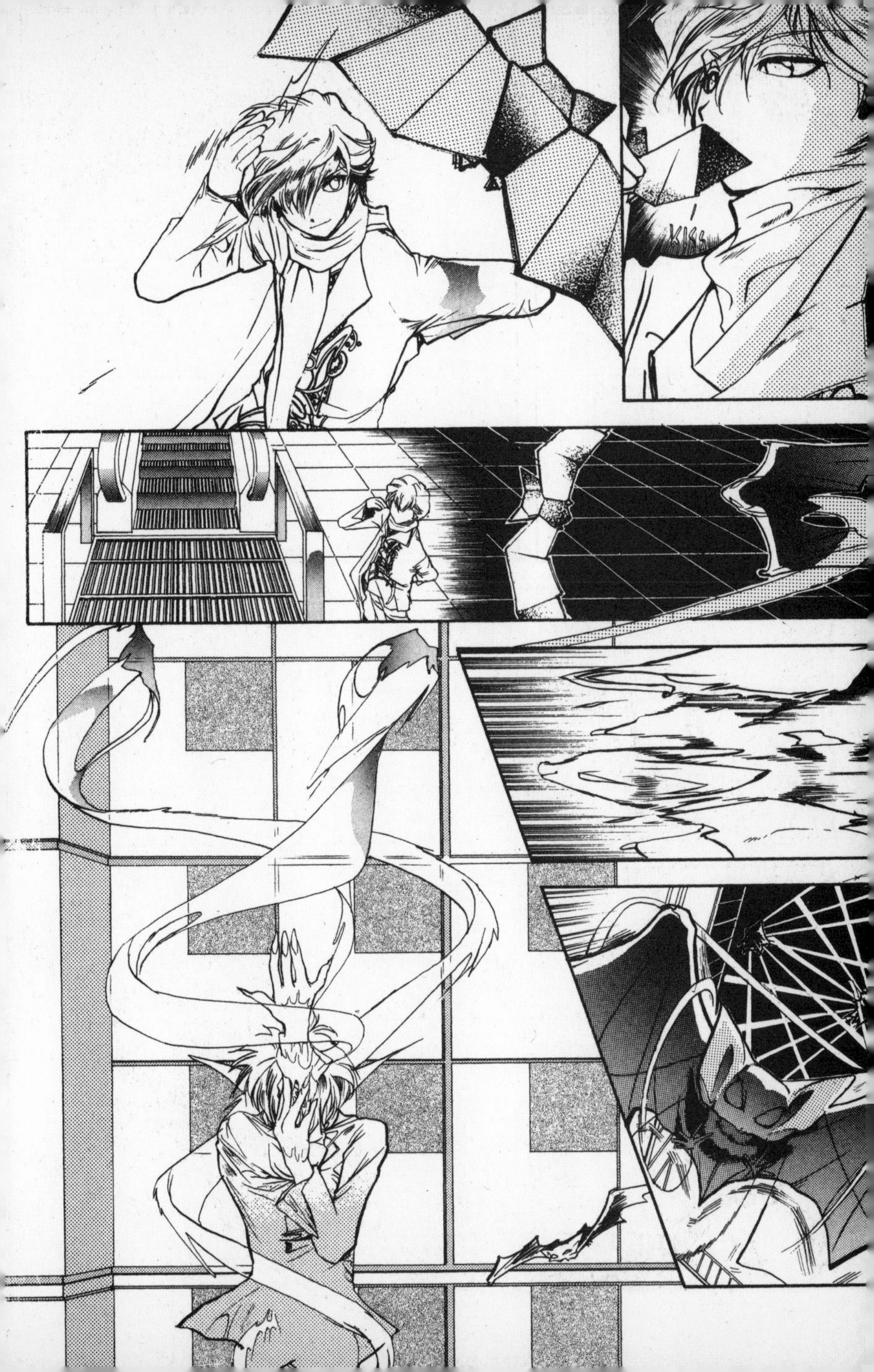
KISS

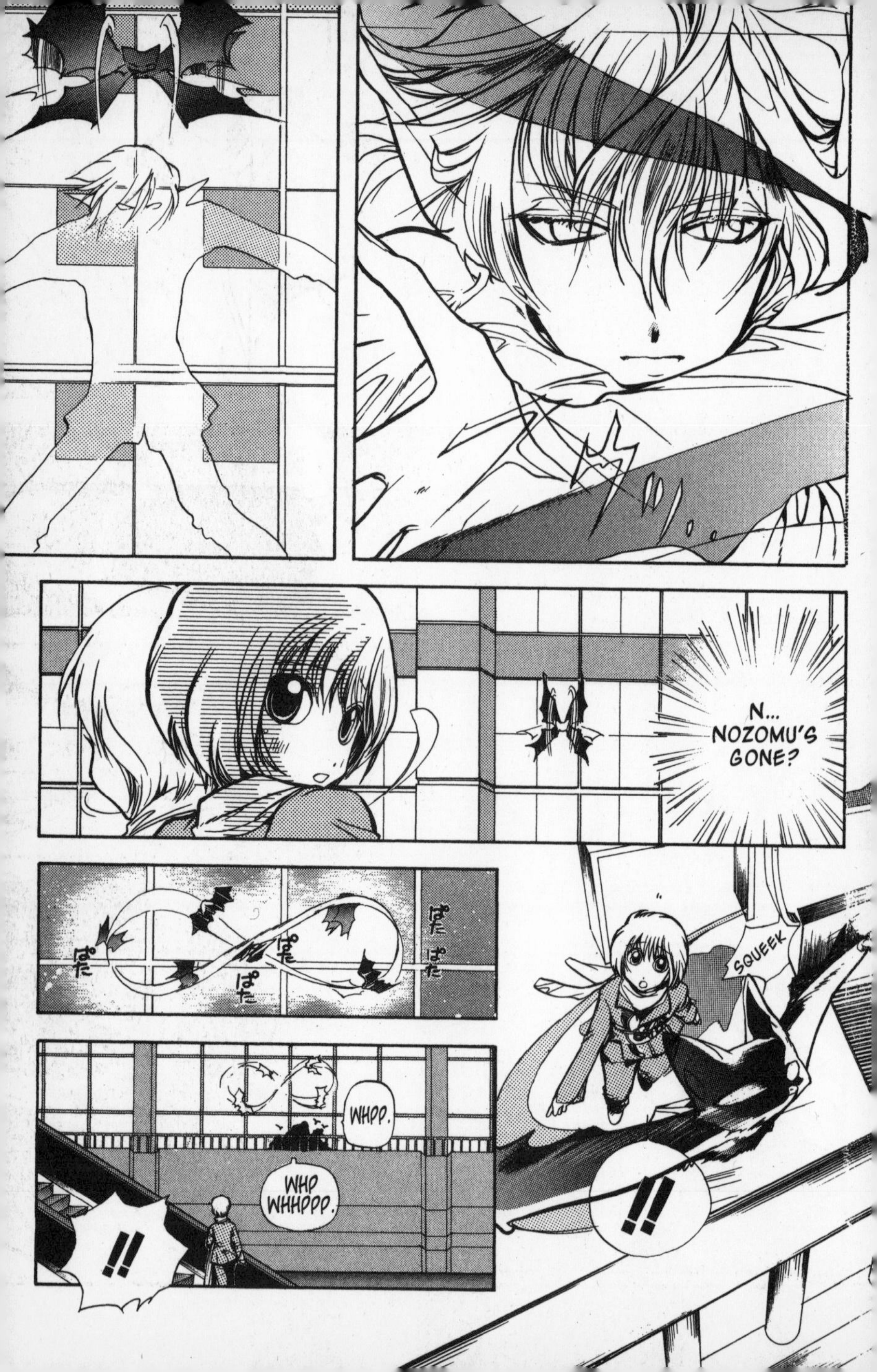
N... NOZOMU'S GONE?
SQUEEK
!!
ぱた ぱた
ぱた
ぱた
ぱた
WHPP.
WHP WHHPPP.
!!

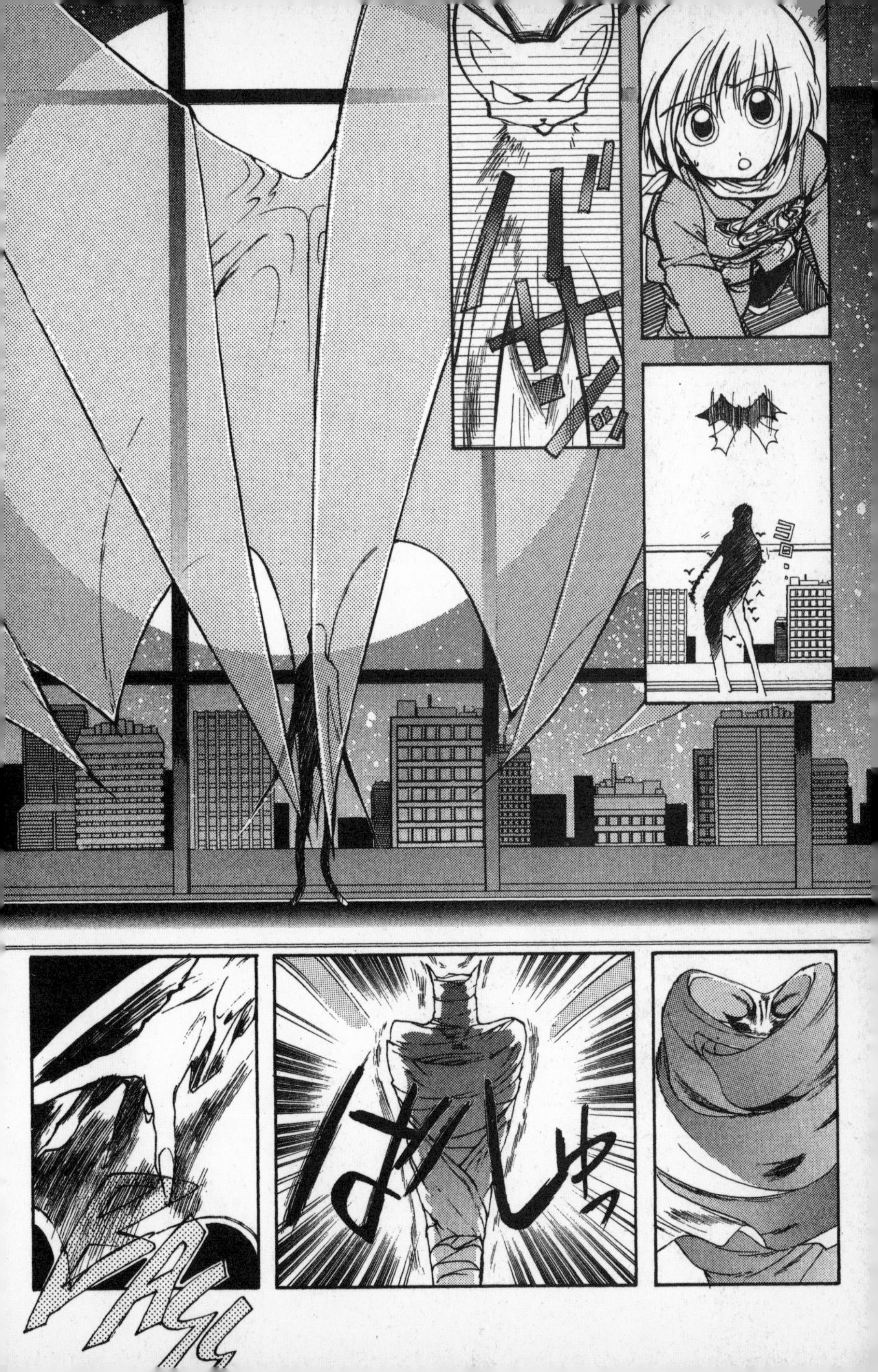

バサッ
ヨロ
はしゅっ

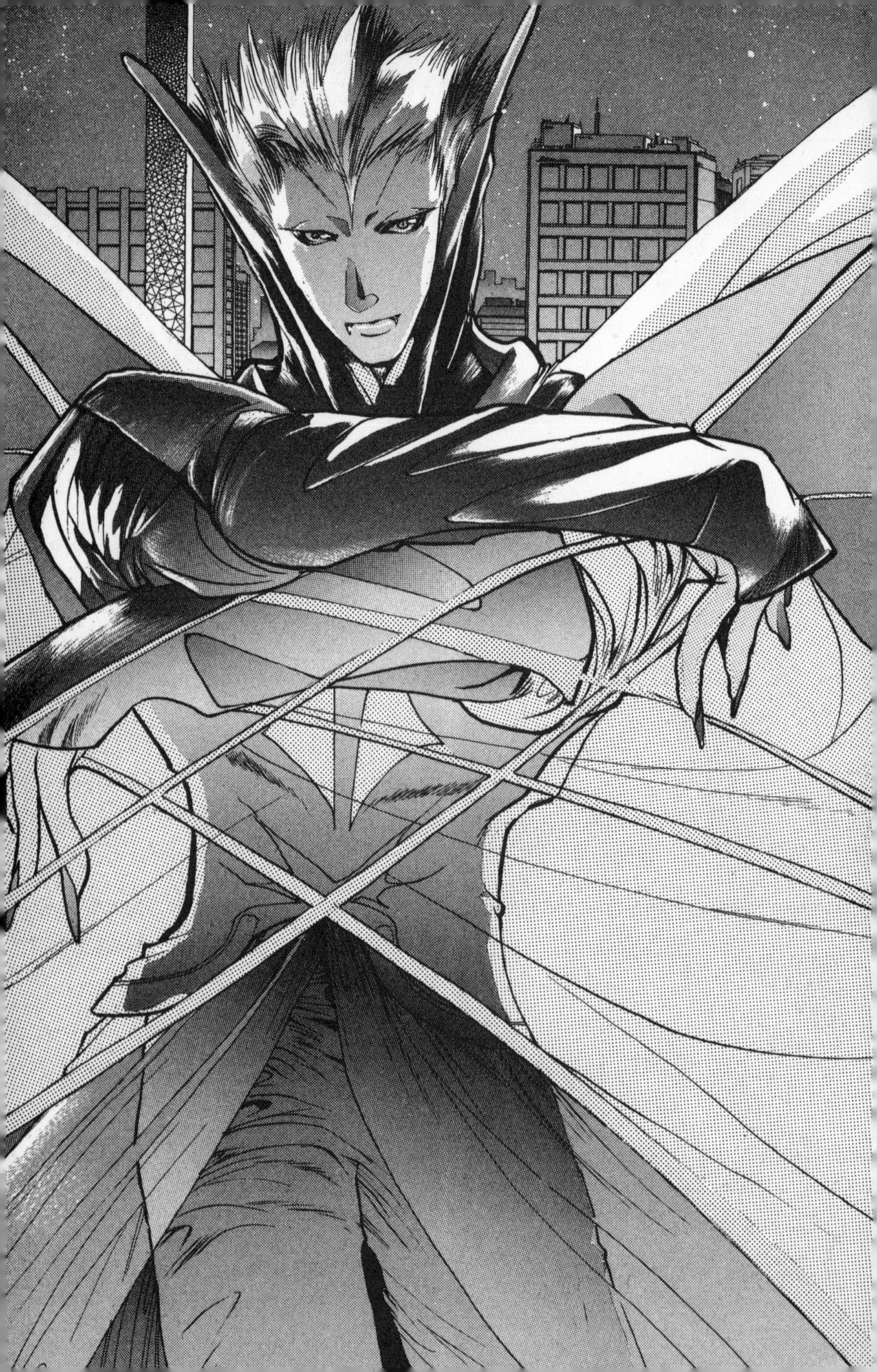

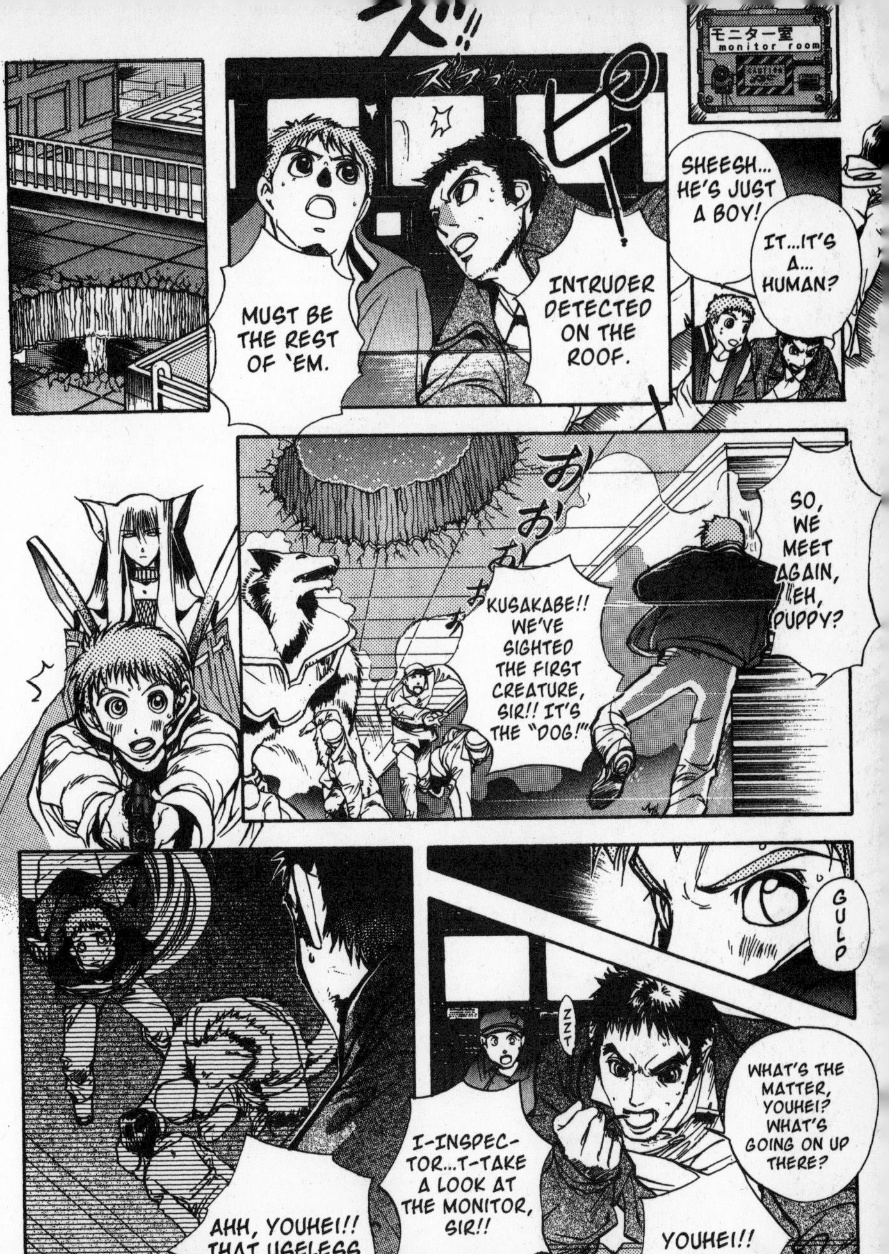
モニター室
monitor room
SHEESH... HE'S JUST A BOY!
IT...IT'S A... HUMAN?
ズ!!
ピー!
INTRUDER DETECTED ON THE ROOF.
MUST BE THE REST OF 'EM.
SO, WE MEET AGAIN, EH, PUPPY?
おおおお
KUSAKABE!! WE'VE SIGHTED THE FIRST CREATURE, SIR!! IT'S THE "DOG!"
GULP
WHAT'S THE MATTER, YOUHEI? WHAT'S GOING ON UP THERE?
YOUHEI!! ??......
ZZT
I-INSPECTOR...T-TAKE A LOOK AT THE MONITOR, SIR!!
AHH, YOUHEI!! THAT USELESS DOLT!!

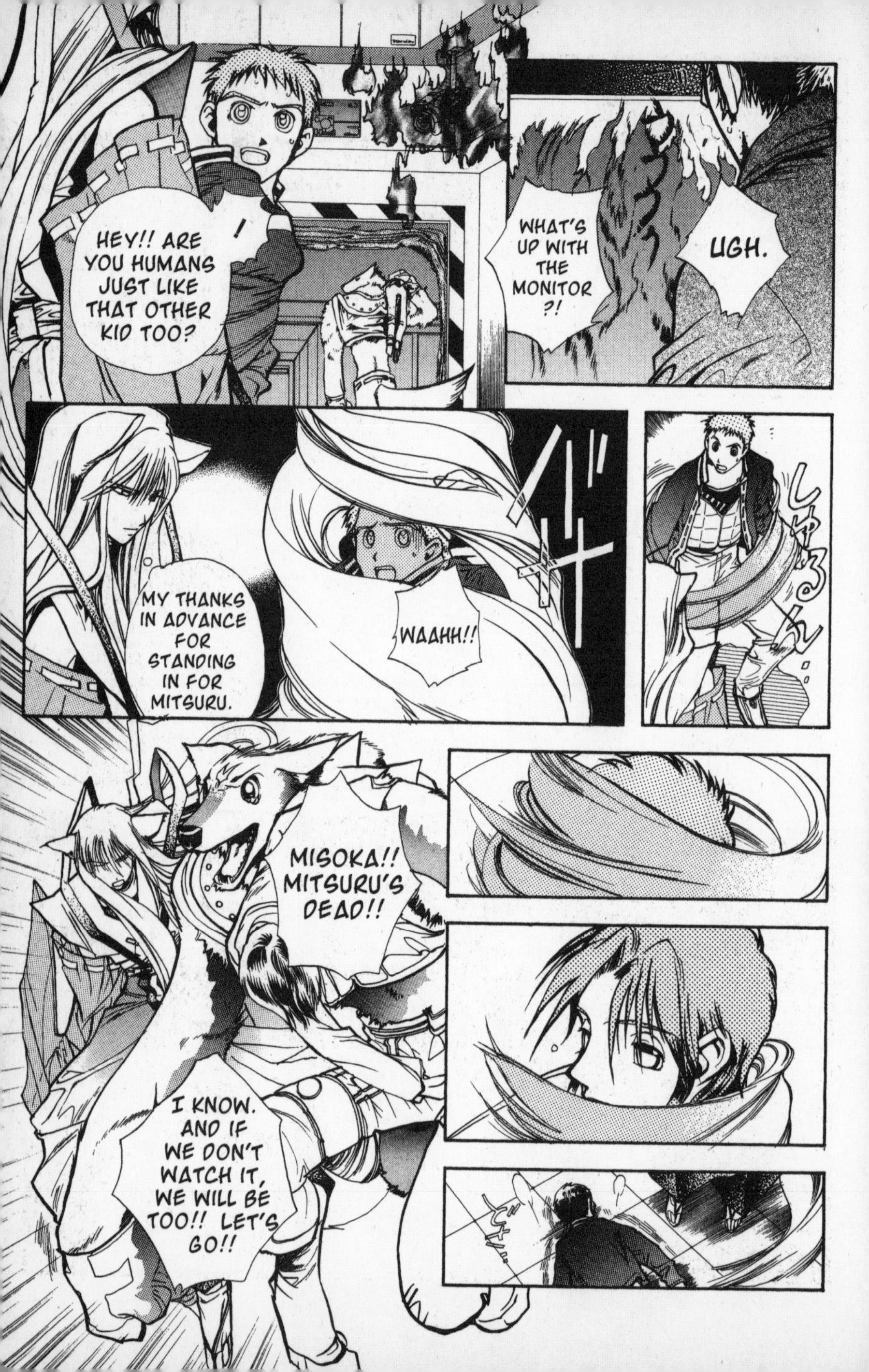
UGH.
WHAT'S UP WITH THE MONITOR?!
!
HEY!! ARE YOU HUMANS JUST LIKE THAT OTHER KID TOO?
WAAHH!!
MY THANKS IN ADVANCE FOR STANDING IN FOR MITSURU.
MISOKA!! MITSURU'S DEAD!!
I KNOW. AND IF WE DON'T WATCH IT, WE WILL BE TOO!! LET'S GO!!

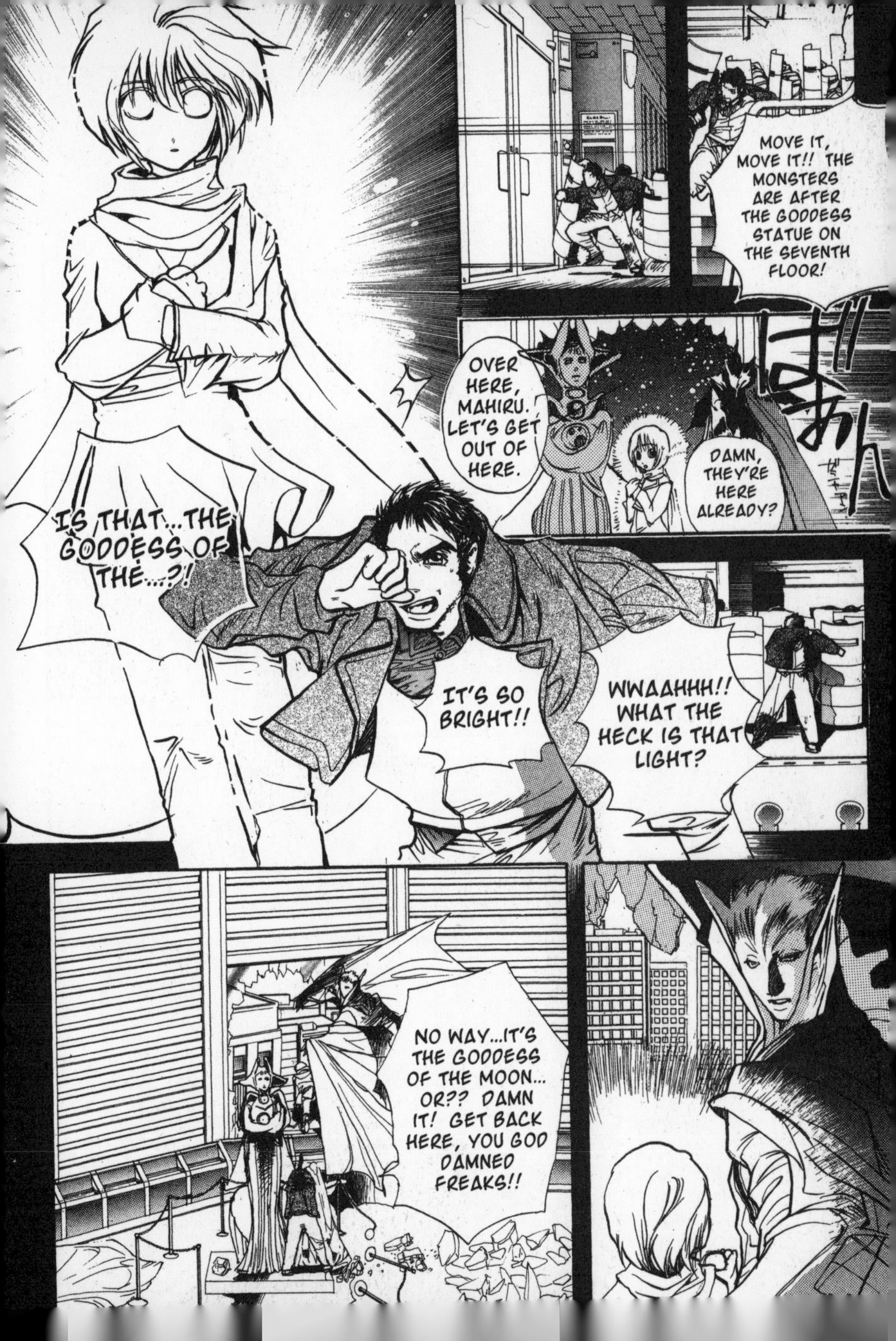
MOVE IT, MOVE IT!! THE MONSTERS ARE AFTER THE GODDESS STATUE ON THE SEVENTH FLOOR!
ばぁん
OVER HERE, MAHIRU. LET'S GET OUT OF HERE.
DAMN, THEY'RE HERE ALREADY?
WWAAHHH!! WHAT THE HECK IS THAT LIGHT?
IT'S SO BRIGHT!!
IS THAT...THE GODDESS OF THE...?!
NO WAY...IT'S THE GODDESS OF THE MOON... OR?? DAMN IT! GET BACK HERE, YOU GOD DAMNED FREAKS!!

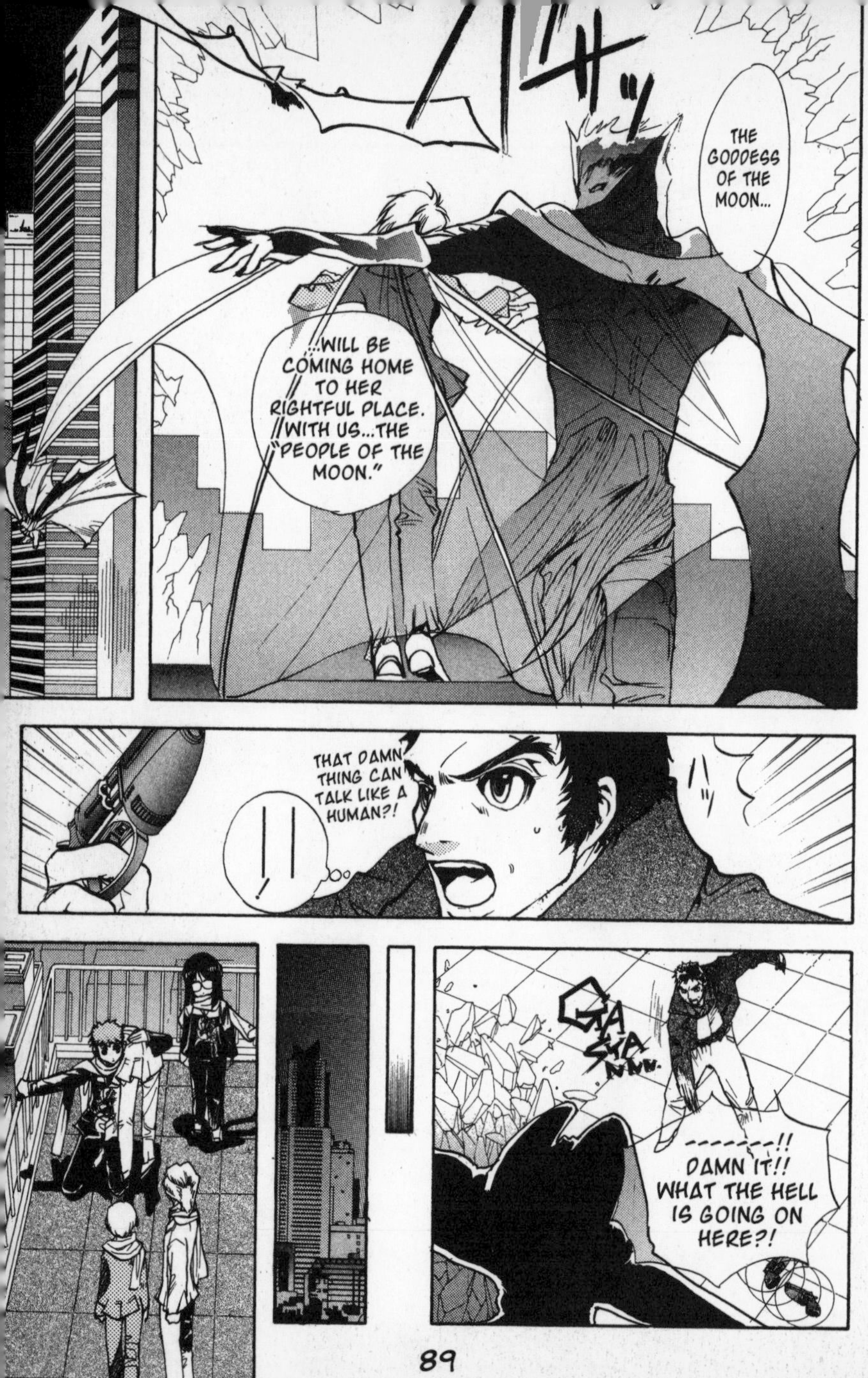
THE GODDESS OF THE MOON...
...WILL BE COMING HOME TO HER RIGHTFUL PLACE. WITH US...THE "PEOPLE OF THE MOON."
!!
THAT DAMN THING CAN TALK LIKE A HUMAN?!
GASHANNN
--------!! DAMN IT!! WHAT THE HELL IS GOING ON HERE?!

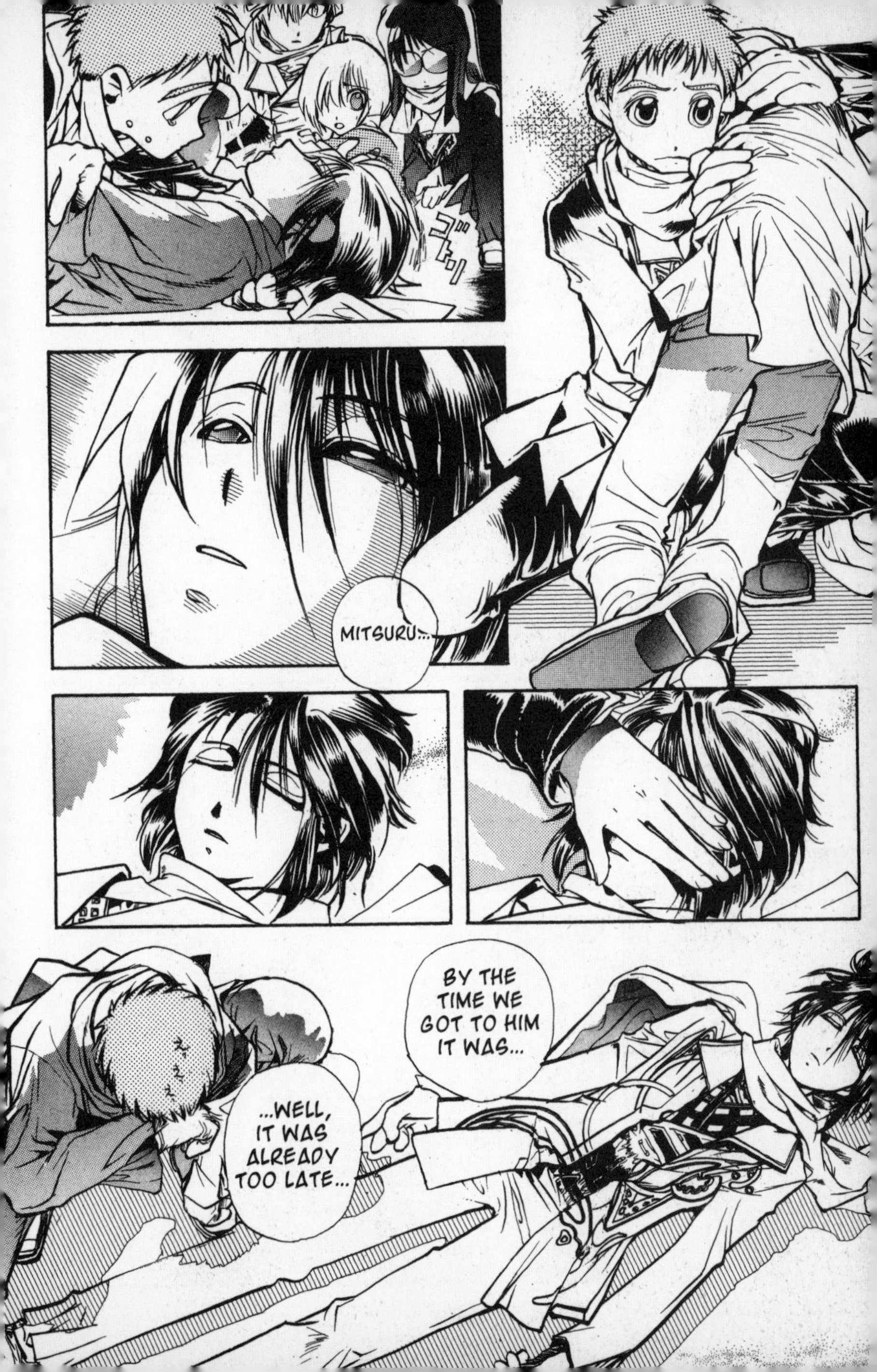
MITSURU...
BY THE TIME WE GOT TO HIM IT WAS...
...WELL, IT WAS ALREADY TOO LATE...

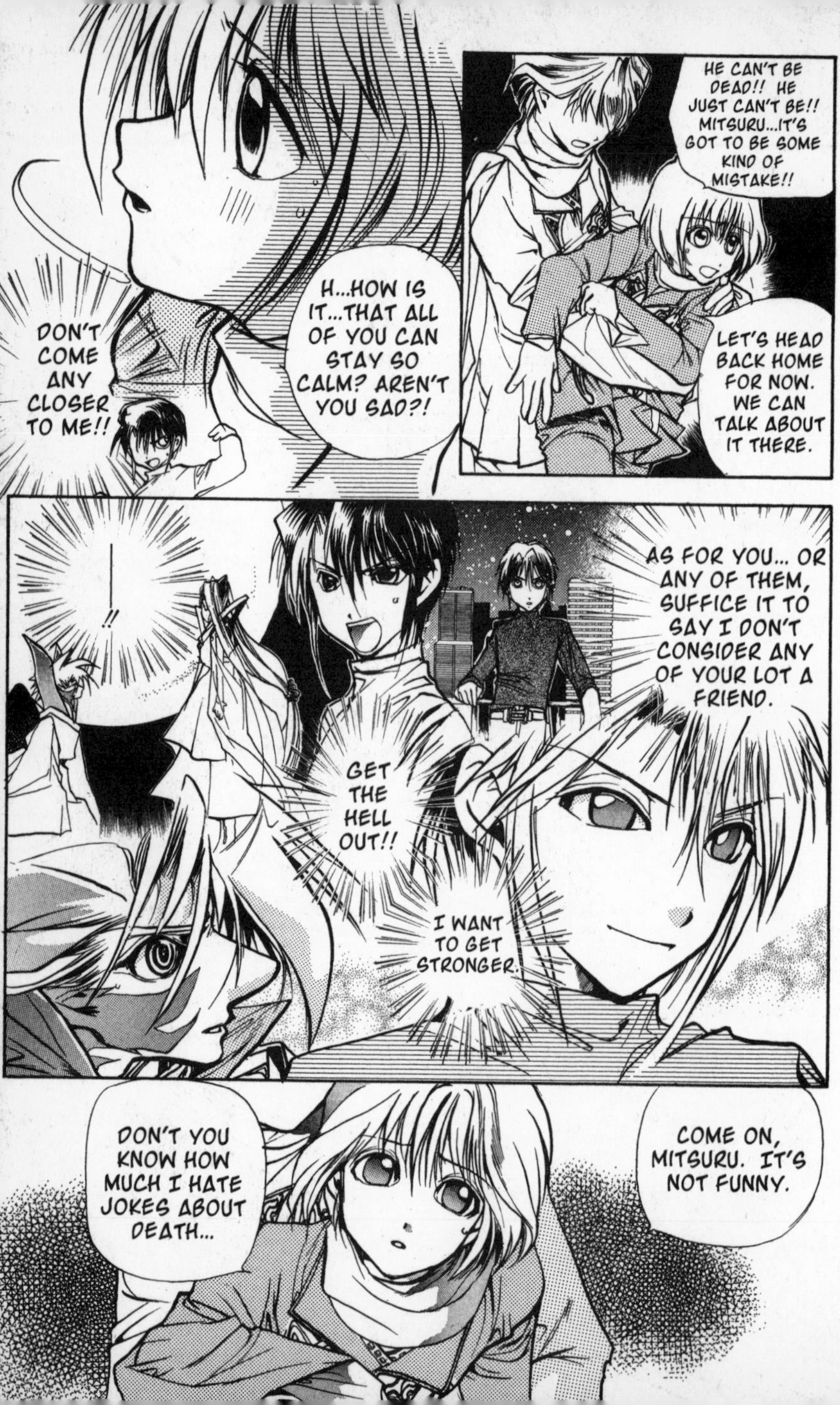
HE CAN'T BE DEAD!! HE JUST CAN'T BE!! MITSURU...IT'S GOT TO BE SOME KIND OF MISTAKE!!
LET'S HEAD BACK HOME FOR NOW. WE CAN TALK ABOUT IT THERE.
H...HOW IS IT...THAT ALL OF YOU CAN STAY SO CALM? AREN'T YOU SAD?!
DON'T COME ANY CLOSER TO ME!!
AS FOR YOU... OR ANY OF THEM, SUFFICE IT TO SAY I DON'T CONSIDER ANY OF YOUR LOT A FRIEND.
—!!
GET THE HELL OUT!!
I WANT TO GET STRONGER.
COME ON, MITSURU. IT'S NOT FUNNY.
DON'T YOU KNOW HOW MUCH I HATE JOKES ABOUT DEATH...

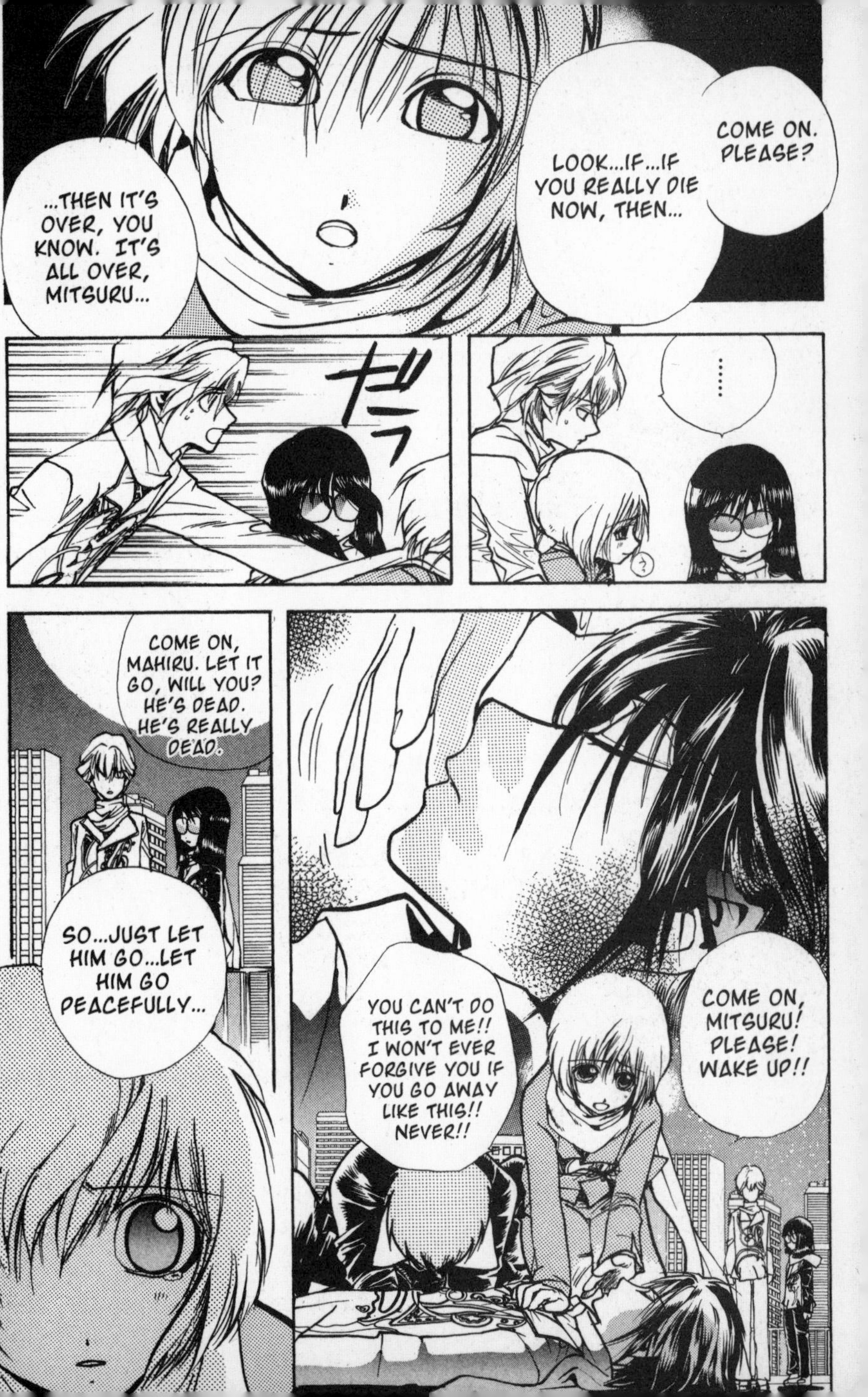
COME ON. PLEASE?
LOOK...IF...IF YOU REALLY DIE NOW, THEN...
...THEN IT'S OVER, YOU KNOW. IT'S ALL OVER, MITSURU...
......
ガラ
COME ON, MITSURU! PLEASE! WAKE UP!!
YOU CAN'T DO THIS TO ME!! I WON'T EVER FORGIVE YOU IF YOU GO AWAY LIKE THIS!! NEVER!!
COME ON, MAHIRU. LET IT GO, WILL YOU? HE'S DEAD. HE'S REALLY DEAD.
SO...JUST LET HIM GO...LET HIM GO PEACEFULLY...

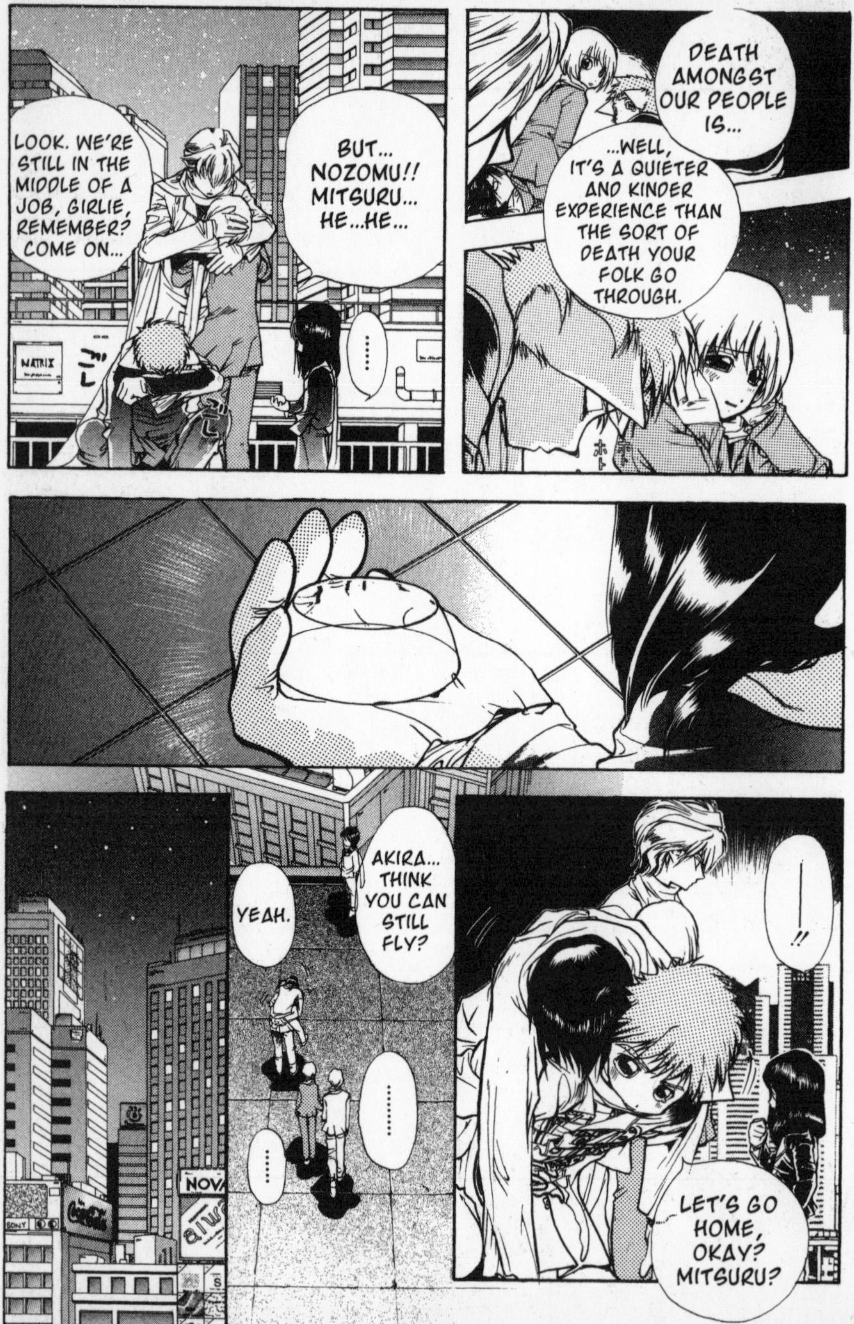
DEATH AMONGST OUR PEOPLE IS...
...WELL, IT'S A QUIETER AND KINDER EXPERIENCE THAN THE SORT OF DEATH YOUR FOLK GO THROUGH.
BUT... NOZOMU!! MITSURU... HE...HE...
LOOK. WE'RE STILL IN THE MIDDLE OF A JOB, GIRLIE, REMEMBER? COME ON...
......
—!!
LET'S GO HOME, OKAY? MITSURU?
AKIRA... THINK YOU CAN STILL FLY?
YEAH.
......
......
NOVA
SONY

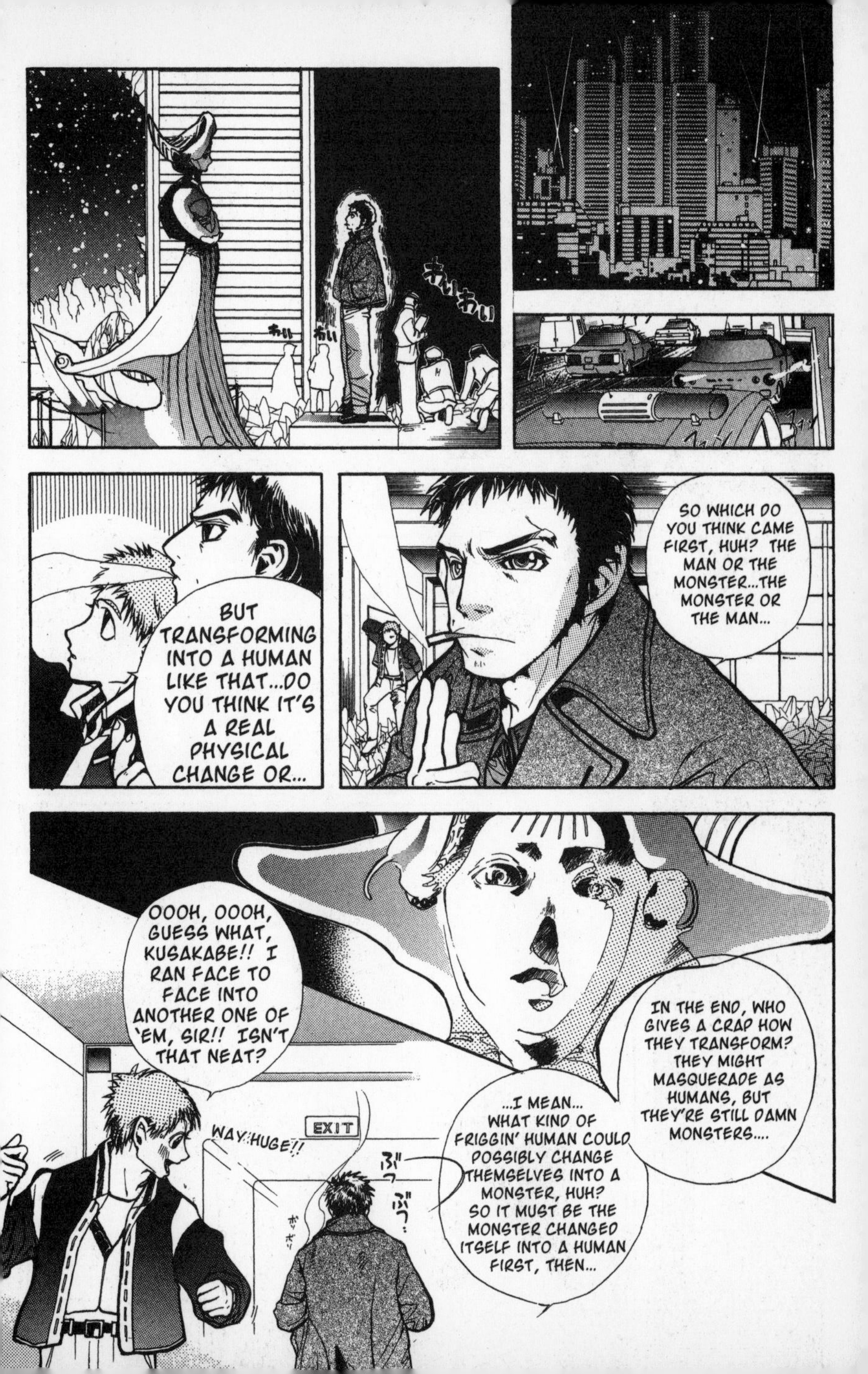
SO WHICH DO YOU THINK CAME FIRST, HUH? THE MAN OR THE MONSTER...THE MONSTER OR THE MAN...
BUT TRANSFORMING INTO A HUMAN LIKE THAT...DO YOU THINK IT'S A REAL PHYSICAL CHANGE OR...
IN THE END, WHO GIVES A CRAP HOW THEY TRANSFORM? THEY MIGHT MASQUERADE AS HUMANS, BUT THEY'RE STILL DAMN MONSTERS....
...I MEAN... WHAT KIND OF FRIGGIN' HUMAN COULD POSSIBLY CHANGE THEMSELVES INTO A MONSTER, HUH? SO IT MUST BE THE MONSTER CHANGED ITSELF INTO A HUMAN FIRST, THEN...
EXIT
OOOH, OOOH, GUESS WHAT, KUSAKABE!! I RAN FACE TO FACE INTO ANOTHER ONE OF 'EM, SIR!! ISN'T THAT NEAT?
WAY HUGE!!

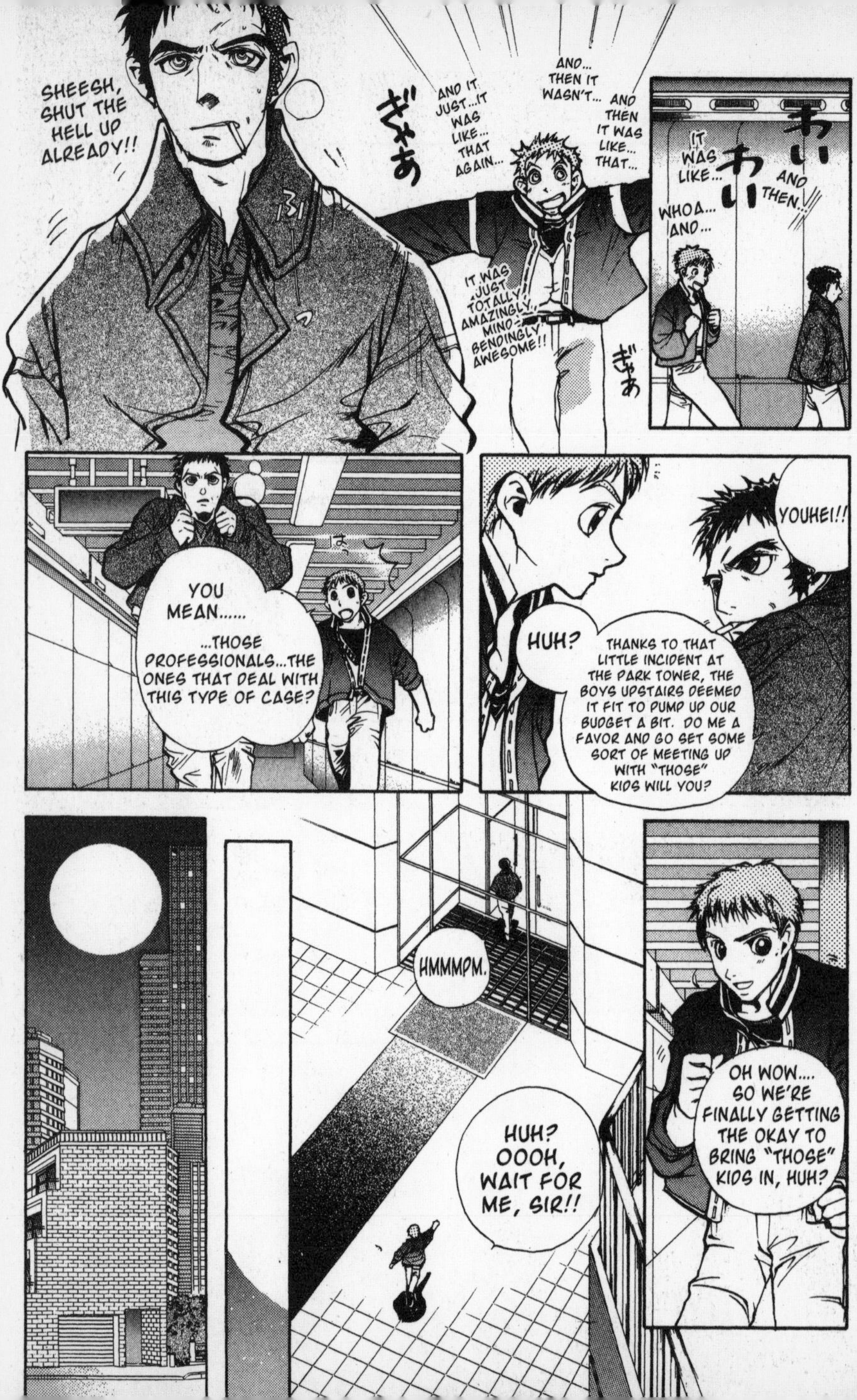
わい わい
AND THEN...
IT WAS LIKE...
WHOA... AND...
AND THEN IT WAS LIKE... THAT...
AND... THEN IT WASN'T...
AND IT JUST...IT WAS LIKE... THAT AGAIN...
IT WAS JUST TOTALLY AMAZINGLY, MIND-BENDINGLY AWESOME!!
ぎゃあ
ぎゃあ
SHEESH, SHUT THE HELL UP ALREADY!!
YOUHEI!!
HUH?
THANKS TO THAT LITTLE INCIDENT AT THE PARK TOWER, THE BOYS UPSTAIRS DEEMED IT FIT TO PUMP UP OUR BUDGET A BIT. DO ME A FAVOR AND GO SET SOME SORT OF MEETING UP WITH "THOSE" KIDS WILL YOU?
YOU MEAN......
...THOSE PROFESSIONALS...THE ONES THAT DEAL WITH THIS TYPE OF CASE?
OH WOW.... SO WE'RE FINALLY GETTING THE OKAY TO BRING "THOSE" KIDS IN, HUH?
HMMMPM.
HUH? OOOH, WAIT FOR ME, SIR!!

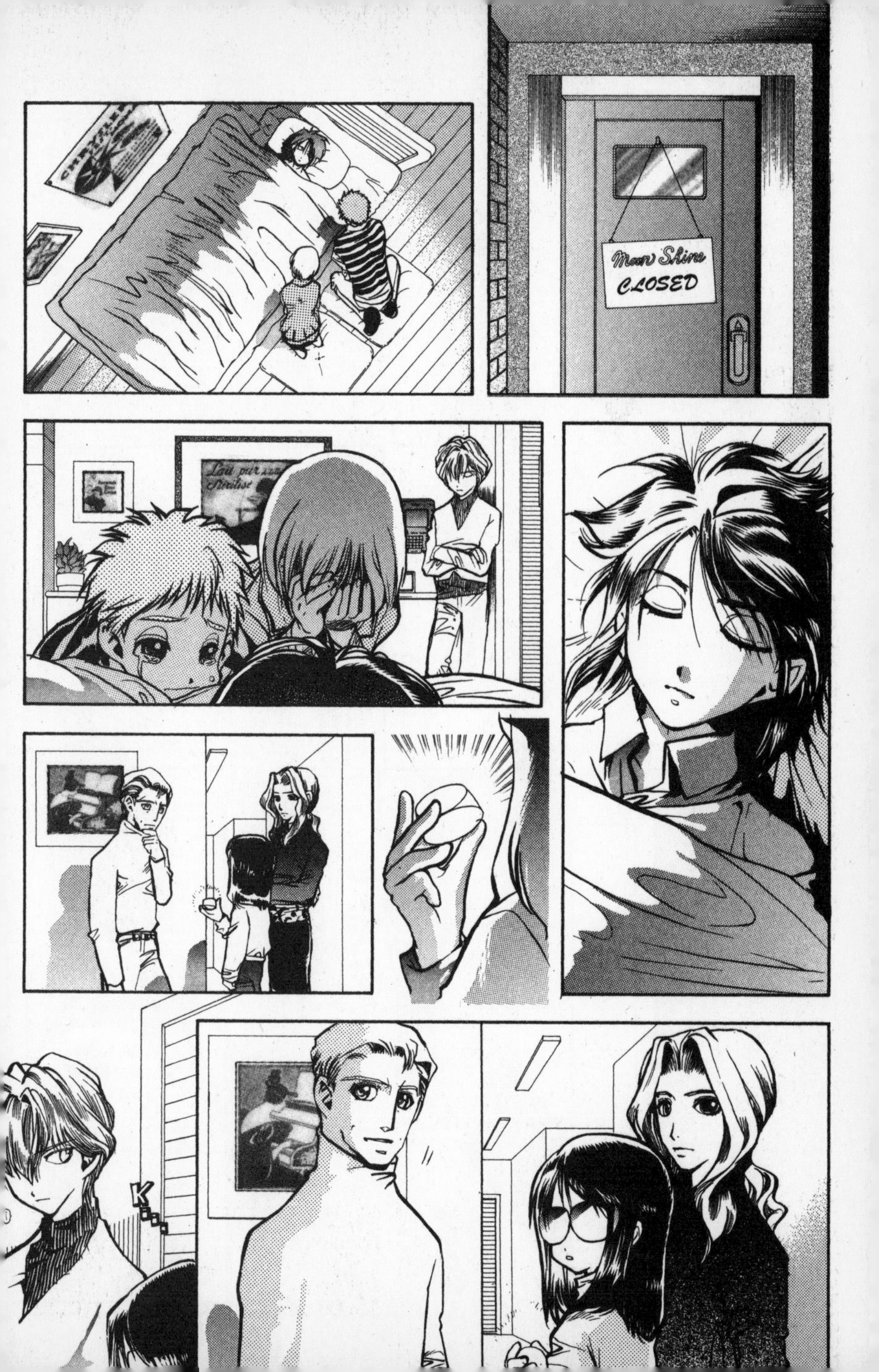
Moon Shine
CLOSED
K

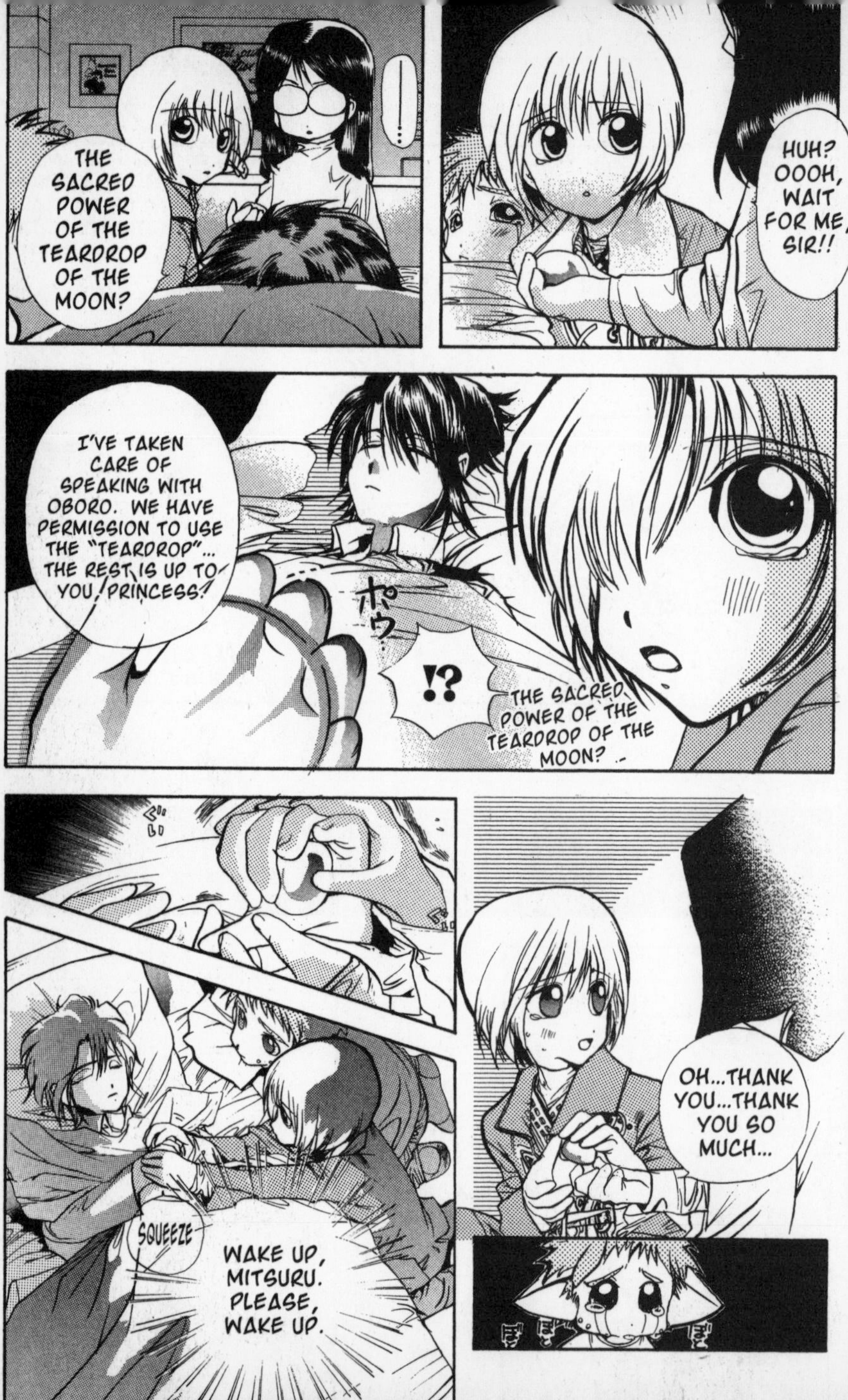
HUH? OOOH, WAIT FOR ME, SIR!!
!...
THE SACRED POWER OF THE TEARDROP OF THE MOON?
I'VE TAKEN CARE OF SPEAKING WITH OBORO. WE HAVE PERMISSION TO USE THE "TEARDROP"... THE REST IS UP TO YOU, PRINCESS!
ポウ
!?
THE SACRED POWER OF THE TEARDROP OF THE MOON?
OH...THANK YOU...THANK YOU SO MUCH...
SQUEEZE
WAKE UP, MITSURU. PLEASE, WAKE UP.

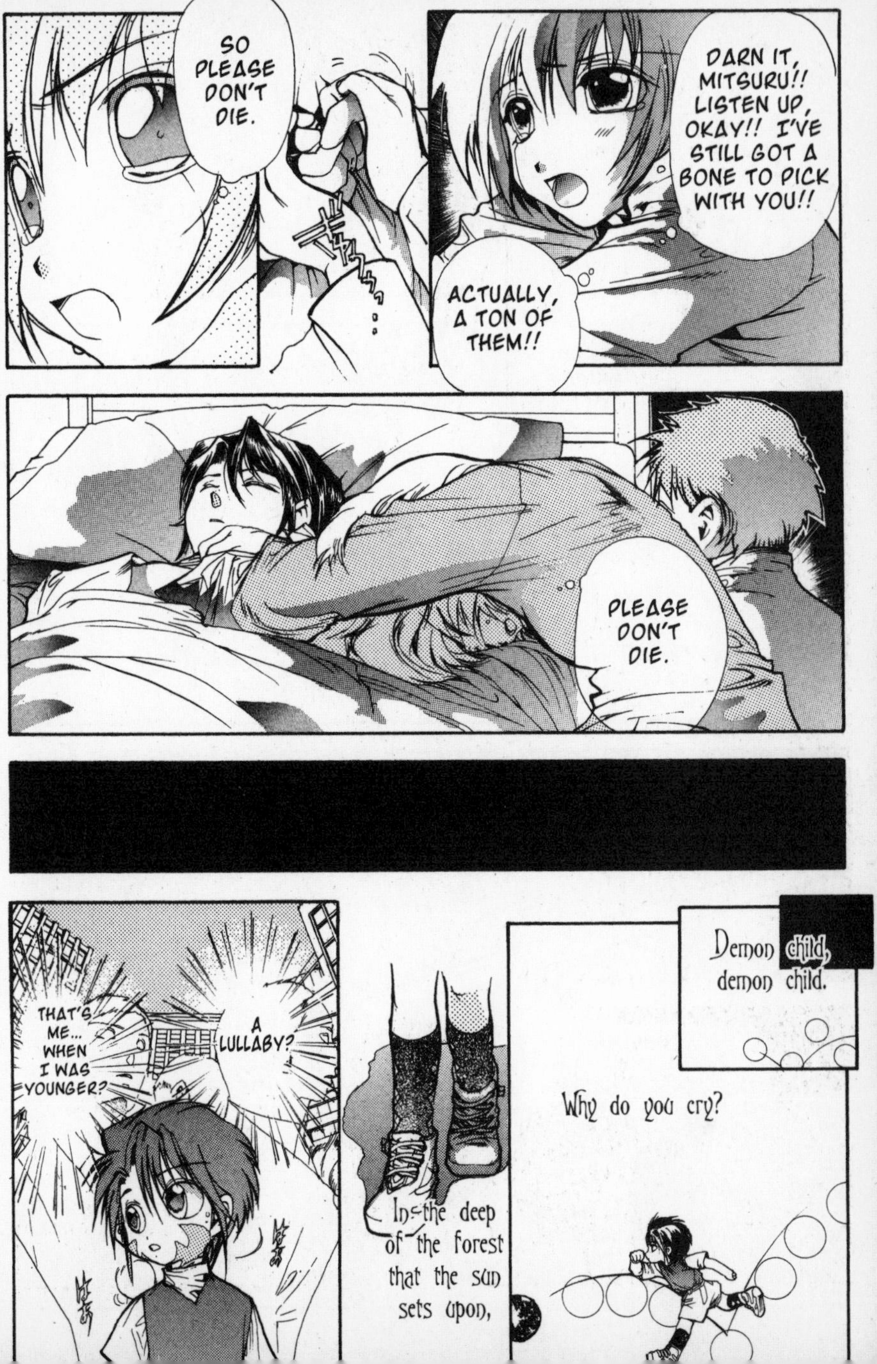
DARN IT, MITSURU!! LISTEN UP, OKAY!! I'VE STILL GOT A BONE TO PICK WITH YOU!!
ACTUALLY, A TON OF THEM!!
SO PLEASE DON'T DIE.
PLEASE DON'T DIE.
Demon child, demon child.
Why do you cry?
In the deep of the forest that the sun sets upon,
A LULLABY?
THAT'S ME... WHEN I WAS YOUNGER?

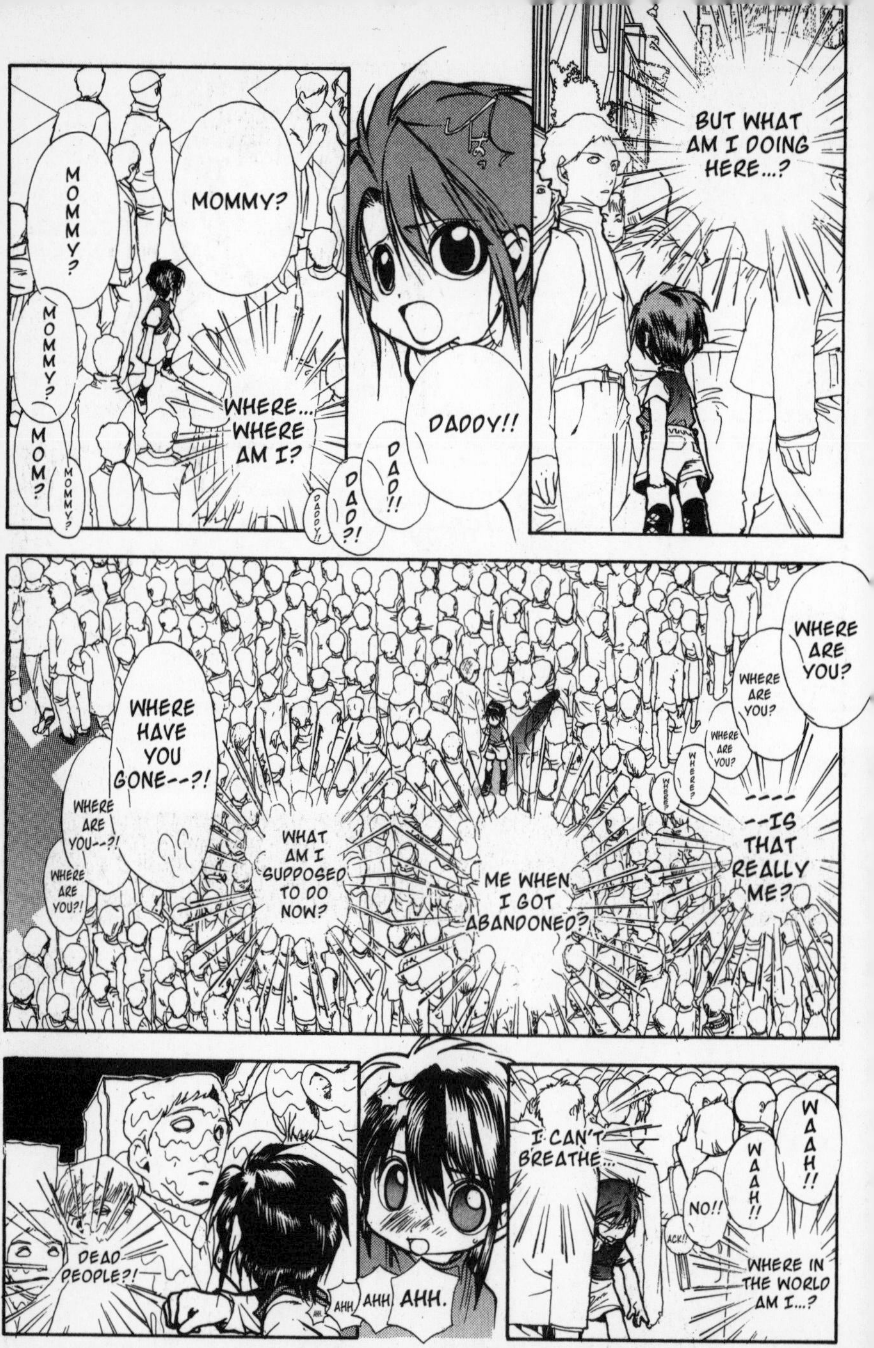
BUT WHAT AM I DOING HERE...?
DADDY!!
DAD!!
DAD?!
DADDY!!
MOMMY?
MOMMY?
MOMMY?!
WHERE... WHERE AM I?
MOM?
MOMMY?
WHERE ARE YOU?
WHERE ARE YOU?
WHERE ARE YOU?
WHERE?
WHERE?

--IS THAT REALLY ME?
ME WHEN I GOT ABANDONED?
WHAT AM I SUPPOSED TO DO NOW?
WHERE HAVE YOU GONE--?!
WHERE ARE YOU--?!
WHERE ARE YOU?!
WAAH!!
WAAH!!
NO!!
ACK!!
I CAN'T BREATHE...
WHERE IN THE WORLD AM I...?
AHH.
AHH
AHH
AHH
DEAD PEOPLE?!

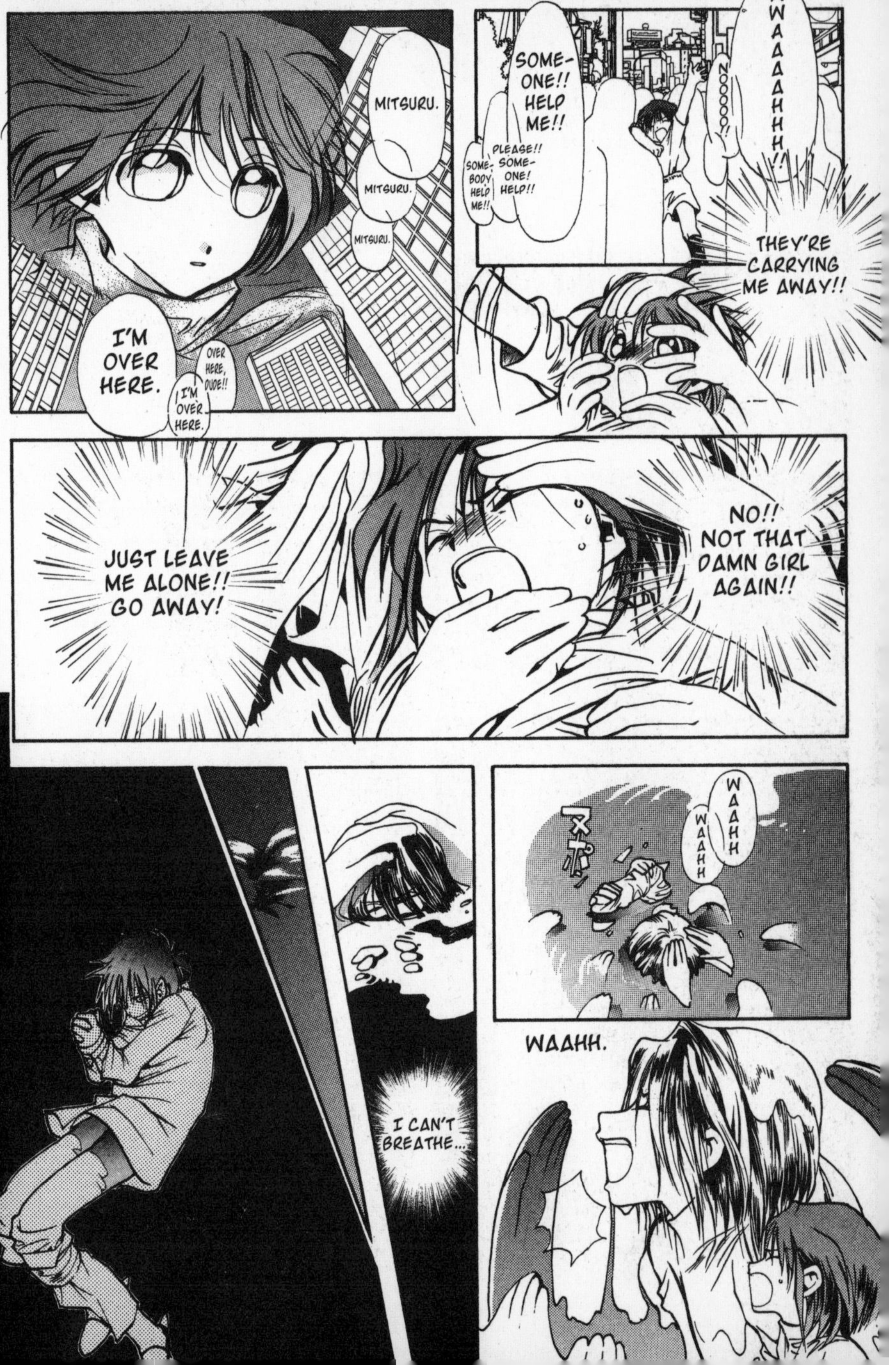
WWAAAAAHHH!!
NOOOOOO!!
SOME-ONE!! HELP ME!!
PLEASE!! SOME-ONE! HELP!!
SOME-BODY HELP ME!!
THEY'RE CARRYING ME AWAY!!
MITSURU.
MITSURU.
MITSURU.
I'M OVER HERE.
OVER HERE, DUDE!!
I'M OVER HERE.
NO!! NOT THAT DAMN GIRL AGAIN!!
JUST LEAVE ME ALONE!! GO AWAY!
WAAHH
WAAHH
WAAHH.
I CAN'T BREATHE...

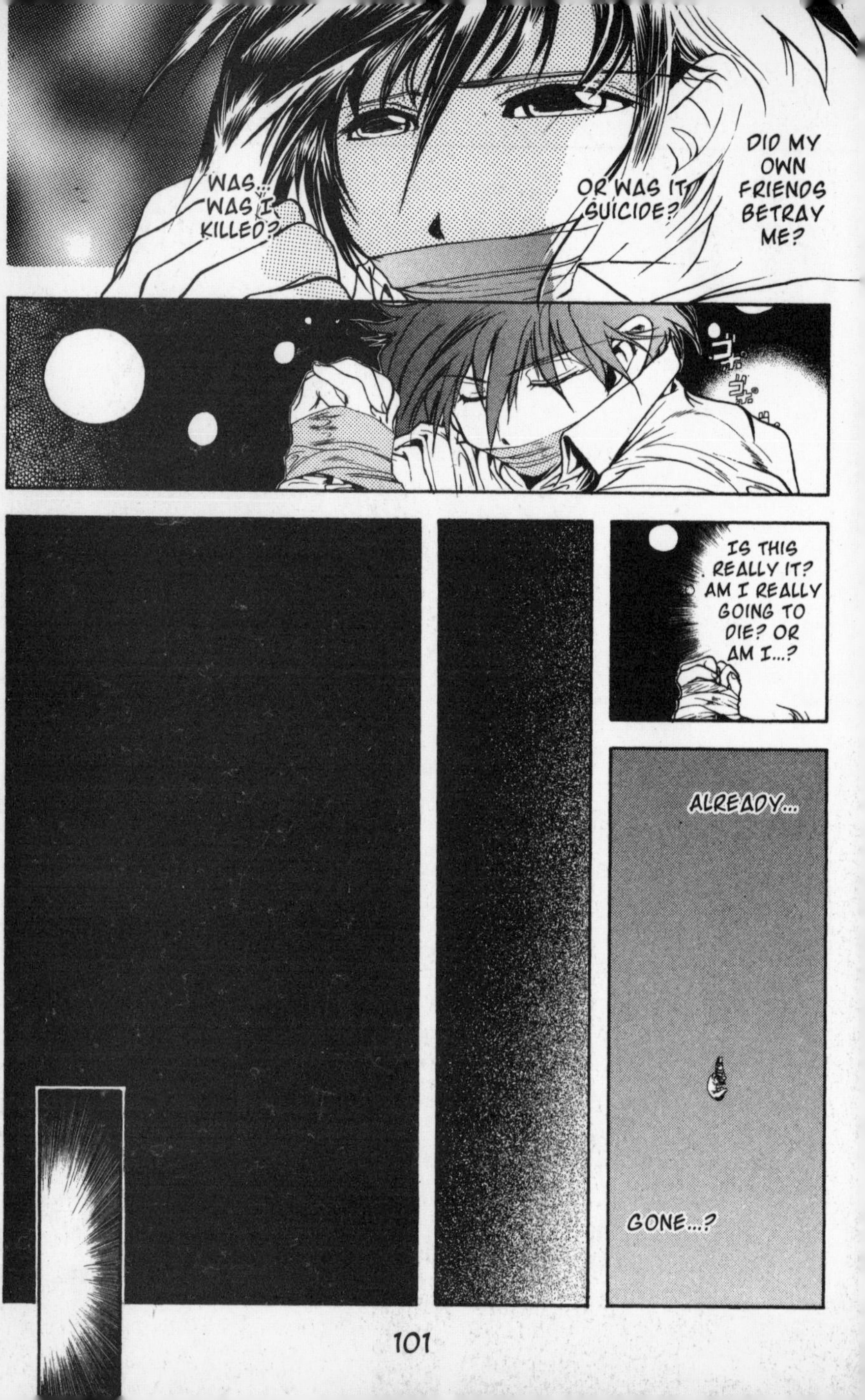
DID MY OWN FRIENDS BETRAY ME?
OR WAS IT SUICIDE?
WAS... WAS I KILLED?
IS THIS REALLY IT? AM I REALLY GOING TO DIE? OR AM I...?
ALREADY...
GONE...?

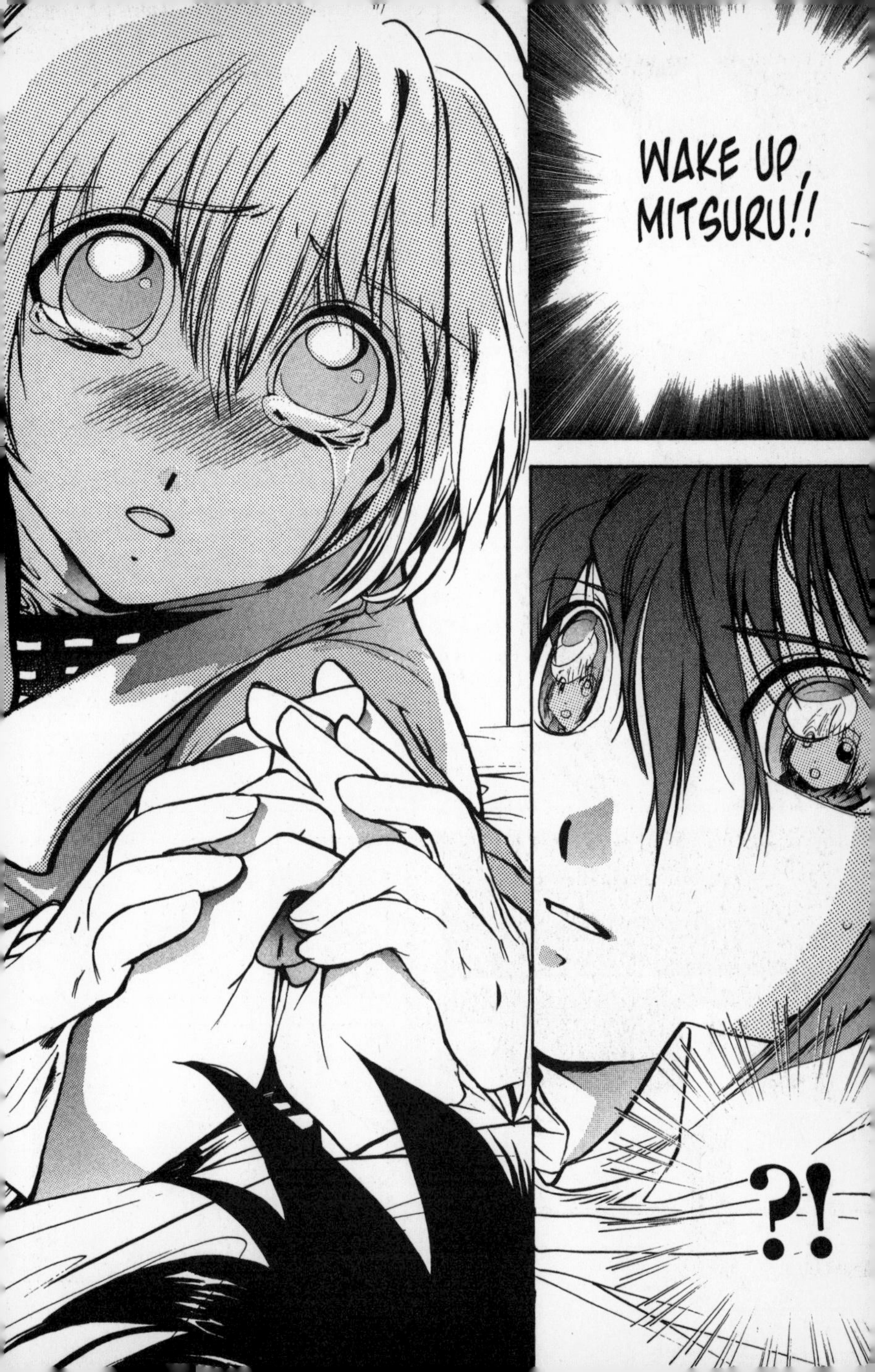
WAKE UP, MITSURU!!
?!

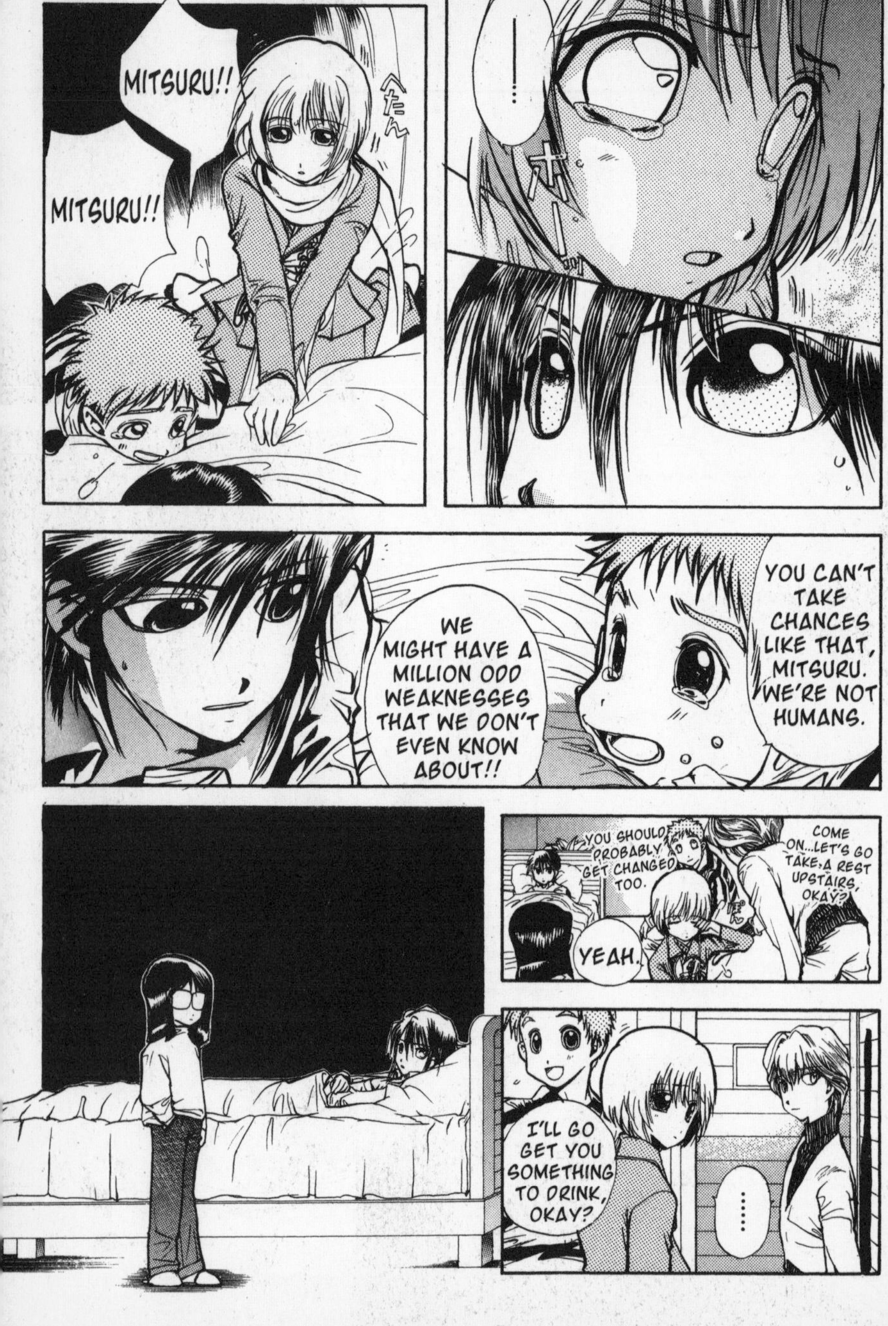
……!
MITSURU!!
MITSURU!!
へたん
YOU CAN'T TAKE CHANCES LIKE THAT, MITSURU. WE'RE NOT HUMANS.
WE MIGHT HAVE A MILLION ODD WEAKNESSES THAT WE DON'T EVEN KNOW ABOUT!!
COME ON...LET'S GO TAKE A REST UPSTAIRS, OKAY?
YOU SHOULD PROBABLY GET CHANGED TOO.
YEAH.
I'LL GO GET YOU SOMETHING TO DRINK, OKAY?
……

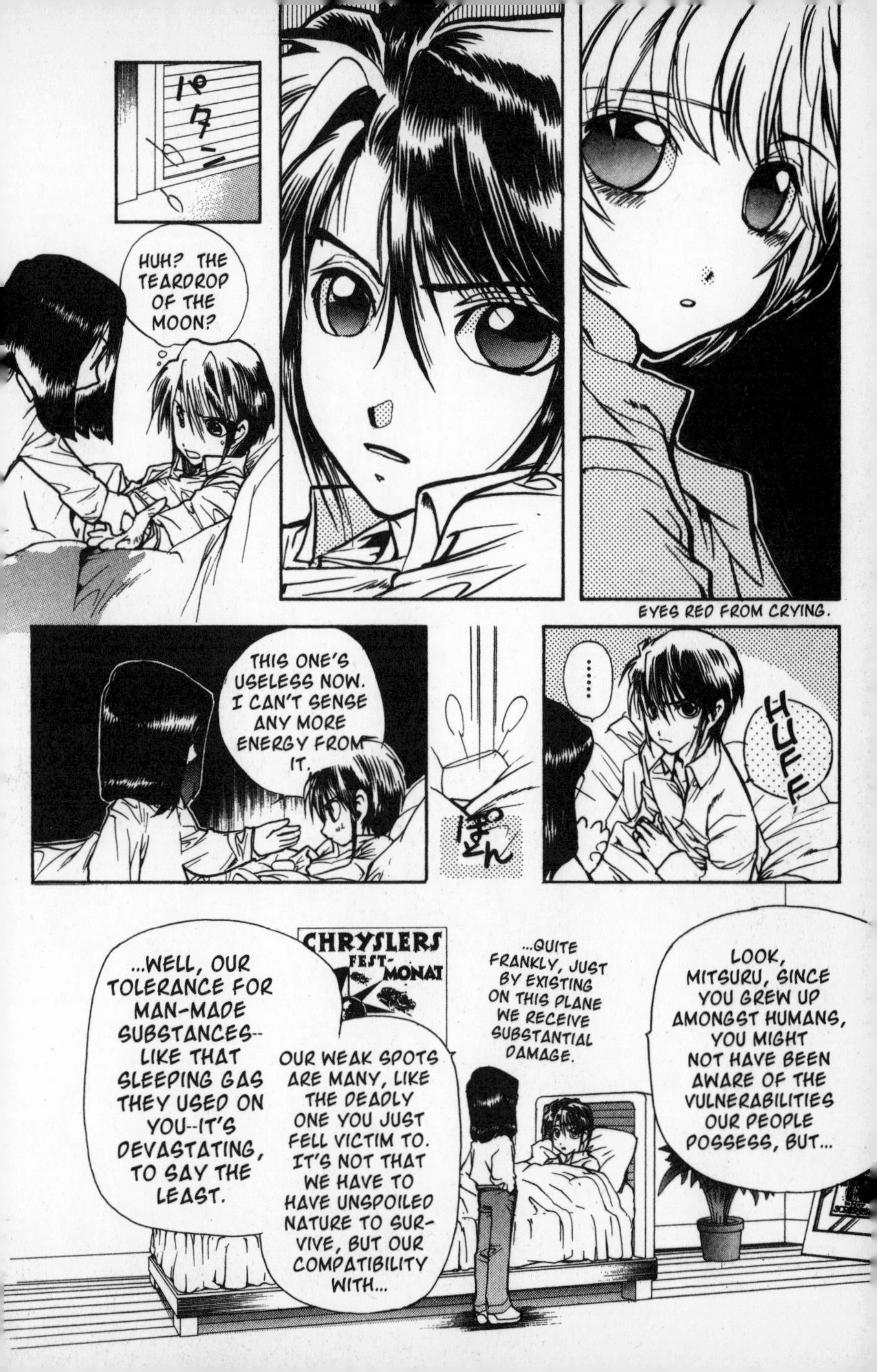
EYES RED FROM CRYING.
パタ—
HUH? THE TEARDROP OF THE MOON?
......
HUFF
ぽとん
THIS ONE'S USELESS NOW. I CAN'T SENSE ANY MORE ENERGY FROM IT.
LOOK, MITSURU, SINCE YOU GREW UP AMONGST HUMANS, YOU MIGHT NOT HAVE BEEN AWARE OF THE VULNERABILITIES OUR PEOPLE POSSESS, BUT...
...QUITE FRANKLY, JUST BY EXISTING ON THIS PLANE WE RECEIVE SUBSTANTIAL DAMAGE.
CHRYSLERS FEST-MONAT
OUR WEAK SPOTS ARE MANY, LIKE THE DEADLY ONE YOU JUST FELL VICTIM TO. IT'S NOT THAT WE HAVE TO HAVE UNSPOILED NATURE TO SURVIVE, BUT OUR COMPATIBILITY WITH...
...WELL, OUR TOLERANCE FOR MAN-MADE SUBSTANCES--LIKE THAT SLEEPING GAS THEY USED ON YOU--IT'S DEVASTATING, TO SAY THE LEAST.

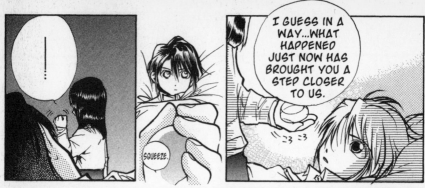

I GUESS IN A WAY...WHAT HAPPENED JUST NOW HAS BROUGHT YOU A STEP CLOSER TO US.
SQUEEZE.
KOTON
THIS WAS THE PRINCESS' CHOICE...HER SOLUTION.
DON'T WASTE HER HELP.

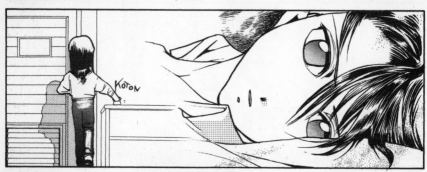

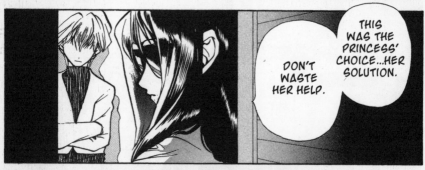

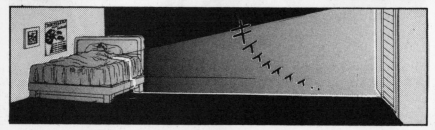

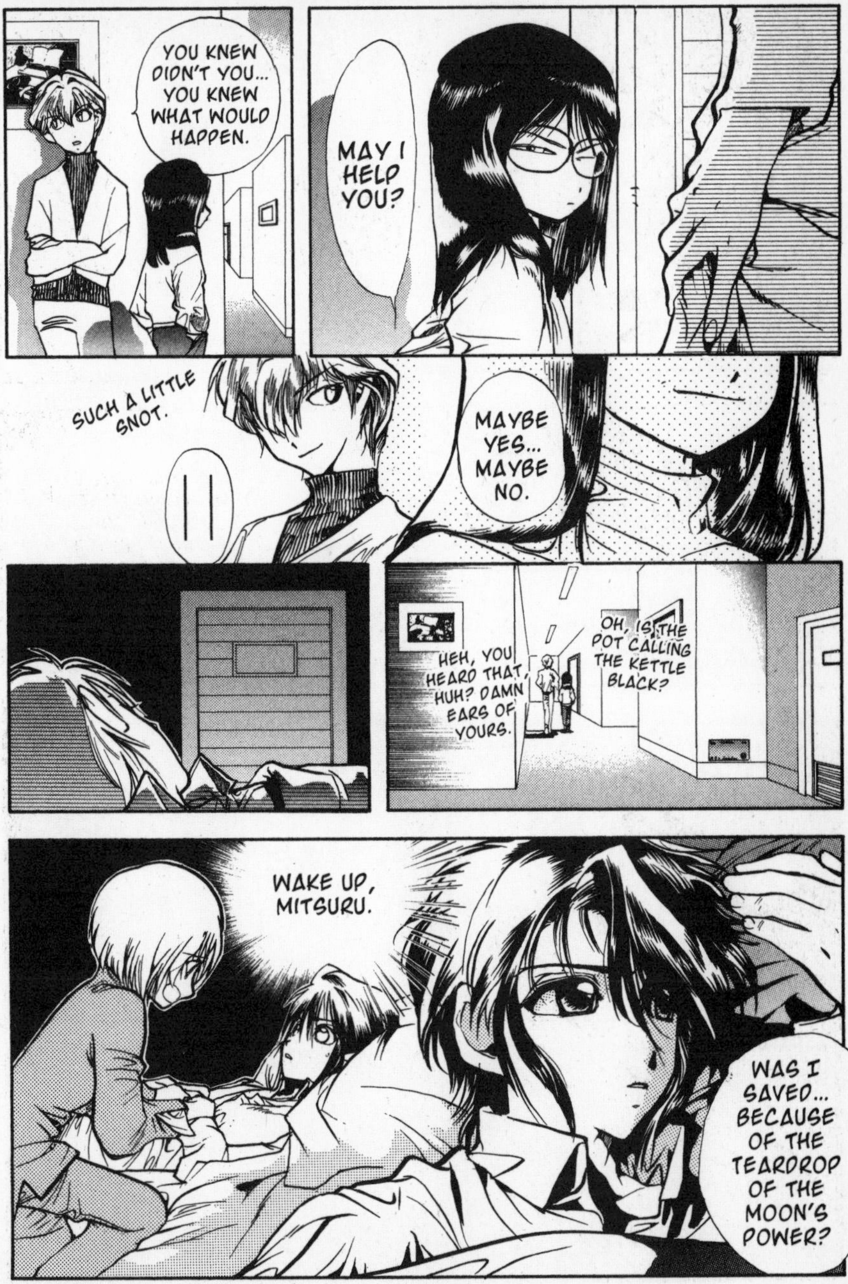
MAY I HELP YOU?
YOU KNEW DIDN'T YOU... YOU KNEW WHAT WOULD HAPPEN.
MAYBE YES... MAYBE NO.
SUCH A LITTLE SNOT.
OH, IS THE POT CALLING THE KETTLE BLACK?
HEH, YOU HEARD THAT, HUH? DAMN EARS OF YOURS.
WAKE UP, MITSURU.
WAS I SAVED... BECAUSE OF THE TEARDROP OF THE MOON'S POWER?

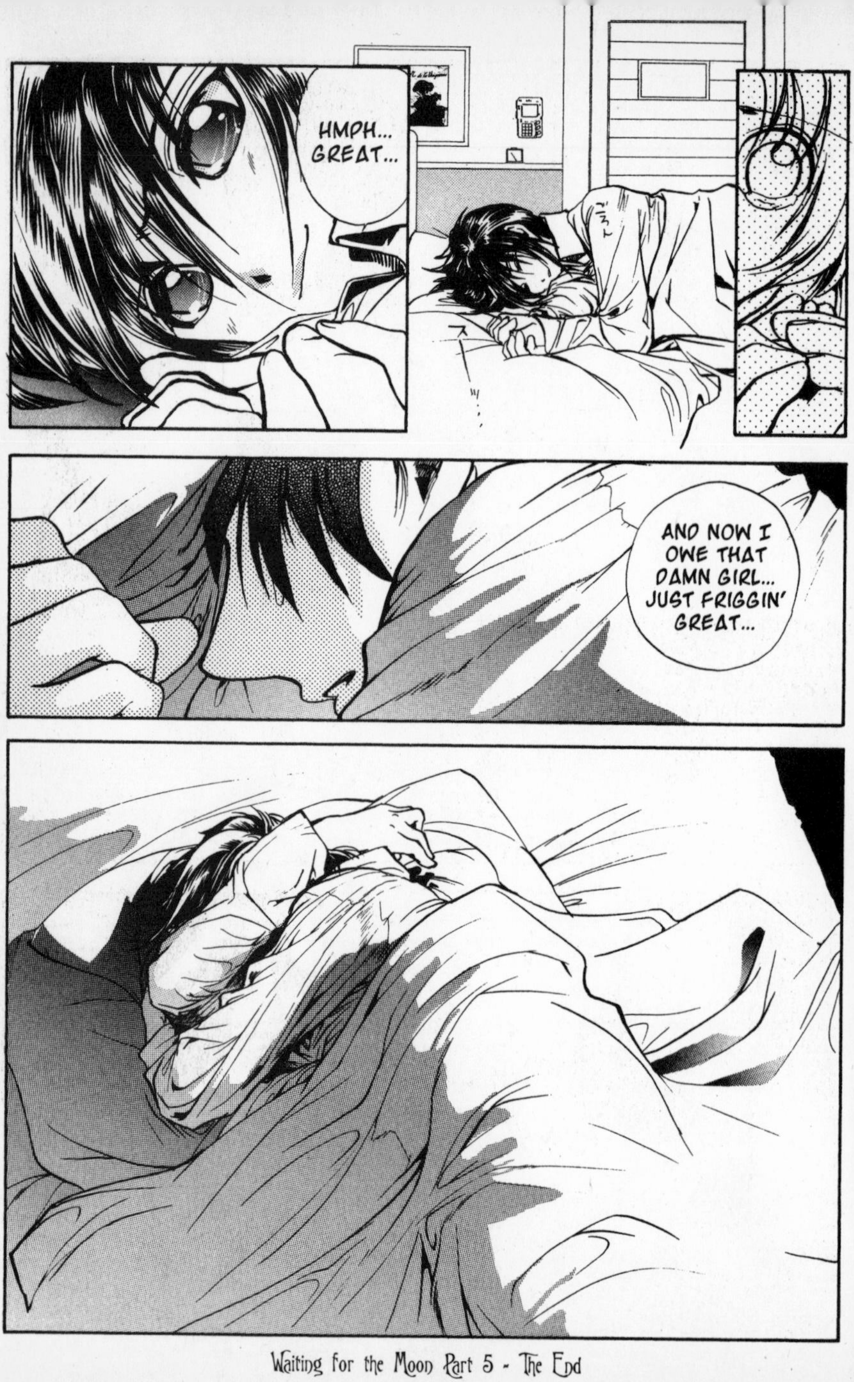
HMPH... GREAT...
AND NOW I OWE THAT DAMN GIRL... JUST FRIGGIN' GREAT...

Waiting for the Moon Part 5 - The End

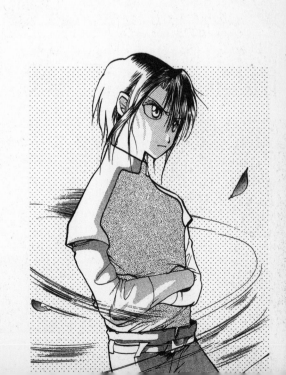

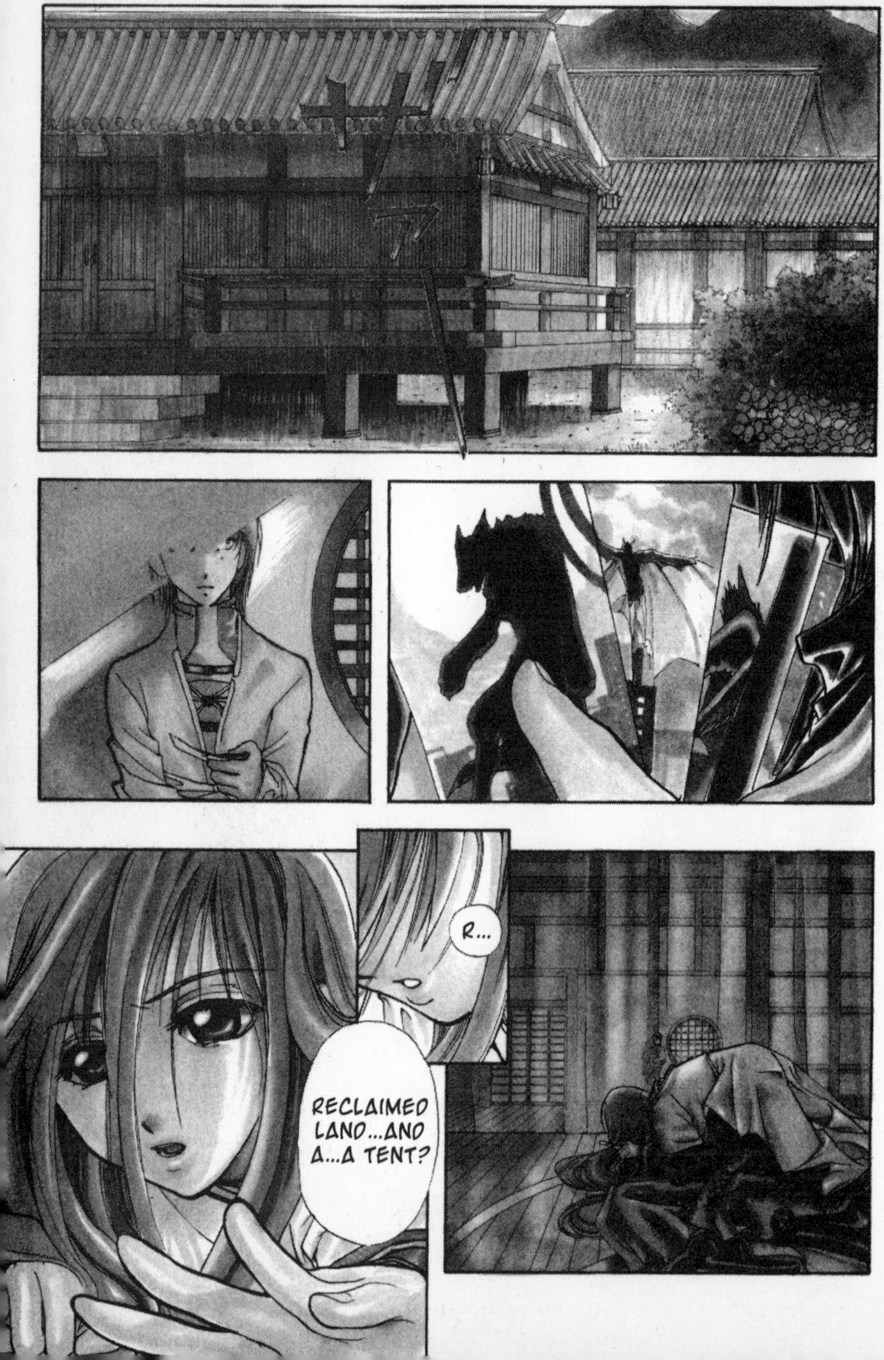
R...
RECLAIMED LAND...AND A...A TENT?

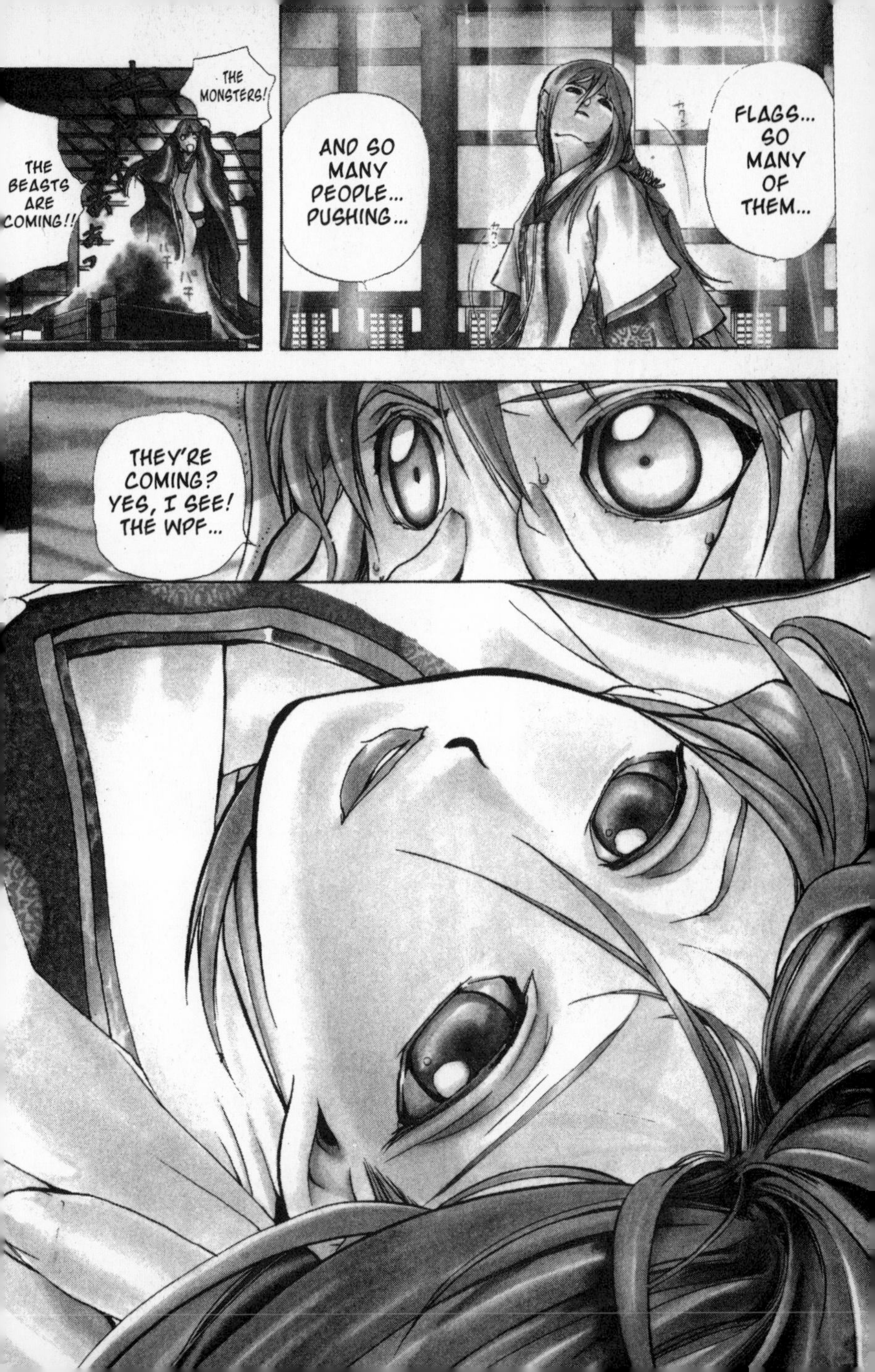
FLAGS... SO MANY OF THEM...
AND SO MANY PEOPLE... PUSHING...
THE MONSTERS!
THE BEASTS ARE COMING!!
THEY'RE COMING? YES, I SEE! THE WPF...

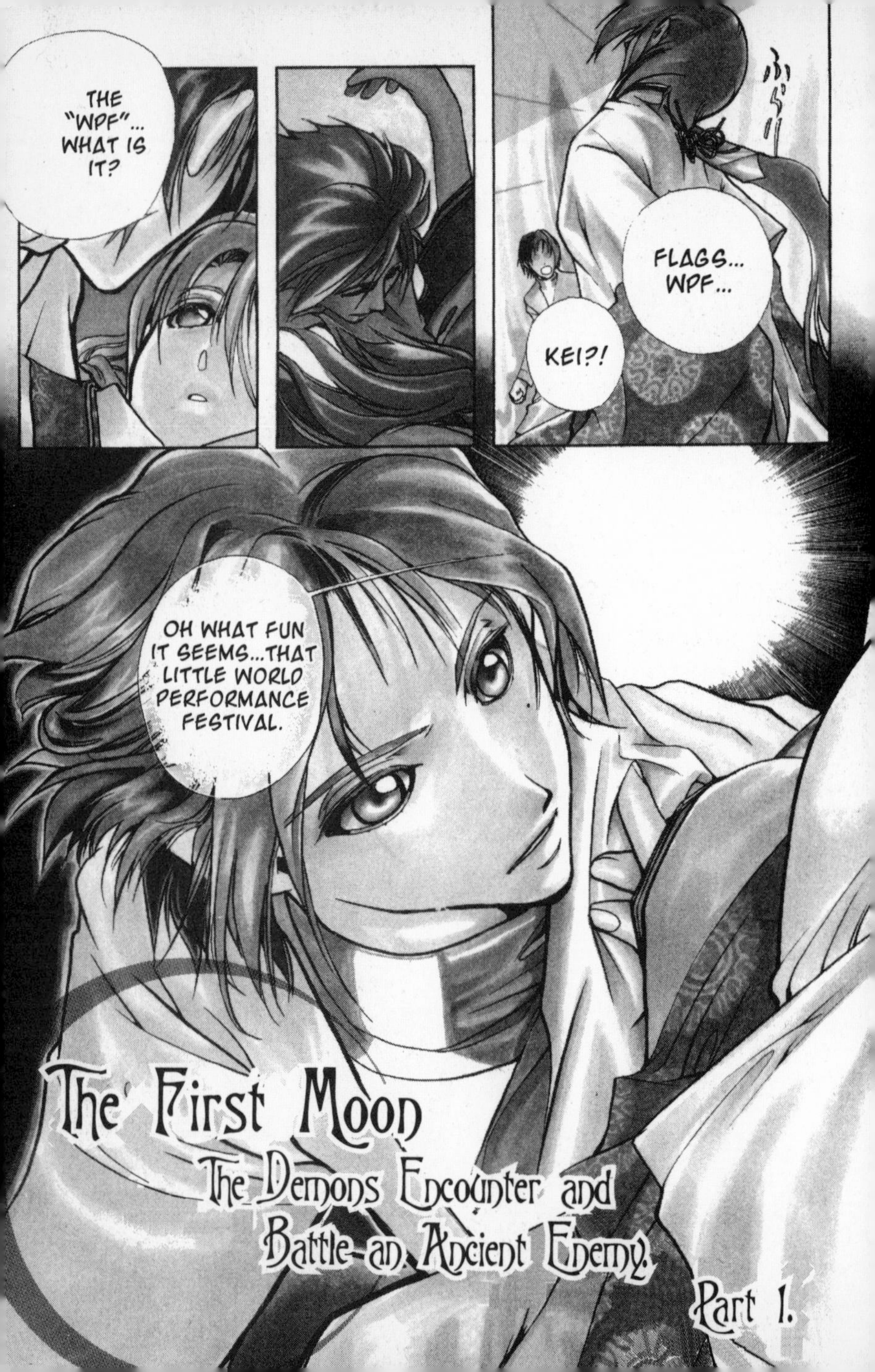
FLAGS... WPF...
KEI?!
THE "WPF"... WHAT IS IT?
OH WHAT FUN IT SEEMS...THAT LITTLE WORLD PERFORMANCE FESTIVAL.
The First Moon
The Demons Encounter and Battle an Ancient Enemy.
Part 1.

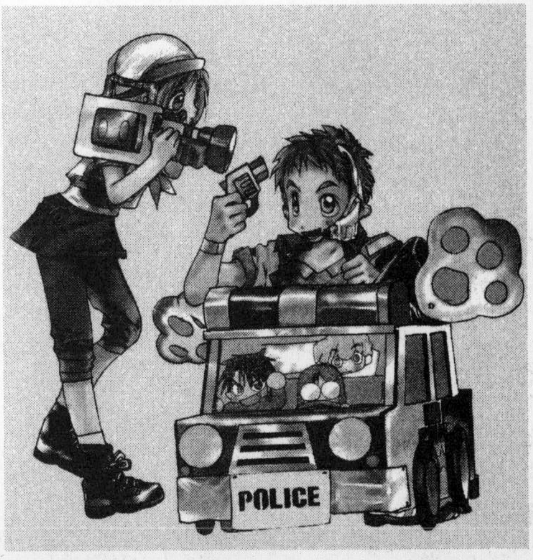
POLICE

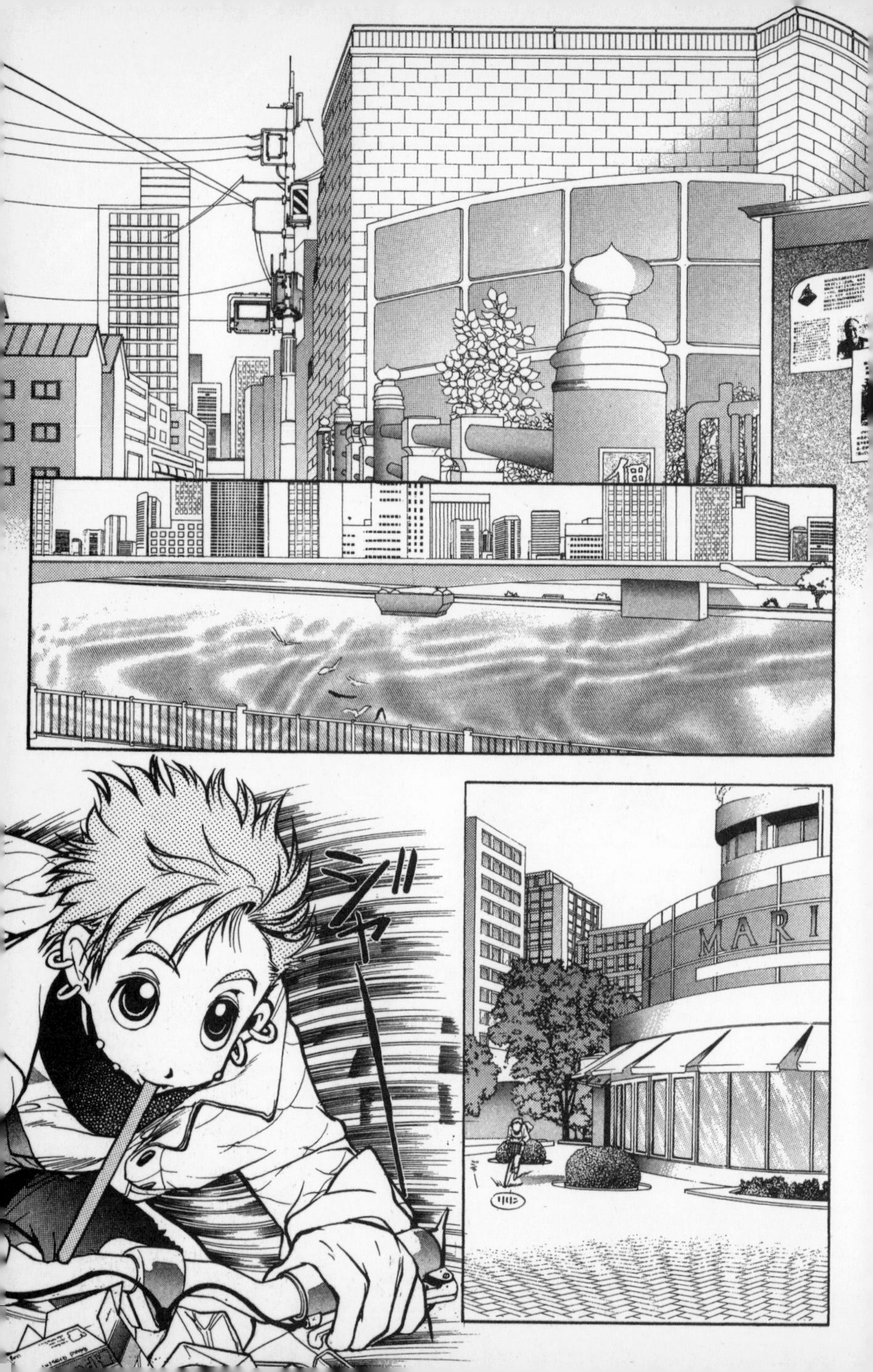
佃
ジャー
MARI

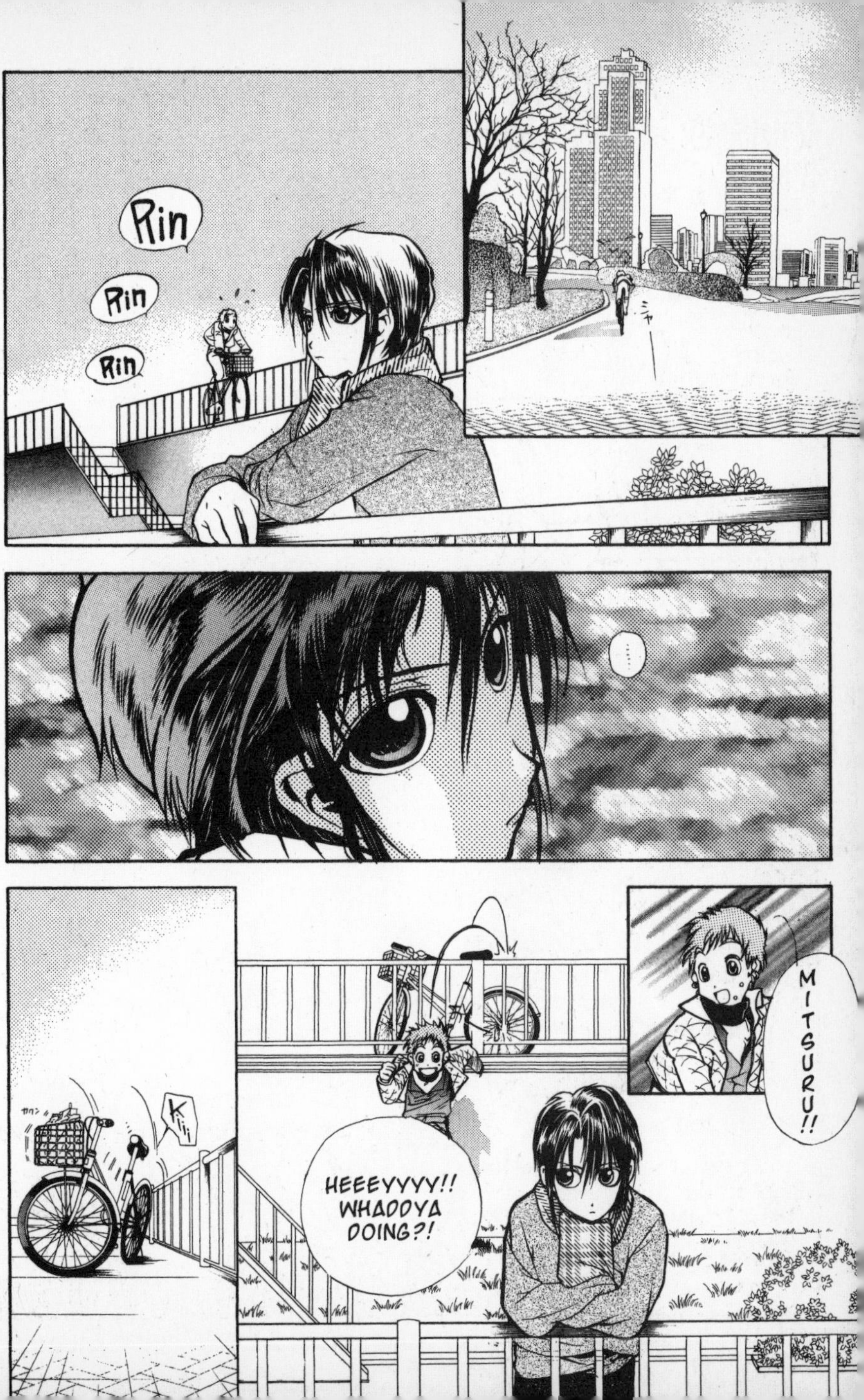
Rin
Rin
Rin
......
MITSURU!!
HEEEYYYY!! WHADDYA DOING?!
Kiii

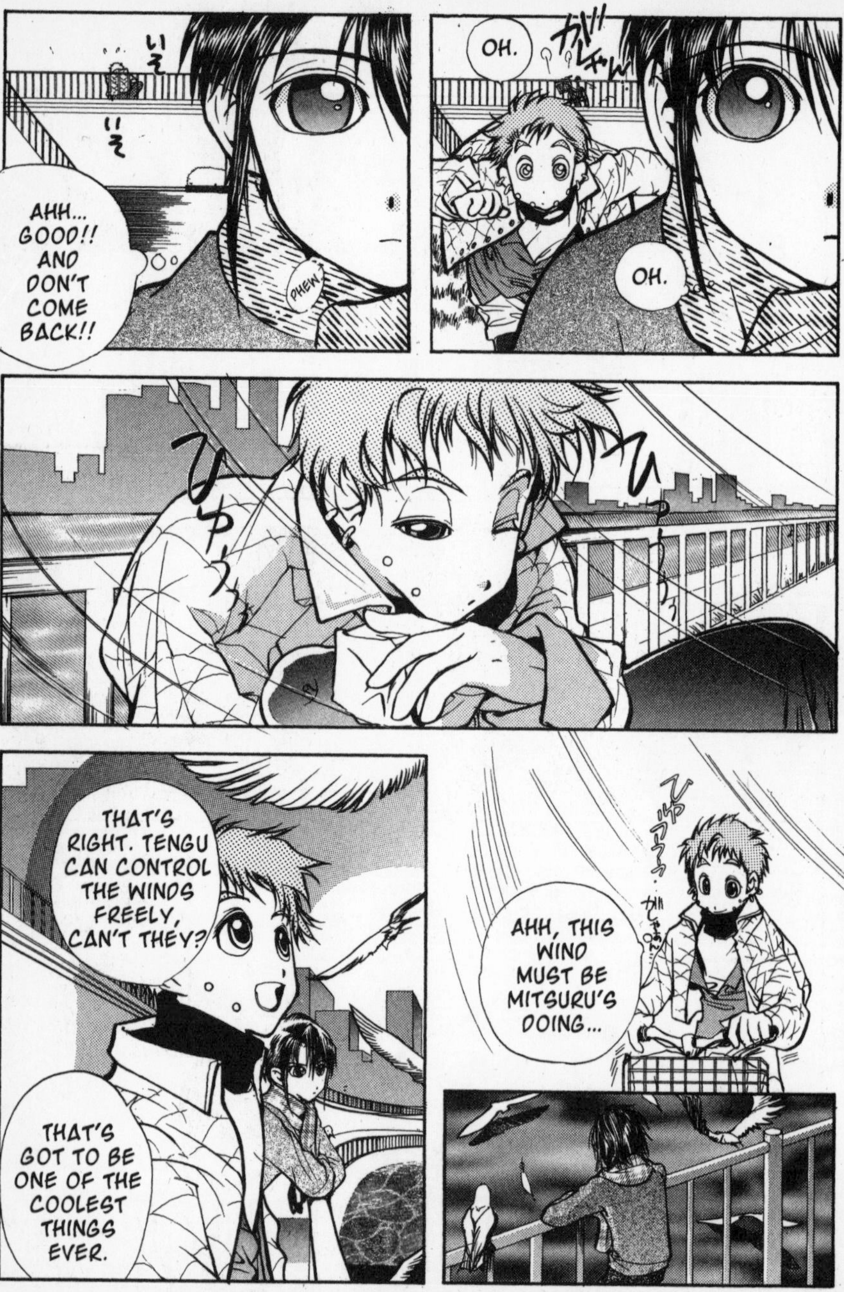
OH.
OH.
いそいそ
AHH... GOOD!! AND DON'T COME BACK!!
PHEW
AHH, THIS WIND MUST BE MITSURU'S DOING...
THAT'S RIGHT. TENGU CAN CONTROL THE WINDS FREELY, CAN'T THEY?
THAT'S GOT TO BE ONE OF THE COOLEST THINGS EVER.

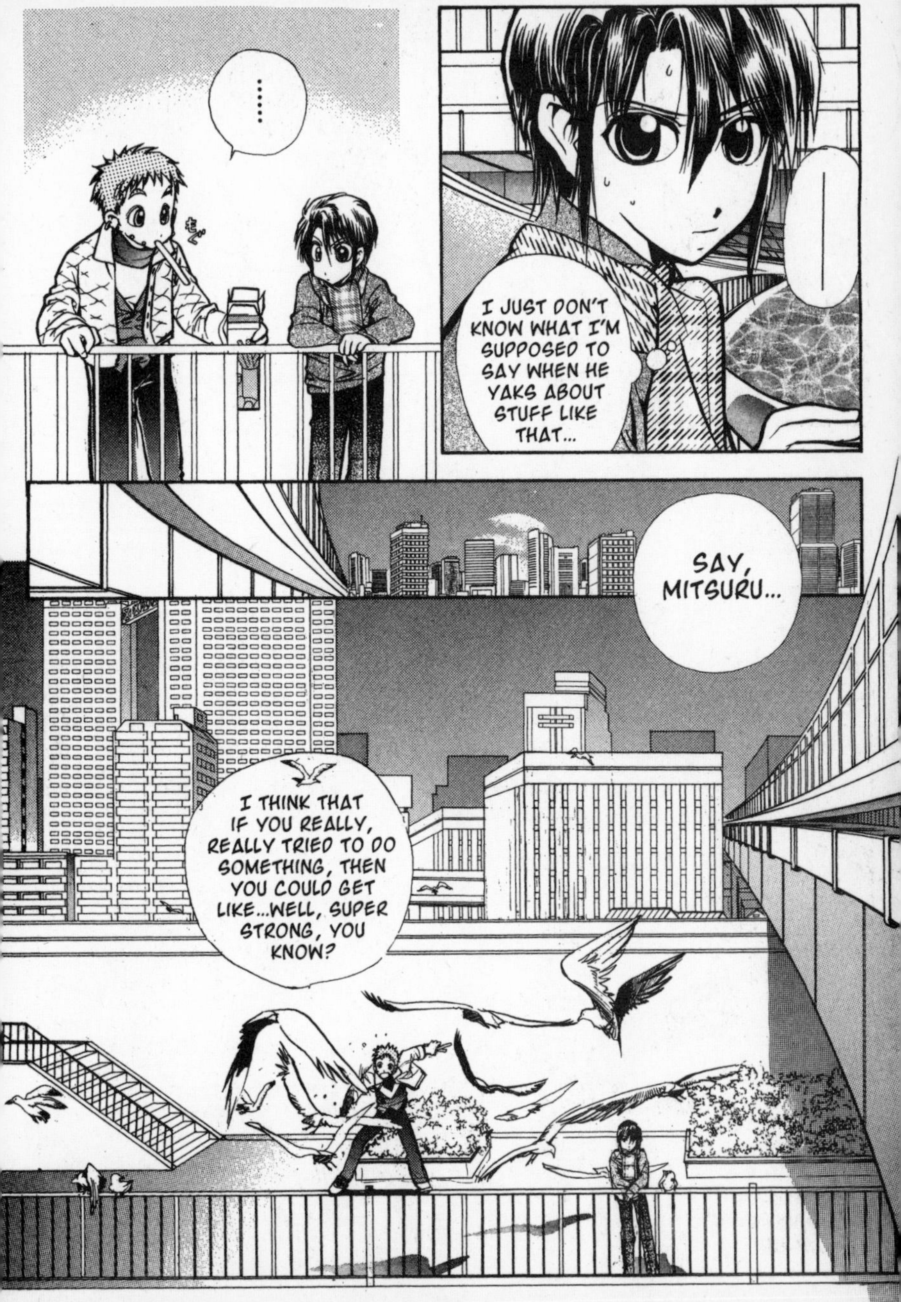
I JUST DON'T KNOW WHAT I'M SUPPOSED TO SAY WHEN HE YAKS ABOUT STUFF LIKE THAT...
......
SAY, MITSURU...
I THINK THAT IF YOU REALLY, REALLY TRIED TO DO SOMETHING, THEN YOU COULD GET LIKE...WELL, SUPER STRONG, YOU KNOW?

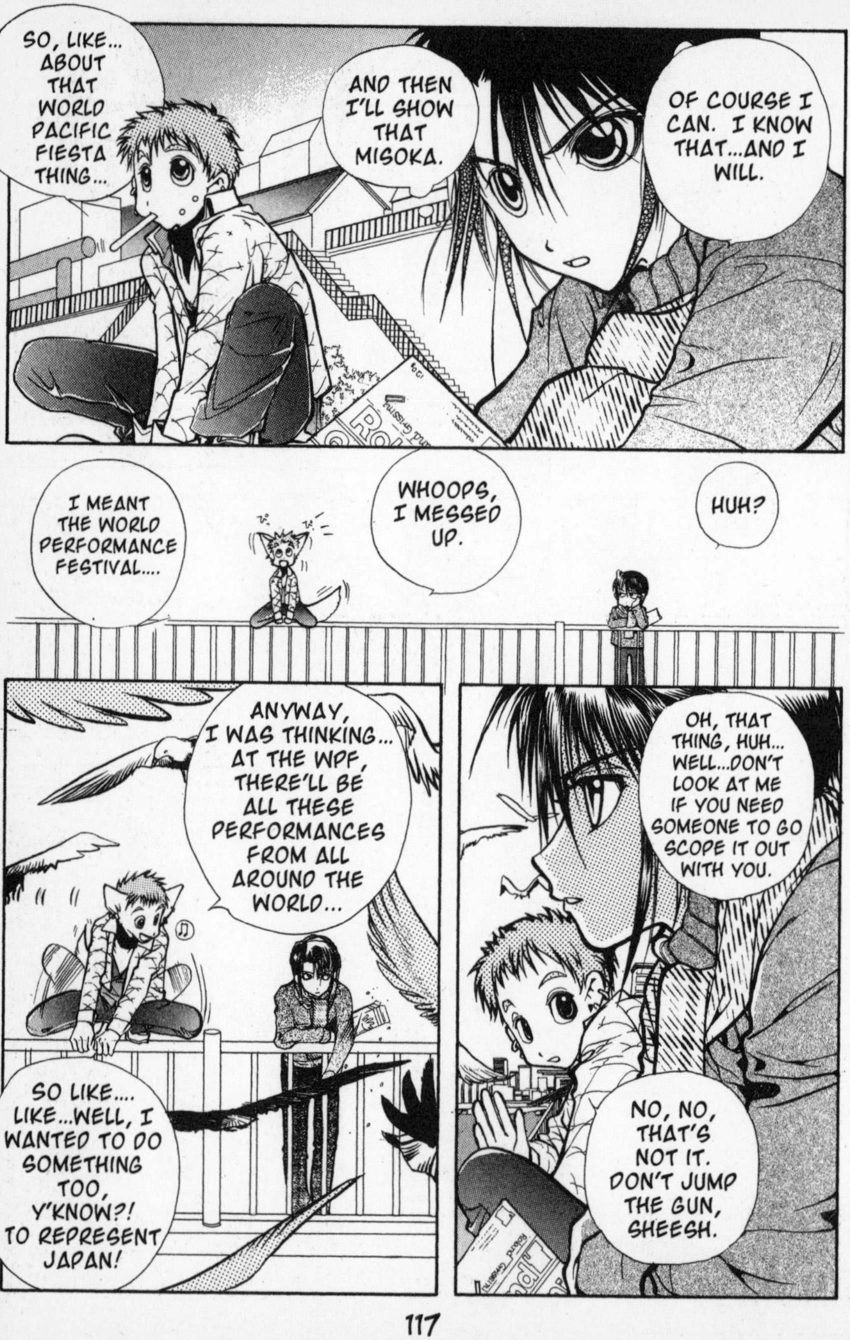
OF COURSE I CAN. I KNOW THAT...AND I WILL.
AND THEN I'LL SHOW THAT MISOKA.
SO, LIKE... ABOUT THAT WORLD PACIFIC FIESTA THING...
HUH?
WHOOPS, I MESSED UP.
I MEANT THE WORLD PERFORMANCE FESTIVAL....
OH, THAT THING, HUH... WELL...DON'T LOOK AT ME IF YOU NEED SOMEONE TO GO SCOPE IT OUT WITH YOU.
NO, NO, THAT'S NOT IT. DON'T JUMP THE GUN, SHEESH.
ANYWAY, I WAS THINKING... AT THE WPF, THERE'LL BE ALL THESE PERFORMANCES FROM ALL AROUND THE WORLD...
SO LIKE.... LIKE...WELL, I WANTED TO DO SOMETHING TOO, Y'KNOW?! TO REPRESENT JAPAN!

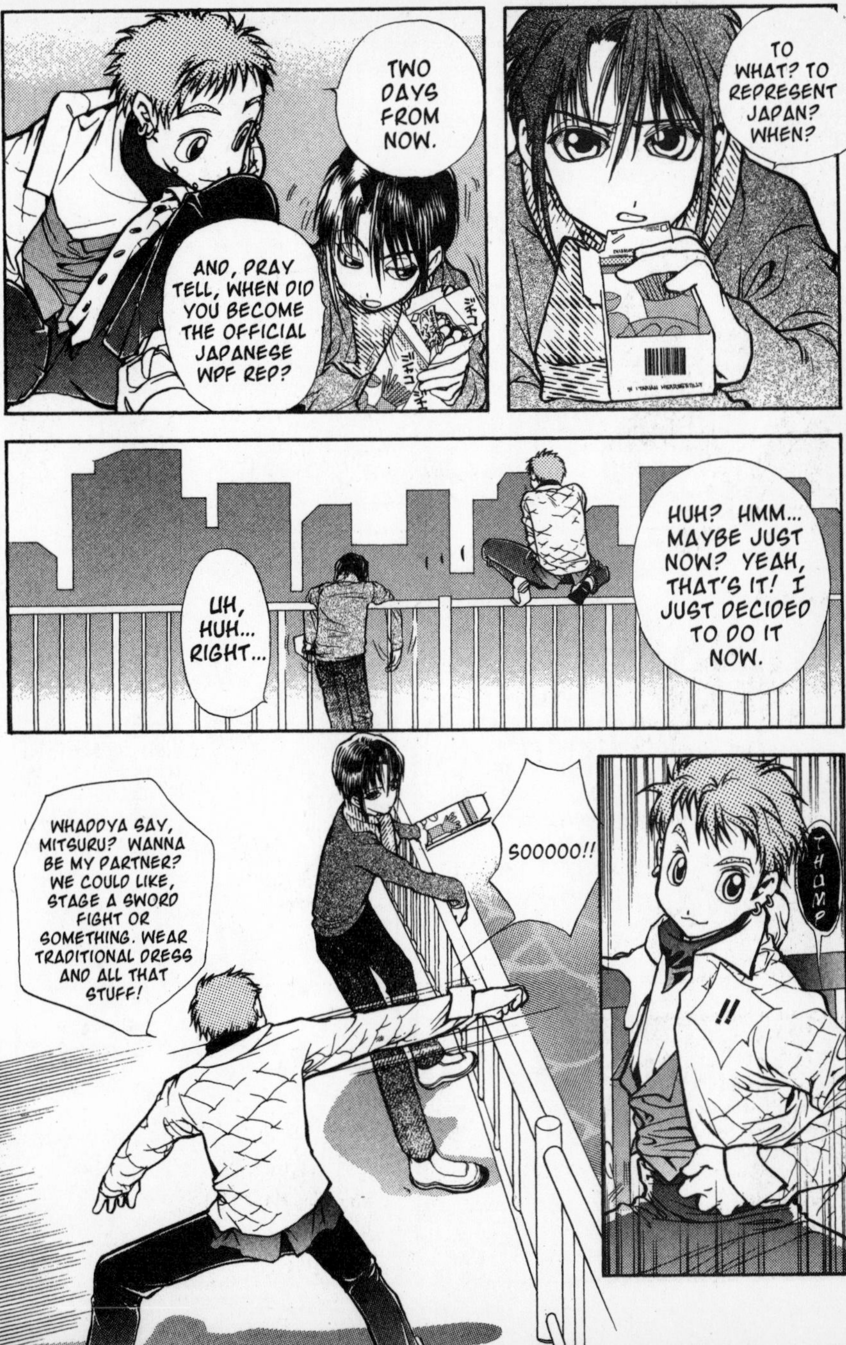
TO WHAT? TO REPRESENT JAPAN? WHEN?
TWO DAYS FROM NOW.
AND, PRAY TELL, WHEN DID YOU BECOME THE OFFICIAL JAPANESE WPF REP?
HUH? HMM... MAYBE JUST NOW? YEAH, THAT'S IT! I JUST DECIDED TO DO IT NOW.
UH, HUH... RIGHT...
THUMP
!!
SOOOOO!!
WHADDYA SAY, MITSURU? WANNA BE MY PARTNER? WE COULD LIKE, STAGE A SWORD FIGHT OR SOMETHING. WEAR TRADITIONAL DRESS AND ALL THAT STUFF!

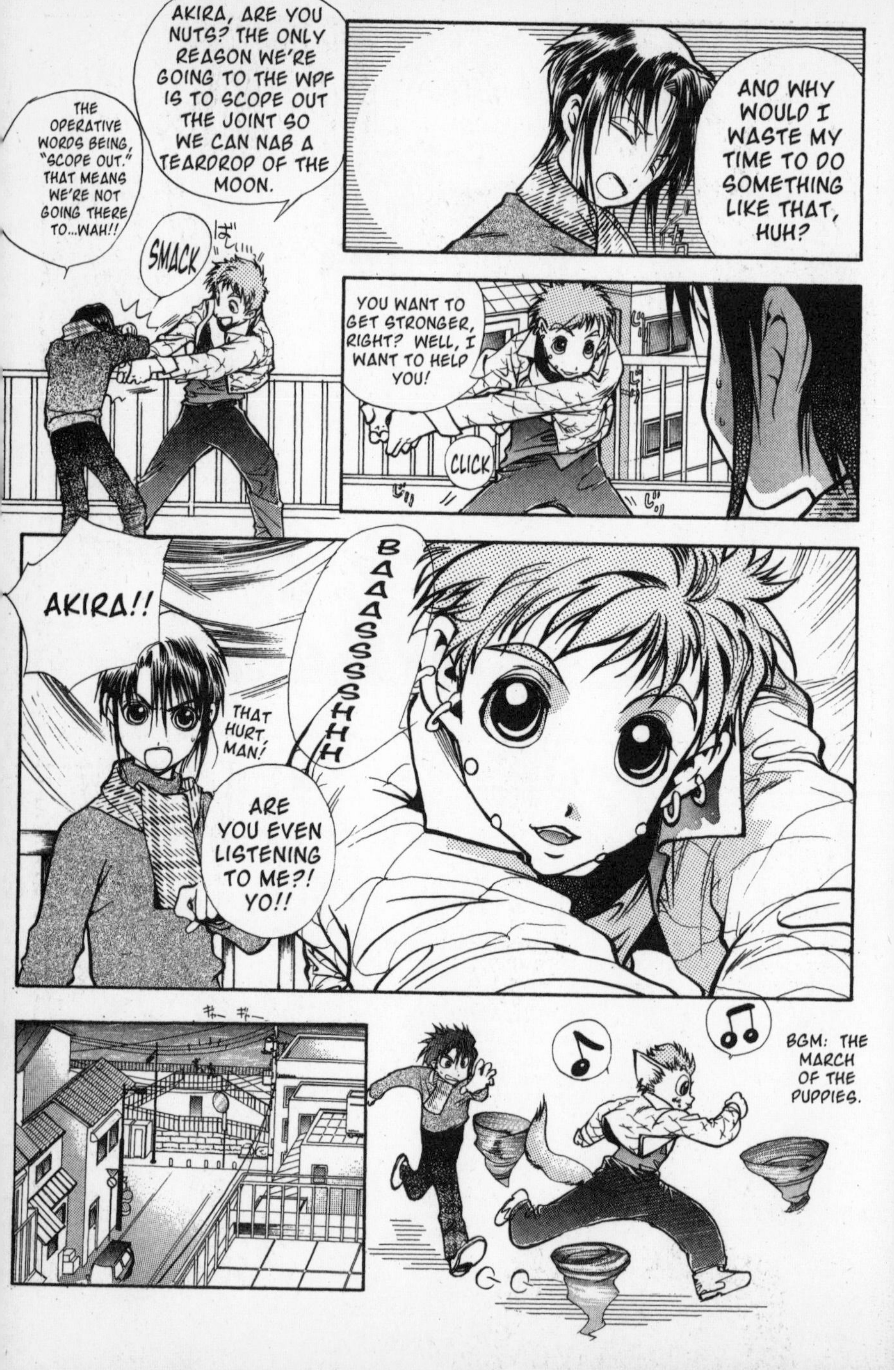
AND WHY WOULD I WASTE MY TIME TO DO SOMETHING LIKE THAT, HUH?
YOU WANT TO GET STRONGER, RIGHT? WELL, I WANT TO HELP YOU!
CLICK
AKIRA, ARE YOU NUTS? THE ONLY REASON WE'RE GOING TO THE WPF IS TO SCOPE OUT THE JOINT SO WE CAN NAB A TEARDROP OF THE MOON.
THE OPERATIVE WORDS BEING, "SCOPE OUT." THAT MEANS WE'RE NOT GOING THERE TO...WAH!!
SMACK
BAAAASSSSSHHH
AKIRA!!
THAT HURT, MAN!
ARE YOU EVEN LISTENING TO ME?! YO!!
BGM: THE MARCH OF THE PUPPIES.

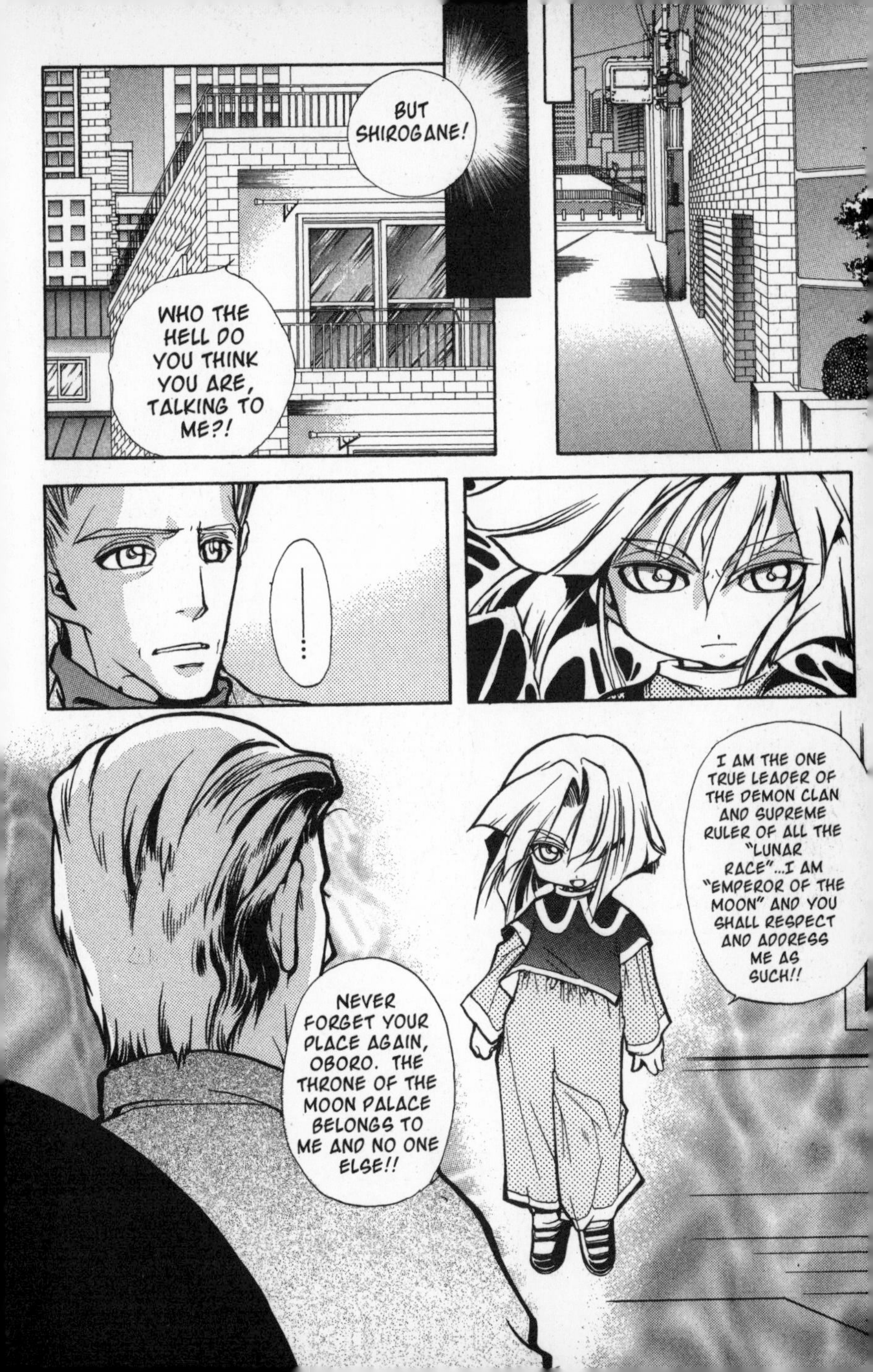
BUT SHIROGANE!
WHO THE HELL DO YOU THINK YOU ARE, TALKING TO ME?!
...!
I AM THE ONE TRUE LEADER OF THE DEMON CLAN AND SUPREME RULER OF ALL THE "LUNAR RACE"...I AM "EMPEROR OF THE MOON" AND YOU SHALL RESPECT AND ADDRESS ME AS SUCH!!
NEVER FORGET YOUR PLACE AGAIN, OBORO. THE THRONE OF THE MOON PALACE BELONGS TO ME AND NO ONE ELSE!!

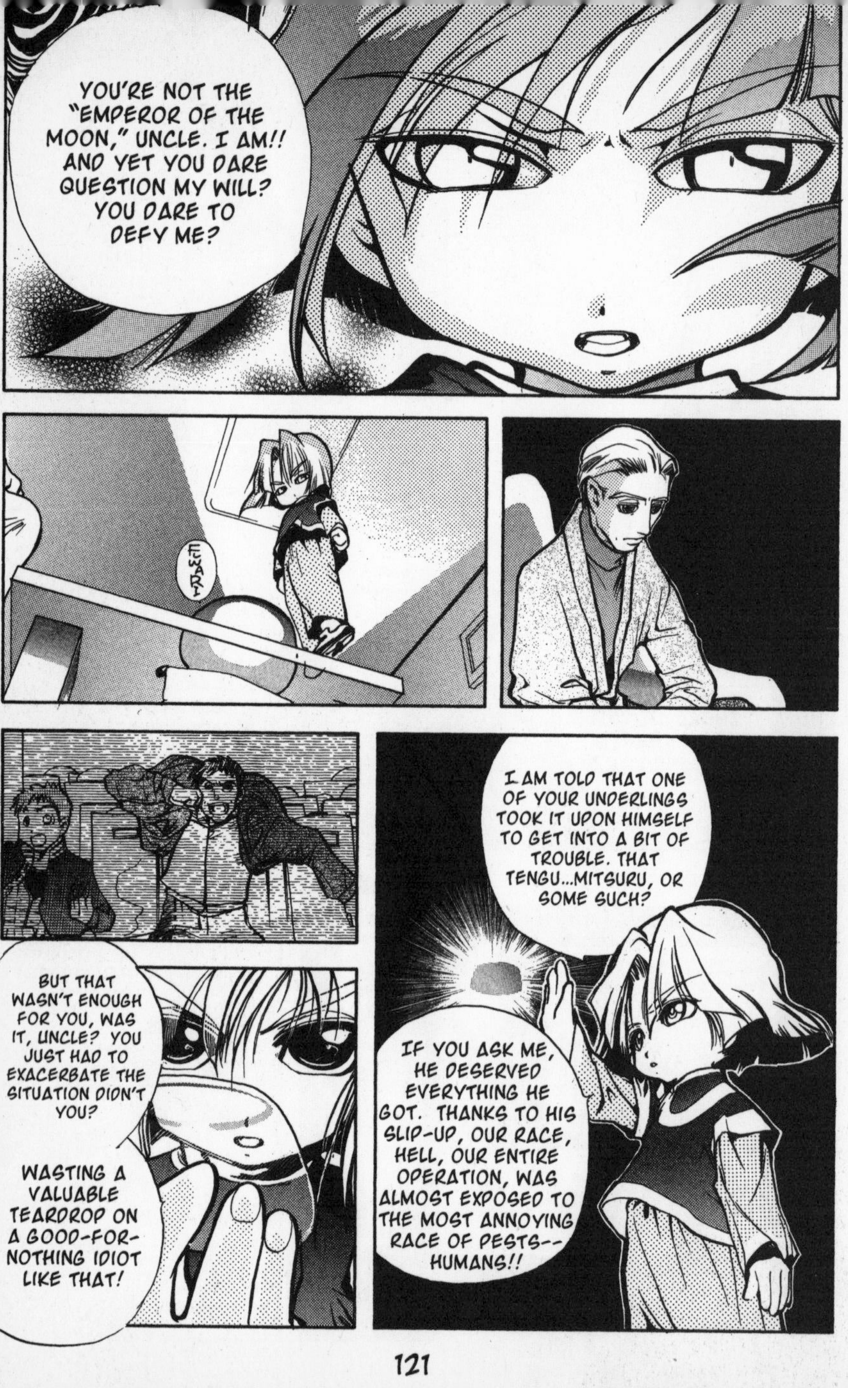
YOU'RE NOT THE "EMPEROR OF THE MOON," UNCLE. I AM!! AND YET YOU DARE QUESTION MY WILL? YOU DARE TO DEFY ME?
FUWARI
I AM TOLD THAT ONE OF YOUR UNDERLINGS TOOK IT UPON HIMSELF TO GET INTO A BIT OF TROUBLE. THAT TENGU...MITSURU, OR SOME SUCH?
IF YOU ASK ME, HE DESERVED EVERYTHING HE GOT. THANKS TO HIS SLIP-UP, OUR RACE, HELL, OUR ENTIRE OPERATION, WAS ALMOST EXPOSED TO THE MOST ANNOYING RACE OF PESTS--HUMANS!!
BUT THAT WASN'T ENOUGH FOR YOU, WAS IT, UNCLE? YOU JUST HAD TO EXACERBATE THE SITUATION DIDN'T YOU?
WASTING A VALUABLE TEARDROP ON A GOOD-FOR-NOTHING IDIOT LIKE THAT!

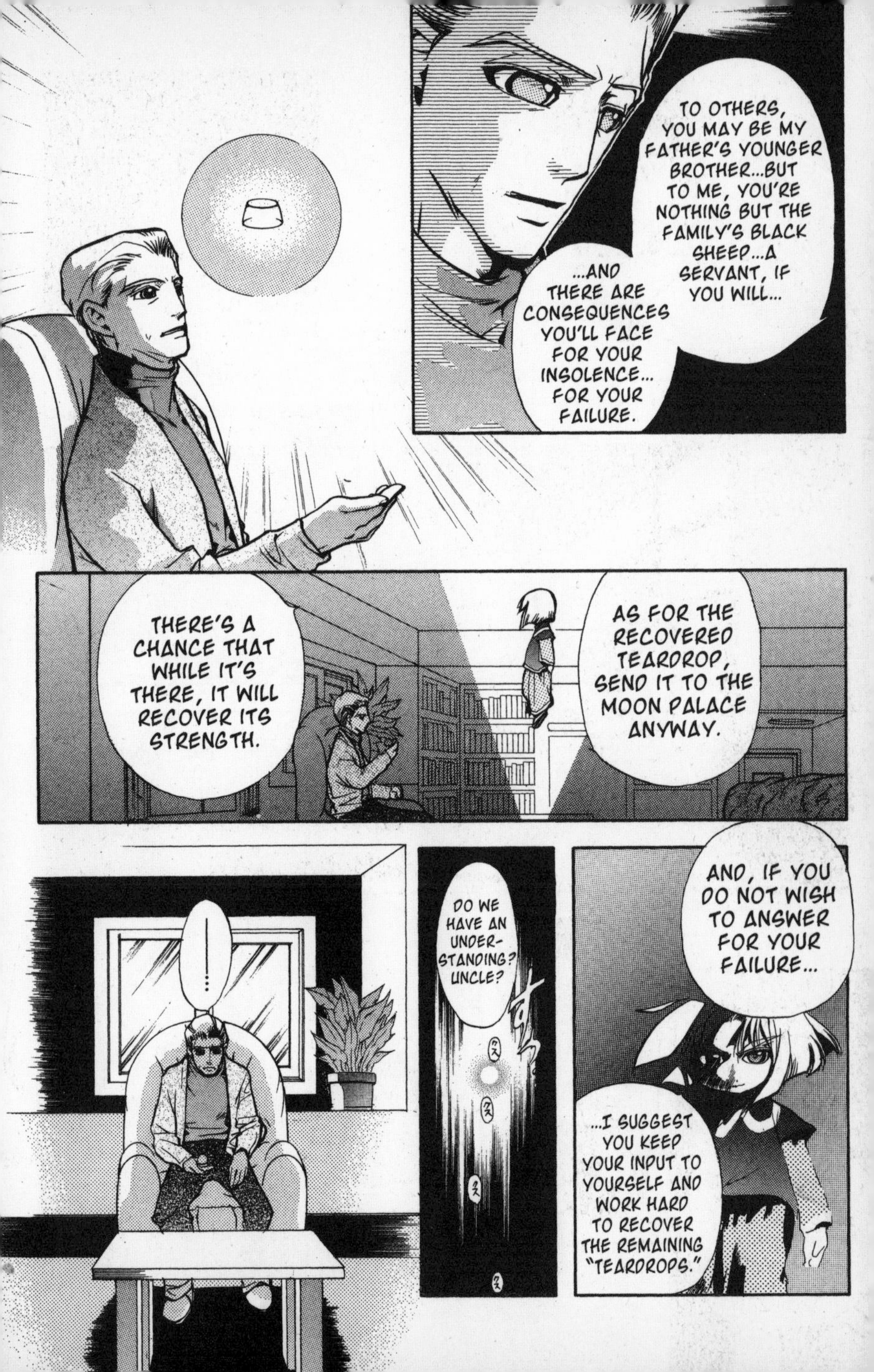
TO OTHERS, YOU MAY BE MY FATHER'S YOUNGER BROTHER...BUT TO ME, YOU'RE NOTHING BUT THE FAMILY'S BLACK SHEEP...A SERVANT, IF YOU WILL...
...AND THERE ARE CONSEQUENCES YOU'LL FACE FOR YOUR INSOLENCE... FOR YOUR FAILURE.
AS FOR THE RECOVERED TEARDROP, SEND IT TO THE MOON PALACE ANYWAY.
THERE'S A CHANCE THAT WHILE IT'S THERE, IT WILL RECOVER ITS STRENGTH.
AND, IF YOU DO NOT WISH TO ANSWER FOR YOUR FAILURE...
...I SUGGEST YOU KEEP YOUR INPUT TO YOURSELF AND WORK HARD TO RECOVER THE REMAINING "TEARDROPS."
DO WE HAVE AN UNDER-STANDING? UNCLE?
......!

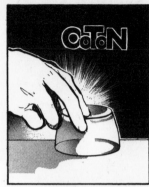

HOW CAN YOU STILL BELIEVE THAT I'M AFTER THE THRONE OF THE EMPEROR OF THE MOON...?

SHIROGANE...

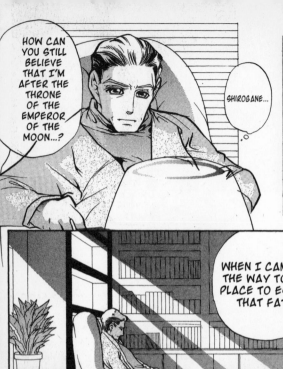

WHEN I CAME ALL THE WAY TO THIS PLACE TO ESCAPE THAT FATE?

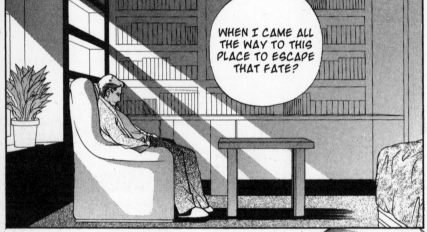

IT IS...TO SAVE THE DYING LUNAR RACE FROM EXTINCTION THAT WE MUST GATHER THE TEARDROPS OF THE MOON AS QUICKLY AS POSSIBLE...TO COLLECT THOSE SACRED GEMS SAID TO POSSESS THE POWER TO STRENGTHEN THE LIFE FORCE OF OUR PEOPLE...THAT IS OUR MISSION.

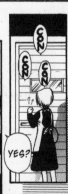

CON CON CON

YES?

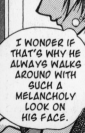

I WONDER IF THAT'S WHY HE ALWAYS WALKS AROUND WITH SUCH A MELANCHOLY LOOK ON HIS FACE.

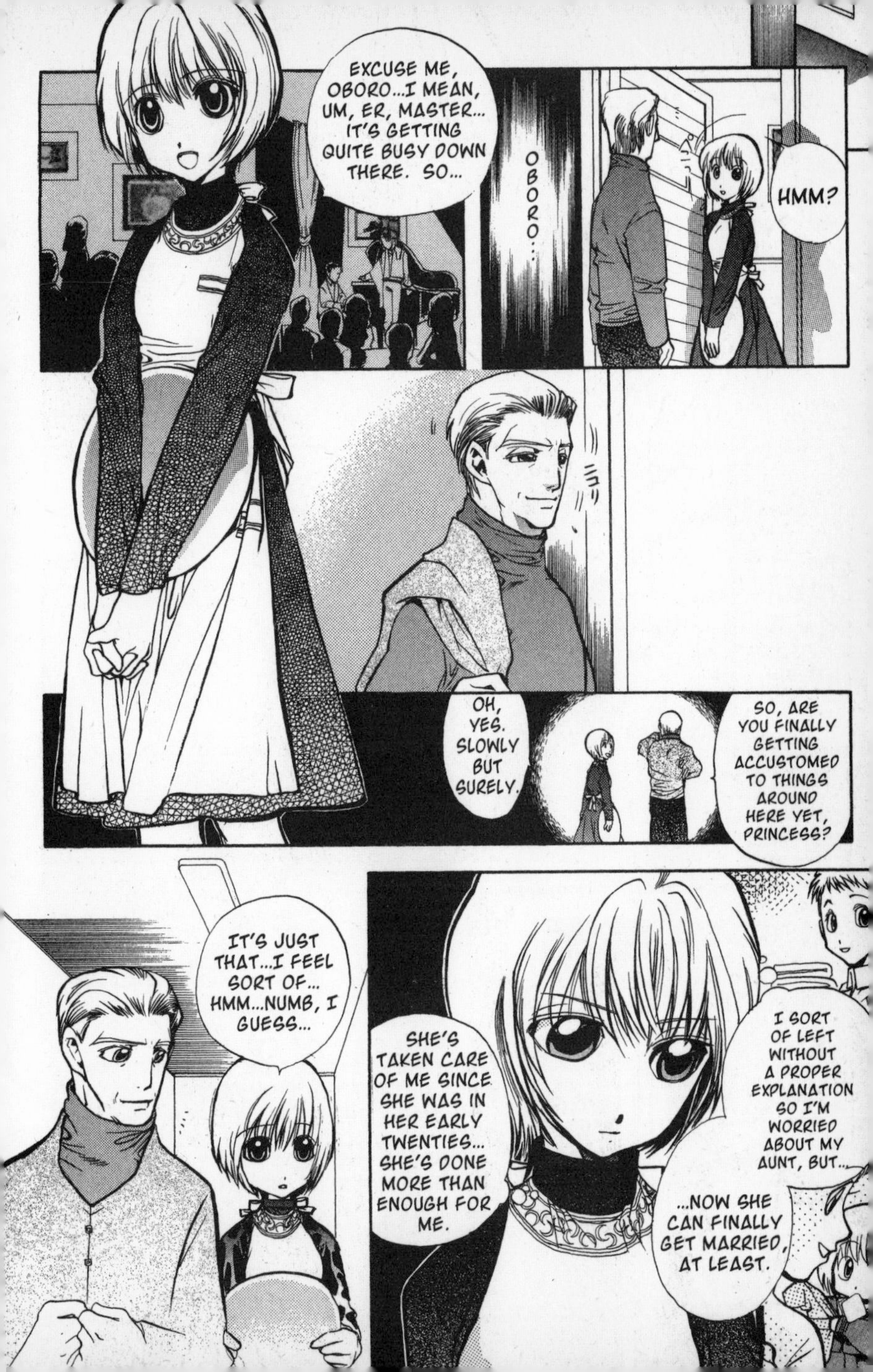
HMM?
OBORO...
EXCUSE ME, OBORO...I MEAN, UM, ER, MASTER... IT'S GETTING QUITE BUSY DOWN THERE. SO...
SO, ARE YOU FINALLY GETTING ACCUSTOMED TO THINGS AROUND HERE YET, PRINCESS?
OH, YES. SLOWLY BUT SURELY.
I SORT OF LEFT WITHOUT A PROPER EXPLANATION SO I'M WORRIED ABOUT MY AUNT, BUT...
SHE'S TAKEN CARE OF ME SINCE SHE WAS IN HER EARLY TWENTIES... SHE'S DONE MORE THAN ENOUGH FOR ME.
...NOW SHE CAN FINALLY GET MARRIED, AT LEAST.
IT'S JUST THAT...I FEEL SORT OF... HMM...NUMB, I GUESS...

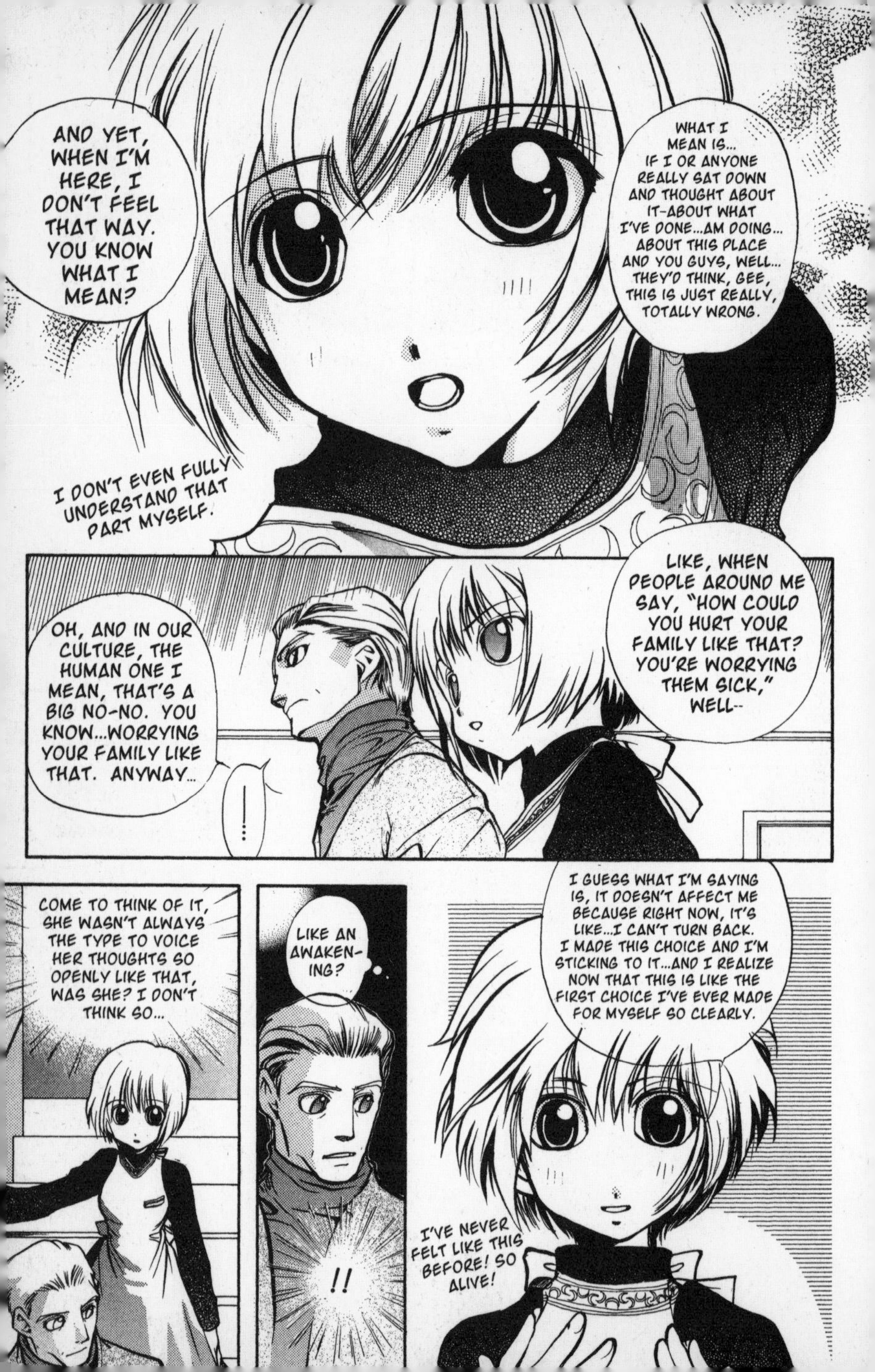
WHAT I MEAN IS... IF I OR ANYONE REALLY SAT DOWN AND THOUGHT ABOUT IT-ABOUT WHAT I'VE DONE...AM DOING... ABOUT THIS PLACE AND YOU GUYS, WELL... THEY'D THINK, GEE, THIS IS JUST REALLY, TOTALLY WRONG.
AND YET, WHEN I'M HERE, I DON'T FEEL THAT WAY. YOU KNOW WHAT I MEAN?
I DON'T EVEN FULLY UNDERSTAND THAT PART MYSELF.
LIKE, WHEN PEOPLE AROUND ME SAY, "HOW COULD YOU HURT YOUR FAMILY LIKE THAT? YOU'RE WORRYING THEM SICK," WELL--
OH, AND IN OUR CULTURE, THE HUMAN ONE I MEAN, THAT'S A BIG NO-NO. YOU KNOW...WORRYING YOUR FAMILY LIKE THAT. ANYWAY...
I GUESS WHAT I'M SAYING IS, IT DOESN'T AFFECT ME BECAUSE RIGHT NOW, IT'S LIKE...I CAN'T TURN BACK. I MADE THIS CHOICE AND I'M STICKING TO IT...AND I REALIZE NOW THAT THIS IS LIKE THE FIRST CHOICE I'VE EVER MADE FOR MYSELF SO CLEARLY.
I'VE NEVER FELT LIKE THIS BEFORE! SO ALIVE!
LIKE AN AWAKEN-ING?
!!
COME TO THINK OF IT, SHE WASN'T ALWAYS THE TYPE TO VOICE HER THOUGHTS SO OPENLY LIKE THAT, WAS SHE? I DON'T THINK SO...

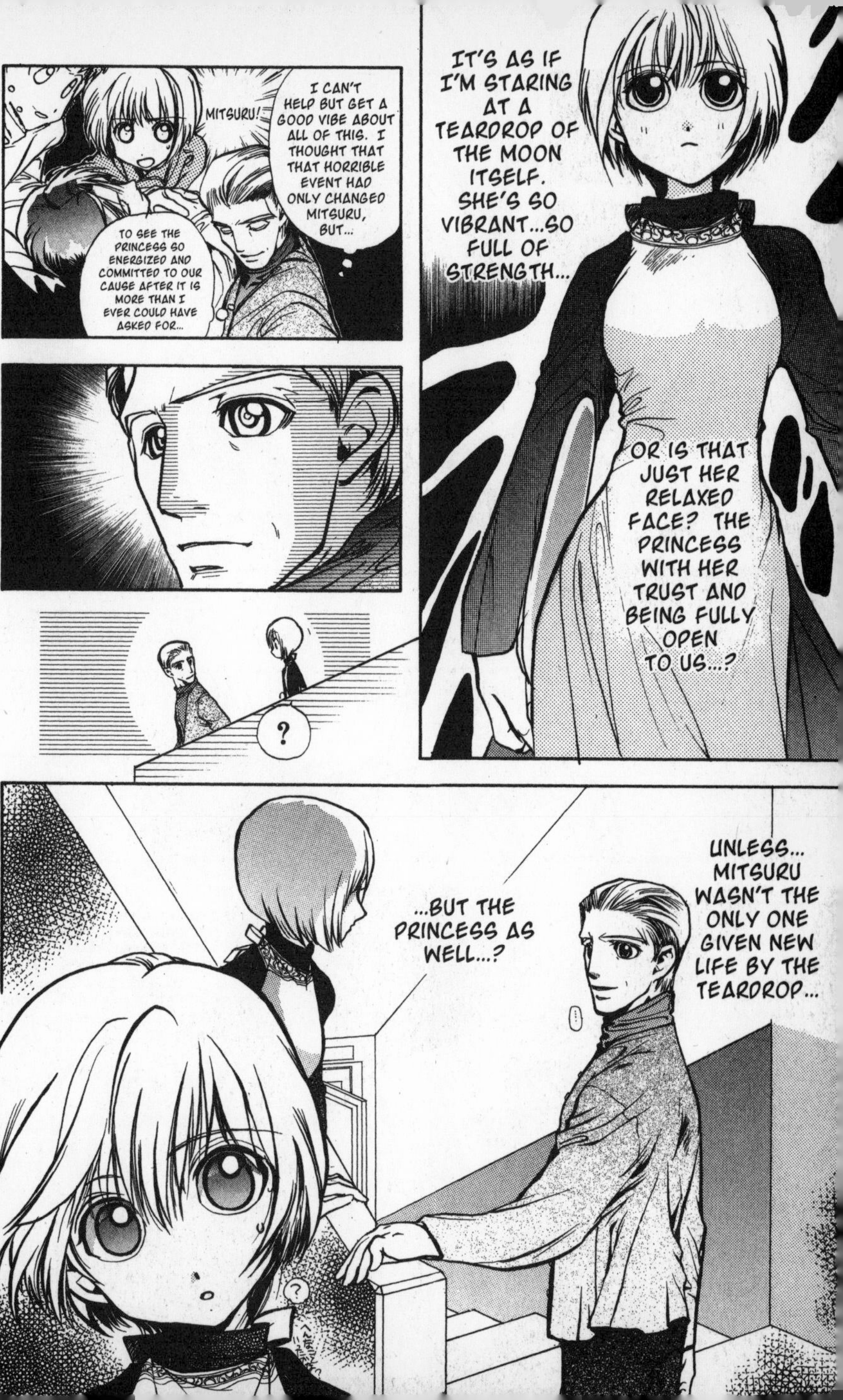
IT'S AS IF I'M STARING AT A TEARDROP OF THE MOON ITSELF. SHE'S SO VIBRANT...SO FULL OF STRENGTH...
OR IS THAT JUST HER RELAXED FACE? THE PRINCESS WITH HER TRUST AND BEING FULLY OPEN TO US...?
I CAN'T HELP BUT GET A GOOD VIBE ABOUT ALL OF THIS. I THOUGHT THAT THAT HORRIBLE EVENT HAD ONLY CHANGED MITSURU, BUT...
MITSURU!
TO SEE THE PRINCESS SO ENERGIZED AND COMMITTED TO OUR CAUSE AFTER IT IS MORE THAN I EVER COULD HAVE ASKED FOR...
?
UNLESS... MITSURU WASN'T THE ONLY ONE GIVEN NEW LIFE BY THE TEARDROP...
...BUT THE PRINCESS AS WELL...?
!
?

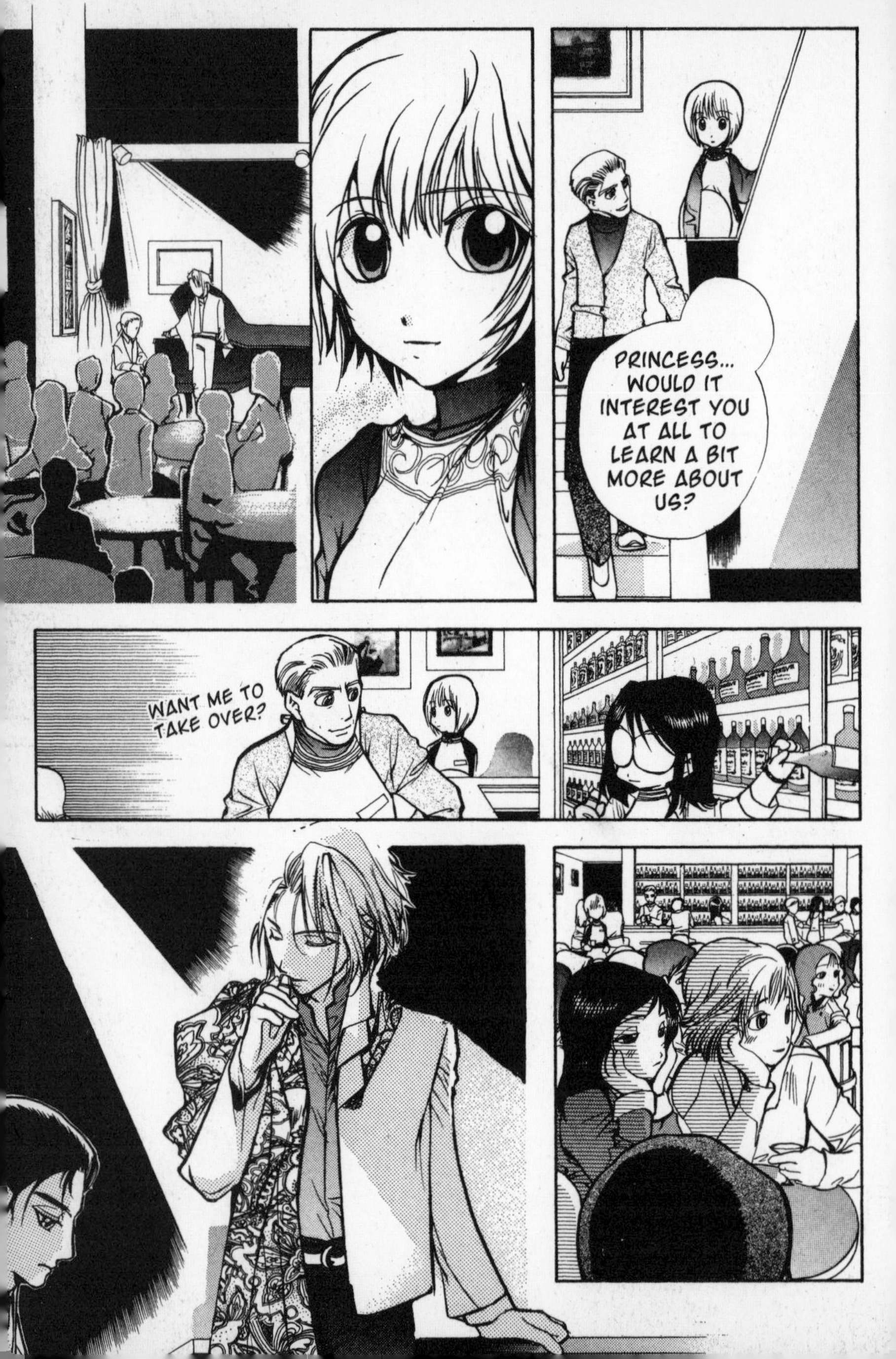
PRINCESS... WOULD IT INTEREST YOU AT ALL TO LEARN A BIT MORE ABOUT US?
WANT ME TO TAKE OVER?

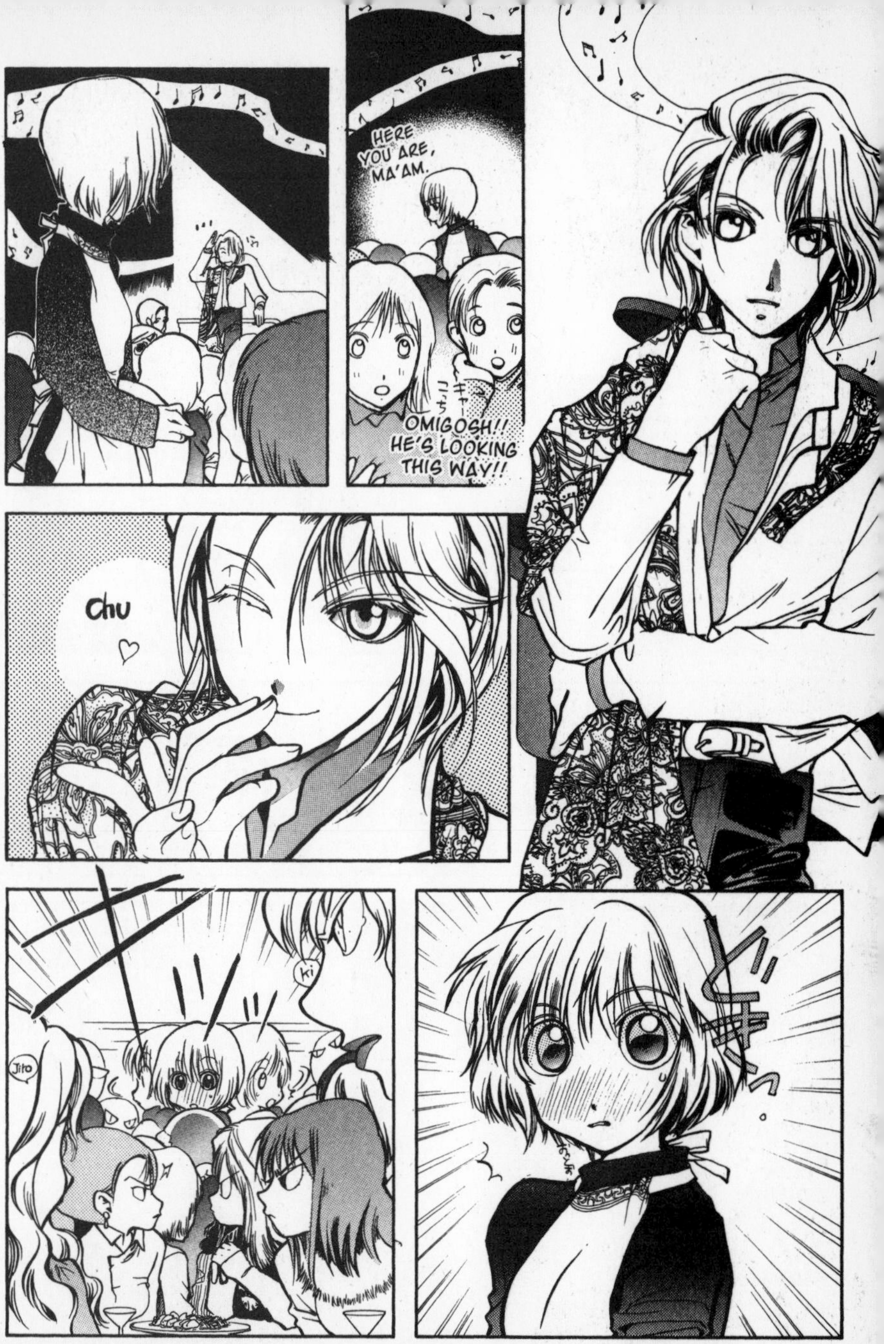
HERE YOU ARE, MA'AM.
OMIGOSH!! HE'S LOOKING THIS WAY!!
Chu
♡
ki
Jito

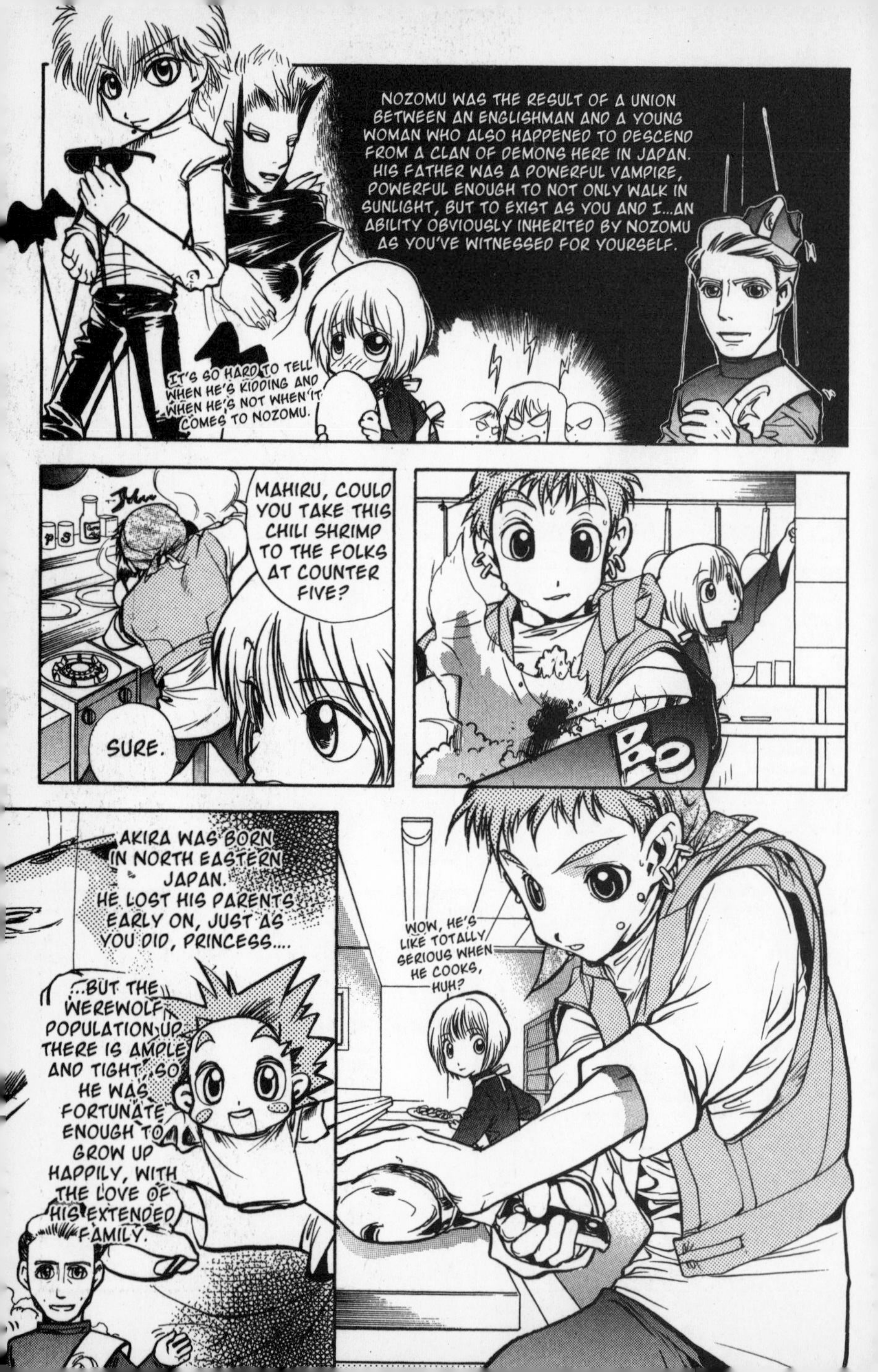
NOZOMU WAS THE RESULT OF A UNION BETWEEN AN ENGLISHMAN AND A YOUNG WOMAN WHO ALSO HAPPENED TO DESCEND FROM A CLAN OF DEMONS HERE IN JAPAN. HIS FATHER WAS A POWERFUL VAMPIRE, POWERFUL ENOUGH TO NOT ONLY WALK IN SUNLIGHT, BUT TO EXIST AS YOU AND I...AN ABILITY OBVIOUSLY INHERITED BY NOZOMU AS YOU'VE WITNESSED FOR YOURSELF.
IT'S SO HARD TO TELL WHEN HE'S KIDDING AND WHEN HE'S NOT WHEN IT COMES TO NOZOMU.
MAHIRU, COULD YOU TAKE THIS CHILI SHRIMP TO THE FOLKS AT COUNTER FIVE?
SURE.
WOW, HE'S LIKE TOTALLY SERIOUS WHEN HE COOKS, HUH?
AKIRA WAS BORN IN NORTH EASTERN JAPAN. HE LOST HIS PARENTS EARLY ON, JUST AS YOU DID, PRINCESS....
...BUT THE WEREWOLF POPULATION UP THERE IS AMPLE AND TIGHT, SO HE WAS FORTUNATE ENOUGH TO GROW UP HAPPILY, WITH THE LOVE OF HIS EXTENDED FAMILY.

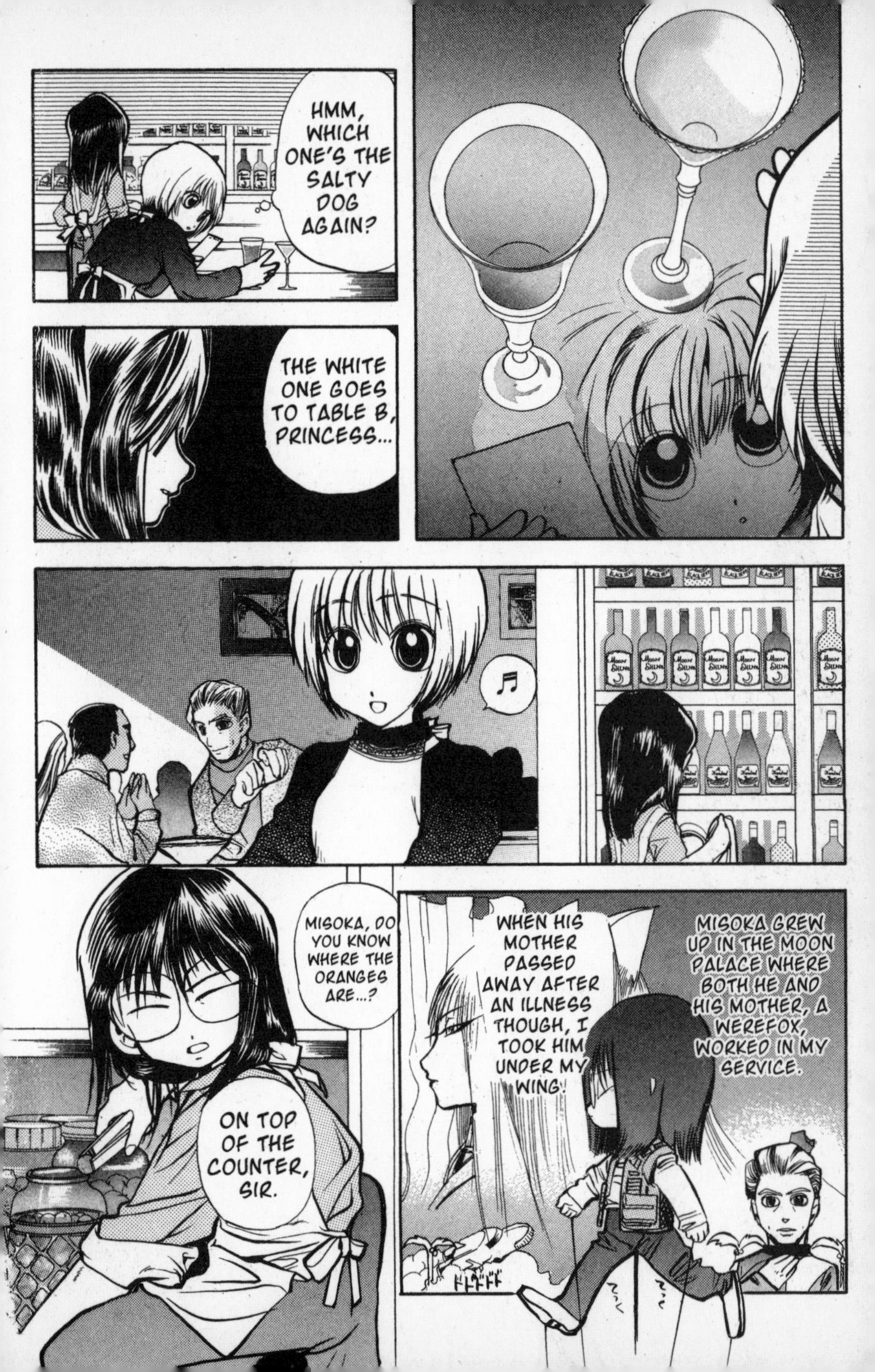
HMM, WHICH ONE'S THE SALTY DOG AGAIN?
THE WHITE ONE GOES TO TABLE B, PRINCESS...
♪
MISOKA GREW UP IN THE MOON PALACE WHERE BOTH HE AND HIS MOTHER, A WEREFOX, WORKED IN MY SERVICE.
WHEN HIS MOTHER PASSED AWAY AFTER AN ILLNESS THOUGH, I TOOK HIM UNDER MY WING.
MISOKA, DO YOU KNOW WHERE THE ORANGES ARE...?
ON TOP OF THE COUNTER, SIR.

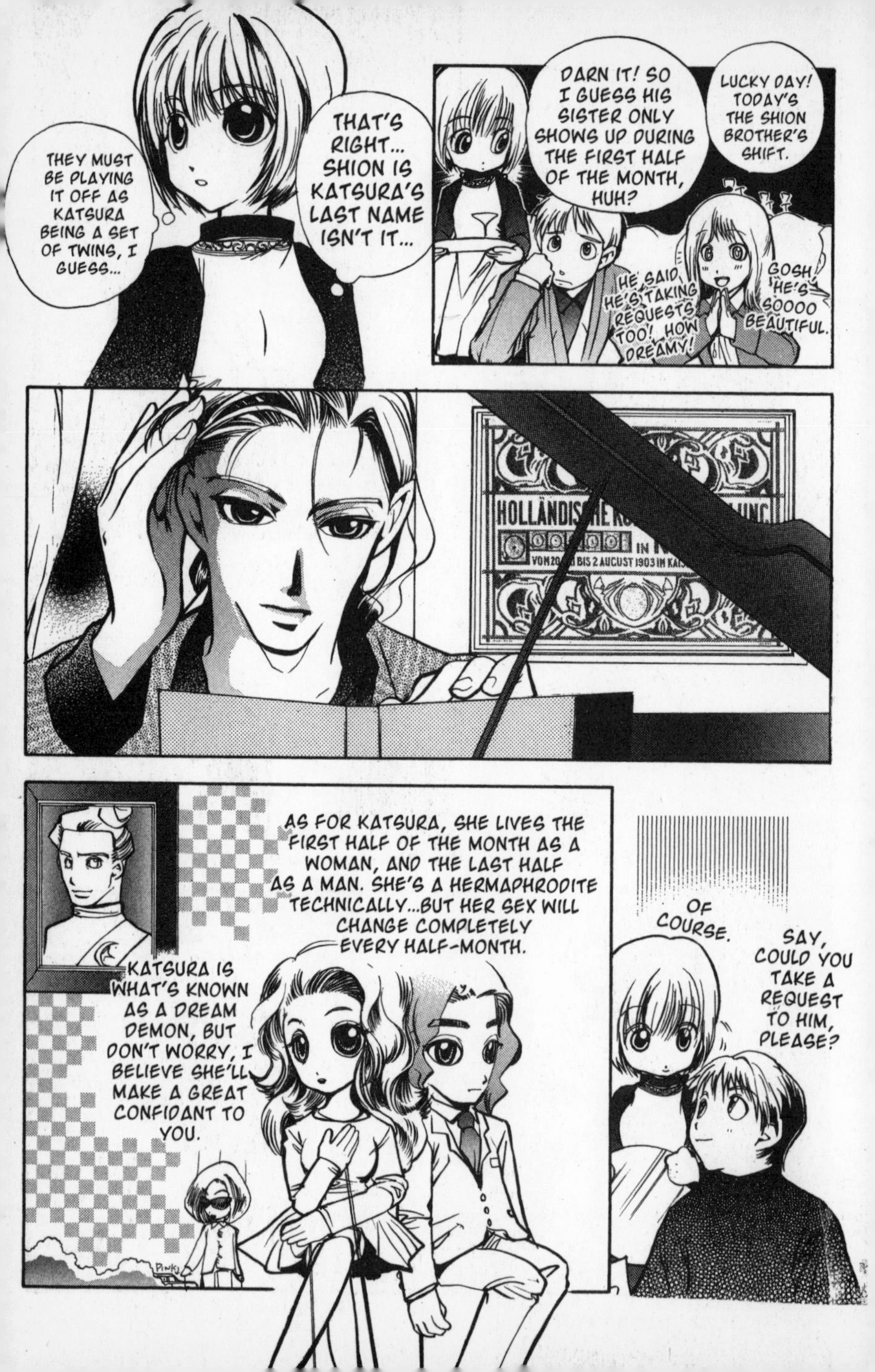
LUCKY DAY! TODAY'S THE SHION BROTHER'S SHIFT.
DARN IT! SO I GUESS HIS SISTER ONLY SHOWS UP DURING THE FIRST HALF OF THE MONTH, HUH?
GOSH! HE'S SOOOO BEAUTIFUL.
HE SAID HE'S TAKING REQUESTS TOO! HOW DREAMY!
THAT'S RIGHT... SHION IS KATSURA'S LAST NAME ISN'T IT...
THEY MUST BE PLAYING IT OFF AS KATSURA BEING A SET OF TWINS, I GUESS...
HOLLÄNDISCHE
BIS 2 AUGUST 1903
OF COURSE.
SAY, COULD YOU TAKE A REQUEST TO HIM, PLEASE?
AS FOR KATSURA, SHE LIVES THE FIRST HALF OF THE MONTH AS A WOMAN, AND THE LAST HALF AS A MAN. SHE'S A HERMAPHRODITE TECHNICALLY...BUT HER SEX WILL CHANGE COMPLETELY EVERY HALF-MONTH.
KATSURA IS WHAT'S KNOWN AS A DREAM DEMON, BUT DON'T WORRY, I BELIEVE SHE'LL MAKE A GREAT CONFIDANT TO YOU.

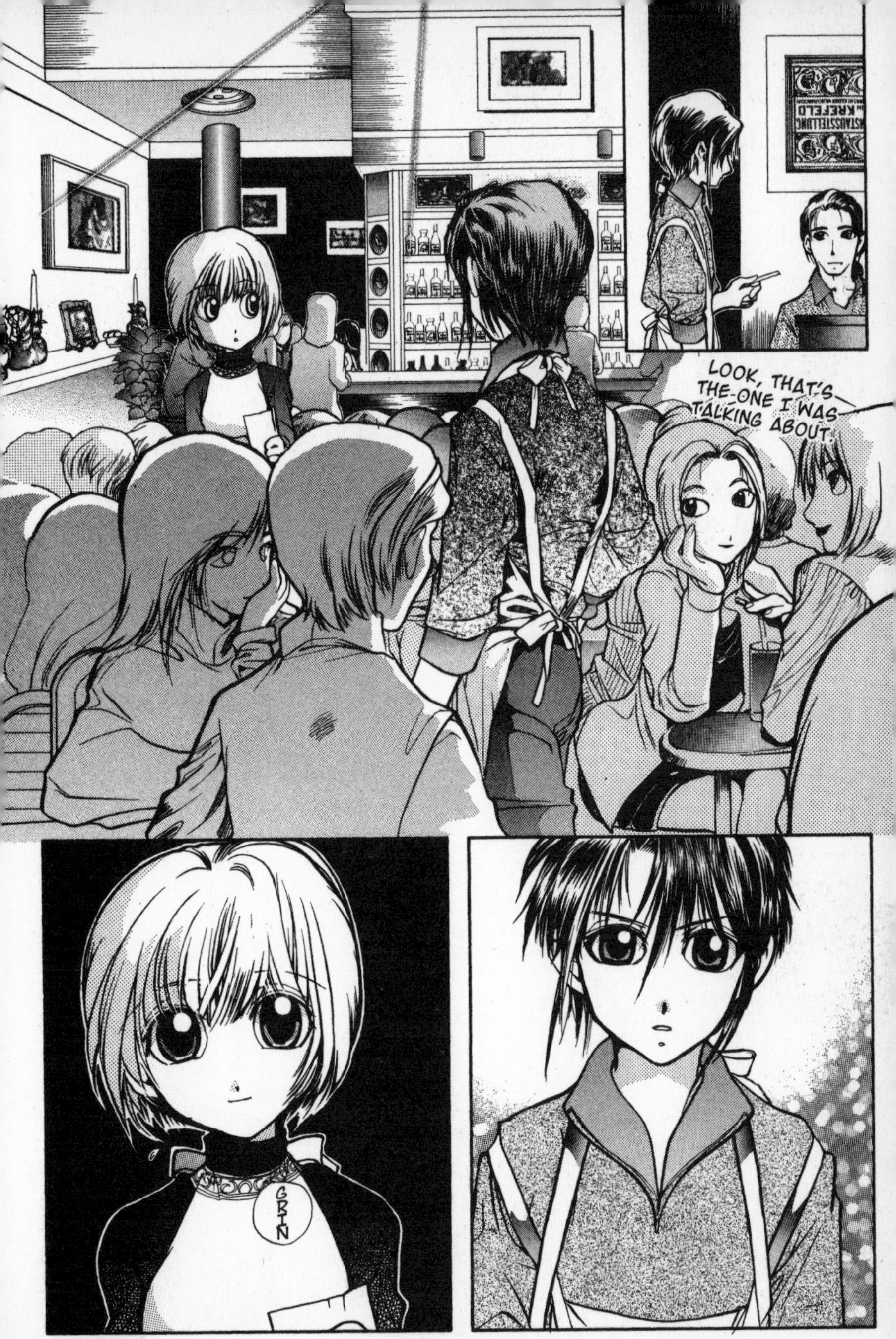
LOOK, THAT'S THE ONE I WAS TALKING ABOUT.
GRIN

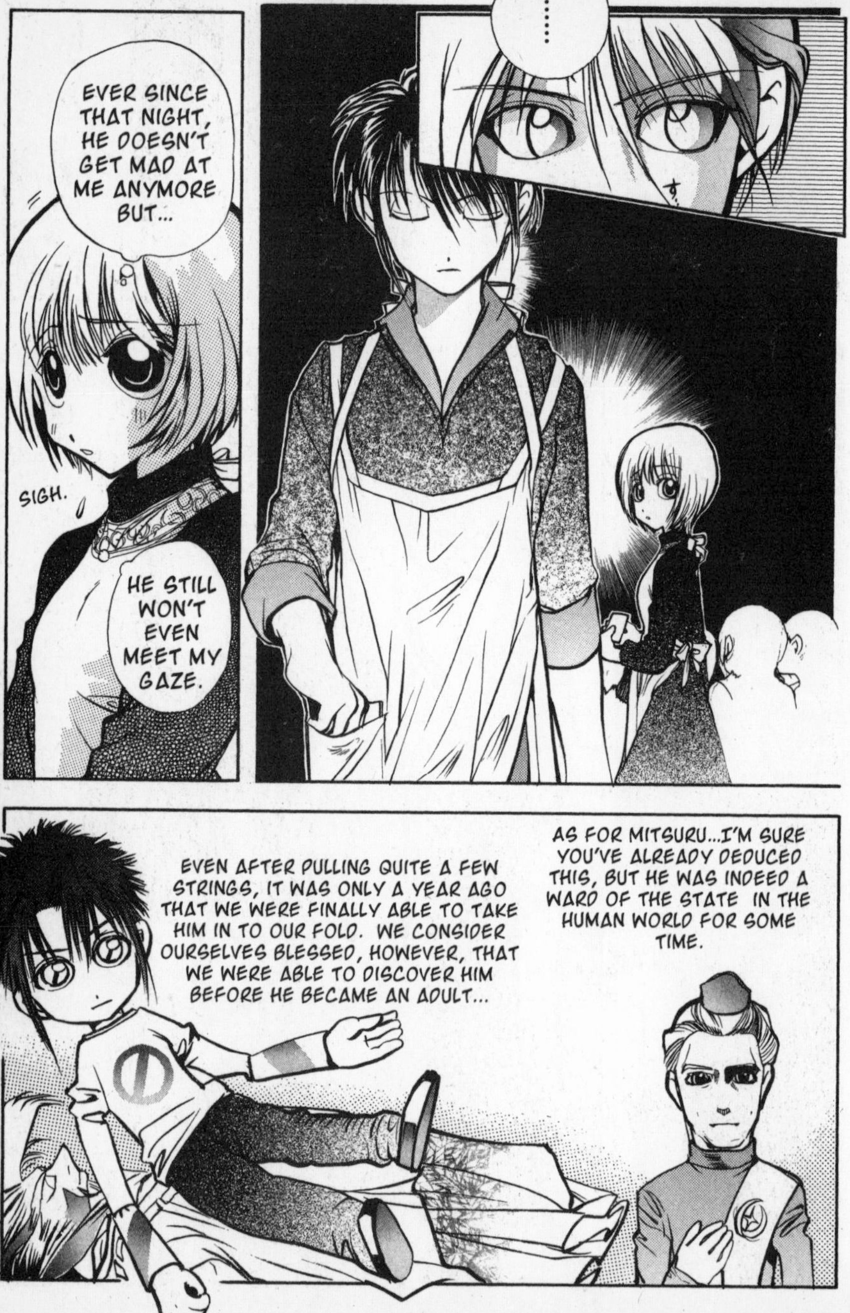
......
EVER SINCE THAT NIGHT, HE DOESN'T GET MAD AT ME ANYMORE BUT...
SIGH.
HE STILL WON'T EVEN MEET MY GAZE.
AS FOR MITSURU...I'M SURE YOU'VE ALREADY DEDUCED THIS, BUT HE WAS INDEED A WARD OF THE STATE IN THE HUMAN WORLD FOR SOME TIME.
EVEN AFTER PULLING QUITE A FEW STRINGS, IT WAS ONLY A YEAR AGO THAT WE WERE FINALLY ABLE TO TAKE HIM IN TO OUR FOLD. WE CONSIDER OURSELVES BLESSED, HOWEVER, THAT WE WERE ABLE TO DISCOVER HIM BEFORE HE BECAME AN ADULT...

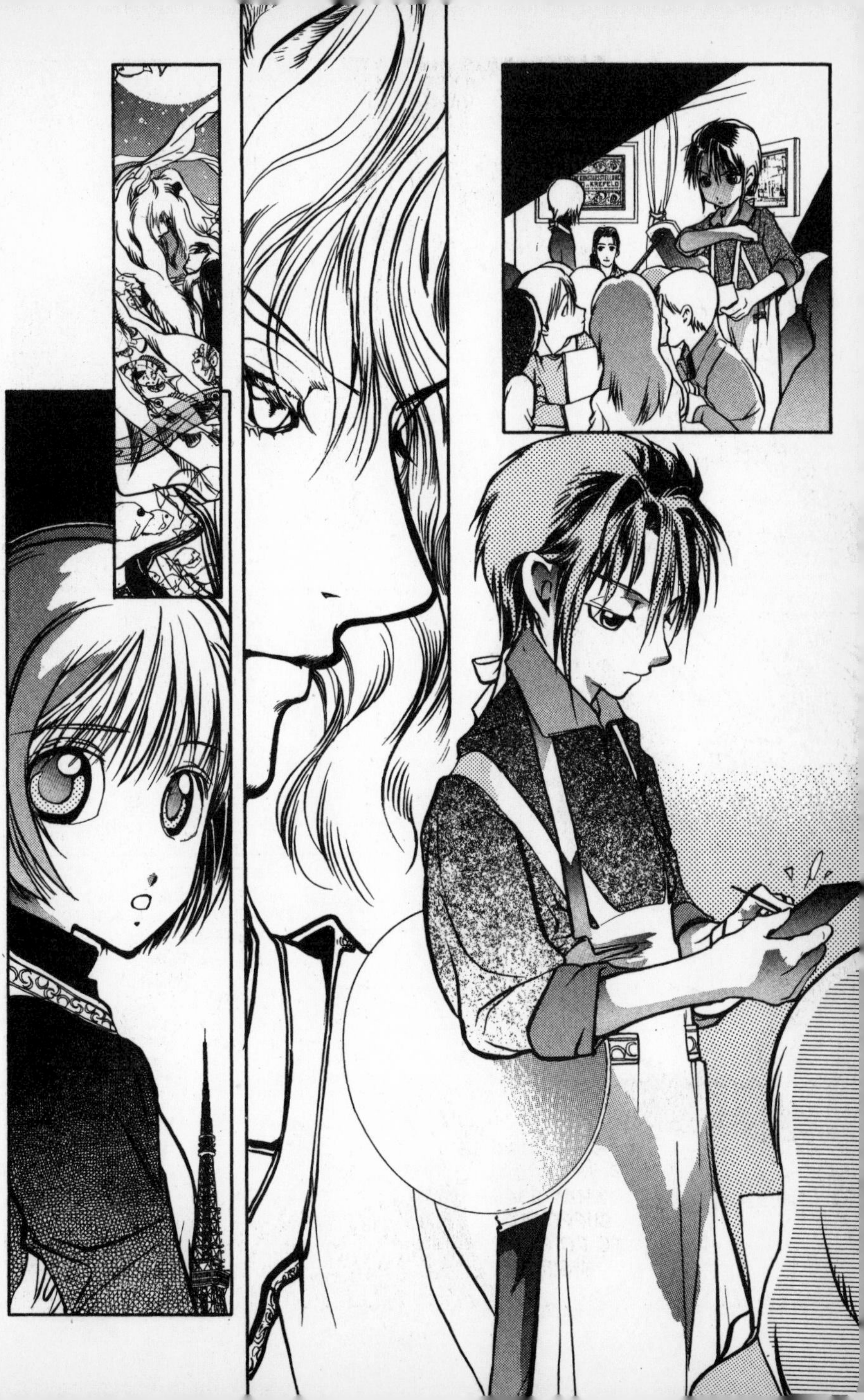
KUNSTAUSSTELLUNG
KREFELD

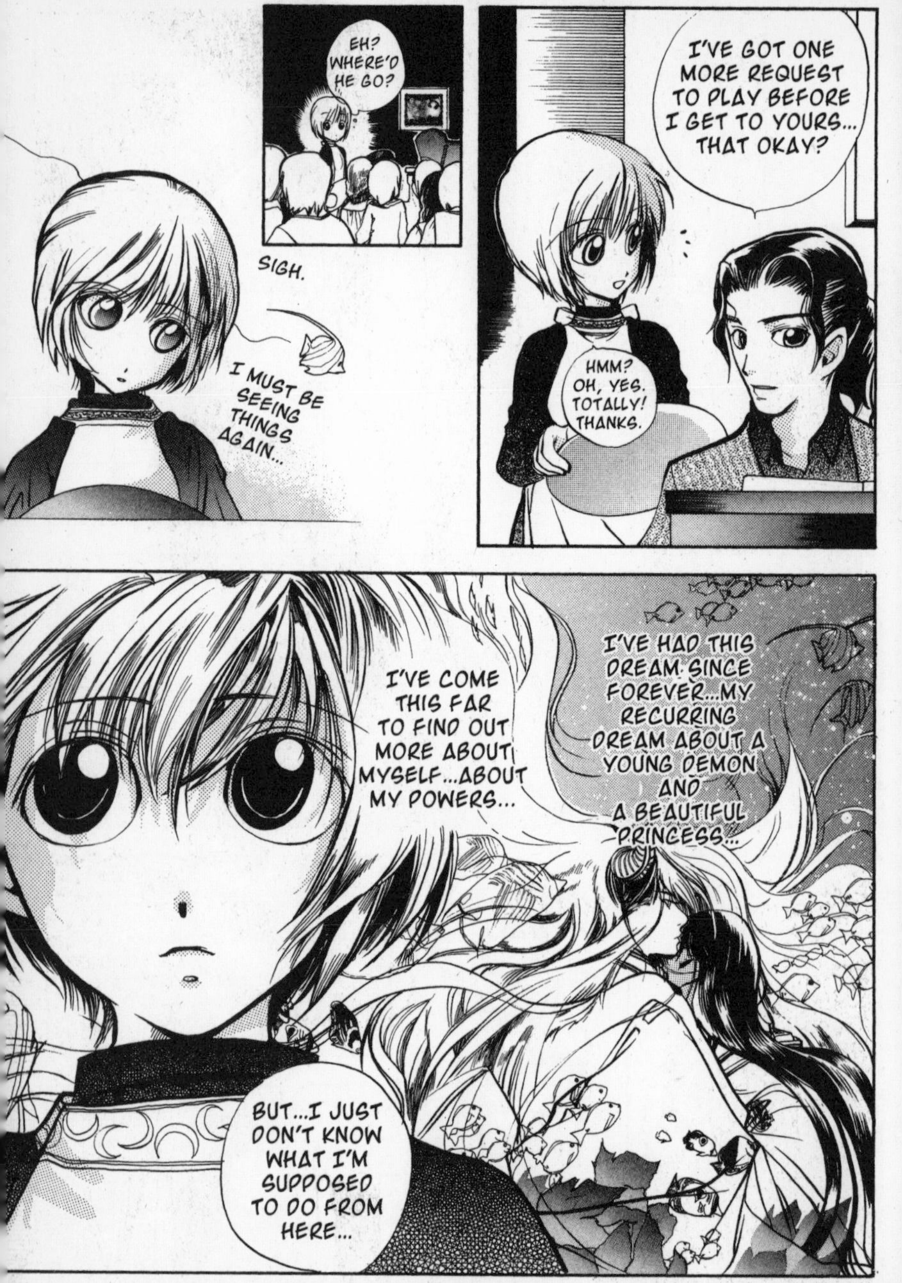

I'VE GOT ONE MORE REQUEST TO PLAY BEFORE I GET TO YOURS... THAT OKAY?
HMM? OH, YES. TOTALLY! THANKS.
EH? WHERE'D HE GO?
SIGH.
I MUST BE SEEING THINGS AGAIN...
I'VE HAD THIS DREAM SINCE FOREVER...MY RECURRING DREAM ABOUT A YOUNG DEMON AND A BEAUTIFUL PRINCESS...
I'VE COME THIS FAR TO FIND OUT MORE ABOUT MYSELF...ABOUT MY POWERS...
BUT...I JUST DON'T KNOW WHAT I'M SUPPOSED TO DO FROM HERE...

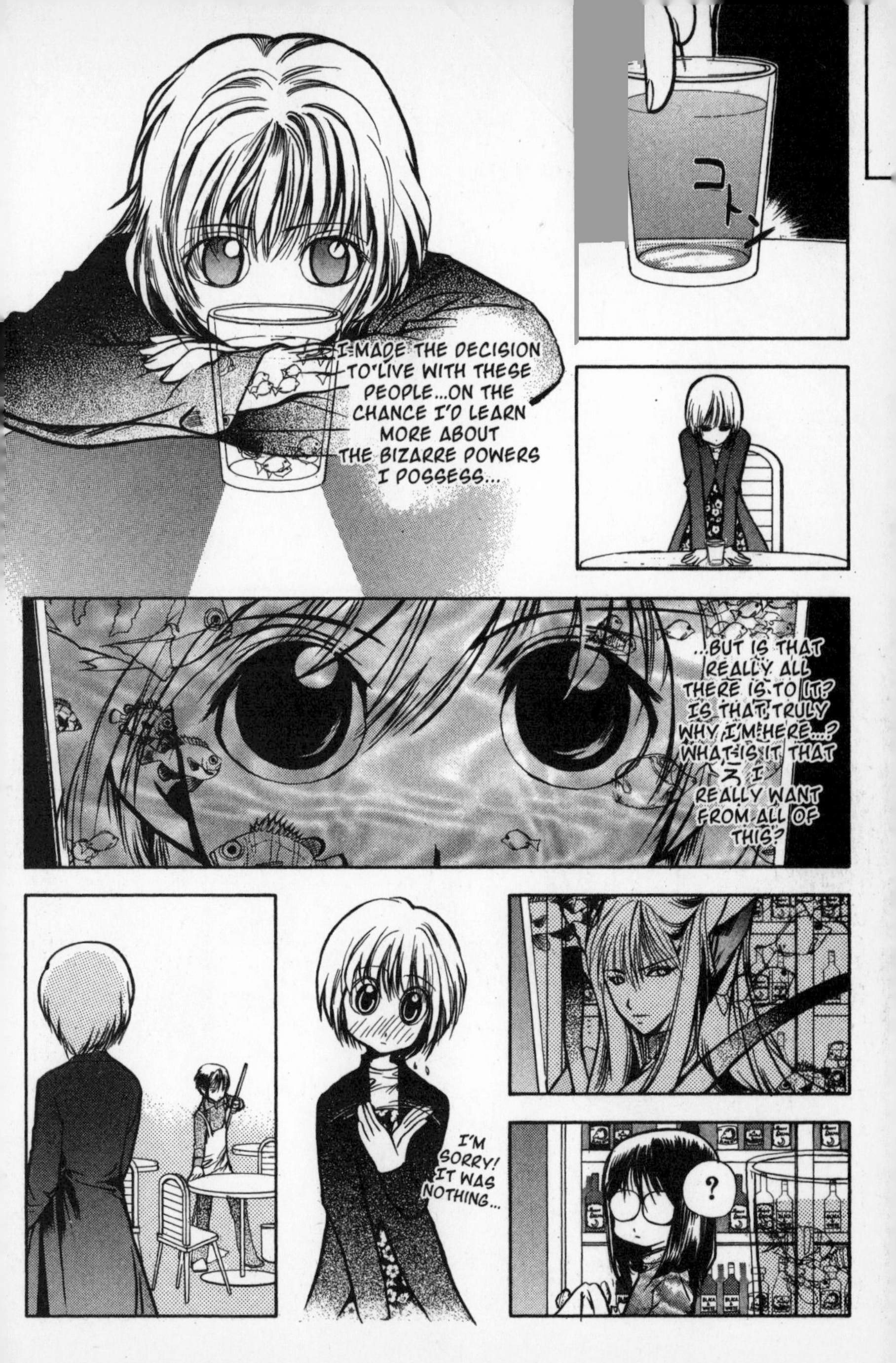
コト
I MADE THE DECISION TO LIVE WITH THESE PEOPLE...ON THE CHANCE I'D LEARN MORE ABOUT THE BIZARRE POWERS I POSSESS...
...BUT IS THAT REALLY ALL THERE IS TO IT? IS THAT TRULY WHY I'M HERE...? WHAT IS IT THAT I REALLY WANT FROM ALL OF THIS?
?
I'M SORRY! IT WAS NOTHING...

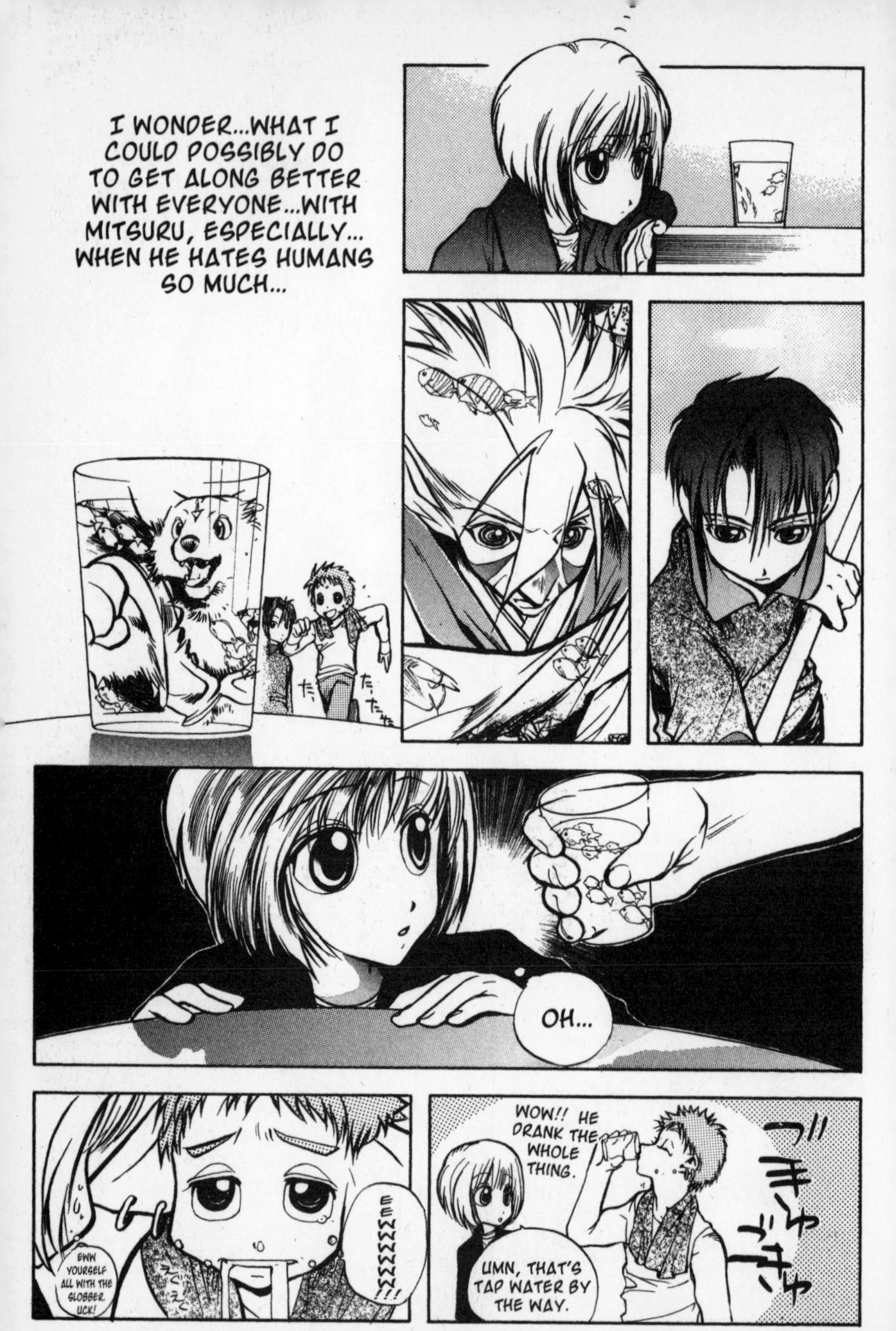
I WONDER...WHAT I COULD POSSIBLY DO TO GET ALONG BETTER WITH EVERYONE...WITH MITSURU, ESPECIALLY... WHEN HE HATES HUMANS SO MUCH...
OH...
WOW!! HE DRANK THE WHOLE THING.
UMN, THAT'S TAP WATER BY THE WAY.
EEWWWWWWW!!!
EWW YOURSELF ALL WITH THE SLOBBER. UCK!

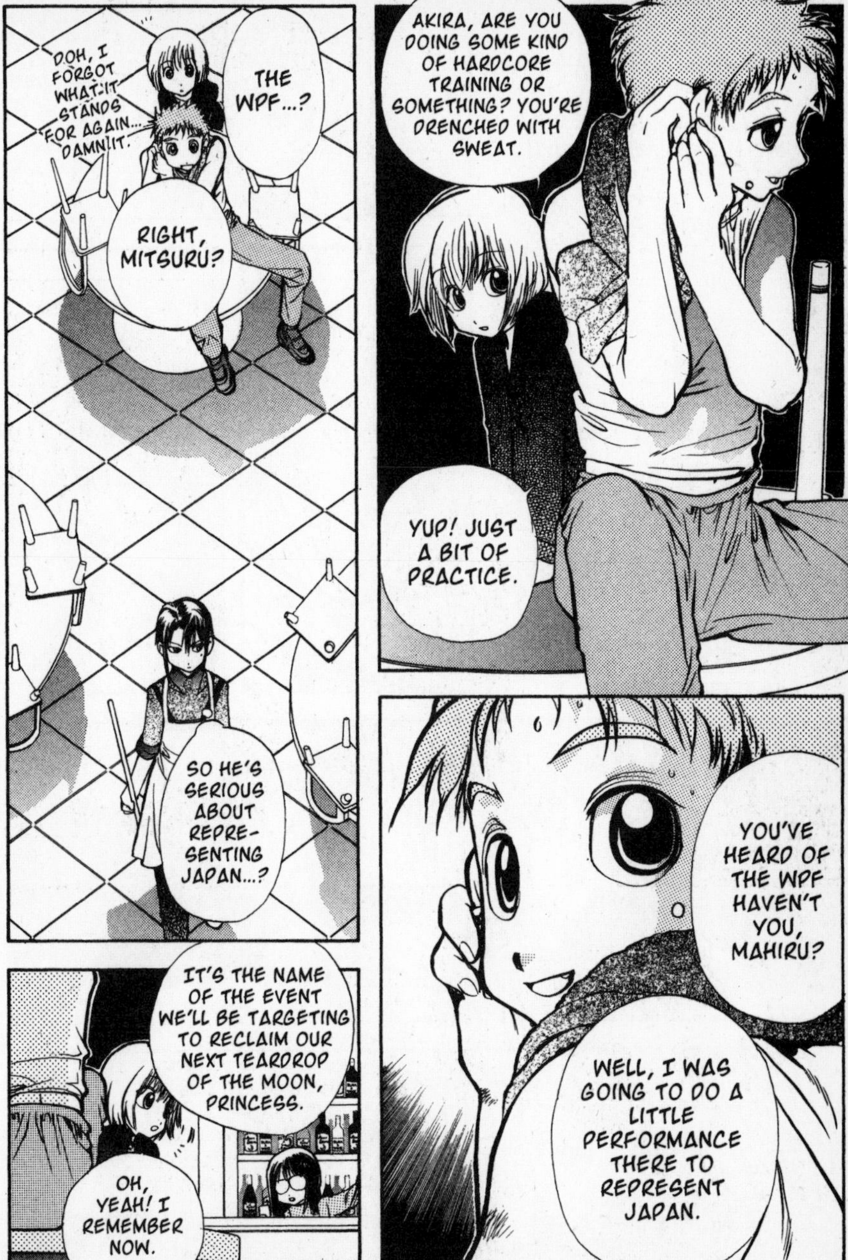

AKIRA, ARE YOU DOING SOME KIND OF HARDCORE TRAINING OR SOMETHING? YOU'RE DRENCHED WITH SWEAT.
YUP! JUST A BIT OF PRACTICE.
YOU'VE HEARD OF THE WPF HAVEN'T YOU, MAHIRU?
WELL, I WAS GOING TO DO A LITTLE PERFORMANCE THERE TO REPRESENT JAPAN.
THE WPF...?
RIGHT, MITSURU?
DOH, I FORGOT WHAT IT STANDS FOR AGAIN... DAMN IT.
SO HE'S SERIOUS ABOUT REPRE-SENTING JAPAN...?
IT'S THE NAME OF THE EVENT WE'LL BE TARGETING TO RECLAIM OUR NEXT TEARDROP OF THE MOON, PRINCESS.
OH, YEAH! I REMEMBER NOW.

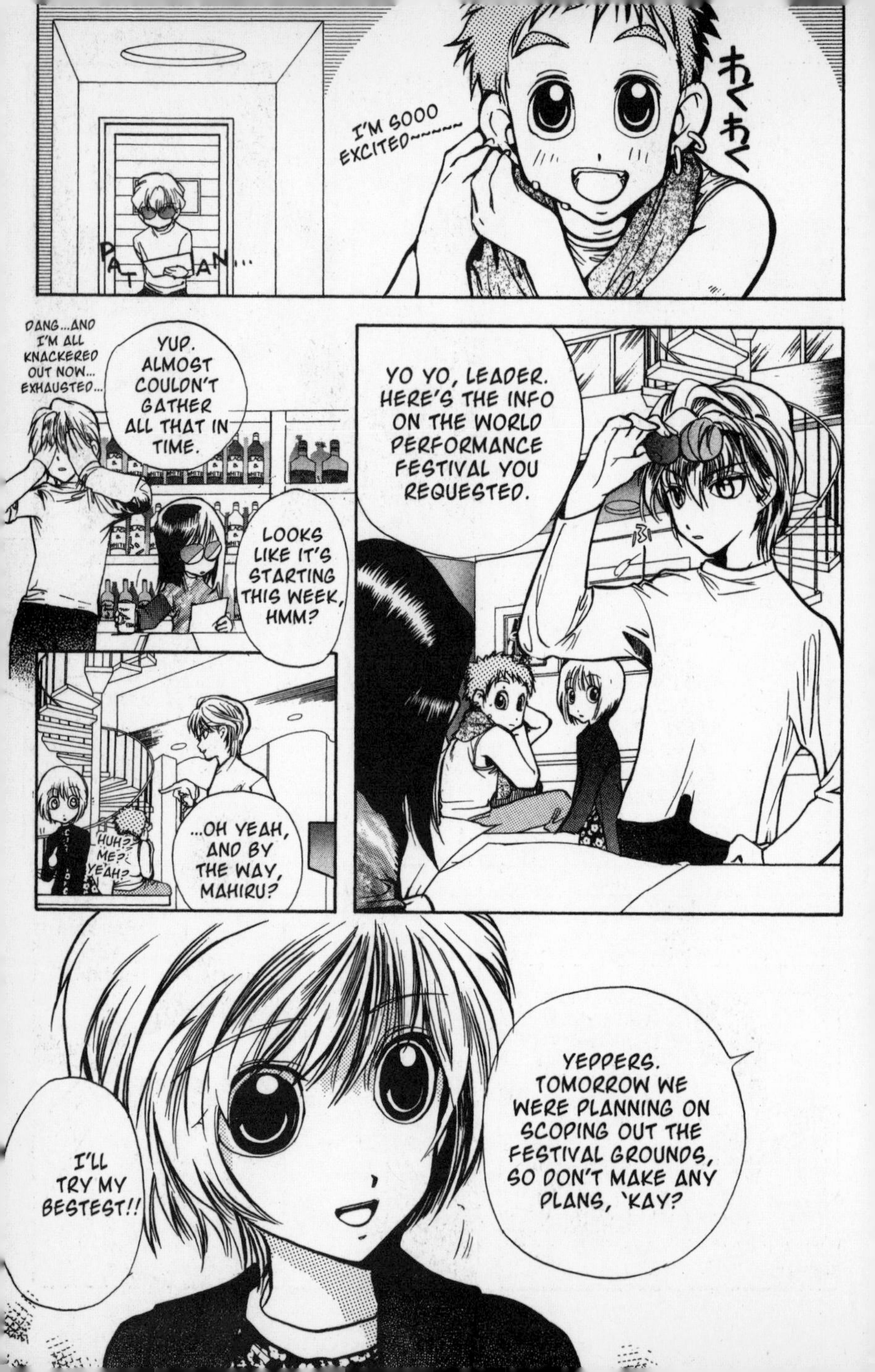

わくわく
I'M SOOO EXCITED~~~~~
PATAN...
YO YO, LEADER. HERE'S THE INFO ON THE WORLD PERFORMANCE FESTIVAL YOU REQUESTED.
LOOKS LIKE IT'S STARTING THIS WEEK, HMM?
YUP. ALMOST COULDN'T GATHER ALL THAT IN TIME.
DANG...AND I'M ALL KNACKERED OUT NOW... EXHAUSTED...
...OH YEAH, AND BY THE WAY, MAHIRU?
HUH? ME? YEAH?
YEPPERS. TOMORROW WE WERE PLANNING ON SCOPING OUT THE FESTIVAL GROUNDS, SO DON'T MAKE ANY PLANS, 'KAY?
I'LL TRY MY BESTEST!!

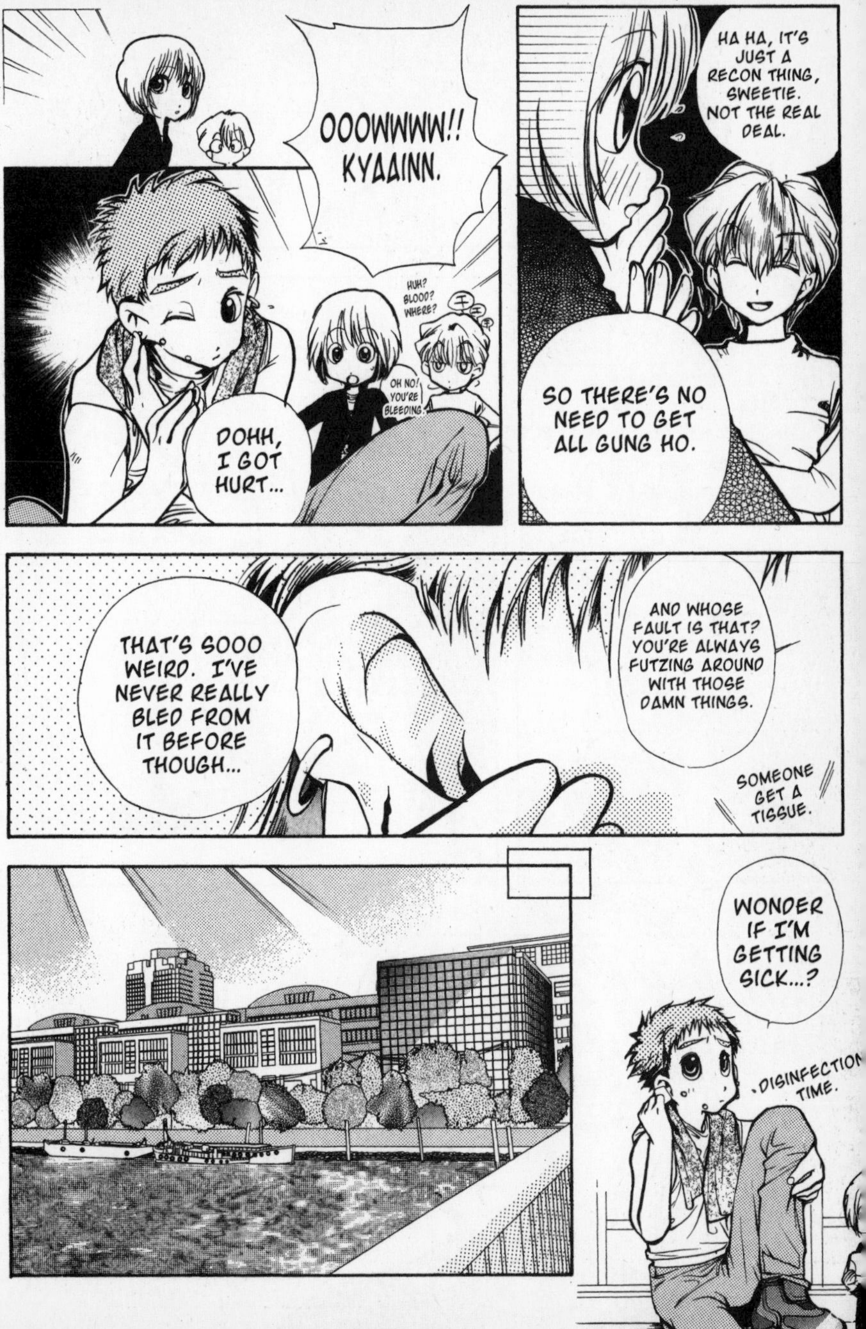
HA HA, IT'S JUST A RECON THING, SWEETIE. NOT THE REAL DEAL.
SO THERE'S NO NEED TO GET ALL GUNG HO.
OOOWWWW!! KYAAINN.
HUH? BLOOD? WHERE?
OH NO! YOU'RE BLEEDING.
DOHH, I GOT HURT...
AND WHOSE FAULT IS THAT? YOU'RE ALWAYS FUTZING AROUND WITH THOSE DAMN THINGS.
SOMEONE GET A TISSUE.
THAT'S SOOO WEIRD. I'VE NEVER REALLY BLED FROM IT BEFORE THOUGH...
WONDER IF I'M GETTING SICK...?
DISINFECTION TIME.

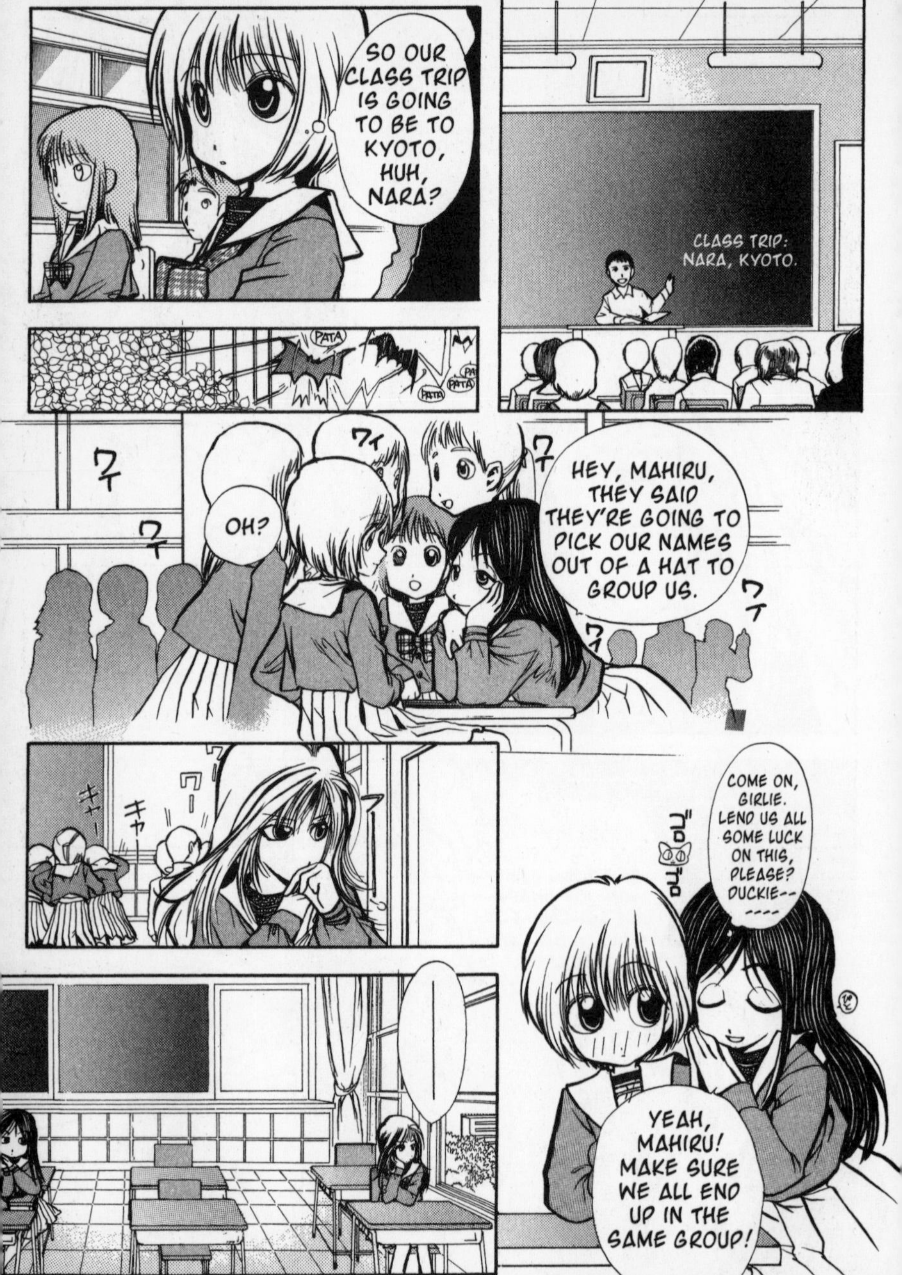
CLASS TRIP: NARA, KYOTO.
SO OUR CLASS TRIP IS GOING TO BE TO KYOTO, HUH, NARA?
PATA PATA PATA PATA
ワイ
HEY, MAHIRU, THEY SAID THEY'RE GOING TO PICK OUR NAMES OUT OF A HAT TO GROUP US.
ワイ
OH?
ワイ
ワイ
COME ON, GIRLIE. LEND US ALL SOME LUCK ON THIS, PLEASE? DUCKIE-- ----
YEAH, MAHIRU! MAKE SURE WE ALL END UP IN THE SAME GROUP!
ワー
ワー
キャー
キャー

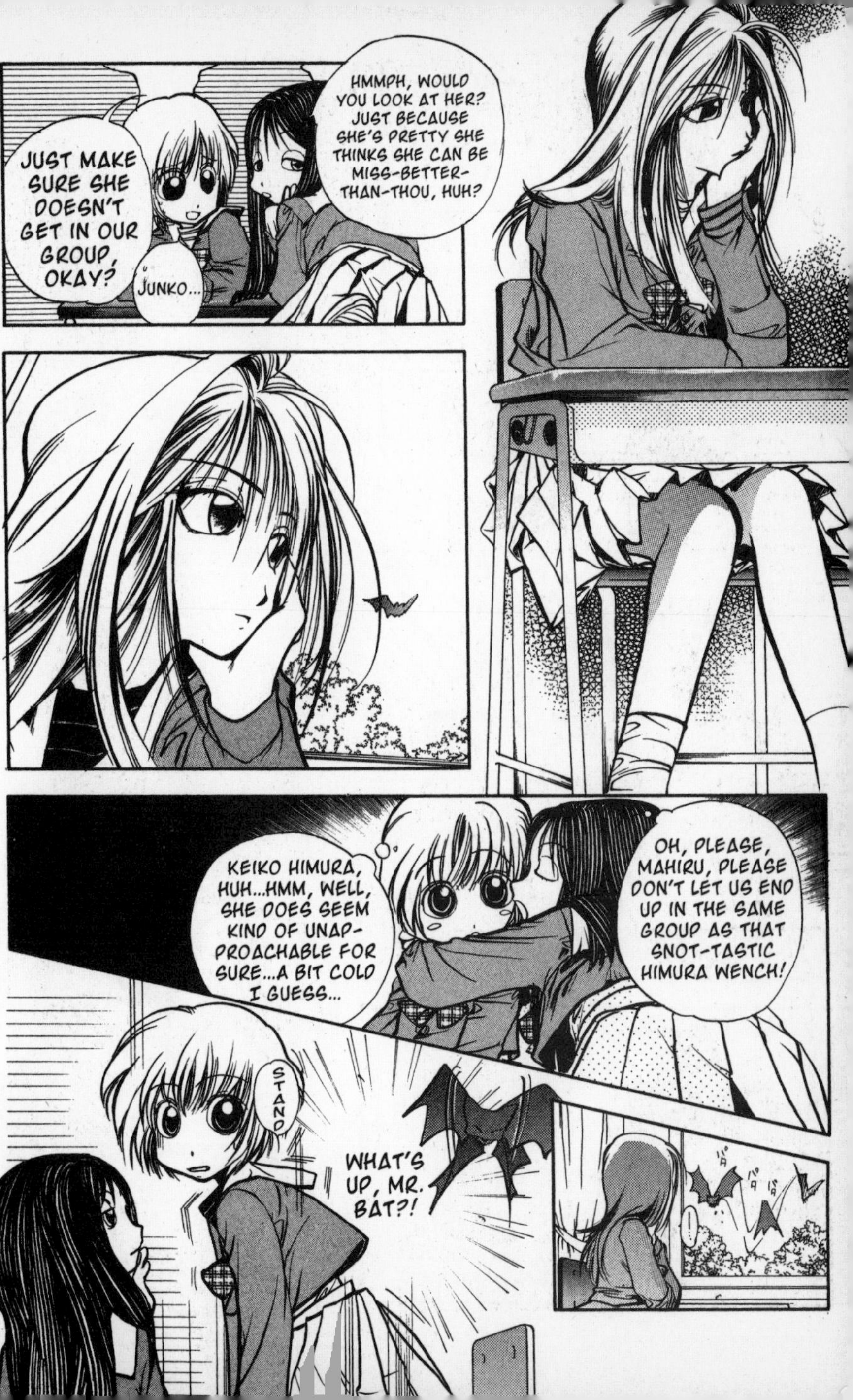
HMMPH, WOULD YOU LOOK AT HER? JUST BECAUSE SHE'S PRETTY SHE THINKS SHE CAN BE MISS-BETTER-THAN-THOU, HUH?
JUST MAKE SURE SHE DOESN'T GET IN OUR GROUP, OKAY?
JUNKO...
OH, PLEASE, MAHIRU, PLEASE DON'T LET US END UP IN THE SAME GROUP AS THAT SNOT-TASTIC HIMURA WENCH!
KEIKO HIMURA, HUH...HMM, WELL, SHE DOES SEEM KIND OF UNAP-PROACHABLE FOR SURE...A BIT COLD I GUESS...
!
STAND
WHAT'S UP, MR. BAT?!

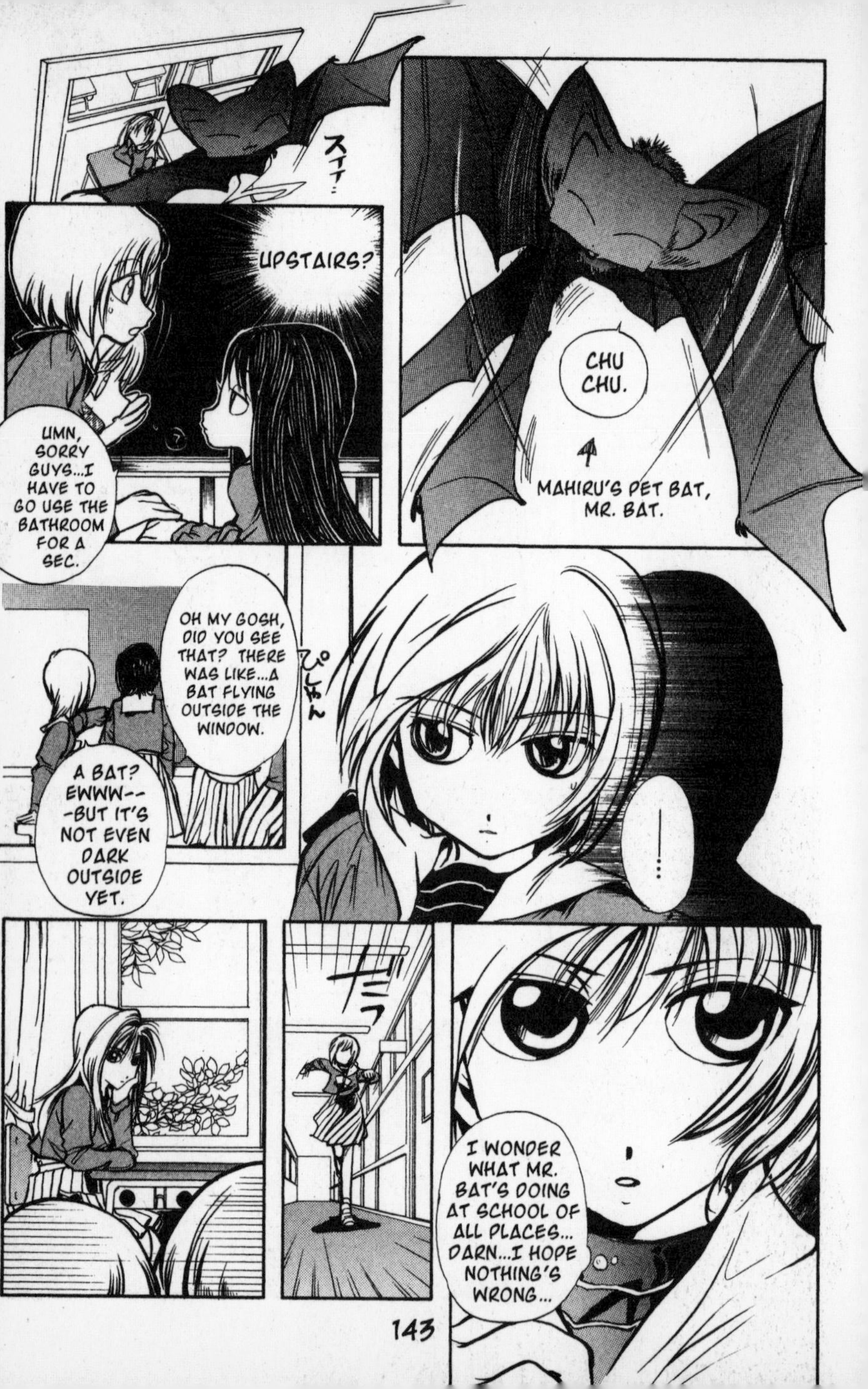
CHU CHU.
MAHIRU'S PET BAT, MR. BAT.
スイイ…
UPSTAIRS?
UMN, SORRY GUYS...I HAVE TO GO USE THE BATHROOM FOR A SEC.
......
ぴしゃん
OH MY GOSH, DID YOU SEE THAT? THERE WAS LIKE...A BAT FLYING OUTSIDE THE WINDOW.
A BAT? EWWW---BUT IT'S NOT EVEN DARK OUTSIDE YET.
I WONDER WHAT MR. BAT'S DOING AT SCHOOL OF ALL PLACES... DARN...I HOPE NOTHING'S WRONG...

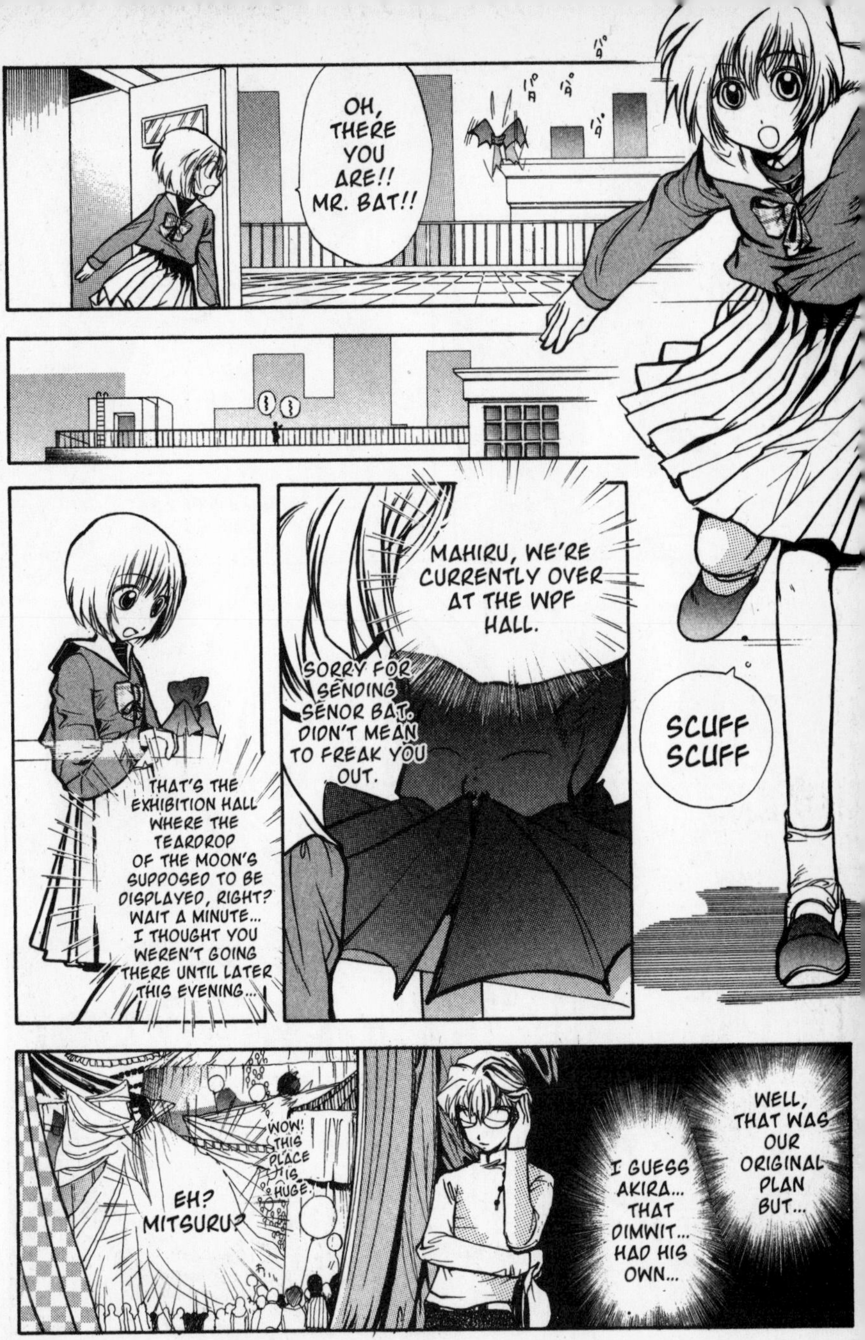
SCUFF SCUFF
OH, THERE YOU ARE!! MR. BAT!!
MAHIRU, WE'RE CURRENTLY OVER AT THE WPF HALL.
SORRY FOR SENDING SENOR BAT. DIDN'T MEAN TO FREAK YOU OUT.
THAT'S THE EXHIBITION HALL WHERE THE TEARDROP OF THE MOON'S SUPPOSED TO BE DISPLAYED, RIGHT? WAIT A MINUTE... I THOUGHT YOU WEREN'T GOING THERE UNTIL LATER THIS EVENING...
WELL, THAT WAS OUR ORIGINAL PLAN BUT...
I GUESS AKIRA... THAT DIMWIT... HAD HIS OWN...
WOW! THIS PLACE IS HUGE.
EH? MITSURU?

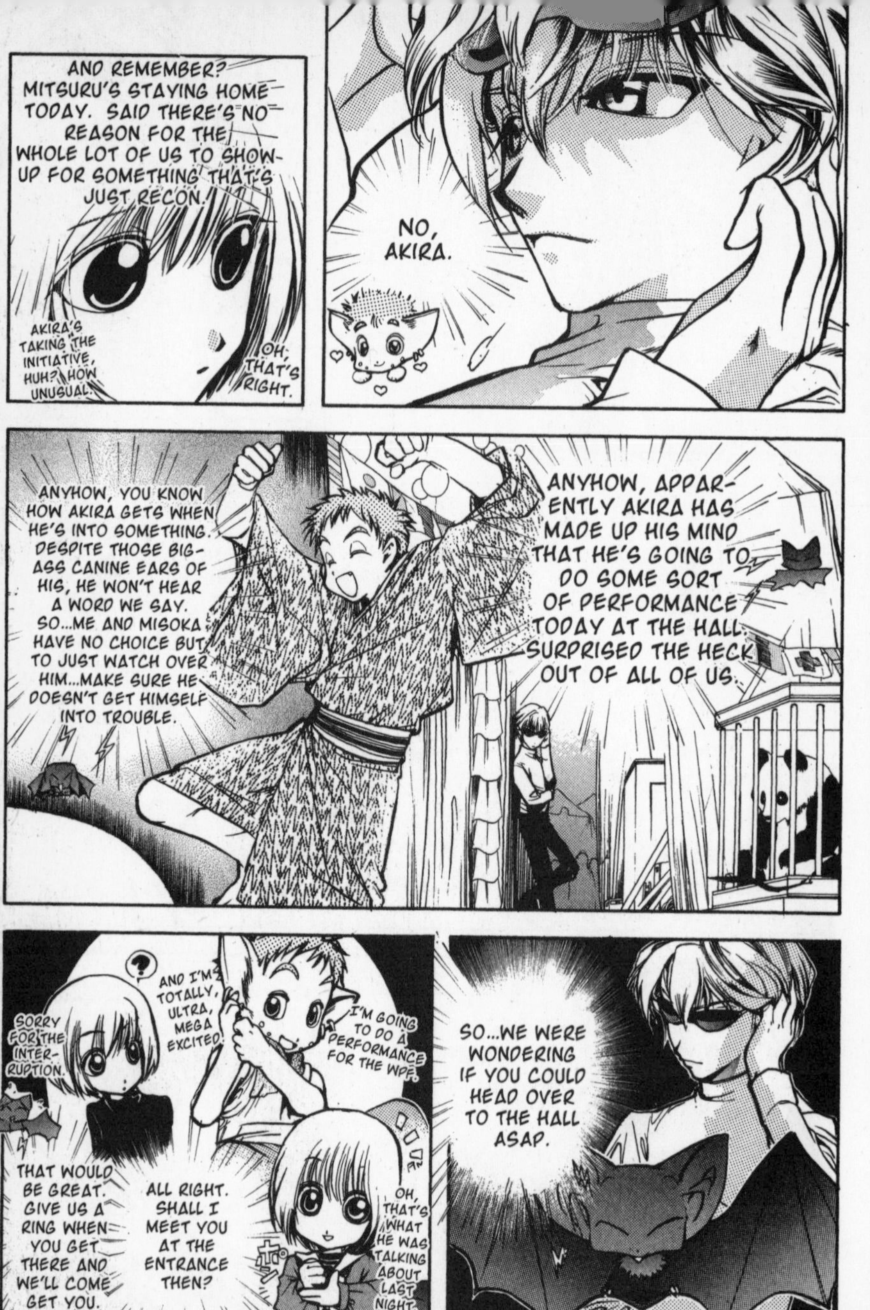
NO, AKIRA.
AND REMEMBER? MITSURU'S STAYING HOME TODAY. SAID THERE'S NO REASON FOR THE WHOLE LOT OF US TO SHOW UP FOR SOMETHING THAT'S JUST RECON.
OH, THAT'S RIGHT.
AKIRA'S TAKING THE INITIATIVE, HUH? HOW UNUSUAL.
ANYHOW, APPARENTLY AKIRA HAS MADE UP HIS MIND THAT HE'S GOING TO DO SOME SORT OF PERFORMANCE TODAY AT THE HALL. SURPRISED THE HECK OUT OF ALL OF US.
ANYHOW, YOU KNOW HOW AKIRA GETS WHEN HE'S INTO SOMETHING. DESPITE THOSE BIG-ASS CANINE EARS OF HIS, HE WON'T HEAR A WORD WE SAY. SO...ME AND MISOKA HAVE NO CHOICE BUT TO JUST WATCH OVER HIM...MAKE SURE HE DOESN'T GET HIMSELF INTO TROUBLE.
SO...WE WERE WONDERING IF YOU COULD HEAD OVER TO THE HALL ASAP.
I'M GOING TO DO A PERFORMANCE FOR THE WPF.
AND I'M TOTALLY, ULTRA, MEGA EXCITED.
SORRY FOR THE INTERRUPTION.
OH, THAT'S WHAT HE WAS TALKING ABOUT LAST NIGHT.
ALL RIGHT. SHALL I MEET YOU AT THE ENTRANCE THEN?
THAT WOULD BE GREAT. GIVE US A RING WHEN YOU GET THERE AND WE'LL COME GET YOU.

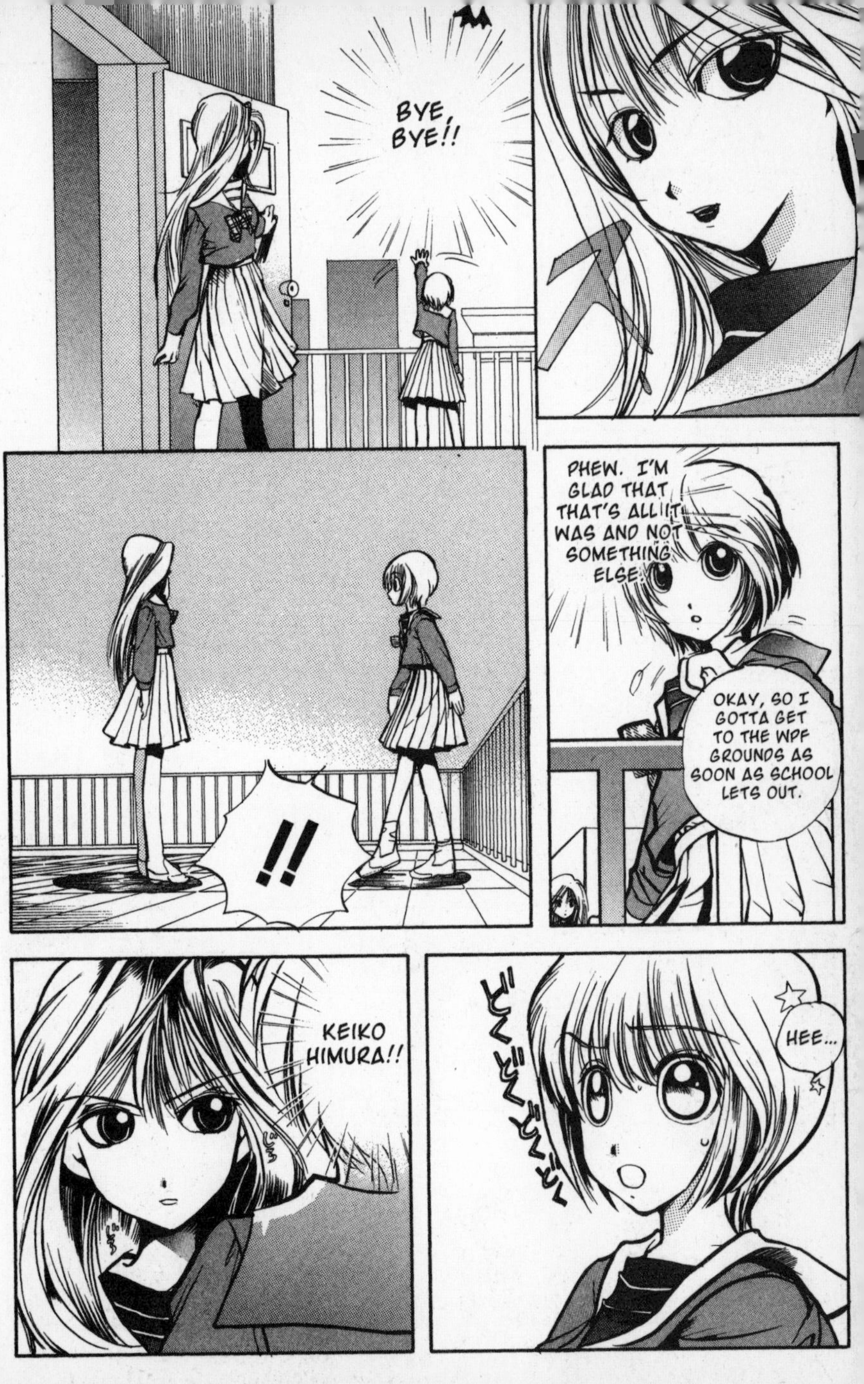
BYE BYE!!
PHEW. I'M GLAD THAT THAT'S ALL IT WAS AND NOT SOMETHING ELSE.
OKAY, SO I GOTTA GET TO THE WPF GROUNDS AS SOON AS SCHOOL LETS OUT.
!!
HEE...
KEIKO HIMURA!!

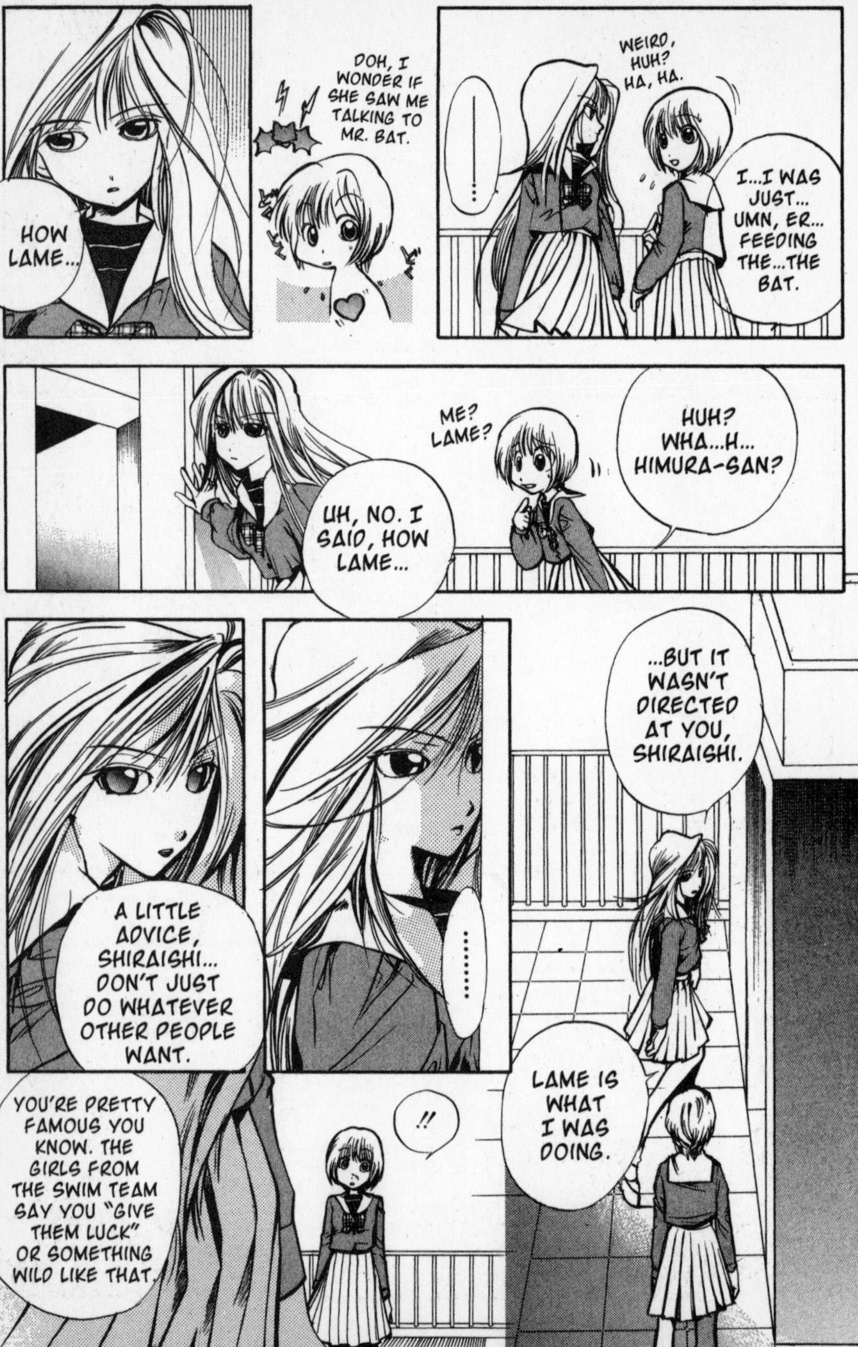
I...I WAS JUST... UMN, ER... FEEDING THE...THE BAT.
WEIRD, HUH? HA, HA.
!......
OOH, I WONDER IF SHE SAW ME TALKING TO MR. BAT.
HOW LAME...
HUH? WHA...H... HIMURA-SAN?
ME? LAME?
UH, NO. I SAID, HOW LAME...
...BUT IT WASN'T DIRECTED AT YOU, SHIRAISHI.
....
A LITTLE ADVICE, SHIRAISHI... DON'T JUST DO WHATEVER OTHER PEOPLE WANT.
LAME IS WHAT I WAS DOING.
!!
YOU'RE PRETTY FAMOUS YOU KNOW. THE GIRLS FROM THE SWIM TEAM SAY YOU "GIVE THEM LUCK" OR SOMETHING WILD LIKE THAT.

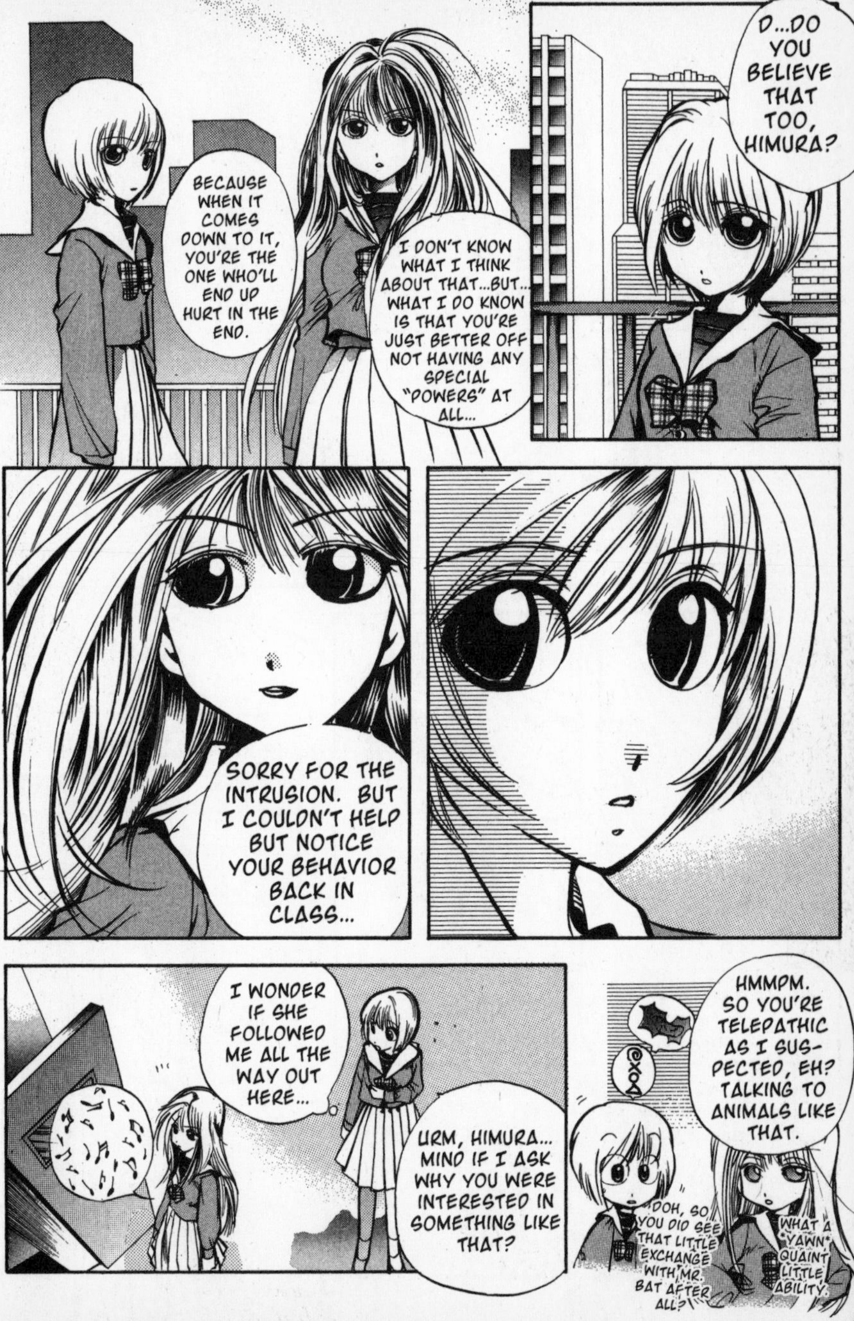
D...DO YOU BELIEVE THAT TOO, HIMURA?
I DON'T KNOW WHAT I THINK ABOUT THAT...BUT... WHAT I DO KNOW IS THAT YOU'RE JUST BETTER OFF NOT HAVING ANY SPECIAL "POWERS" AT ALL...
BECAUSE WHEN IT COMES DOWN TO IT, YOU'RE THE ONE WHO'LL END UP HURT IN THE END.
SORRY FOR THE INTRUSION. BUT I COULDN'T HELP BUT NOTICE YOUR BEHAVIOR BACK IN CLASS...
HMMPM. SO YOU'RE TELEPATHIC AS I SUSPECTED, EH? TALKING TO ANIMALS LIKE THAT.
WHAT A *YAWN* QUAINT LITTLE ABILITY.
@XO
DOH, SO YOU DID SEE THAT LITTLE EXCHANGE WITH MR. BAT AFTER ALL?
I WONDER IF SHE FOLLOWED ME ALL THE WAY OUT HERE...
URM, HIMURA... MIND IF I ASK WHY YOU WERE INTERESTED IN SOMETHING LIKE THAT?

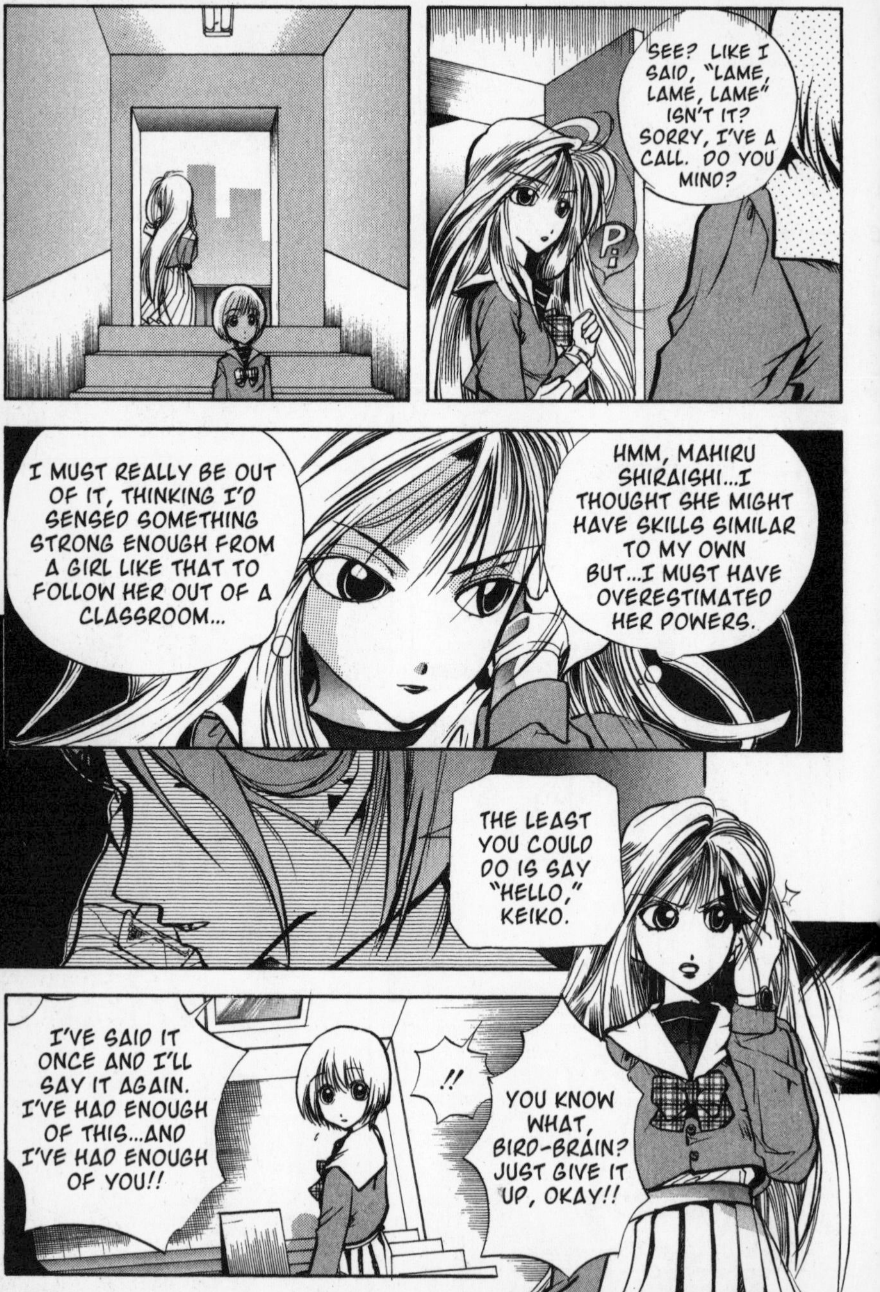
SEE? LIKE I SAID, "LAME, LAME, LAME" ISN'T IT? SORRY, I'VE A CALL. DO YOU MIND?
P!
HMM, MAHIRU SHIRAISHI...I THOUGHT SHE MIGHT HAVE SKILLS SIMILAR TO MY OWN BUT...I MUST HAVE OVERESTIMATED HER POWERS.
I MUST REALLY BE OUT OF IT, THINKING I'D SENSED SOMETHING STRONG ENOUGH FROM A GIRL LIKE THAT TO FOLLOW HER OUT OF A CLASSROOM...
THE LEAST YOU COULD DO IS SAY "HELLO," KEIKO.
YOU KNOW WHAT, BIRD-BRAIN? JUST GIVE IT UP, OKAY!!
!!
I'VE SAID IT ONCE AND I'LL SAY IT AGAIN. I'VE HAD ENOUGH OF THIS...AND I'VE HAD ENOUGH OF YOU!!

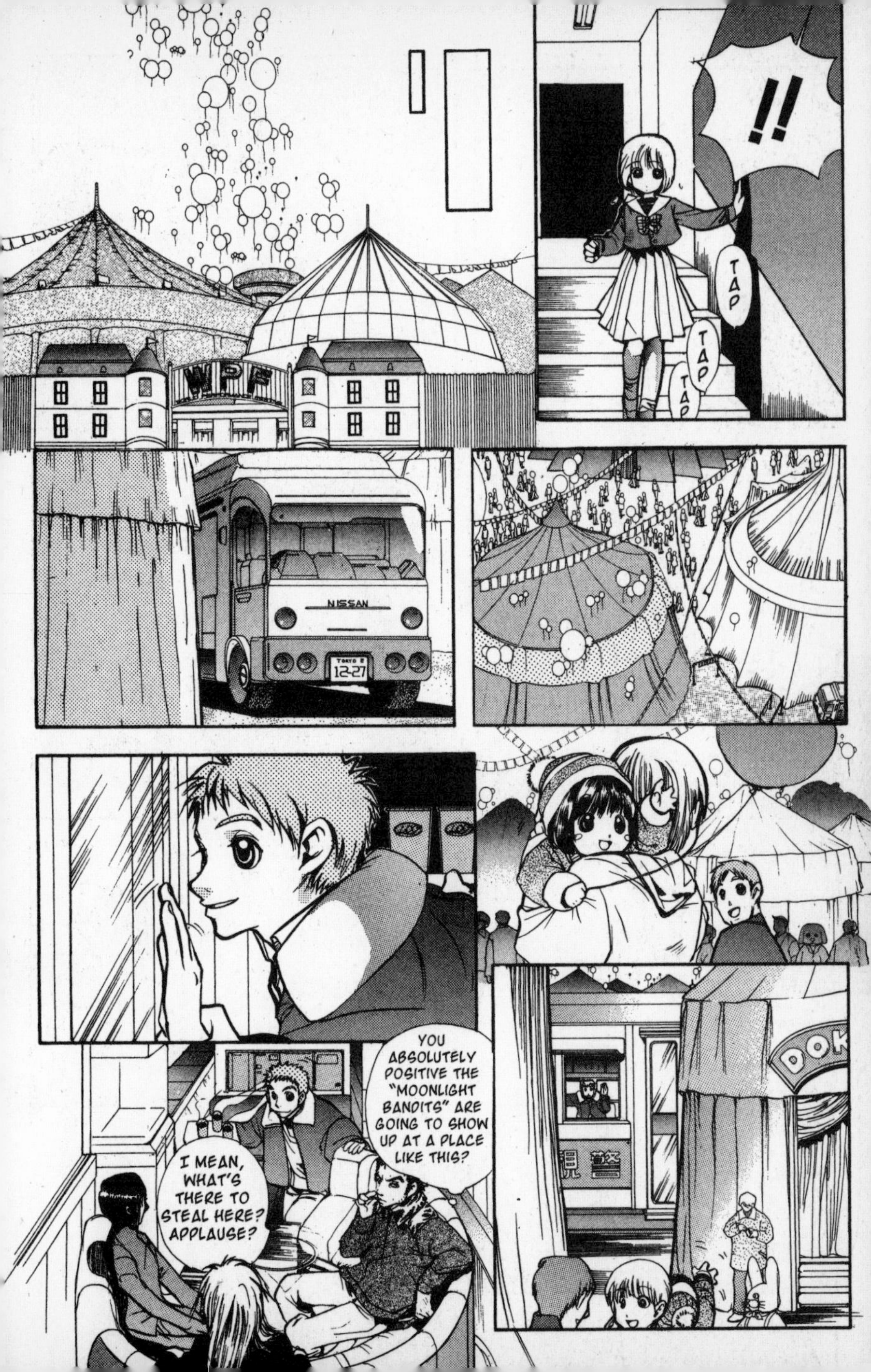

!!
TAP
TAP
TAP
TAP
WPF
NISSAN
12-27
DOK
YOU ABSOLUTELY POSITIVE THE "MOONLIGHT BANDITS" ARE GOING TO SHOW UP AT A PLACE LIKE THIS?
I MEAN, WHAT'S THERE TO STEAL HERE? APPLAUSE?

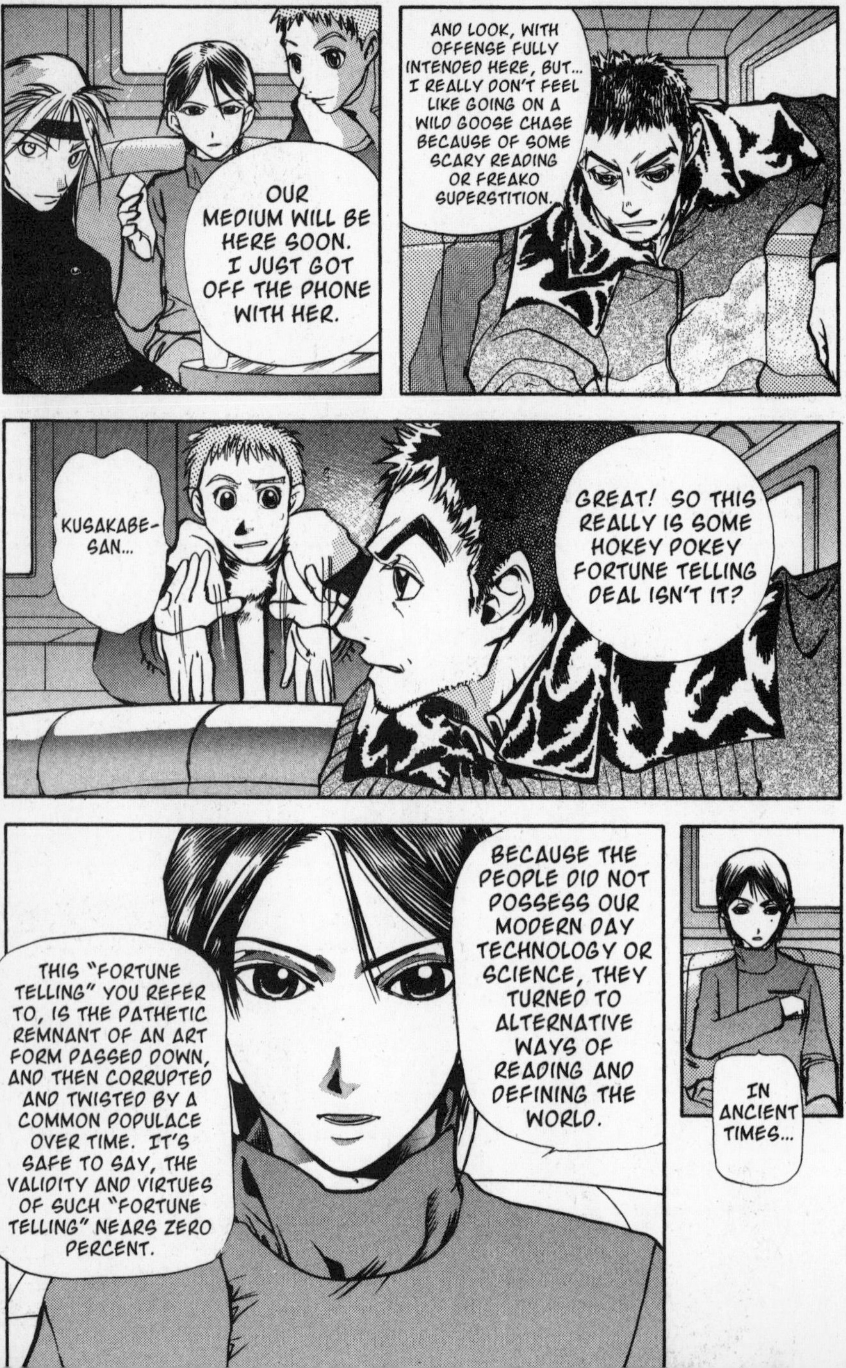
AND LOOK, WITH OFFENSE FULLY INTENDED HERE, BUT... I REALLY DON'T FEEL LIKE GOING ON A WILD GOOSE CHASE BECAUSE OF SOME SCARY READING OR FREAKO SUPERSTITION.
OUR MEDIUM WILL BE HERE SOON. I JUST GOT OFF THE PHONE WITH HER.
GREAT! SO THIS REALLY IS SOME HOKEY POKEY FORTUNE TELLING DEAL ISN'T IT?
KUSAKABE-SAN...
IN ANCIENT TIMES...
BECAUSE THE PEOPLE DID NOT POSSESS OUR MODERN DAY TECHNOLOGY OR SCIENCE, THEY TURNED TO ALTERNATIVE WAYS OF READING AND DEFINING THE WORLD.
THIS "FORTUNE TELLING" YOU REFER TO, IS THE PATHETIC REMNANT OF AN ART FORM PASSED DOWN, AND THEN CORRUPTED AND TWISTED BY A COMMON POPULACE OVER TIME. IT'S SAFE TO SAY, THE VALIDITY AND VIRTUES OF SUCH "FORTUNE TELLING" NEARS ZERO PERCENT.

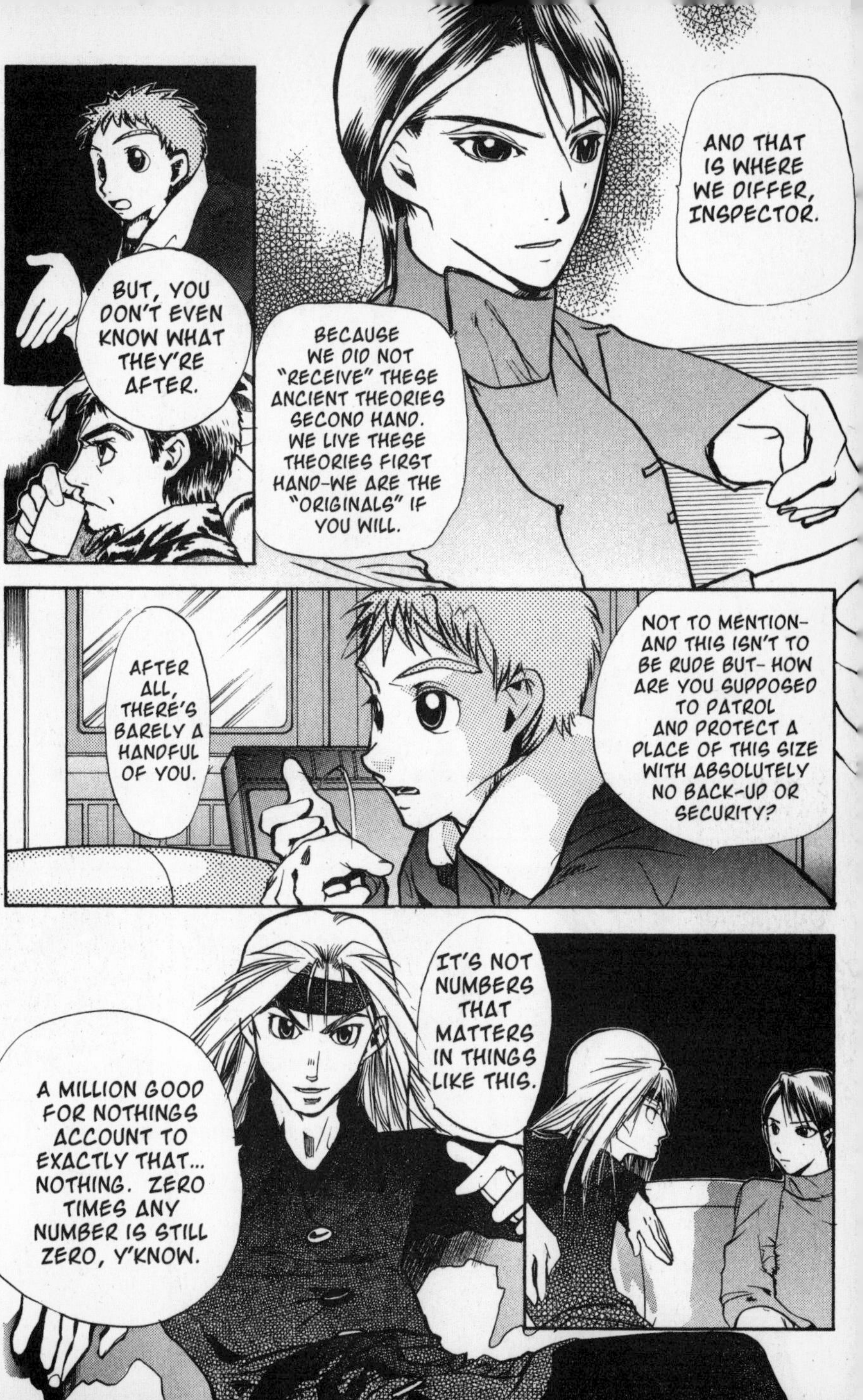
AND THAT IS WHERE WE DIFFER, INSPECTOR.
BECAUSE WE DID NOT "RECEIVE" THESE ANCIENT THEORIES SECOND HAND. WE LIVE THESE THEORIES FIRST HAND–WE ARE THE "ORIGINALS" IF YOU WILL.
BUT, YOU DON'T EVEN KNOW WHAT THEY'RE AFTER.
NOT TO MENTION– AND THIS ISN'T TO BE RUDE BUT– HOW ARE YOU SUPPOSED TO PATROL AND PROTECT A PLACE OF THIS SIZE WITH ABSOLUTELY NO BACK-UP OR SECURITY?
AFTER ALL, THERE'S BARELY A HANDFUL OF YOU.
IT'S NOT NUMBERS THAT MATTERS IN THINGS LIKE THIS.
A MILLION GOOD FOR NOTHINGS ACCOUNT TO EXACTLY THAT... NOTHING. ZERO TIMES ANY NUMBER IS STILL ZERO, Y'KNOW.

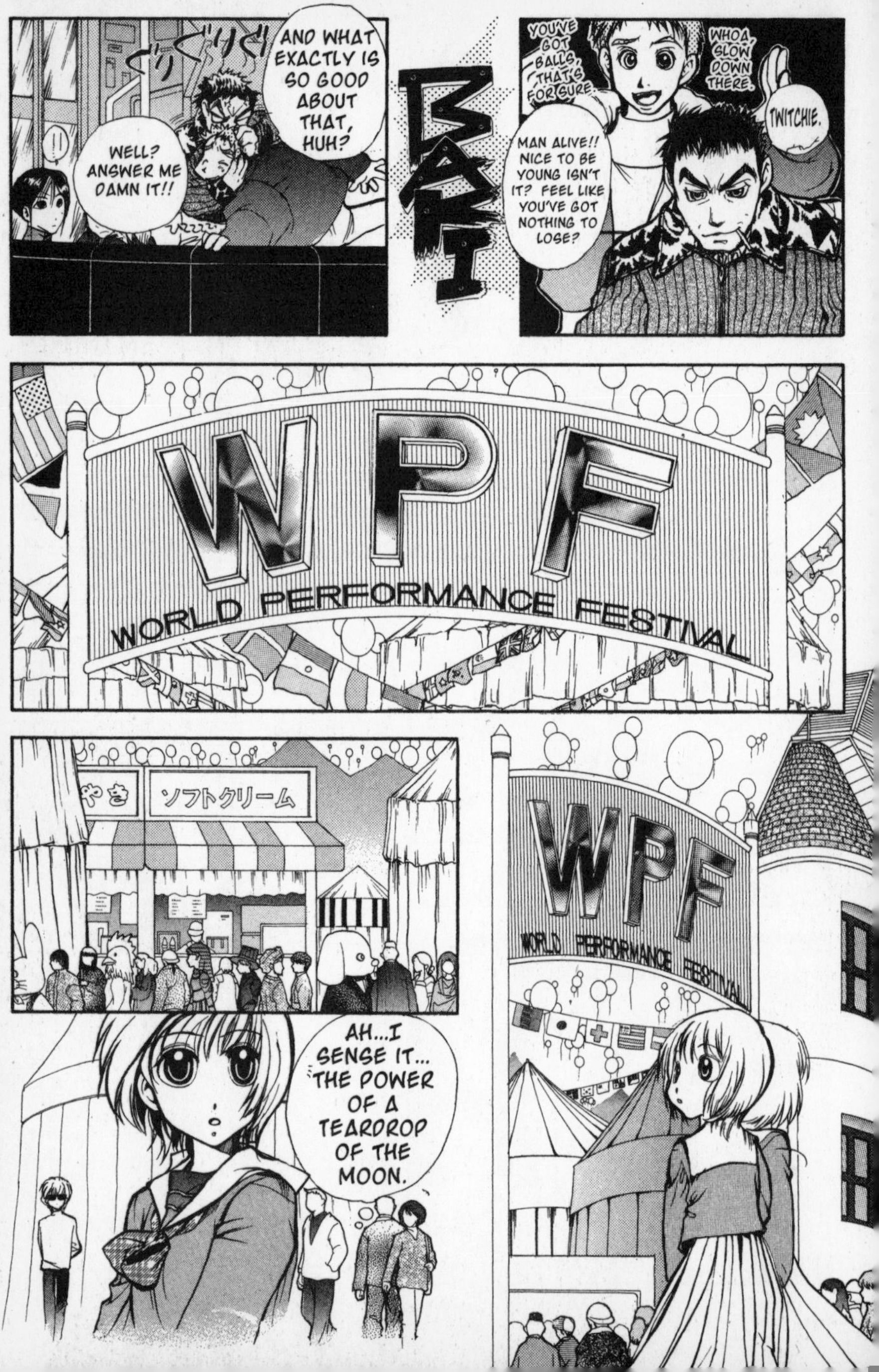
WHOA, SLOW DOWN THERE.
TWITCHIE.
YOU'VE GOT BALLS, THAT'S FOR SURE.
MAN ALIVE!! NICE TO BE YOUNG ISN'T IT? FEEL LIKE YOU'VE GOT NOTHING TO LOSE?
BAKI
AND WHAT EXACTLY IS SO GOOD ABOUT THAT, HUH?
ぐりぐりぐ
WELL? ANSWER ME DAMN IT!!
!!
WPF
WORLD PERFORMANCE FESTIVAL
WPF
WORLD PERFORMANCE FESTIVAL
やき
ソフトクリーム
AH...I SENSE IT... THE POWER OF A TEARDROP OF THE MOON.

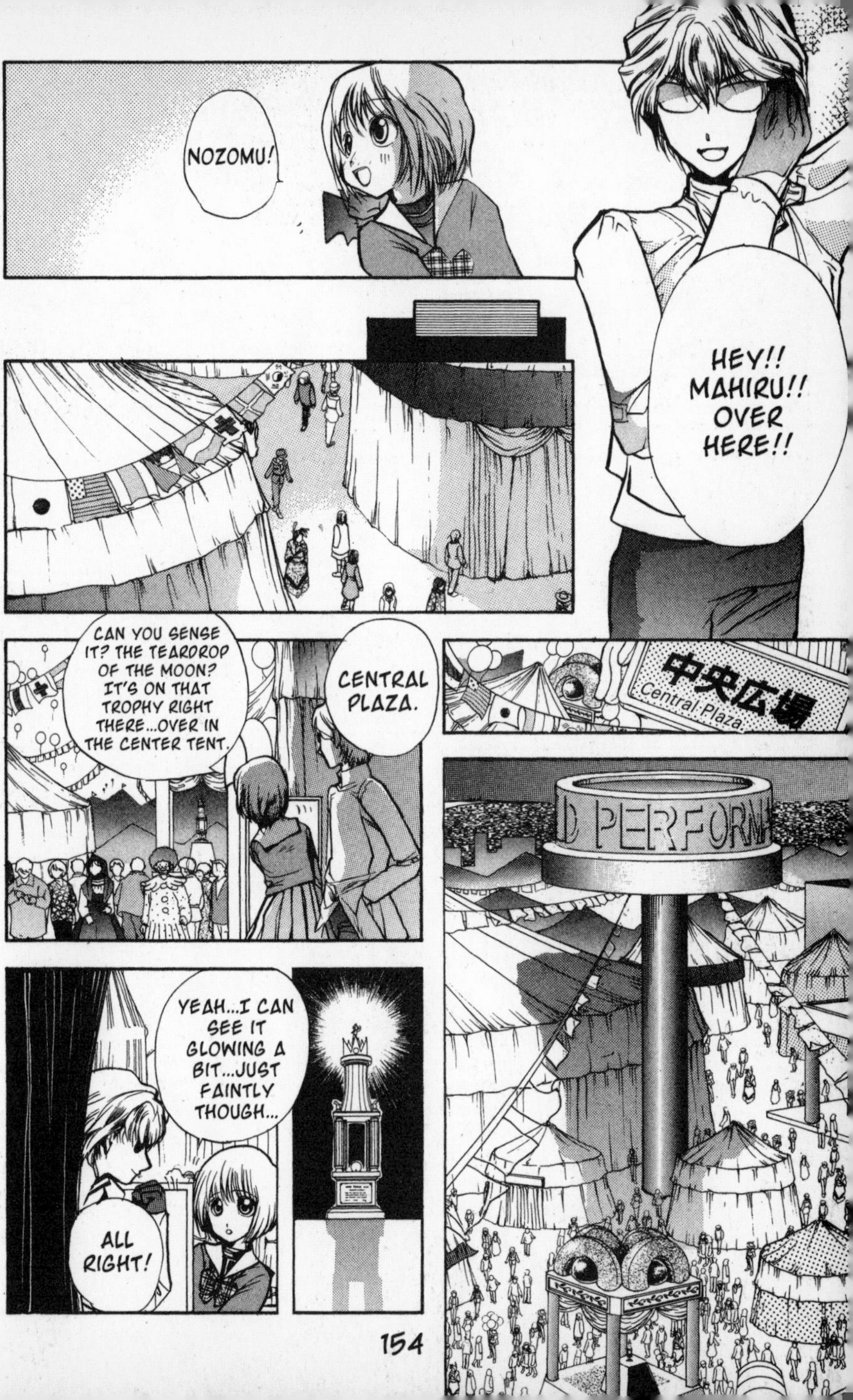
HEY!! MAHIRU!! OVER HERE!!
NOZOMU!
中央広場
Central Plaza
D PERFORM
CENTRAL PLAZA.
CAN YOU SENSE IT? THE TEARDROP OF THE MOON? IT'S ON THAT TROPHY RIGHT THERE...OVER IN THE CENTER TENT.
YEAH...I CAN SEE IT GLOWING A BIT...JUST FAINTLY THOUGH...
ALL RIGHT!

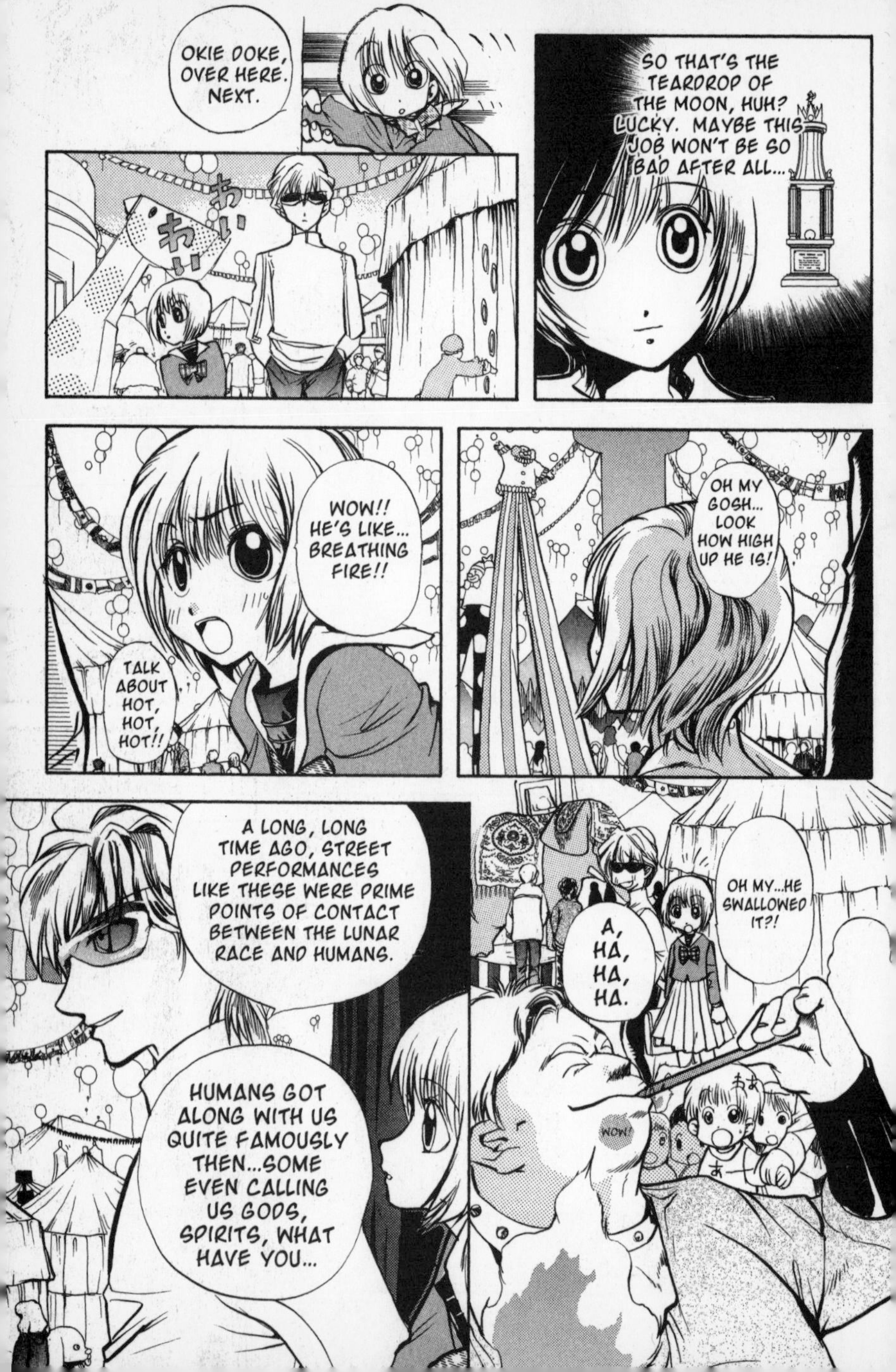
SO THAT'S THE TEARDROP OF THE MOON, HUH? LUCKY. MAYBE THIS JOB WON'T BE SO BAD AFTER ALL...
OKIE DOKE, OVER HERE. NEXT.
OH MY GOSH... LOOK HOW HIGH UP HE IS!
WOW!! HE'S LIKE... BREATHING FIRE!!
TALK ABOUT HOT, HOT, HOT!!
OH MY...HE SWALLOWED IT?!
A, HA, HA, HA.
WOW!
A LONG, LONG TIME AGO, STREET PERFORMANCES LIKE THESE WERE PRIME POINTS OF CONTACT BETWEEN THE LUNAR RACE AND HUMANS.
HUMANS GOT ALONG WITH US QUITE FAMOUSLY THEN...SOME EVEN CALLING US GODS, SPIRITS, WHAT HAVE YOU...

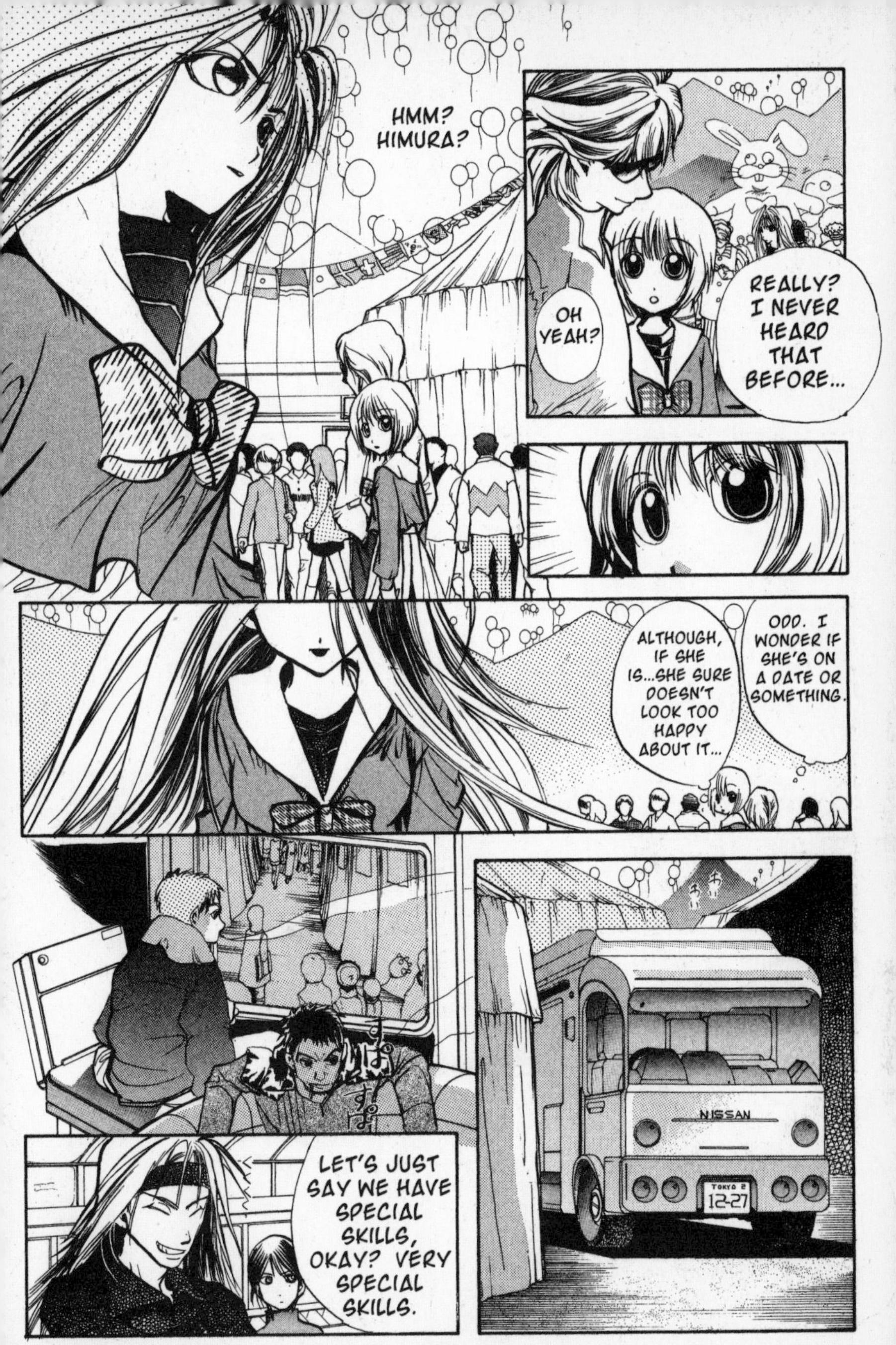
REALLY? I NEVER HEARD THAT BEFORE...
OH YEAH?
HMM? HIMURA?
ODD. I WONDER IF SHE'S ON A DATE OR SOMETHING.
ALTHOUGH, IF SHE IS...SHE SURE DOESN'T LOOK TOO HAPPY ABOUT IT...
NISSAN
TOKYO 2 12-27
LET'S JUST SAY WE HAVE SPECIAL SKILLS, OKAY? VERY SPECIAL SKILLS.

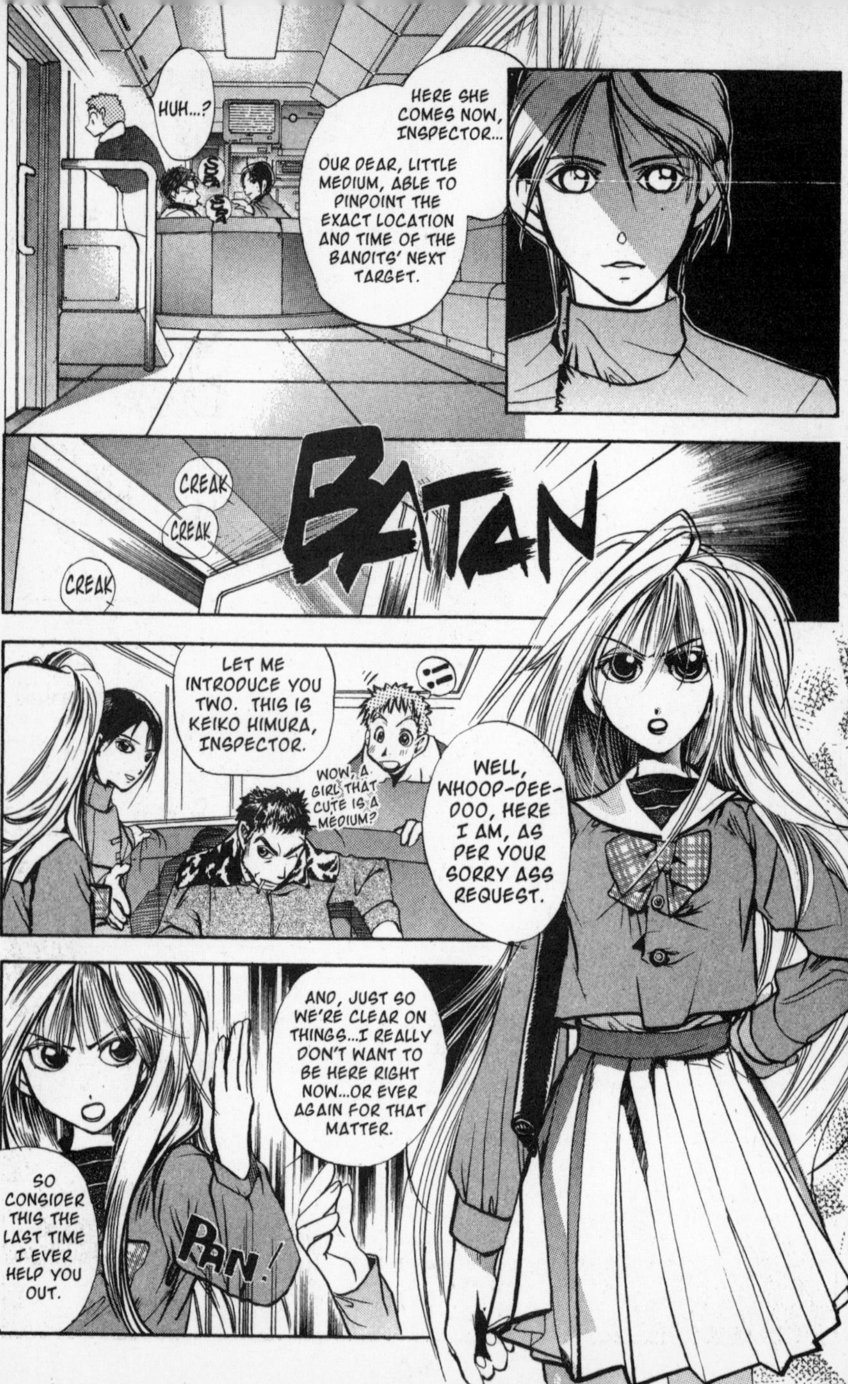
HERE SHE COMES NOW, INSPECTOR...
OUR DEAR, LITTLE MEDIUM, ABLE TO PINPOINT THE EXACT LOCATION AND TIME OF THE BANDITS' NEXT TARGET.
HUH...?
BATAN
CREAK
CREAK
CREAK
WELL, WHOOP-DEE-DOO, HERE I AM, AS PER YOUR SORRY ASS REQUEST.
LET ME INTRODUCE YOU TWO. THIS IS KEIKO HIMURA, INSPECTOR.
WOW, A GIRL THAT CUTE IS A MEDIUM?
AND, JUST SO WE'RE CLEAR ON THINGS...I REALLY DON'T WANT TO BE HERE RIGHT NOW...OR EVER AGAIN FOR THAT MATTER.
PAN!
SO CONSIDER THIS THE LAST TIME I EVER HELP YOU OUT.

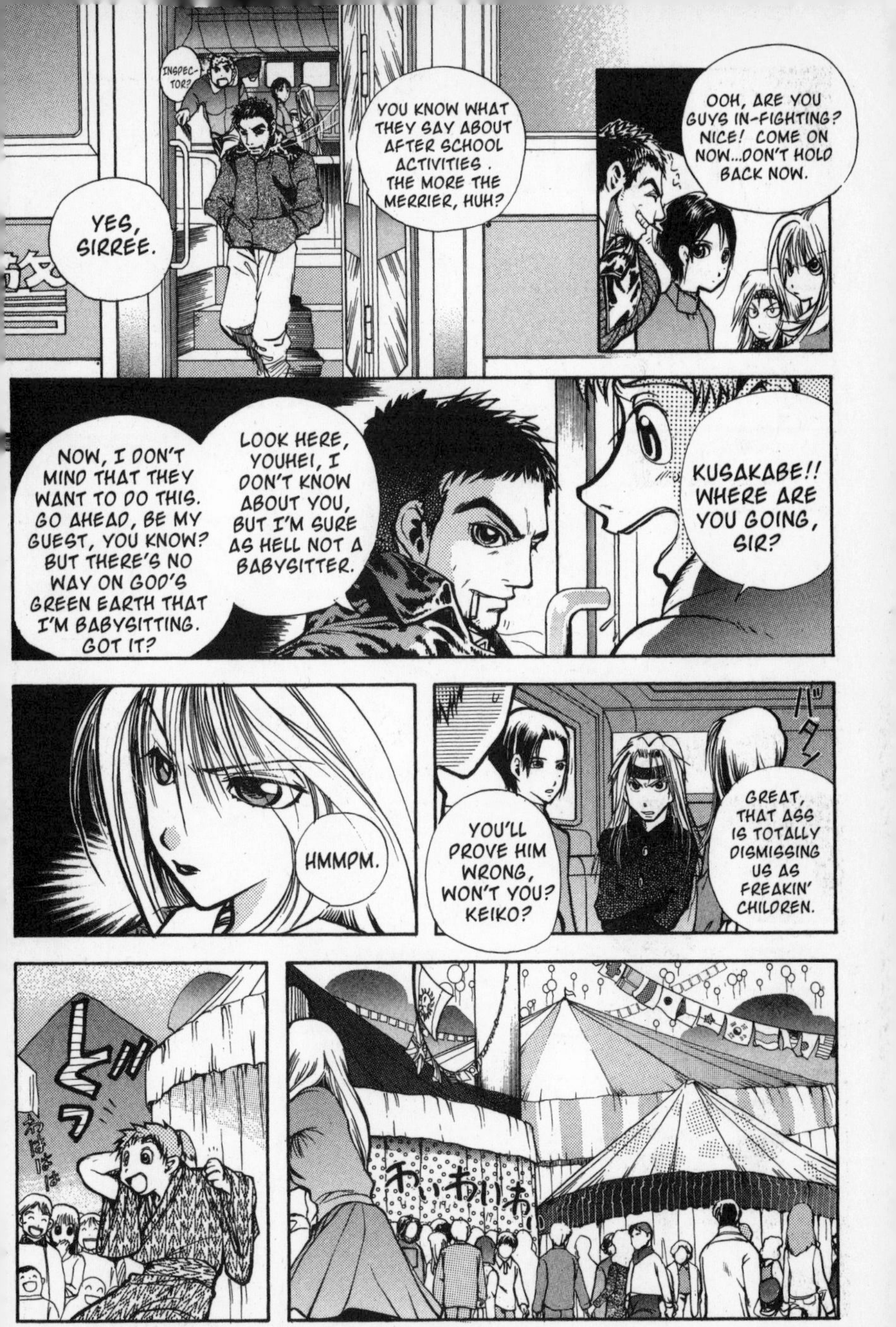
OOH, ARE YOU GUYS IN-FIGHTING? NICE! COME ON NOW...DON'T HOLD BACK NOW.
YOU KNOW WHAT THEY SAY ABOUT AFTER SCHOOL ACTIVITIES . THE MORE THE MERRIER, HUH?
INSPEC-TOR?
YES, SIRREE.
KUSAKABE!! WHERE ARE YOU GOING, SIR?
LOOK HERE, YOUHEI, I DON'T KNOW ABOUT YOU, BUT I'M SURE AS HELL NOT A BABYSITTER.
NOW, I DON'T MIND THAT THEY WANT TO DO THIS. GO AHEAD, BE MY GUEST, YOU KNOW? BUT THERE'S NO WAY ON GOD'S GREEN EARTH THAT I'M BABYSITTING. GOT IT?
GREAT, THAT ASS IS TOTALLY DISMISSING US AS FREAKIN' CHILDREN.
YOU'LL PROVE HIM WRONG, WON'T YOU? KEIKO?
HMMPM.

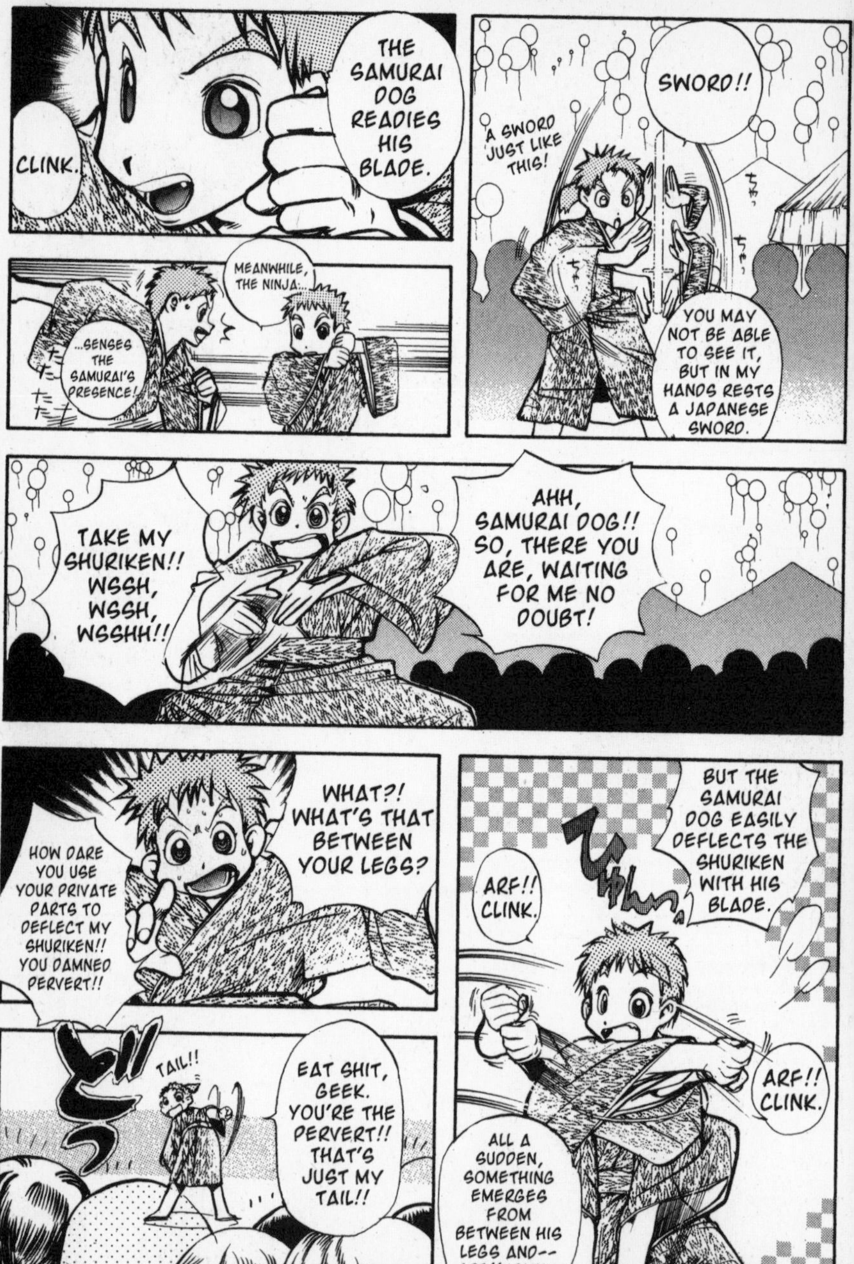
SWORD!!
A SWORD JUST LIKE THIS!
YOU MAY NOT BE ABLE TO SEE IT, BUT IN MY HANDS RESTS A JAPANESE SWORD.
THE SAMURAI DOG READIES HIS BLADE.
CLINK.
MEANWHILE, THE NINJA...
...SENSES THE SAMURAI'S PRESENCE!
AHH, SAMURAI DOG!! SO, THERE YOU ARE, WAITING FOR ME NO DOUBT!
TAKE MY SHURIKEN!! WSSH, WSSH, WSSHH!!
BUT THE SAMURAI DOG EASILY DEFLECTS THE SHURIKEN WITH HIS BLADE.
ARF!! CLINK.
ARF!! CLINK.
ALL A SUDDEN, SOMETHING EMERGES FROM BETWEEN HIS LEGS AND-- ARF!! CLINK.
WHAT?! WHAT'S THAT BETWEEN YOUR LEGS?
HOW DARE YOU USE YOUR PRIVATE PARTS TO DEFLECT MY SHURIKEN!! YOU DAMNED PERVERT!!
TAIL!!
EAT SHIT, GEEK. YOU'RE THE PERVERT!! THAT'S JUST MY TAIL!!

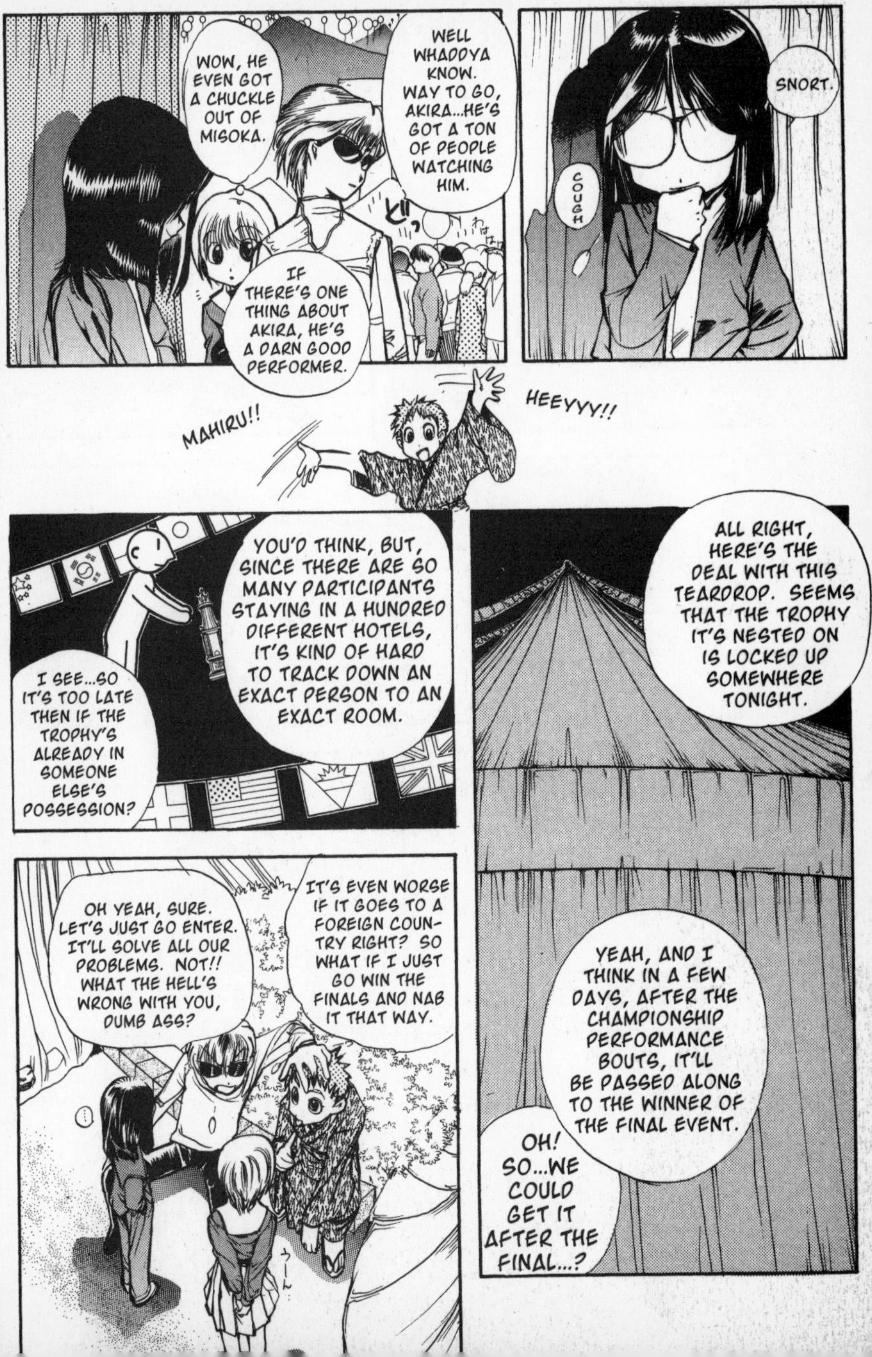
SNORT.
COUGH
WELL WHADDYA KNOW. WAY TO GO, AKIRA...HE'S GOT A TON OF PEOPLE WATCHING HIM.
WOW, HE EVEN GOT A CHUCKLE OUT OF MISOKA.
IF THERE'S ONE THING ABOUT AKIRA, HE'S A DARN GOOD PERFORMER.
HEEYYY!!
MAHIRU!!
ALL RIGHT, HERE'S THE DEAL WITH THIS TEARDROP. SEEMS THAT THE TROPHY IT'S NESTED ON IS LOCKED UP SOMEWHERE TONIGHT.
YEAH, AND I THINK IN A FEW DAYS, AFTER THE CHAMPIONSHIP PERFORMANCE BOUTS, IT'LL BE PASSED ALONG TO THE WINNER OF THE FINAL EVENT.
OH! SO...WE COULD GET IT AFTER THE FINAL...?
YOU'D THINK, BUT, SINCE THERE ARE SO MANY PARTICIPANTS STAYING IN A HUNDRED DIFFERENT HOTELS, IT'S KIND OF HARD TO TRACK DOWN AN EXACT PERSON TO AN EXACT ROOM.
I SEE...SO IT'S TOO LATE THEN IF THE TROPHY'S ALREADY IN SOMEONE ELSE'S POSSESSION?
IT'S EVEN WORSE IF IT GOES TO A FOREIGN COUNTRY RIGHT? SO WHAT IF I JUST GO WIN THE FINALS AND NAB IT THAT WAY.
OH YEAH, SURE. LET'S JUST GO ENTER. IT'LL SOLVE ALL OUR PROBLEMS. NOT!! WHAT THE HELL'S WRONG WITH YOU, DUMB ASS?
...
うーん

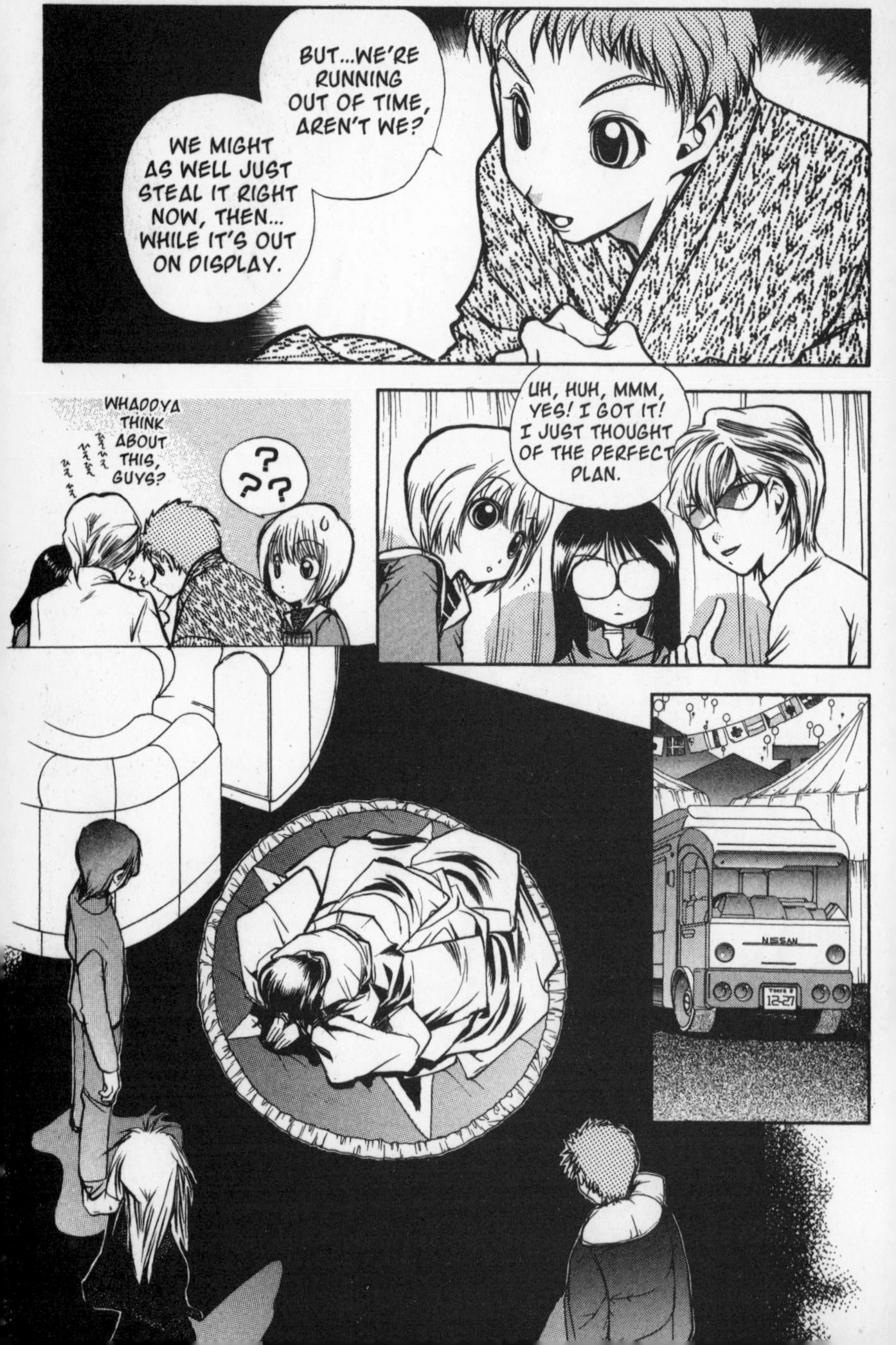
BUT...WE'RE RUNNING OUT OF TIME, AREN'T WE?
WE MIGHT AS WELL JUST STEAL IT RIGHT NOW, THEN... WHILE IT'S OUT ON DISPLAY.
UH, HUH, MMM, YES! I GOT IT! I JUST THOUGHT OF THE PERFECT PLAN.
WHADDOYA THINK ABOUT THIS, GUYS?
???
NISSAN

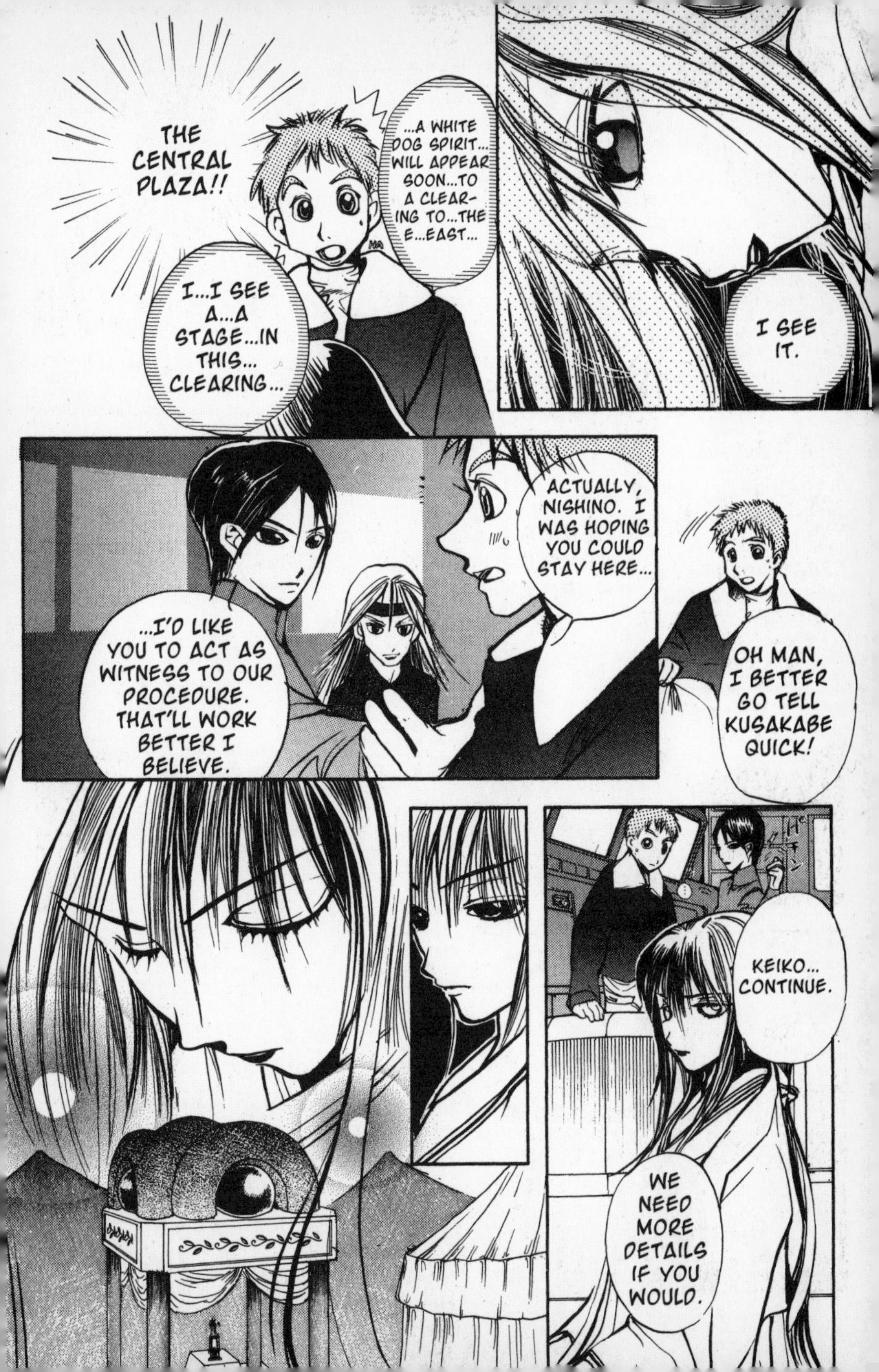
I SEE IT.
...A WHITE DOG SPIRIT... WILL APPEAR SOON...TO A CLEARING TO...THE E...EAST...
I...I SEE A...A STAGE...IN THIS... CLEARING...
THE CENTRAL PLAZA!!
OH MAN, I BETTER GO TELL KUSAKABE QUICK!
ACTUALLY, NISHINO. I WAS HOPING YOU COULD STAY HERE...
...I'D LIKE YOU TO ACT AS WITNESS TO OUR PROCEDURE. THAT'LL WORK BETTER I BELIEVE.
KEIKO... CONTINUE.
WE NEED MORE DETAILS IF YOU WOULD.

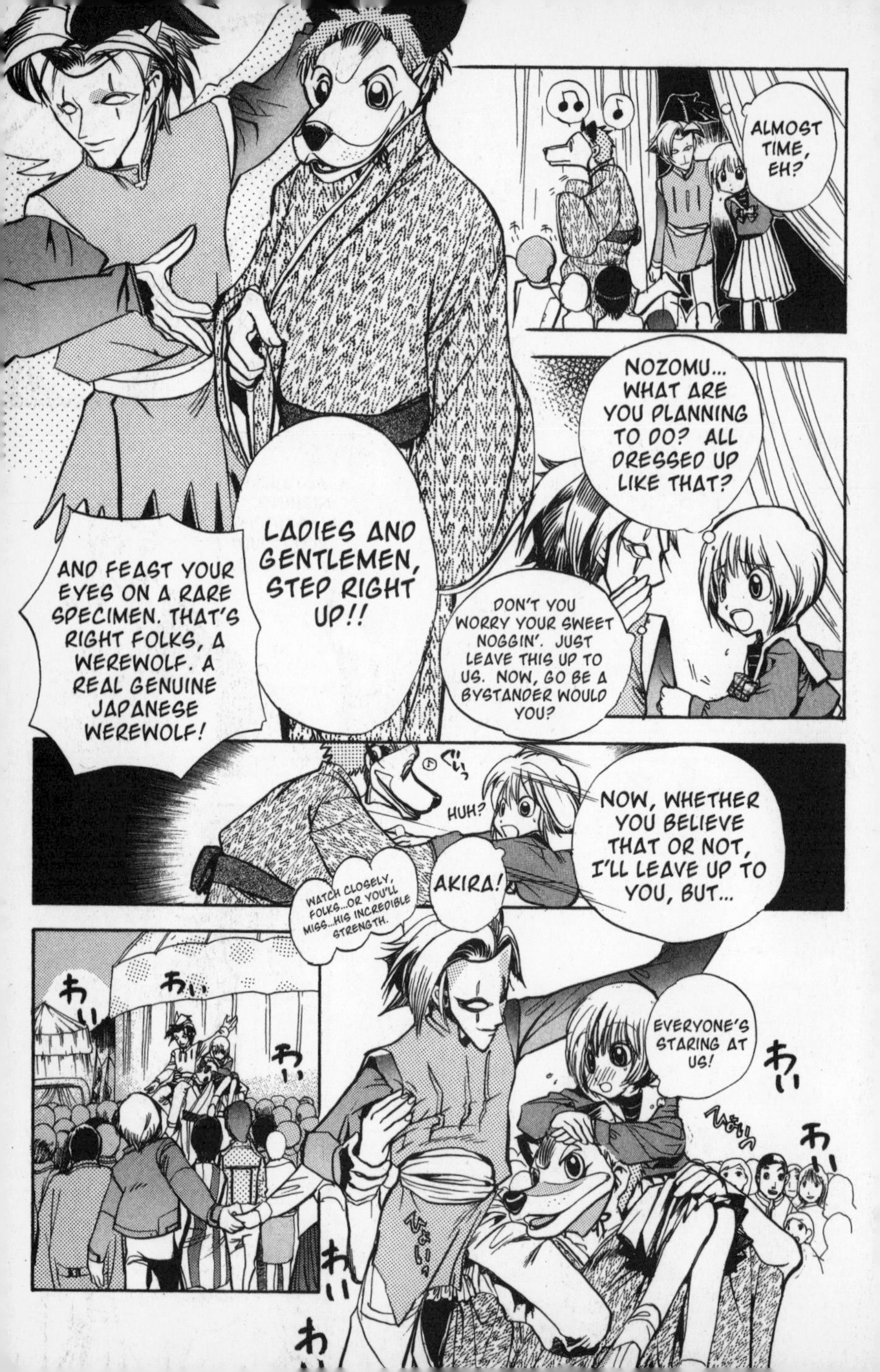
ALMOST TIME, EH?
NOZOMU... WHAT ARE YOU PLANNING TO DO? ALL DRESSED UP LIKE THAT?
DON'T YOU WORRY YOUR SWEET NOGGIN'. JUST LEAVE THIS UP TO US. NOW, GO BE A BYSTANDER WOULD YOU?
LADIES AND GENTLEMEN, STEP RIGHT UP!!
AND FEAST YOUR EYES ON A RARE SPECIMEN. THAT'S RIGHT FOLKS, A WEREWOLF. A REAL GENUINE JAPANESE WEREWOLF!
NOW, WHETHER YOU BELIEVE THAT OR NOT, I'LL LEAVE UP TO YOU, BUT...
HUH?
AKIRA!
WATCH CLOSELY, FOLKS...OR YOU'LL MISS...HIS INCREDIBLE STRENGTH.
EVERYONE'S STARING AT US!
わい
わい
わい
わい
わい

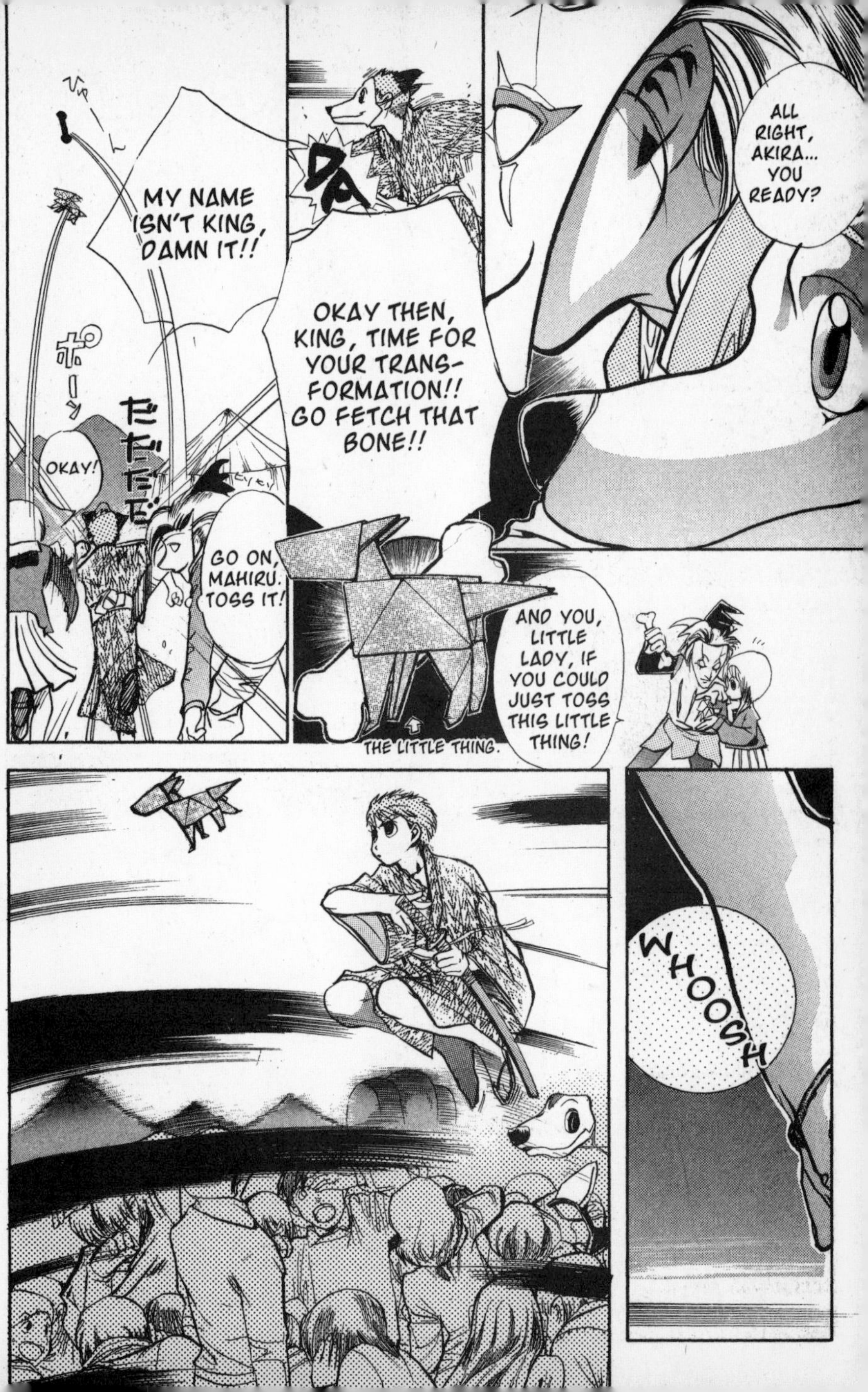
ALL RIGHT, AKIRA... YOU READY?
DA
OKAY THEN, KING, TIME FOR YOUR TRANS-FORMATION!! GO FETCH THAT BONE!!
AND YOU, LITTLE LADY, IF YOU COULD JUST TOSS THIS LITTLE THING!
THE LITTLE THING.
MY NAME ISN'T KING, DAMN IT!!
OKAY!
GO ON, MAHIRU. TOSS IT!
WHOOSH

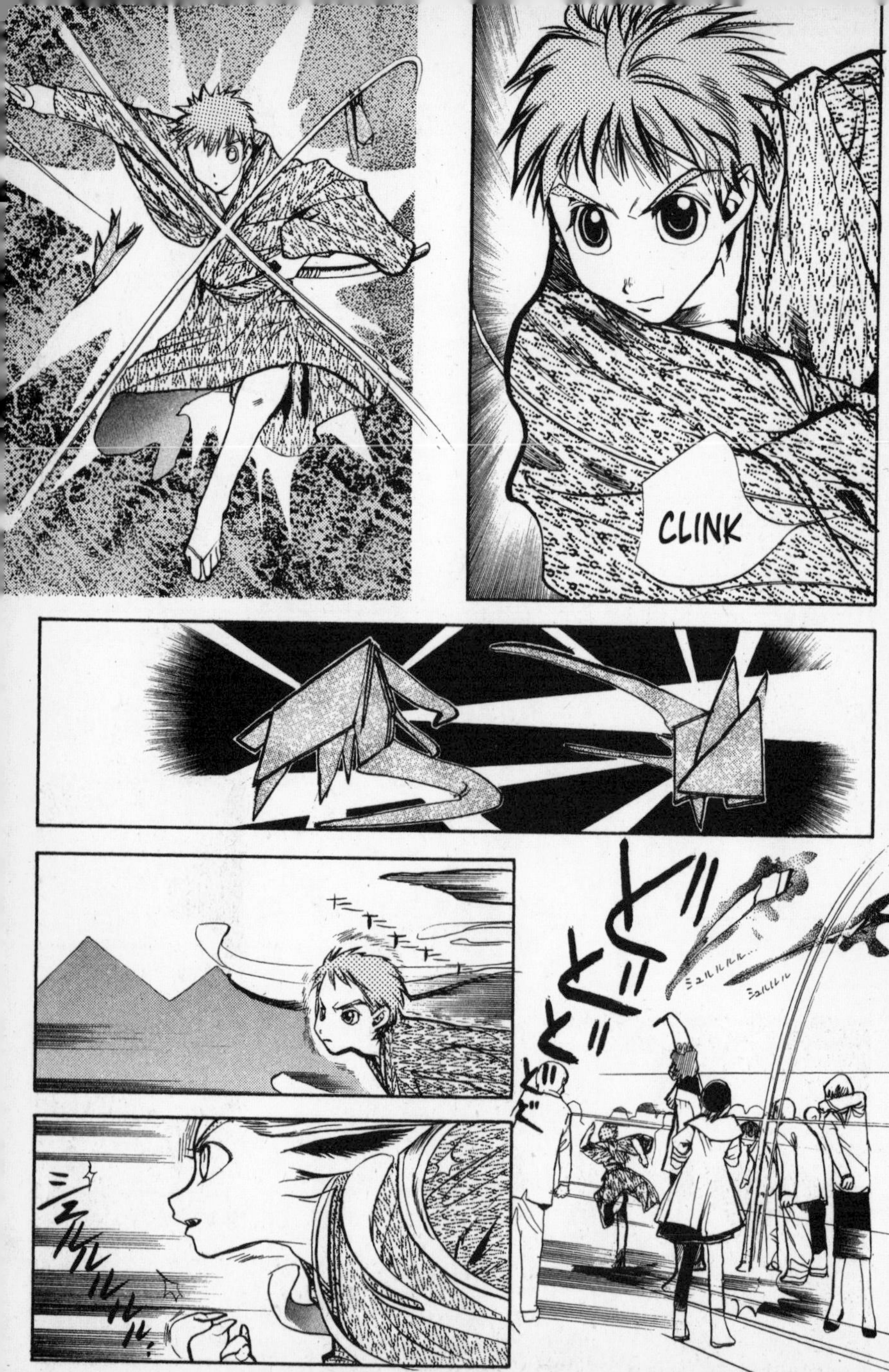
CLINK
どどどど
シュルルルル...
シュルルル
シュルルルルッ

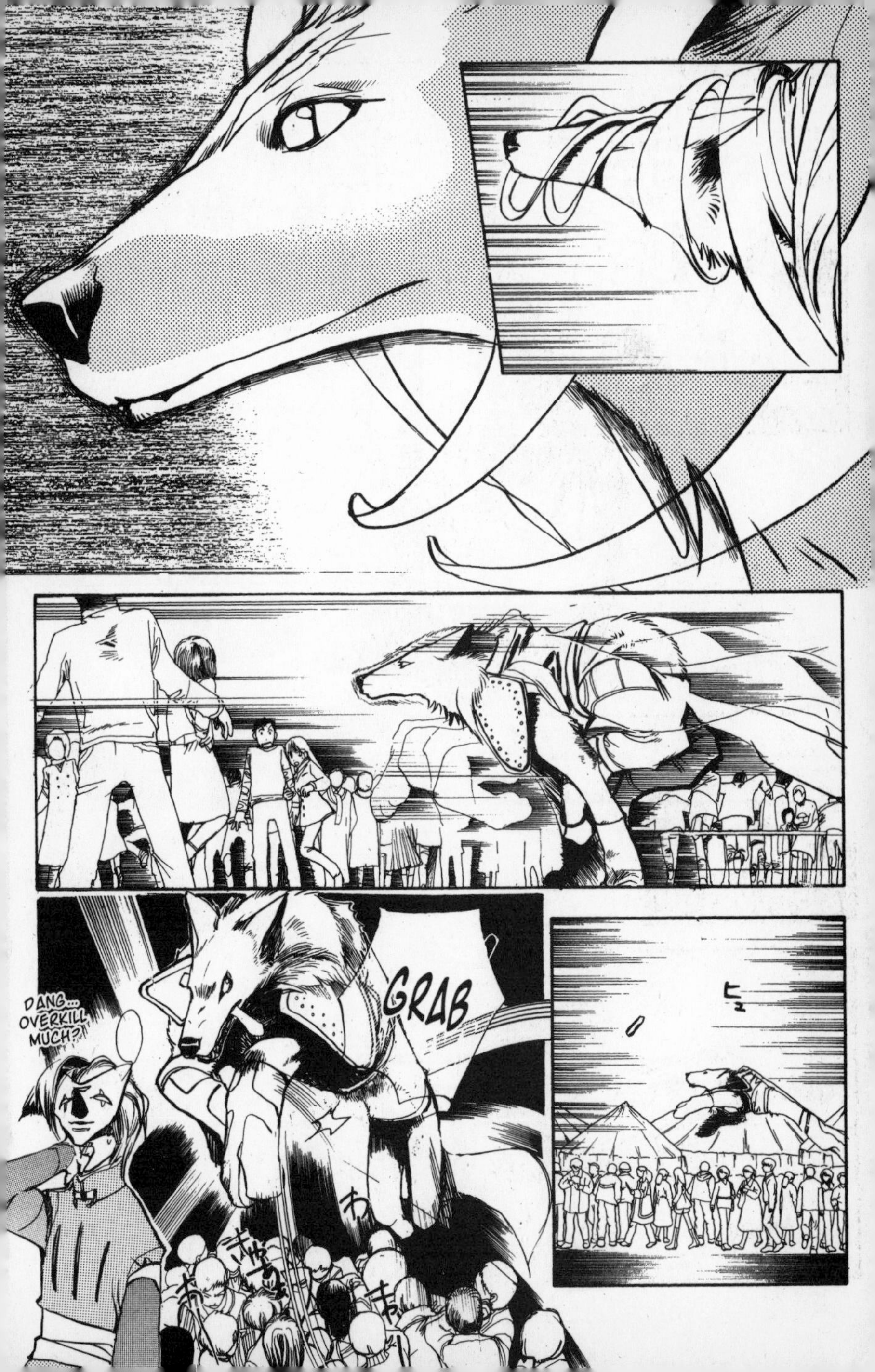
ヒュ
GRAB
DANG... OVERKILL MUCH?

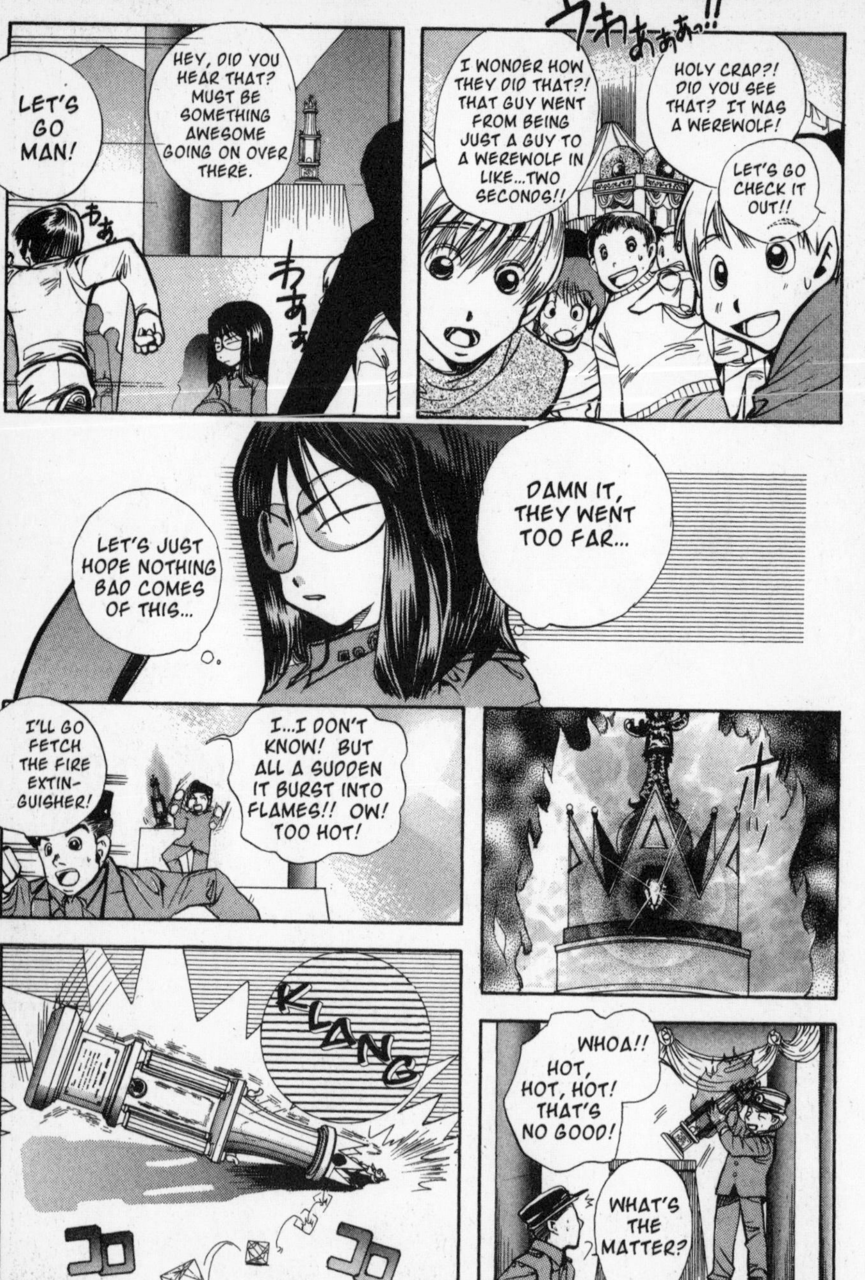
HOLY CRAP?! DID YOU SEE THAT? IT WAS A WEREWOLF!
I WONDER HOW THEY DID THAT?! THAT GUY WENT FROM BEING JUST A GUY TO A WEREWOLF IN LIKE...TWO SECONDS!!
LET'S GO CHECK IT OUT!!
HEY, DID YOU HEAR THAT? MUST BE SOMETHING AWESOME GOING ON OVER THERE.
LET'S GO MAN!
DAMN IT, THEY WENT TOO FAR...
LET'S JUST HOPE NOTHING BAD COMES OF THIS...
I...I DON'T KNOW! BUT ALL A SUDDEN IT BURST INTO FLAMES!! OW! TOO HOT!
I'LL GO FETCH THE FIRE EXTIN-GUISHER!
WHOA!! HOT, HOT, HOT! THAT'S NO GOOD!
WHAT'S THE MATTER?
KLANG

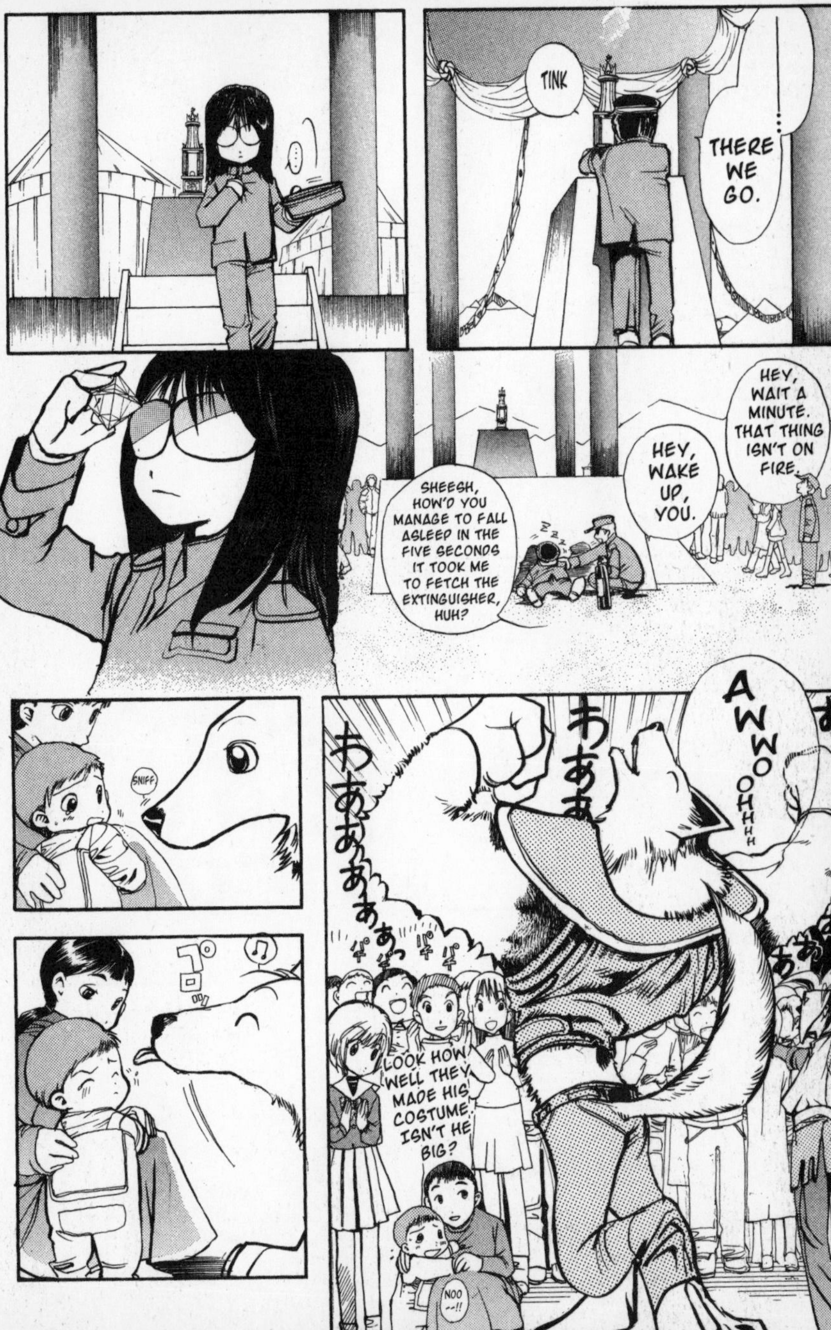
TINK
...... THERE WE GO.
...
HEY, WAIT A MINUTE. THAT THING ISN'T ON FIRE.
HEY, WAKE UP, YOU.
SHEESH, HOW'D YOU MANAGE TO FALL ASLEEP IN THE FIVE SECONDS IT TOOK ME TO FETCH THE EXTINGUISHER, HUH?
AWWOOOHHHH
LOOK HOW WELL THEY MADE HIS COSTUME. ISN'T HE BIG?
NOO --!!
SNIFF
♪

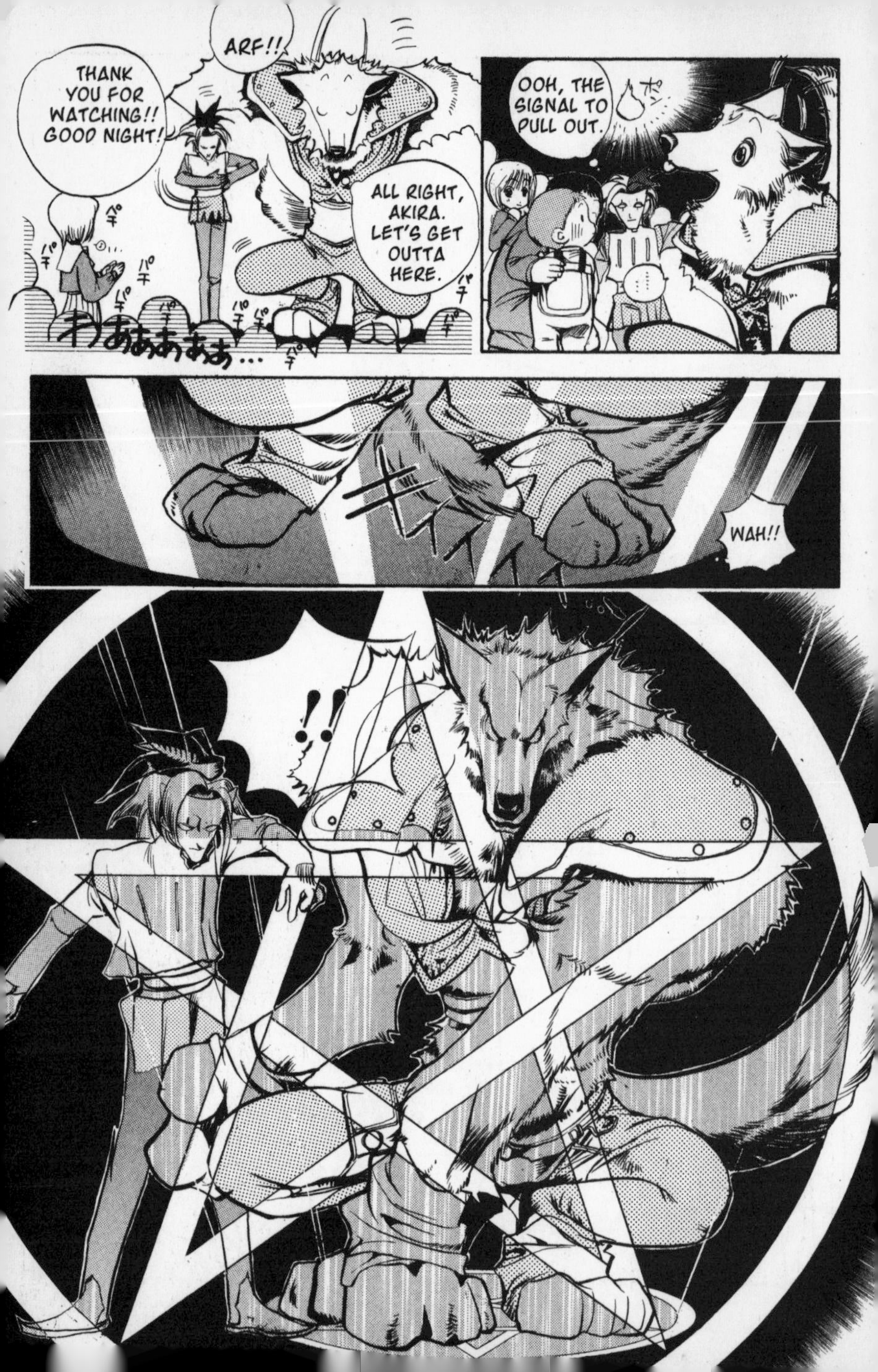
OOH, THE SIGNAL TO PULL OUT.
ポン
ARF!!
THANK YOU FOR WATCHING!! GOOD NIGHT!
ALL RIGHT, AKIRA. LET'S GET OUTTA HERE.
パチ
わあああああ…
WAH!!
!!

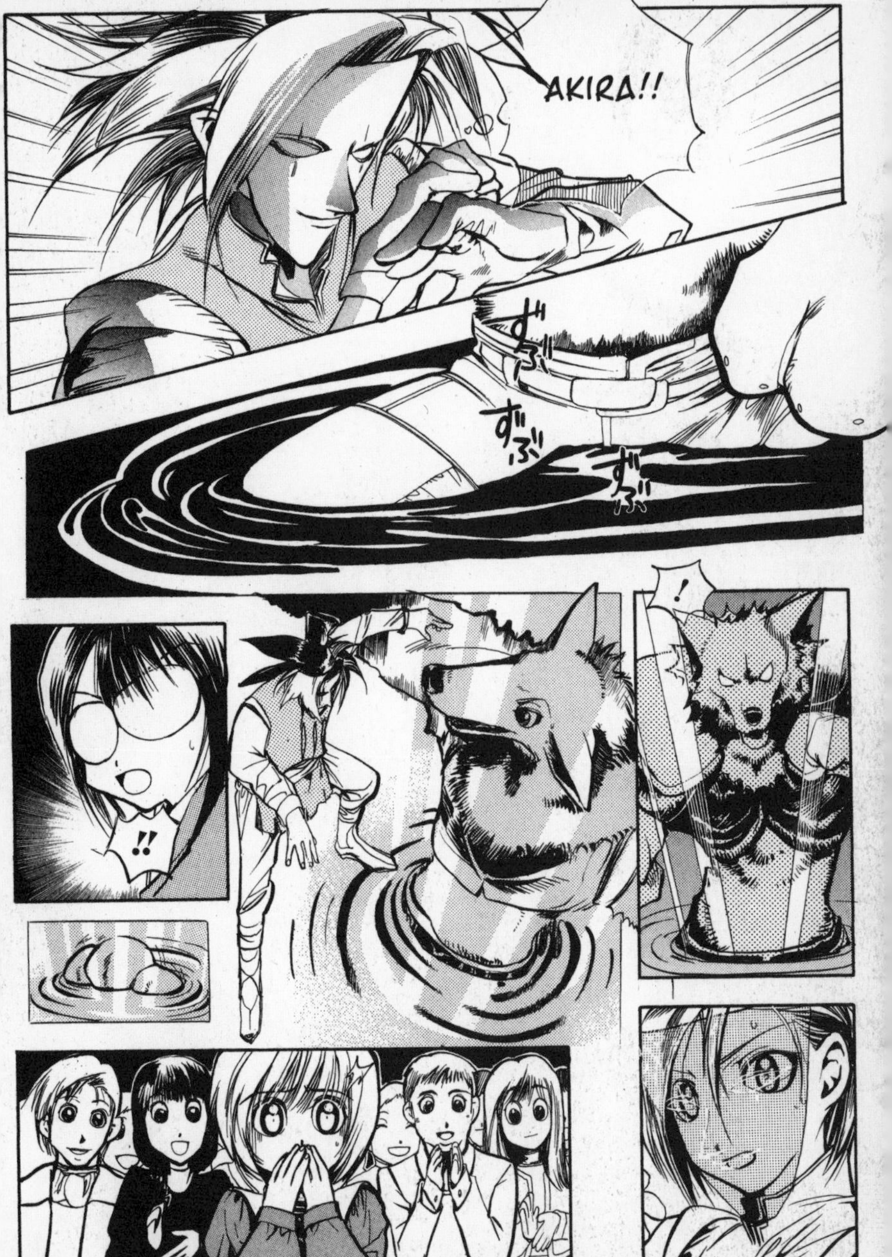
AKIRA!!
ずぶ
ずぶ
ずぶ
!
!!

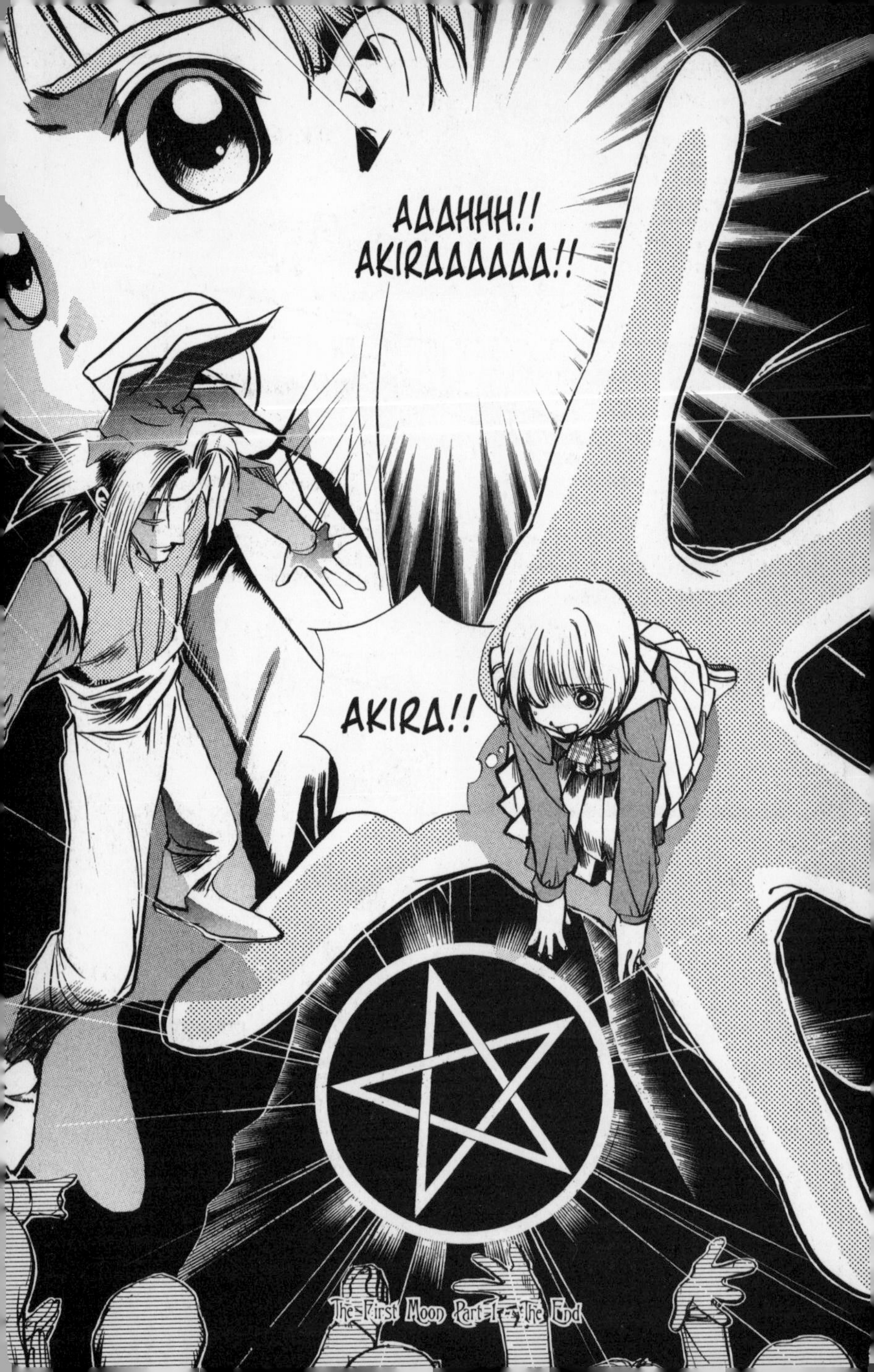
AAAHHH!! AKIRAAAAAAA!!
AKIRA!!
The First Moon Part I ~ The End

AFTER WORD

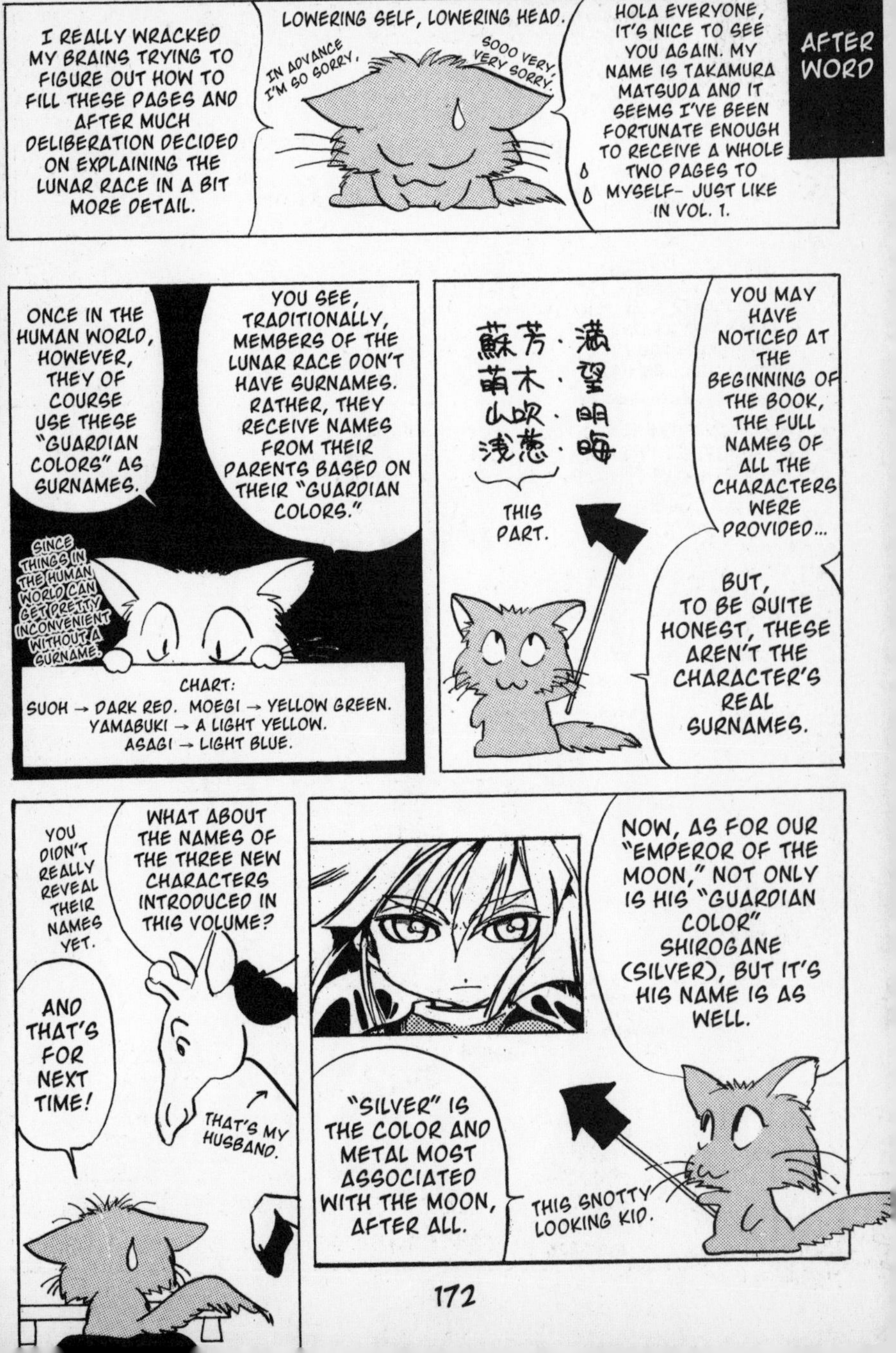
HOLA EVERYONE, IT'S NICE TO SEE YOU AGAIN. MY NAME IS TAKAMURA MATSUDA AND IT SEEMS I'VE BEEN FORTUNATE ENOUGH TO RECEIVE A WHOLE TWO PAGES TO MYSELF- JUST LIKE IN VOL. 1.
LOWERING SELF, LOWERING HEAD.
SOOO VERY, VERY SORRY.
IN ADVANCE I'M SO SORRY.
I REALLY WRACKED MY BRAINS TRYING TO FIGURE OUT HOW TO FILL THESE PAGES AND AFTER MUCH DELIBERATION DECIDED ON EXPLAINING THE LUNAR RACE IN A BIT MORE DETAIL.
YOU MAY HAVE NOTICED AT THE BEGINNING OF THE BOOK, THE FULL NAMES OF ALL THE CHARACTERS WERE PROVIDED...
蘇芳・満
萌木・望
山吹・明
浅葱・晦
THIS PART.
BUT, TO BE QUITE HONEST, THESE AREN'T THE CHARACTER'S REAL SURNAMES.
YOU SEE, TRADITIONALLY, MEMBERS OF THE LUNAR RACE DON'T HAVE SURNAMES. RATHER, THEY RECEIVE NAMES FROM THEIR PARENTS BASED ON THEIR "GUARDIAN COLORS."
ONCE IN THE HUMAN WORLD, HOWEVER, THEY OF COURSE USE THESE "GUARDIAN COLORS" AS SURNAMES.
SINCE THINGS IN THE HUMAN WORLD CAN GET PRETTY INCONVENIENT WITHOUT A SURNAME.
CHART:
SUOH → DARK RED. MOEGI → YELLOW GREEN.
YAMABUKI → A LIGHT YELLOW.
ASAGI → LIGHT BLUE.
NOW, AS FOR OUR "EMPEROR OF THE MOON," NOT ONLY IS HIS "GUARDIAN COLOR" SHIROGANE (SILVER), BUT IT'S HIS NAME IS AS WELL.
THIS SNOTTY LOOKING KID.
"SILVER" IS THE COLOR AND METAL MOST ASSOCIATED WITH THE MOON, AFTER ALL.
WHAT ABOUT THE NAMES OF THE THREE NEW CHARACTERS INTRODUCED IN THIS VOLUME?
YOU DIDN'T REALLY REVEAL THEIR NAMES YET.
AND THAT'S FOR NEXT TIME!
THAT'S MY HUSBAND.

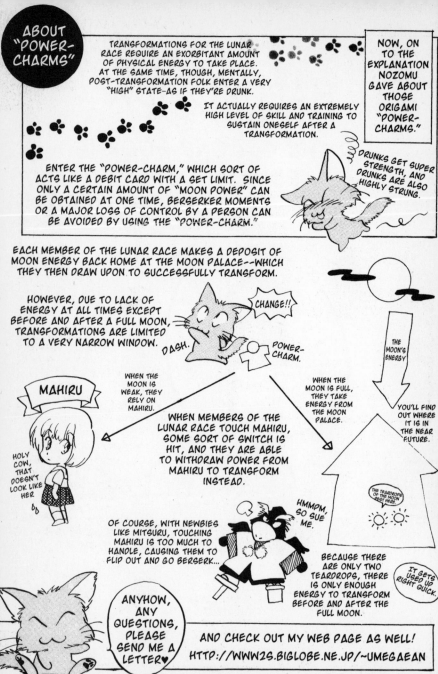

ABOUT "POWER-CHARMS"

NOW, ON TO THE EXPLANATION NOZOMU GAVE ABOUT THOSE ORIGAMI "POWER-CHARMS."

TRANSFORMATIONS FOR THE LUNAR RACE REQUIRE AN EXORBITANT AMOUNT OF PHYSICAL ENERGY TO TAKE PLACE. AT THE SAME TIME, THOUGH, MENTALLY, POST-TRANSFORMATION FOLK ENTER A VERY "HIGH" STATE-AS IF THEY'RE DRUNK.

IT ACTUALLY REQUIRES AN EXTREMELY HIGH LEVEL OF SKILL AND TRAINING TO SUSTAIN ONESELF AFTER A TRANSFORMATION.

DRUNKS GET SUPER STRENGTH, AND DRUNKS ARE ALSO HIGHLY STRUNG.

ENTER THE "POWER-CHARM," WHICH SORT OF ACTS LIKE A DEBIT CARD WITH A SET LIMIT. SINCE ONLY A CERTAIN AMOUNT OF "MOON POWER" CAN BE OBTAINED AT ONE TIME, BERSERKER MOMENTS OR A MAJOR LOSS OF CONTROL BY A PERSON CAN BE AVOIDED BY USING THE "POWER-CHARM."

EACH MEMBER OF THE LUNAR RACE MAKES A DEPOSIT OF MOON ENERGY BACK HOME AT THE MOON PALACE--WHICH THEY THEN DRAW UPON TO SUCCESSFULLY TRANSFORM.

HOWEVER, DUE TO LACK OF ENERGY AT ALL TIMES EXCEPT BEFORE AND AFTER A FULL MOON, TRANSFORMATIONS ARE LIMITED TO A VERY NARROW WINDOW.

CHANGE!!
DASH.
POWER-CHARM.

WHEN THE MOON IS WEAK, THEY RELY ON MAHIRU.

WHEN THE MOON IS FULL, THEY TAKE ENERGY FROM THE MOON PALACE.

MAHIRU
HOLY COW, THAT DOESN'T LOOK LIKE HER

WHEN MEMBERS OF THE LUNAR RACE TOUCH MAHIRU, SOME SORT OF SWITCH IS HIT, AND THEY ARE ABLE TO WITHDRAW POWER FROM MAHIRU TO TRANSFORM INSTEAD.

THE MOON'S ENERGY
YOU'LL FIND OUT WHERE IT IS IN THE NEAR FUTURE.
THE TEARDROPS OF THE MOON REST HERE.

OF COURSE, WITH NEWBIES LIKE MITSURU, TOUCHING MAHIRU IS TOO MUCH TO HANDLE, CAUSING THEM TO FLIP OUT AND GO BERSERK...

HMMPM, SO SUE ME.

BECAUSE THERE ARE ONLY TWO TEARDROPS, THERE IS ONLY ENOUGH ENERGY TO TRANSFORM BEFORE AND AFTER THE FULL MOON.

IT GETS USED UP RIGHT QUICK.

ANYHOW, ANY QUESTIONS, PLEASE SEND ME A LETTER♥

AND CHECK OUT MY WEB PAGE AS WELL!

HTTP://WWW2S.BIGLOBE.NE.JP/~UMEGAEAN

HARUKO IIDA

SO THE SECOND BOOK IS FINALLY OUT.

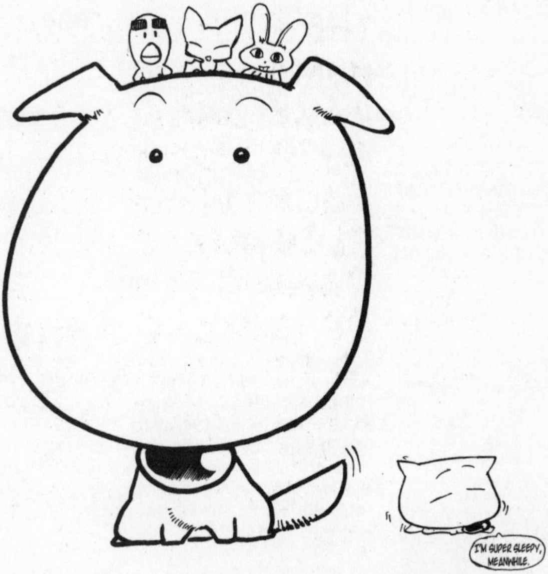
I'M SUPER SLEEPY, MEANWHILE.

THANKS SO MUCH FOR PURCHASING IT.

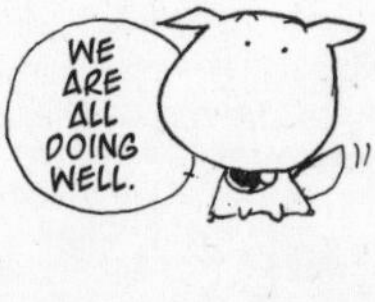
WE ARE ALL DOING WELL.

-AFTER WORD- END.

Crescent Moon

Preview: Volume 3

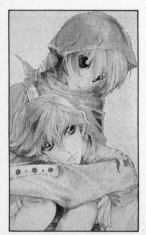

THE BATTLE BETWEEN HUMANS AND THE LUNAR RACE ESCALATES! MAHIRU SUPPORTS THE LUNAR RACE, WHILE HER PSYCHIC CLASSMATE KEIKO BACKS DAWN'S VENUS— A GROUP OF HUMANS WHOSE GOAL IS TO ANNIHILATE THE LUNAR RACE. AS THE CONFLICT DRAWS EVERYONE CLOSER INTO THE SHADOW OF THE VALLEY OF DEATH, MAHIRU REALIZES THAT THE ONLY WAY TO END THE BLOODY CONFLICT IS TO GIVE PEACE A CHANCE.

ALSO AVAILABLE FROM ⚙TOKYOPOP®

PLANET LADDER
PLANETES
PRIEST
PRINCESS AI
PSYCHIC ACADEMY
QUEEN'S KNIGHT, THE
RAGNAROK
RAVE MASTER
REALITY CHECK
REBIRTH
REBOUND
REMOTE
RISING STARS OF MANGA
SABER MARIONETTE J
SAILOR MOON
SAINT TAIL
SAIYUKI
SAMURAI DEEPER KYO
SAMURAI GIRL REAL BOUT HIGH SCHOOL
SCRYED
SEIKAI TRILOGY, THE
SGT. FROG
SHAOLIN SISTERS
SHIRAHIME-SYO: SNOW GODDESS TALES
SHUTTERBOX
SKULL MAN, THE
SNOW DROP
SORCERER HUNTERS
STONE
SUIKODEN III
SUKI
THREADS OF TIME
TOKYO BABYLON
TOKYO MEW MEW
TOKYO TRIBES
TRAMPS LIKE US
UNDER THE GLASS MOON
VAMPIRE GAME
VISION OF ESCAFLOWNE, THE
WARRIORS OF TAO
WILD ACT
WISH
WORLD OF HARTZ
X-DAY
ZODIAC P.I.

NOVELS

CLAMP SCHOOL PARANORMAL INVESTIGATORS
KARMA CLUB
SAILOR MOON
SLAYERS

ART BOOKS

ART OF CARDCAPTOR SAKURA
ART OF MAGIC KNIGHT RAYEARTH, THE
PEACH: MIWA UEDA ILLUSTRATIONS

ANIME GUIDES

COWBOY BEBOP
GUNDAM TECHNICAL MANUALS
SAILOR MOON SCOUT GUIDES

TOKYOPOP KIDS

STRAY SHEEP

CINE-MANGA™

ALADDIN
CARDCAPTORS
DUEL MASTERS
FAIRLY ODDPARENTS, THE
FAMILY GUY
FINDING NEMO
G.I. JOE SPY TROOPS
GREATEST STARS OF THE NBA
JACKIE CHAN ADVENTURES
JIMMY NEUTRON: BOY GENIUS, THE ADVENTURES OF
KIM POSSIBLE
LILO & STITCH: THE SERIES
LIZZIE MCGUIRE
LIZZIE MCGUIRE MOVIE, THE
MALCOLM IN THE MIDDLE
POWER RANGERS: DINO THUNDER
POWER RANGERS: NINJA STORM
PRINCESS DIARIES 2
RAVE MASTER
SHREK 2
SIMPLE LIFE, THE
SPONGEBOB SQUAREPANTS
SPY KIDS 2
SPY KIDS 3-D: GAME OVER
THAT'S SO RAVEN
TOTALLY SPIES
TRANSFORMERS: ARMADA
TRANSFORMERS: ENERGON
VAN HELSING

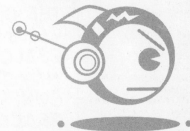

**You want it? We got it!
A full range of TOKYOPOP
products are available now at:
www.TOKYOPOP.com/shop**

04.23.04T

ALSO AVAILABLE FROM 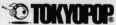 TOKYOPOP®

MANGA

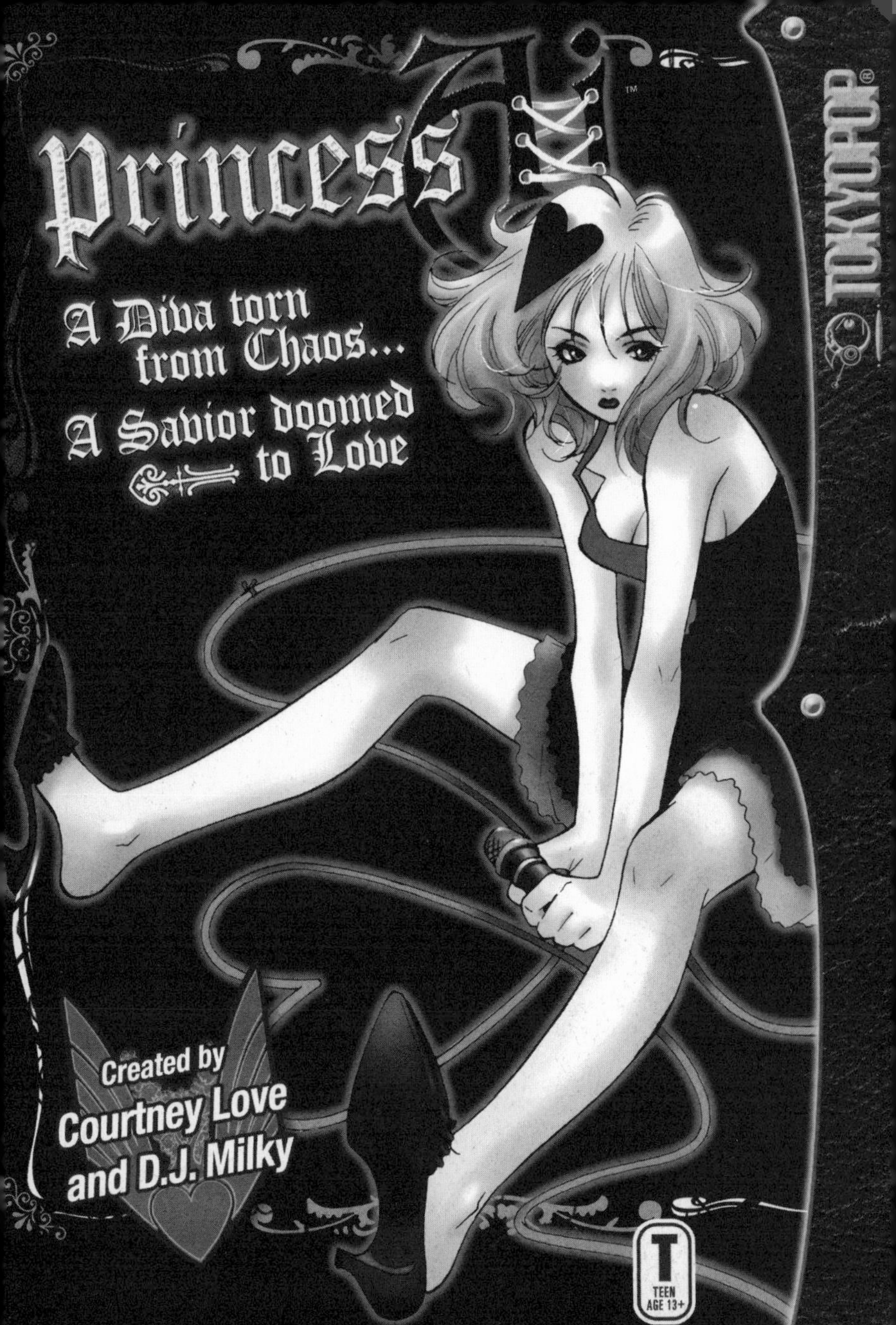

Princess Ai™
A Diva torn from Chaos...
A Savior doomed to Love
TOKYOPOP®
Created by
Courtney Love
and D.J. Milky
T
TEEN
AGE 13+

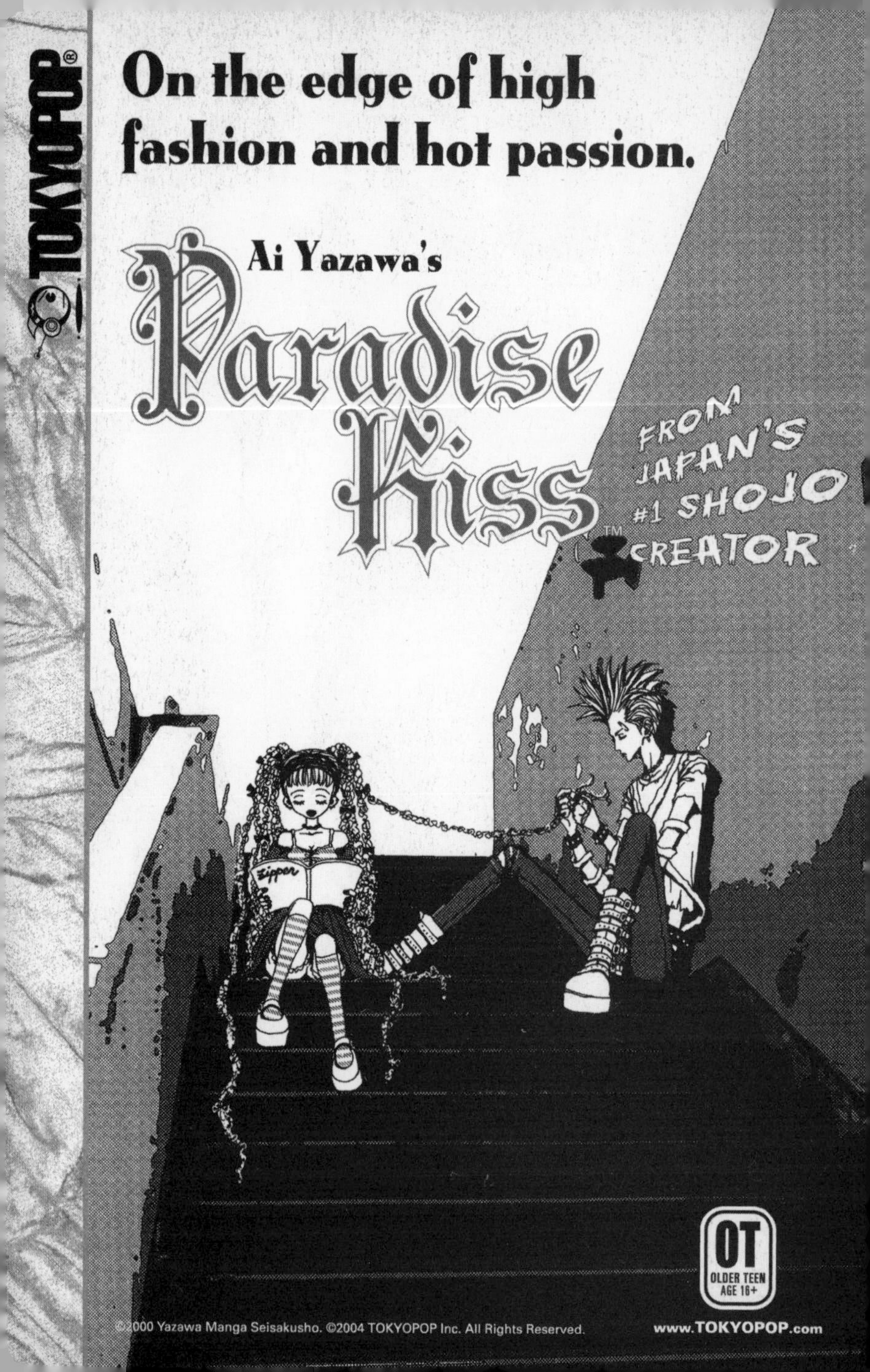

On the edge of high fashion and hot passion.

Ai Yazawa's

Paradise Kiss

FROM JAPAN'S #1 SHOJO CREATOR

OT
OLDER TEEN
AGE 16+

www.TOKYOPOP.com

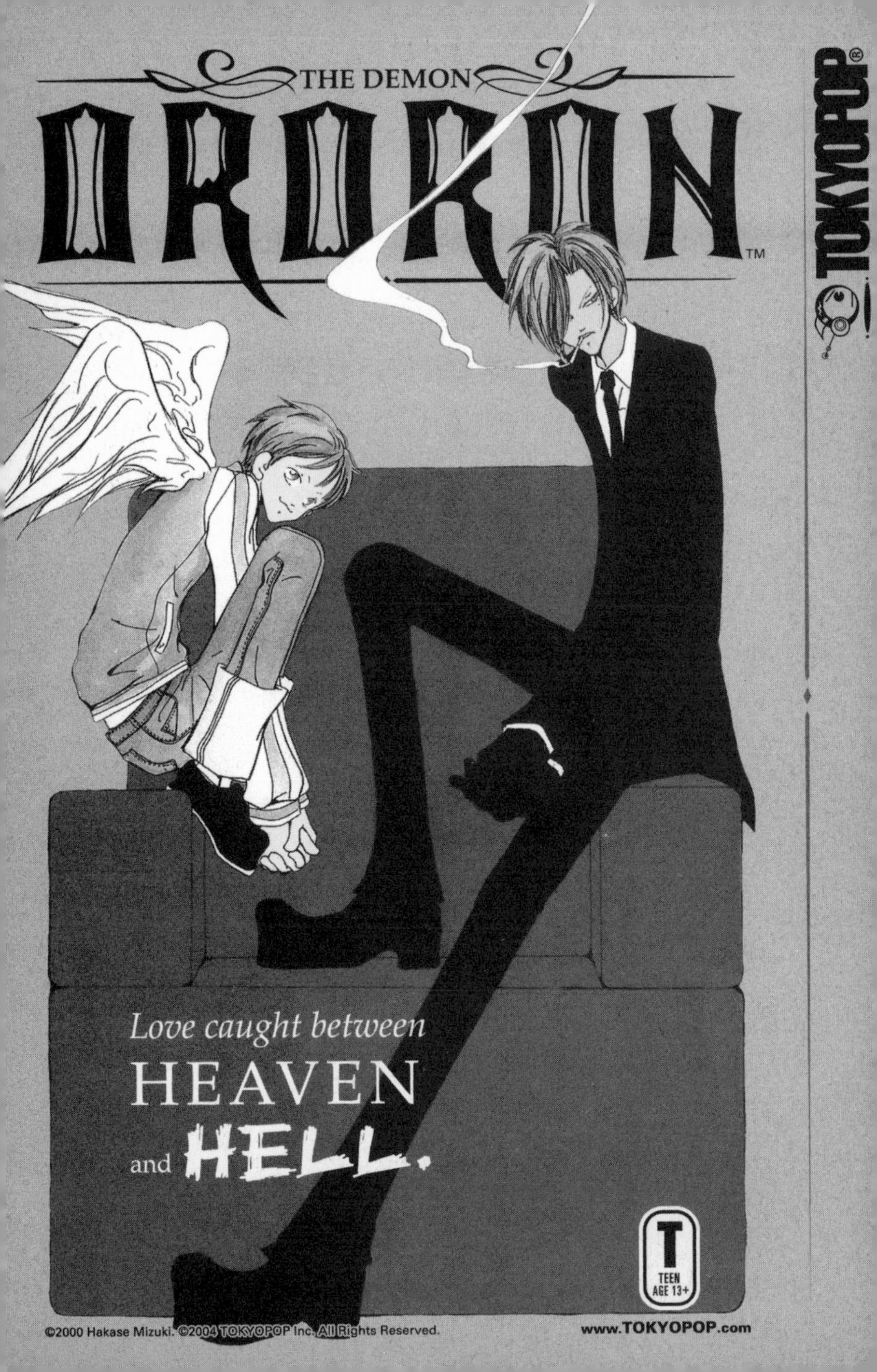
THE DEMON
ORORON™
TOKYOPOP
Love caught between
HEAVEN
and HELL.
T TEEN AGE 13+
©2000 Hakase Mizuki. ©2004 TOKYOPOP Inc. All Rights Reserved.
www.TOKYOPOP.com

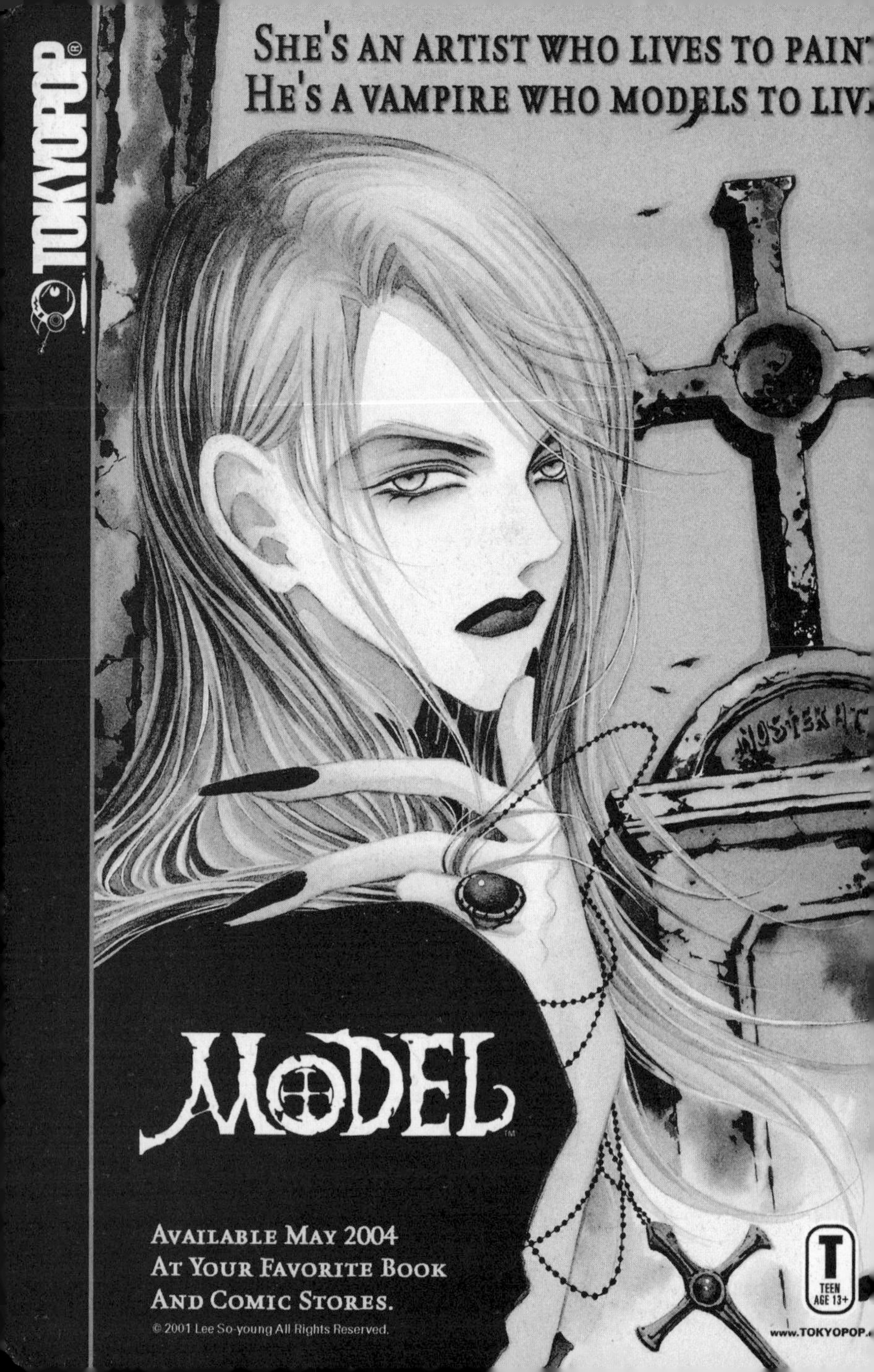
TOKYOPOP®
SHE'S AN ARTIST WHO LIVES TO PAIN
HE'S A VAMPIRE WHO MODELS TO LIV
MODEL™
AVAILABLE MAY 2004
AT YOUR FAVORITE BOOK
AND COMIC STORES.
© 2001 Lee So-young All Rights Reserved.
T
TEEN
AGE 13+
www.TOKYOPOP.

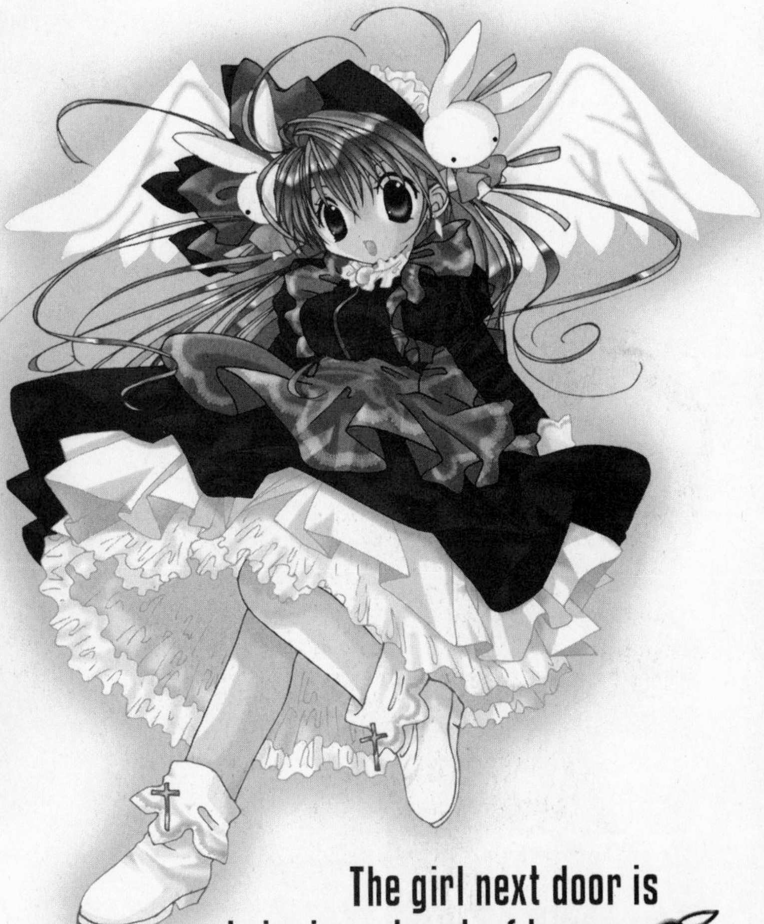

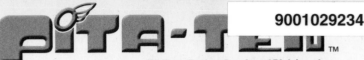

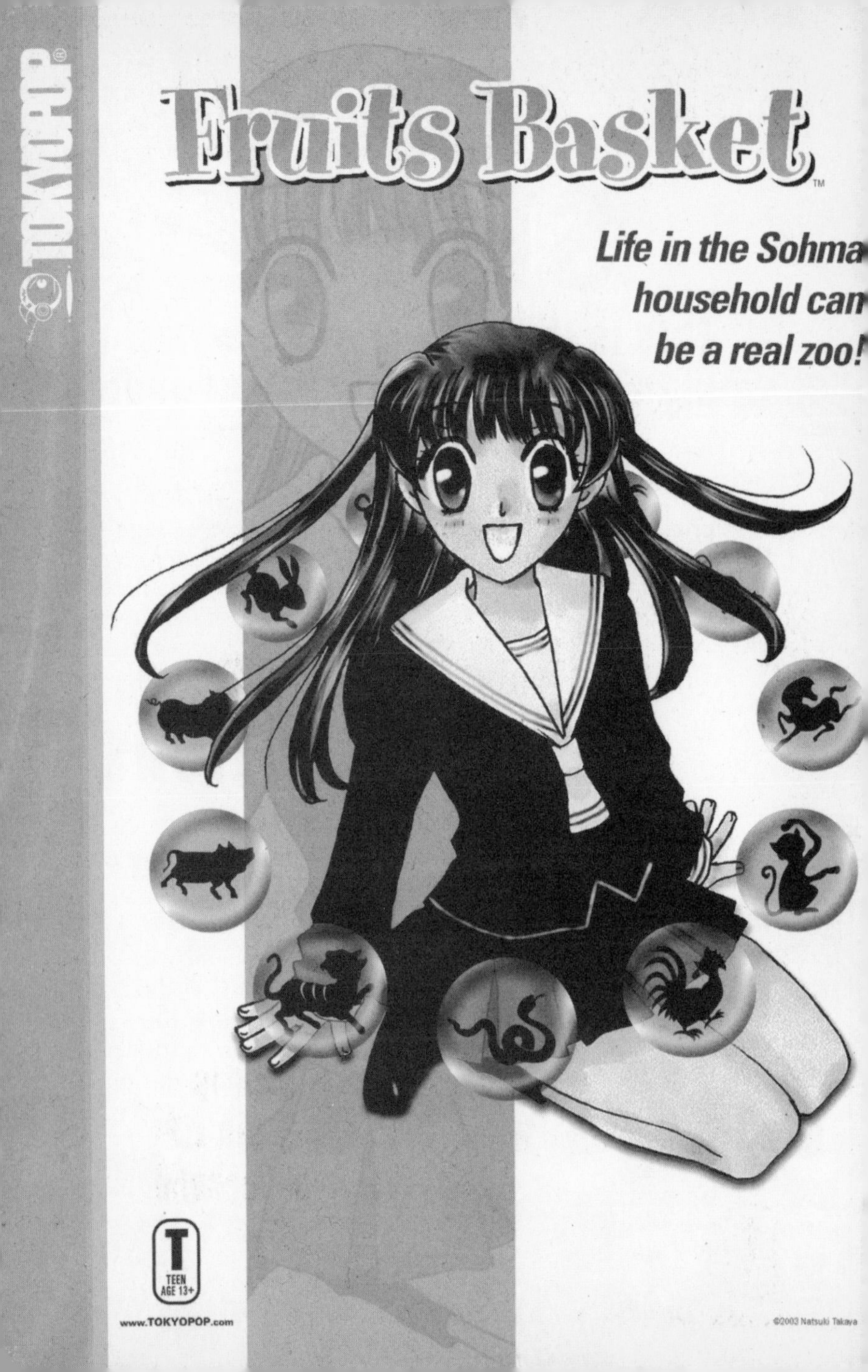
TOKYOPOP
Fruits Basket™
Life in the Sohma household can be a real zoo!
T TEEN AGE 13+
www.TOKYOPOP.com
©2003 Natsuki Takaya

STOP!

This is the back of the book.
You wouldn't want to spoil a great ending!

This book is printed "manga-style," in the authentic Japanese right-to-left format. Since none of the artwork has been flipped or altered, readers get to experience the story just as the creator intended. You've been asking for it, so TOKYOPOP® delivered: authentic, hot-off-the-press, and far more fun!

DIRECTIONS

If this is your first time reading manga-style, here's a quick guide to help you understand how it works.

It's easy... just start in the top right panel and follow the numbers. Have fun, and look for more 100% authentic manga from TOKYOPOP®!

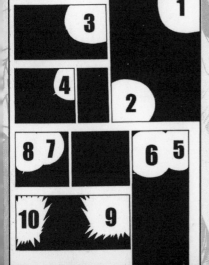

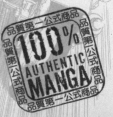